# Dark Fiber

## Electronic Culture: History, Theory, Practice
Timothy Druckrey, series editor

**Ars Electronica: Facing the Future**

edited by Timothy Druckrey with Ars Electronica, 1999

**net_condition: art and global media**

edited by Peter Weibel and Timothy Druckrey, 2001

**Dark Fiber: Tracking Critical Internet Culture**

Geert Lovink

# Dark Fiber

## Tracking Critical Internet Culture

Geert Lovink

The MIT Press

Cambridge, Massachusetts          London, England

Set in Bell Gothic and Courier by The MIT Press. Printed and bound in the United States of America.

Library of Congress Cataloging-in-Publication Data

Lovink, Geert.
Dark fiber : tracking critical internet culture / Geert Lovink.
p. cm. — (Electronic culture—history, theory, practice)
Includes bibliographical references.
ISBN 0-262-12249-9 (hc. : alk. paper)
1. Internet—Social aspects. 2. Information society. 3. Culture. I. Title. II. Series.
HM851 .L68 2002
303.48'33—dc21                                                    2001059641

**D a r k   f i b e r** refers to unused fiber-optic cable. Often times companies lay more lines than what's needed in order to curb costs of having to do it again and again. The dark strands can be leased to individuals or other companies who want to establish optical connections among their own locations. In this case, the fiber is neither controlled by nor connected to the phone company. Instead, the company or individual provides the necessary components to make it functional.

—www.webopedia.internet.com

# Contents

## Travelogues

## Dynamics of Net Culture

## Reality Check

## Towards a Political Economy

# Acknowledgements

This study has the Internet as its natural environment. It is there that the ideas first developed and ought be contextualized. These days, the book is no longer the dominant storage medium of knowledge. Yet, it offers an opportunity for the author to reassess and filter thoughts into a comprehensive body of files. The copy-paste feature is no longer a disdainful, shameful feature of writing. Rather, it is exciting to see how text crystals travel through the net, are translated or pop up in different contexts, get deleted only to reappear elsewhere.

Most of the texts in this book appeared in earlier versions on mailing lists and web sites, in particular nettime and Telepolis, sometimes under different titles. Concepts have grown out of dialogues and interviews, electronic and real-life conversations with hundreds of colleague media theorists, activists, journalists, programmers, and designers. Even though this book bears my name (indeed, it is the first book of essays in English with my name on it), I regard it as a collective body of knowledge.

A considerable part of my thinking, and of this book, has been developed from collaborations. My media theory framework goes back to the years I spent in Berlin in the 1980s and the early 1990s and to my work in the Netherlands as an editor of *Mediamatic* magazine (1989–1994) and as a member of the Adilkno group (the Foundation for the Advancement of Illegal Knowledge; Agentur; Bilwet in Dutch or German). In particular, the long-standing collective writing experience with Adilkno member Arjen Mulder has been one of great joy and inspiration. One text in this book, "Organized Innocence and War in the New Europe: Adilkno, Culture and the Independent Media," explicitly bridges the Adilkno canon with my own theoretical work.

As one of the founders of the Amsterdam Digital City project, I promoted and closely monitored this large Internet community project from an early stage. Traveling as a "cultural ambassador" of Amsterdam new media culture, I have done a lot of promotion and critical work in this context. "The Digital City—Metaphor and Community" draws heavily on collaborative writings with Patrice Riemens. The Digital City ideas sprang out of collaborations since the late 1980s with Caroline Nevejan and Marleen Stikker around projects within the framework of Paradiso, De Balie, Digital City, and the Society for Old and New Media.

My friendship and working relationship with Pit Schultz during the stormy period 1995–1998 was intensively productive. A great deal of the thinking on net criticism was developed during our collaboration, while building up the nettime list and other publishing activities. Perhaps at some stage our Netzkritik essays, written in German, will become available in English.

Tactical media and debates on net activism should be credited to the Amsterdam Next Five Minutes circles, in particular Eveline Lubbers, Jo van der Spek, Patrice Riemens, David Garcia, Menno Grootveld, and Andreas Broeckmann. Writings on this topic have been published under David Garcia's name and under mine, and parts of these have been used here. Extensive exchanges and collaborations with DeeDee Halleck, Florian Schneider, Sam de Silva, Ravi Sundaram, and other Sarai members have been instrumental in formulating media activist strategies.

My ongoing collaboration with the designer Mieke Gerritzen should be mentioned here separately. This book is only one of the many projects we have worked on together, the results of which continue to astonish me.

Over the years the following persons and media outlets have supported me in my work and been a source of inspiration: Basjan van Stam, Janos Sugar, Peter Lunenfeld, Lev Manovich, Arthur and Marilouise Kroker, Siegfried Zielinski, Thorsten Schilling, Toek of DFM Radio/TV International, the Amsterdam free radio stations Radio 100 and Radio Patapoe, Stefaan Decostere, the editors of the journal *Andere Sinema,* Peter Lamborn Wilson, Jim Fleming and others of the Autonomedia collective, Katharina Teichgräber, Wim Nijenhuis, Andreas Kallfelz, Nel and Ben and the others of Kloof 57, Telepolis editor Armin Medosch, the crew from *Mute* magazine, Bart Schut of VPRO Radio, Mark Dery, Graham Harwood, Marita Liulia, McKenzie Wark, Toshiya Ueno, Howard Rheingold, and Saskia Sassen. Without having met them I would most certainly have taken other paths.

I have to mention Klaus Theweleit and Friedrich Kittler here separately. Their work has been a great source of inspiration in finding my own style and place within media theory.

As a non-native English speaker, editorial support from many has played a key role in the decision to bring the texts together and the actual work. Because of the special status of English as lingua franca of the Internet, I decided to include a text on the issue of "Euro-English," written in the time when I realized that waiting for publishers to translate my work into English was a waste of time. I am no longer sure which English is apparent in my writing and spoken accent: it's a melange of the old Dutch layer in me, the lovely long and complex German sentences (which I have to miss now), the stiff sentences of BBC Worldservice, Internet pidgin, and the English of Australia, the country I now call home.

Since 1995 Matthew Fuller, Ted Byfield, Geneva Anderson, Patrice Riemens, Linda Wallace, David Hudson, Anita Mage, and McKenzie Wark have been doing great work polishing my texts, editorial work which all flew into this book. Laura Martz translated both ISEA 94 and 95 lectures from Dutch, parts of which were used. For this book Willard Uncapher, jonathan jay, Scott McQuire, Ed Phillips, Ned Rossiter, and in particular Katie Mondloch were all helpful with comments and contributed greatly in copy editing different parts. Because of all the fragments shifting through the manuscript I refrained from mentioning who exactly copy edited which part. Timothy Druckrey and Linda Wallace went through the manuscript with great care. [Only light editing was done at The MIT Press.]

Thanks to Chris Swart Sr. and Michael van Eeden for their ongoing software and hardware support. In particular I would like to mention Felipe Rodriquez for his generous contribution in helping to make it all happen. I would also like to acknowledge the financial support of the Dutch ThuisKopie Fonds and the Fonds voor Beeldende Kunsten, Vormgeving en Bouwkunst (Netherlands Foundation for Visual Arts, Design and Architecture).

It was series editor Timothy Druckrey, during a visit to New York in late October 2000, who invited me to do this book and gave me the courage to write it, directly in English. Details were finalized in March 2001. Writing and editorial work took place in May, June, and July of 2001. I would like to thank him especially for his confidence in my work and his determination to get the work done in such a short period of time.

This book would not have been realized without the initial and ongoing support of Linda Wallace, the love of my life and my wife. This book is dedicated to her.

An archive of texts by Geert Lovink can be found on the World Wide Web at www.laudanum.net/geert.

# Dark Fiber

# Introduction: Twilight of the Digirati

After discovery and colonization, what remains is the socialization of cyberspace. This is the early-21st-century post-heroic age of "massification" of the Internet. The downfall of the cybergods is predicted. A growing group of engaged users openly question the conservative, corporate-biased "digital revolution."

The "net criticism" discussed in this book is not targeted against the values of Internet pioneers from the pre-dotcom age—those with a belief in decentrality, the right to own your own words, the idea of sharing resources, code, and content, and anonymity remain essential and worth defending. Rather, there is a growing disbelief that "the market" is the appropriate partner in defending, and defining, Internet freedom. The hackers' version of a do-it-yourself capitalism, with worthy, anti-monopolistic intentions, promoting true market forces, has proved unable to beat the big software, telecom, and media players, who all have their own vested interests in dismantling core Internet values.

The texts assembled here point to the economic and political bias and blind spots of the still dominant cyber-libertarian ideology. Central to this is the belief that the state is the main enemy of the Internet and only market forces can create a decentralized communication system, accessible for everyone. Even now, despite the dotcom crash and growing monopolies, the net is still presented to an ever growing group of usually young (and usually male) developers as a "pure" medium; an abstract mathematical environment, untouched by society, neutral of class, gender or race, capable of "routing around"[1] problems caused by the dirty world outside.

However, computer networks are no longer an insider's phenomenon in the hands of a few academics and programmers, as was the case until the mid 1990s. Software engineers no longer decide over the future of the medium, not even over technical matters. Technology standards have become an economic and political battleground. Ever since the boom of World Wide Web browsers in 1995, the Internet has come under the control of telecom carriers, content-driven access providers such as AOL, software giants, and the media industry. Many in the IT industry are working in close harmony with legislators, further privatizing what is left of the Internet public domain, restricting privacy, demanding anti-"cyber terrorism" legislation, installing content filters and tolerating monopolies. The list goes on and on. Internet is more than a medium for transactions. How much more will be sacrificed in order to further increase the illusion of the web as a "safe" place for e-commerce and e-business interests? If the only thing business can do is to demand repressive laws against society, the scenario of a global civil war is going to be an obvious one.

Presenting the current consolidation period as gloomy is not what I intend to do. Not all is lost. There is always another future. What is needed is a firm injection of political and economic competence into the freedom loving electric minds. The aim would be to harness Internet liberty against both corporate domination and state control. So far, "cyberselfish" libertarians only saw danger coming from a demonized Big Brother, deliberately overseeing corporate agendas, for whom the Internet merely has been a vehicle to make money as fast as possible, certainly not a sustainable and open many-to-many medium. The overemphasis on the "evil" role of the state within Internet circles can be explained historically. In the 1990s academic networks and national telecoms had to give up their exclusive access rights. A decade later the overall picture is a radically different one. The avant-garde role of the dotcom entrepreneur was over, even before outsiders noticed. Those who rise out of the tech wreck ashes will set the techno-economic standards and divide the audience share among a small group of converging conglomerates. File exchange within peer-to-peer networks, net activism against global capitalism and a further proliferation of free software (as program and metaphor) can only endanger volatile, bearish markets and burned-out

IT/telecom firms on the fragile road of recovery from the 2001 recession. It is in the light of these ongoing conflicts of interest that the material gathered here should be read.

The topic discussed is not so much about the birth stage of Internet cultures. Nor do I speculative about the future. Like Lev Manovich in his groundbreaking study *The Language of New Media* (2001), I am looking into Internet culture as it actually develops. My concern aims less at a media archeology as it is to investigate the dynamics of the post-euphoric period in which ideas transform into social networks, institutions, and informal structures. I did not feel the need to put the net culture of the 1990s under the scrutiny of a historical analogy with, for example, radio or mail art. The topic discussed here is how concepts transform into actual networks. After a brief period of excitement, the newly founded web sites, lists, servers, media labs etc. have to find ways to deal with growth, economic issues, internal hierarchies, ever-changing standards, ongoing convergence problems between platforms, and incompatible software while establishing a form of cybernetic normalcy in the process.

Analyzing the closure of the net has the danger of sliding into cultural pessimism and unreconstructed forms of Marxism. I am the last one to give a cynical laugh about the burn rate of Internet idealism. It is easy to call for a synthesis of critical micro practices and the vista of a macro-size speculative theory, combining radical pragmatism with negative thinking, escape, presence, resistance, and utopia. A fictional virtual realism, giving shelter to radical informality. Which is easier said than done.

During the crucial mid 1990s, intellectuals, struggling with the French post-structuralist legacy had little to contribute to the making of an independent Internet culture. Constantly, high resolution offline VR animations, mainly produced for blockbuster movies, got mixed up with the slow reality of the 2D web browser. The flashy Hollywood imagination of criminal yet heroic info warriors in numerous hacker films created its own mythology. However, the Internet of the early days was exciting but not spectacular. With the exception of a few fields such as critical urban studies, (virtual) architecture, and the globalization debate, the theory sector carefully avoided the real existing net and its clumsy practicalities and left the task of defining the bubbling field to business gurus. Internet culture thus got easily crushed between popular imagination and equally unrealistic economic models.

On the other side of the theory line, reservations within engineer circles and geek circles against humanities and theory in general are still there. Marvin Minsky's famous remark of culture as "bad science" has not faded away. Electronic artists might be interested in a serious collaboration with scientists, but leaving out the few exceptions it is not the case the other way round. Science and industry would like to acquire some cultural capital, thereby helping to prop up their image by making them look more human, but that's not a good starting point for a fair dialogue. Whose interested in such unequal trade-offs? It is therefor better to take a more cautious stand and not overemphasize the catalyst role of "creative industries" in the development of the technology sector.

Soon the Internet will not be new anymore. Email is becoming part of everyday life, as did television, the vacuum cleaner, and the refrigerator. The fact that one can surf the web on a hand-hold device has not turned the world upside down. Instead of taking the cynical stand, complaining about eternal return of the sin fall, the proposal made is to develop a reflexive theory. An open discourse, able to incorporate a wide range of experiences, beyond the good, the bad, and the ugly, expressing an engaged environment which is both keen to further development technology (standards) while fully aware this process is happening within society with all its layers of social, economic, gender, and race relations.

An example of a reflexive text in dialogue with earlier assumptions could be the long chapter Howard Rheingold appended to his influential book *Virtual Communities*, originally published in 1992. Writing in late 1999 for the second edition, published by The MIT Press, he made a critical re-assessment of his former, perhaps somewhat idealistic ideas. Rheingold had the courage to point out where he was wrong and what he learned from his critics, while maintaining the basic belief in the (progressive) power of online collaboration and exchange. Combining experience with theory makes this a unique document, one worth presenting in detail. In a careful style, he takes the reader through his stormy West Coast experiences throughout the 1990s. He then describes and criticizes the takeup of the virtual community meme within hyped-up business circles, and his own ambivalence toward the commodification of a once-fashionable term. While reading the work of social scientists such as Barry Wellmann, Rheingold takes apart the romantic, closed aspects of the notion and practice of "community."

In his last chapter, Rheingold looks into contemporary literature, discussing phenomena such as Internet addiction, confronting his present thoughts on "online social networks" (Wellman) with classic texts from Mumford, Adorno, Horkheimer, Ellul, and Winner. This leads towards a revision of technological determinism. "It's not healthy to assume we don't have a choice. Tools aren't always neutral. But neither do they determine our destinies, immune to human efforts." However, Rheingold has not completely relinquished the deterministic aspects of technology. "Mindless acceptance of tools and toys that tune our lives and sensibilities more and more acutely to the needs of machinery is dangerous. But extracting the humane powers from the diabolical forces enabled by technology is not a simple task. It might not even be possible. I see no alternative but to make the effort to find out." This works sets out on the path, elaborated by Rheingold, to find out what a critical practice could look like within the development of Internet as a medium could look like.

The original 1992 *Virtual Communities* story is still full of positive energy and constructive feedback among community members. Eight years later Rheingold notes: "While people often jump to disagree, dispute, disparage, or mock something they dislike, people don't spend as much time telling each other online how much they appreciate one another's contributions. Online peanut galleries are incubators for kibitzing—online book discussions can include heated arguments among people who haven't read the book yet. Character assassins and passive aggressive organizers of other people's feuds, gossips and snitches, bullies, charlatans, con-artists all make their way online, along with the authentically goodwilled."

About the early days of *HotWired* (1994) Rheingold has the following to say: "If *Wired* publisher Louis Rossetto had taken the time for a cup of coffee or a walk around the block with me, it would have been clear to both of us that we would never work together harmoniously. He looked at our new e-zine and saw it as an extension of *Wired*'s brand into cyberspace, which it certainly was, and an extension of *Wired*'s role as fashion arbiter of the emerging digital culture, which many of us thought to be the wrong role online among technical sophisticates. I looked at the same enterprise and saw a community of the best of the digital culture on line, the best of whose world-wide multimedia jam sessions would be featured in the e-zine. But Rossetto didn't want to provide resources for the community role. It was an electronic extension of letters to the editor, from where he sat. "I don't want to be the bozofilter for the net," he barked when I talked about user-generated content.

The clash with Madison Avenue's running dog Rossetto led to Rheingold's own start-up, a mixture of a magazine and a web conferencing system, a place on the web where content and those in discussion are integrated.[2] After a good eight months Electric Minds went out of business in May 1997. Howard sums up: "I had turned something that was fun into something that wasn't fun. When I had the time to think about where I had gone wrong, it became clear to me that if I had simply added simple conferencing software and continued doing my amateur editing and design, then grew a virtual community on my own, I could have grown something less fancy but more sustainable in cultural if not in financial terms. Venture capital, I concluded, might be a good way to ramp up a Yahoo or create a market for a kind of technology product that never existed before. But perhaps it isn't a healthy way to grow a social enterprise."

Rheingold's critical investigations led him to conclude that peer-to-peer communication alone will not do the job of securing Internet freedom. "There is no guarantee that the potential power of many to many communications will make a difference in political battles about the shape of our future. Indeed, the odds are against a media-literate population seizing the opportunities the Internet offers." In order to tackle disintegration, flame wars, and cries over censorship, online communities need experienced, empowering initiators. "The forces that draw people and our attention away from anything as abstract as written discussions in cyberspace are strong, and action must be taken to glue people together. Skilled facilitation, well thought-out social contracts, social mechanisms and multimedia material for initiating newcomers in the use of the medium—the 'social infrastructure' for success in virtual-community building—has become valuable, now that tools are free."

Throughout this study, the key axiomatic for me resides in the feedback between theory and practice. The emerging discipline of Internet studies, if it wants to be innovative, has to be enriched with a critical involvement in both technical, user-related matters and content matters. A "digital dialectic," as Peter Lunenfeld calls it (2000, p. 171), grounding "the insights of theory in the constraints of practice, combining the critical investigations of contemporary culture with the hands-on analysis of the possibilities (and limitations) of new technologies." There is no need for positive New Age talk. I am not looking for spiritual enlightenment, neither inside, nor outside the machine. I don't feel extropian needs to leave my body behind and store my brains on disk, nor do I call for a return to some ("natural") body. Being cyborg is a 21st-century condition, not a lifestyle identity option. Nor is a withdrawal into a scientific positivism desirable. The response to cyber mysticism should not be usability statistics. Stressing the complexity of the situation, with so many players involved in the making of an inherently unstable medium, often remains an empty phrase, clouding the things which need to be said. What is required is an evaluation of what has happened over the last few years. Stories need to be told. Only then it is time to move on to create a matrix for decisive action. Too many concepts and phrases remain empty and uncontested. Before coming up with yet another blueprint of "the future," the recent past, with its hyper growth and conceptual inflation, needs further excavation. In Rheingold's words: "Before we can take actions that influence our future in more positive directions, however, we need to know how to act, and understand why."

The New does not emerge. It erupts, then fades away. It always begins with brief moments of undefinedness. Everyone involved in the development and implementation of technology must have experienced this. Technology is not a God-given entity, its standards can be changed, our understanding can be triggered, altered, undermined, revolutionized, especially in the beginnings of a medium when convention has not yet set in. Networks can be built from scratch, and generate unheard excitement in a matter of weeks, days, minutes. After the rupture of the New, there is a decision to be made. Either one disappears and switches channels, on the look out for the next thing, or one gets involved in a long-term engagement. What needs to be critiqued is the notion of unavoidable speed and growth, like the advertisement logic of technology being developed on "Internet time." It is not. Hardware and software can be installed overnight, but not developed overnight. A database can be set up in a blitz, but to produce the content for it might take time. Java scripts are not by definition innovative, or even a marketable item. Putting an HTML document on the web is not software development. The next version of an application may as well be a setback. Changes in technological paradigms take years. It's questionable whether human nature, with all its fatal flaws and charming defects, will ever change. It is therefore good to distinguish between true excitement during ruptures and long reality waves, and not to mix them.

In *Generation Berlin*, referring to reunified Germany after 1989 with Berlin as its new capital, the German social theorist Heinz Bude called for "definitions" instead of the critical pose of the 1968 generation. I will here briefly relate his ideas to the case of Internet: no more vapor theory anymore. Enough techno-mysticism and digital Darwinism. Neither do we need techno-cultural pessimism. Bude (2001; my translation): "What counts is to start somewhere, not so much to grasp the entire picture.

Defining the beginning is essentially different from the decision in a state of emergency. Defining is not creating. Rather is it is implementation of a new combination." This, in my opinion, describes the experimental yet decisive attitude of the "net criticism" I have in mind, and try to give shape. Now that futurologists have left cyberspace in the aftermath of the dotcom fallout, the Internet is heading towards a conceptual void. Neither predominantly library, shopping mall, nor banking office, it is seen as a "source of information," a neutral, bleak, and somewhat passive definition.[3] The care, expressed here, is growing out a daily experience with the net as a site of infection, disseminating viruses and worms, pornography, money scams, and other unaccountable information. Space of reason or paranoia pressure cooker? You choose.

Beyond resignation and the romance of revolt a lot of critical work can be done on the level of the implementation of ideas into software, interfaces, network architecture, discourse, design. Unlike Bude's Germany, the Internet is not exactly "lamed" by negativism. While faced with an overproduction of German *Kritik*, the Internet by and large is still missing its own class of global (virtual) intellectuals, mainly due to its heritage as a (white male) engineering culture. However, this situation might come to a close. What's next, rephrasing Bude, is the implementation of a new combination which brings development humanities, user groups, social movements, NGOs, artists, and critics into the core of Internet development. Internet culture should not reduce itself to content. Not so much as a call for "accountability" from the outside, but as a diverse set of critical practices, ready to mediate and intervene in the technological, political, and economic debate that defines the Internet.

One of the steps in this process is the recognition of the importance of arts and culture in IT and the implementation of a cultural policy of new media, which consists of more than installing a few terminals in technologically deprived social spaces. It is not about bringing computers inside the museum or digitizing cultural heritage. What is at stake here is the acceptance that we are living in an "technological culture." Culture and the arts should not be instrumentalized as spiritual compensations for technological brutality of the everyday. On the other side, technologists are not more advanced compared to those working inside the culture industry. Issues of a critical techno-culture include, for example, the support of a innovative interface culture, open content licenses, research partnerships between new media arts and the science and technology sectors, inquiries into the working conditions in the IT industry, bandwidth policy (broadband for all), of support of free software development and network research, merits of remote learning, the changing role of public libraries, and the organization of public debates about the parameters of a sustainable network society.

Heinz Bude's "defining" has nothing to do with the "will to decide" of German conservative constitutional lawyer-theorist Carl Schmitt. His authoritarian "decisionism" was proposed in contrast to the weak parliamentary democracy during the Weimar Republic. Rather, Bude wanted to get away from the "comfortable position of 'observing from a secondary position' and define the situation." Defining is different from creating. A definition, according to Bude, is the implementation of a new combination. "In demand is a style of responsibility, born out of curiosity. A position beyond weakness in shape and identity mania." Those growing up with the anger of new social movements (feminism, ecology), having proved their skepticism towards power while studying post-structuralism, are now called upon to put their vision, if they still have any, in place. "For those who define, both skepticism and criticism are escapist attitudes, which take flight in a state beyond disappointment and entanglement. However, those with the will to define are vulnerable and liable, because they neither believe in the cleansing aspect of 'separation,' nor in the cathartic effect of 'crossing.'" (Bude 2001, p. 50)

The "net criticism" proposed here is obviously not escapist and not even looking for an "alien" outsider position. With Bude, it calls for engagement and responsibility, out of a deep concern that the Internet, bit by bit, is being closed down, sealed off by filters, firewalls, and security laws, in a joint operation by corporations and governments in order to create a "secure" and "safe" information environment, free of dissents and irritants to capital flows. With the technical and law enforcement measures in place every bit can be labeled dissent. Radical pragmatists, like myself, believe that this is not a gloomy picture and that there's still enough space for intervention and freedom for off-the-radar initiatives. This confidence, however, builds on the presumption of an active minority of net users willing to act, skilled enough to lobby, equipped with enough experience to build social alliances in order to uphold closed systems (profit and control for few), while reinforcing open, innovative standards, situated in the public domain (to be accessed by all). One could think of Eric Raymond's metaphorical battle between the cathedral and the bazaar, or Manuel Delanda's useful yet somewhat idealistic distinction between markets and anti-markets (based on Ferdinand Braudel). Radical media pragmatism is not satisfied with some ideal notion of how capitalism or socialism could work in theory, assisted by well-intentioned engineers who found the perfect technology to run a GPL society based on open money. A net pragmatism requires vigilant efforts to articulate the net with materiality, for herein lies the possibility of a politics that recognizes the embeddedness of social practices.

Sloganomics (a word I use, along with 'Sloganism', to highlight eccentric notions): "Those who do not know history have the freedom to bypass it" (Johan; Sjerpstra); Deleuze Not Found: Complexity and Indifference (book title); Das Prinzip Vernetzung; sticky theory; landscapes of power (dream); unwiring digital desperation; Revolt of the mook and midriff multitudes; Internet revisited; "Stop reading Benjamin, start living Benjamin"; "Access to hope" (Ghassan Hage).

The ideas and experiences gathered here do not openly draw from contemporary debates on the philosophy of technology. Theory is presented here as a set of proposals, preliminary propositions, applied knowledge, collected in a time of intense social-technological acceleration. It is not yet time for a General Network Theory. There is a lot to be learned and borrowed, from both vanished and neighboring fields of study like cybernetics, system theory, mass psychology, etc. before this is achieved. In this period of "permanent transition," scholars are stuck between print and online forms of knowledge hierarchies. Despite the hype, huge investments and commercial take-off, there is no systematic networked knowledge to speak of in the "Western" world around the turn of the millennium, presumed that such a Grand Theory is even possible in the wake of "postmodernity." Institutional power remains wary of network potentials, particularly the danger of losing intellectual property and privileges.

By and large, humanities has been preoccupied with the impact of technology, from a quasi-outsider's perspective, as if society and technology can be still be separated. This also counts for (Euro-Continental) media theory, texts which are frequently not available in English translation or on line. The transfer of critical knowledge and activities into the networks still has to take place, a process which might take decades if not generations, pushed by a growing number of "netizens," who take risks by ignoring publisher's contracts, old media reputation systems and academic publication requirements. The "napsterization" of text is at hand. Content clearance houses are under construction, based on peer-to-peer file exchange principles to ensure that essential reading does not get locked up behind firewalls. But we are not yet there. The general tendency is in the opposite direction. Closed image databases, filled up with cultural heritage which once belonged to the general public, are likely to hold up if not stifle wide use of the net. A growing awareness of the potentialities of the "technologies of freedom" (Ithiel De Sola Pool) goes hand in hand with an ever faster growing control, fueled by uncertainty and fear among users.

The free and open Internet is running out of time. "As Microsoft and AOL play out their corporate duel, each will inevitably seek to lock in customers and lock out competitors," Scott Rosenberg writes in the online magazine *Salon*.[4] "I think a significant number of web users, myself included, would be happy to see these two giants cripple each other in the process. The trouble is, their moves are more likely to injure bystanders—and could wreck the net in itself." He points out that the "paradoxical and perplexing impasse" is leading the Internet back to how the commercial world worked before 1994. AOL and Microsoft don't like the Internet and never have. "MSN and AOL were closed, proprietary networks when the web exploded. Both companies hooked up their networks to the open net, while conniving to keep their users just a little fuzzy about where the 'branded' AOL or Microsoft turf ended and the rest of the net began."

In the "grim summer of 2001" Rosenberg finds the net "still too anarchic to be made a completely smooth, convenient, ready-for-prime-time experience; but it's also losing the vital ferment of its 'let a hundred flowers bloom' youth to the gray monotony of corporate control. We are reaping the worst of both worlds, networked chaos and monopolistic consolidation. In other words, we're screwed." He concludes that AOL and Microsoft are itching to turn back the clock. "If they push too hard, those who care about the survival of an independent web might simply vote with their feet and wallets. It they don't—and only if they don't—it will be time to sing the requiem of the net." I would argue here that a consumer boycott will not be able to secure the Internet's open future. The presumption of the "we" as consumers is itself a setback and points at the fading awareness that only user empowerment, not consumer behavior, can make a difference. A critique of media concentration, as Rosenberg gives here, should be combined with a better understanding of the "inner experience" of networked communities, lists, art servers, cyber-rights campaigns, copyleft projects, etc., because they have also moved on since 1994. It is necessary to go beyond principles and study the inner dynamics of hackers' groups, net activists, and artists. The net is not just a tool. The longer it exists the more important it is to understand the social laws of online life. It is only then that a possible campaign against such heavyweights as AOL and Microsoft might have a chance. The fact is that Internet advocacy groups are still mainly focused on issues related to government regulation, with a blind spot for corporate power. A re-assessment of the cyber-libertarian dominance over the Internet discourse is therefore necessary before a "Reclaim the Net" campaign can possibly take off.

The call for "net criticism" is first and foremost a quest for quality research. Only a few years ago, the only texts available were computer manuals. A medium used by hundred of millions deserves to have a sophisticated and imaginative criticism which is intrinsically part of the technical, legal, and commercial development. As is the case with books, films, and theatre, the net is in need of a lively public debate over its content and direction. However, the prisms envisioned here are not to smooth cultural anxieties of the elites. In the early days the role of the "critic" was taken by science fiction writers, followed by academic researchers and business gurus. Now the time of the net critic has come. It is not enough to produce images of the future (there are plenty of them anyway). Instead, net theory could map the limits and possibilities of materiality. The net wars are multi-spatial—fought out in electronic, material (physical/sex/gender/race, institutional, geographical), and imaginary ways. The Internet is not a parallel world, and it is increasingly becoming less dominated by its technicalities. Computer networks are penetrating society in a deep way. They are spreading so fast and so farthat it is becoming next to impossible to define net specificity towards society at large.

To get a better understanding of the web and all its functionalities would already be a monumental task. I am not just aiming at the technical level, even though software critique as found in the few good computer magazines, discussing operating systems, network architecture, and applications, could benefit from an encounter with a broader audience outside the circles of programmers and system administrators. The criticism I have in mind is as polymorphous and perverse as its topic, having the difficult task to bring together aesthetic and ethical concerns and issues of navigation and usability while keeping in mind the cultural and economic agendas of those running the networks, on the level of hardware, software, content, design, and delivery. That's a lot. Still, the scope may be large but the task is small and precise. Whereas the fox knows many things, the hedgehog knows one big thing. The Internet, in this case.

Hannah Arendt, in a letter to Mary McCarthy dated December 21, 1968, wrote: "The students are perhaps the modern machine smashers, except that they don't even know where the machines are located, let alone how to smash them." (Arendt and McCarty 1995) This observation is increasingly becoming questionable. Today's machines are on everyone's desk, hands, and pockets. There is more and more information available on the "invisible" power should be located—and so is there information on how to smash the information infrastructure. Disdain of adolescent hackers capable only of scratching the surface of the military, finance, and the media is no longer valid. Cyber war is on the rise, and this more than just a construct of the Rand Corporation financed by the Pentagon. Even without having faced fatal data loss it is obvious how the general mood on the open Internet has changed into a space of suspicion filled with untraceable tension and despair. Electronic civil disobedience is only one aspect of the many strategies available. Counterattacks can come from inside or from outside. Us-and-them divisions are not very useful here. Hackers' knowledge is generally available. Mostly playful and innocent so far, testing possibilities, online attacks can easily change character and become ideological, against the World Bank—and against you.

The spirit of the information age has turned nasty. 2001, the recession year in which this book was finalized, has been one of electronic tensions and email overload. Energies and desires were flowing to wider debates on globalization, global warming and missile defense systems, away from the Internet as such. People wake up from the libertarian consensus dream of the neutral, positive hacker ethic. Unlike Pekka Himanen in *The Hacker Ethic*, I believe that the distinction between good hackers and bad crackers, endlessly reproduced by mainstream media, is a thing of the past.[5] There is more to hackers than their "post-Protestant work ethic," as Himanen classifies them. A polarization is becoming visible between those sticking to the outworn New Economy tales of "good capitalism" and others, questioning the free market a priori. The critique of globalization is not a backlash movement, as conservatives like

Thomas E. Friedman suggest. The movements active under the "Seattle" umbrella all have a clear blueprint of global justice and economic democracy on offer. Their communication is as global as ever. Opposite to the branch model there are active trans-local exchanges between a "multitude" of nodes. The days of the offline activists, condemned to do street actions while fighting with the print media for recognition and to get their arguments heard, are numbered. Being both hacker and activist is no longer a contradiction.

There is a renaissance of media activism on both a global and a local level. Protests during numerous summits of politicians and business leaders have boosted local activities which strengthen the global, highly publicized confrontations. Different cultures of techno-geeks and eco-ferals are mingling. "Hacktivism," with its collective denial-of-service attacks on government and corporate web sites, even though controversial, is on the rise. But there are also signs of a global civil war among hackers (Chinese against US-American, Serbs against Albanian sites, Israeli and Palestinian hackers fighting each other, etc.). Unexpected feedback symptoms could occur. Backups should be made. There will be breaks in the circuitry. Activist methods, pointed at foes, backfire, leading to an arms race of even more sophisticated info "weapons" and a further rise in restrictive network security, corporate countercampaigns, and repressive state measures, sold under the name of "increased usability."

The making of "net criticism," the practice-driven Internet theory that I am presenting here, has grown from within a field of dialogue which the nettime mailing list take a central position. A special essay in this book is dedicated to the history and context of nettime. Most of the texts included here were posted and discussed on that list in a first version. I consider all artists, theorists, designers, and code hackers active on nettime as net critics. Others would say they're all net artists. That's fine with me. I am not sure if they're all net activists, but I consider each of their net works nonetheless deeply political.

My passion for "net criticism" should not be read as yet another obsession to carve out a terrain. I am not so much interested in the label as in the activity itself. Others might want to take up the interesting task to take the Gutenberg knowledge of literary criticism, critical theory, and art history in order to lay the epistemological foundations for Internet studies as an academic discipline. It's likely that historical circumstances will overrule the short term concerns expressed in this study. It is common sense that the window of opportunity for the unfinished Internet are closing, even before the medium has reached a mature stage. Still the net is not yet a monolithic broadcast medium. This might be a last call for participation. Before making public claims it could be of use to map the interiority. Offline sentiments, alarmed by the digital darkness, are calling for a halt of the ubiquitous 24-7 electronic availability. Soon it will be time to search for the non-identical, take the alien position and develop a negative network dialectics. The glorification of action and counterculture will prove no match for corporations and nation states to contain the web. Taking the cynical stand and debunking failing utopias is the easy part. There is a necessity for self-irony and the 1990s Internet will prove to be a willing victim. Following Adorno here, precisely when the libertarian project is failing, it is expressing, unintentionally, social truth.[6] Cyclical media histories should not distress anyone. Truth in this context is only an after-effect. What counts is the creation of concepts, images, and code, while resisting both digital mythos and logos.

It is time to say goodbye to the short summer of the Internet. There is no need to focus on past potentialities or future restrictions. Faced with autumn gale winds, it is not an ideal moment to think up a 2.0 version of network utopia. There is enough to explore between alienated superficialities and actual encounters in the virtual. Imagination or critique is a false choice, and the New York-based German philosopher Wolfgang Schirmacher pointed out to me the possibility of thinking and practicing them both and reconciling the contradiction. In May of 2000, at a Computer Programmers for a Social Responsibility conference in Seattle, the MIT computer theorist Joseph Weizenbaum urged me not to give up, since ideas *do* have power. The 19th-century German writer Heinrich Heine warned not to underestimate them. Ideas can destroy mighty regimes and install even worse ones. They can make and break a medium.[7] This study should be read as a contribution to the history of Internet ideas. Concerning the future, there are no firm moral principles to return to. With the American pragmatist philosopher Richard Rorty (1999, p. xxix), one could say that "principles are abbreviations of past practices." There is no way back to the golden days of text-only ascii, telnet, and pine. And there is more to say than the 30-second pitch to a venture capitalist. The digital commons, this third space in between the state and the market, is more than a separate, well-defined zone. A lively public net culture is always one in the making, free of governance and agency, representing everyone and no one, recovering a domain that never was. No code or network is imaginable for good causes only. There can only be designs, concepts, essays, versions—and requests for comment.

## < N o t e s >

1. Here I refer to John Gilmore's famous saying that the Internet "treats censorship as a malfunction and routes around it."

2. For an earlier account of Howard Rheingold's account of the 1990s, see "My Experience with Electric Minds," in Nettime 1999. Originally posted on nettime February 1, 1998, this can also be found in Rheingold 2000. The quotes here are from an earlier electronic version.

3. Opinion research, sponsored by the Markle Foundation (www.markle.org). From the press release: ". . . the research finds that the public identifies the Internet primarily as a source of information—with 45% saying their dominant image of the Internet is that of a 'library' as opposed to 17% who compare it to a 'shopping mall' or 'banking and investment office.'" Yet, despite the Internet's popularity, nearly half of all Americans (45%) see the Internet as a source of worry, and 70% of the public says "You have to question most

things you read on the Internet." By a margin of 54% to 36%, the public believes it does not enjoy the same rights and protections on line than it has in the off-line world, and 59% say they don't know who they would turn to if they had a problem on line." (www.markle.org, July 10, 2001)

4. Scott Rosenberg, "Assimilating the Web,"www.salon.com, June 26, 2001, reprinted as "The Net Closes In," *Weekend Australian Financial Review*, July 14–15, 2001, pp. 1–5.

5. In Pekka Himanen's *The Hacker Ethic* (2001), hackers are portrayed as playful, passionate programmers, combing entertainment with doing something interesting, as Linus Torvalds puts it in his preface to the book. Crackers on the other hand are portrayed as computer criminals, "virus writers and intruders" and "destructive computer users" (p. viii). Himanen does not mention the historical fact that many hackers had to gain access before the net became publicly accessible in the early 1990s. Breaking the security on a system is not by definition a criminal act, especially not if you put it into the context of another hacker ethic, "information wants to be free" (which is more than just code).

6. Paraphrased from Susan Buck-Morss, *The Origin of Negative Dialectics* (Free Press, 1997), p. 189.

7. See Isaiah Berlin, "Two Concepts of Liberty," in Berlin 1998.

# Essay on Speculative Media Theory

Arthur Kroker once pointed out that "media" are "too slow."[1] The term is no longer appropriate to express the speed culture of the digital age. "Media" still refers to information, communication, and black boxes, not to pure mediation, straight into the body. Media, almost by definition, are about filters, switches, technical limitations, silly simulations, and heartless representations. Focused on particular senses, they still need access and selection mechanisms. There are only *particular media*. We should therefore look for terms that are even more fluid, able to break through all interfaces, geographical conditions, and human imperfections. This is the ultimate "speculative" media theory, the wish to overcome the actual object of our studies and passions, heading for "The World after the Media," as one of the early texts of the Adilkno (see Adilkno 1998, pp. 209–211) called it.

The speculative view defines the net as the "medium to end all media," the "Metamedium." But at this very moment, there is not yet a General Net Theory. Cyberspace is still a work in progress. We are facing the realization (and therefore decline) of a specific kind of "partial" media theory (being "too slow"). It is in this ideological vacuum that the temporary autonomous project called "net criticism" shows up. This is a radical pragmatic form of negative thinking, in the aftermath of a period dominated by speculative thinking which tried to capture the "new."

My generation, which entered the intellectual arena in the late 1970s, witnessed the collusion of Marxism-in-crisis with the rising post-modern theory and got crushed in between the two. The dirt of punk was still too political and existential for cool people and free-thinking academics. Most issues centered around the writings of

Althusser, Gramsci, Lukacs, Poulantzas, and Foucault. We were obsessed with the question of power and ideology, beyond historicism, humanism, and the deadly economic determinism. How could the workings of ideology be thought without falling back into idealism or positivism? Media were a part of the ideological realm (but nothing more than that). Like other instances, media had their own "relative autonomy," a term that sounded like a profound revelation. And media were not only repressive, but productive, as Foucault pointed out. So where to locate power, if it is no longer in the corporate headquarters and the government? Capitalism dominates through its ideology. And slowly ideology became more and more identical with the media and its emerging technologies.

When I got involved in the "new social movements" (squatters, anti-militarist, and radical ecologist movements) in the early 1980s, it became clear that is was no longer useful to reflect on the problems of the previous generation, the generation of 1968. But it was not entirely clear whether elements of the "new French thinking" were of any use either. We did not think "micro politics," but rather practiced them (a Deleuzean era in that sense). We did not just want a piece of the cake, but "the whole bloody bakery," as the phrase of the time stated. It was not enough to be a "patchwork of minorities"—the radical movements had much stronger desires but not much actual power. The fear and anger were much stronger; no future involved here, less theory, just action. Deleuze and Guattari only became popular in the 1990s, after all these movements had dissolved into the virtual, to reappear as pop cultures, in rap, techno, and jungle.

During the political and social clashes of the 1980s another change in society had to be faced. Activists were well aware of the explosion of the media realm. I studied political science and mass communication and I remember we did not speak about media in plural, only about "mass media" as a monolithic block, media in the singular, out there. The main focus was the change of "public opinion." The movements of the early 1980s questioned the rigid definitions of politics as such, but did not yet position themselves within the media realm. The mysterious laws of "public opinion" dealt with mentality, consciousness, attitudes; a semiotic process that would ultimately bring about social and political changes without requiring reformist compromises or self-marginalization as embittered, dogmatic Marxists.

The number of channels on TV and radio, and the growing availability of micro-electronics and the PC in the mid 1980s, gave us more access to media which changed the nature of the political fight. The do-it-yourself media strengthened the position of rising movements, especially in the ongoing attempt to influence the journalists of the established media, without depending on them entirely. For me, the rise and the expansion of this media experience went together with the birth of German media theory. When my (direct) involvement as a squatter and eco-activist transformed itself into a commitment to "the media question," I discovered the emerging media theory in Germany. I even got involved in it, although I was no longer in the university and had abandoned academic rituals like footnotes, doing a Ph.D., etc. Just to name a few: Friedrich Kittler in Berlin; Siegfried Zielinski, for a long time head of the Cologne Academy of New Media Arts; Nobert Bolz in the design department in Essen; Christoph Tholen, who used to be in Kassel, a meeting place of German media theorists in the 1980s. There are influences from Jean Baudrillard and Paul Virilio (others would list Derrida and Deleuze). But also Avital Ronell from the United States. For me, the predominant leader is the Jewish-German-Brazilian media philosopher Vilém Flusser. And then there are Peter Weibel and Florian Rötzer, who built bridges between media theory, new media arts, and the visual arts establishment. Such name dropping can only be subjective. The intellectual output since the mid 1980s has been massive.[2]

Let's try to summarize this specific type of media theory. It is not exactly academic or even scientific. There is a strong emphasis on style. At its best, it is techne-poetry, brilliant in its search for new, historical patterns. At its worst it is dry, academic hermeneutics. There is a strong affection for art and aesthetics, and it has a strong relationship to literature and philosophy. If English-speaking colleagues could read all this, it would be fun to read their critique of its metaphysical, 18th- and 19th-century style and premises. Take the works of Martin Heidegger, Carl Schmitt,

Walter Benjamin, Sigmund Freud, Ernst Jünger, Friedrich Nietzsche, J. G. Hamann, Novalis, and J. W. Goethe, simmer them in the sauce of latest media technologies, flavor it with a dash of French Theory. That is the basic recipe.

Postmodern media theory tries implicitly to negate and in many cases deny its 1968 past. Also typical is the rejection of the existence of rival and neighboring media theories. There are no references to the existing media studies like "mass communication" or cultural studies (with McLuhan being the exception). Its dislike of social sciences remains a secret. In the German context, a public condemnation of the Frankfurt School remains necessary (Habermas in particular). German media theory, as I got to know it, dislikes ideology criticism. It reduces media to the essence of the machine logic. It is not interested in the meaning of its message, which was once assumed to be propaganda. Speaking about the fascist past of some the authors in an open way still seems highly problematic. It is not done to just enjoy dubious thinkers and appreciate Heidegger as a fascist (despite his short fascist engagement). A secret or unconscious fascination for authoritarian models is still there. The elitist disdain over the rituals of parliamentary democracy echoes in many texts. Don't laugh about the totalitarian heritage of the Big Thinkers, it is all taken very seriously. In this sense, the Cold War, being the project to freeze-dry the fatal European passions, had not yet ended in the this particular branch of theory.

Central to the specific German media theory discussed here is the definition of media as technical media. This should be seen as a polemic gesture to remove all references to an economic, political, social or even cultural context. First and foremost, media have to be described in the language of the technical, in the language of the technology itself. Strangely enough, this is a precise expression of the further rise of media as an "autonomous" realm, the victory of ideology over the other instances. When media starts to float (and become "immaterial"), it first of all has to cut all references to journalism, social sciences, ideas of progress and enlightenment, state propaganda and public opinion (being a tool to educate and entertain the people).

Media from now on are merely spin-off products of the military that basically deal with the war of perception. The rest is merely noise.

It is important to see that there is a continuity from the debate about ideology and power as a first phase, the notions of discourse and structures as a second, and the centrality of the technical media as a third. Crucial for all three stages is their relation to Jacques Lacan and the question of language. We can see a shift here and a continuous process of redefinition of "language" from being just the spoken and written word toward "language" as a general structural mechanism, ending up with a very abstract definition, the language of the technology, which can no longer be deconstructed as an ideology so easily. Although "language" became so crucial, at the same time these thinkers were confronted with the so-called crisis of linearity, the crisis of the text. With the rise of the personal computer, the status of the text in society changed; so did the role of writing in the electronic age.

Essential for these thinkers is that they have to introduce the "new" in the terms of the old. They always have to proclaim the new and condemn the old while still keeping a channel open to the traditional disciplines. So there is a constant oscillation between the new and the old, both of which must be incorporated in the theory. Also characteristic is a melancholic position towards the old terminology and sources, combined with a deep, philosophic fascination for the new, though never in a truly futuristic manner. The destruction of the old seems an alien notion in this context. Being post-political intellectuals, it is difficult for most of them to act like the hippie prophets and other spiritual propagandists for the new. They can't easily be transformed into Siemens salesmen. Instead, their task remains the careful exploration and explanation of the objectives of the "new" in the language of the old. Their success lies in presenting new media to a conservative cultural elite.

The postwar generation is used to constantly undermining its own premises (an old leftist habit, by the way). In particular in deconstructing the premises of the May 1968 slogans. This became an obsession for most of them—especially for Baudrillard.

They are even more influenced by the trauma of the Second World War. All of them make references to the crucial period between the two world wars, both historically and theoretically. The War is the father of all media, and the founding fathers of media theory are Heidegger and Benjamin (McLuhan being the good third). Combine all these elements and you have an impressive and productive research program for decades to come.

German media theory is like the prophet Moses writing the media laws on tablets, staying behind, unable to travel with his people into the promised new media land. 1980s media theory is in essence a philosophy of The End. Seen in a larger context, it works its way up to its historical height in 1989. It contemplates The End (of the social, history, ideology etc.), but because of its refusal to be radically modern, it is unwilling to overcome its own ideological framework which was formed in the period 1968–1989. As for many of the intellectuals of the same generation, it seems impossible to fit the Fall of the Berlin Wall into the aesthetic program. Most of them do not want to be bothered by the East and its communist history and can only interpret it as an atavistic, disturbing factor, just another sign of ongoing disintegration and fragmentation. Technology is hardware in the first place. It has no users that play with it in a productive way. That is why pop culture can be ignored so easily. Hardware is the driving force, not people, let alone East European revolutions. It sounds almost Marxist, this technological determinism, but that is what happens when theory has freed itself from the categories of (class) subjectivity. A techno materialism with the military in the driver's seat.

There are two methods in use. On the one hand the fascinating "media archaeology" to be found in the works of Werner Künzel, Siegfried Zielinski, Bernhard Siegert, and Christoph Asendorf, to name a few. Well known examples of media archeology are Paul Virilio's *War and Cinema*, Friedrich Kittler's *Grammophone, Film, Typewriter* and Avital Ronell's *The Telephone Book*. On the other hand, there is the tradition of hermeneutics, the essay or theory as such, which can easily be used to speculative about the future possibilities of new media, built on historical references, combining etymology with technological forecasts. But it can also go into the direction of the historical anthropology (as in Dietmar Kamper, Peter Sloterdijk, et al.) or stay within the academic borders of the science of literature (Hans-Ulrich Gumbrecht, Jochen Hörisch, et al.). And then there are the hard core computer scientists with literary ambitions like Otto Rössler, Heinz von Foerster, and Oswald Wiener. It is impossible to give an overview here—99 percent of all this has not been translated, but that's another story.

A crucial term, if we want to study this media theory, seems to me the definition of aesthetics. Media theory rejects the classical definition of aesthetics used by art historians (a set of rules to judge the artwork) and comes up with a new one, focusing on the technical determination of perception. We can no longer speak about a pure aesthetics which is just an expression of visual pleasure. This kind of aesthetics is guided by military perception. It is technical because it is defined by all the tools we are using. There is no aesthetics anymore besides or beyond the technical. All these thinkers were relatively unknown until the late 1980s. But this all changed when the Western societies went through a narcotic period of intense speculation—in bonds and currencies, real estate, painting, and . . . theory. This happened during the 1980s. We see academic theory bursting out of its small circle, making an alliance with the visual art scene and the emerging media-art scene, which by then was mainly video art.

It is also exactly in this period, dominated by speculation, that we see the rise of cyberculture, with its virtual reality, multi-media, and computer networks (BBS and the pre-WWW Internet). Until the late 1980s there were only the rumors one could read in the novels of William Gibson and other cyberpunk writers. This suddenly changed in 1989 with the appearance of the visionaries who not only dreamt, but also had access to the actual technology. By and large, German media theory has been, and still is, offline—old-fashioned Gutenberg knowledge stored in books. Despite a few hypertext attempts (Heiko Idensen), the theory itself is not technical. Is it because of this shortcoming of the institution-focused baby boom generation that 1980s

German media theory is stepping back, ruled over by the Internet wave, mainly dominated by American authors. The history-driven speculative approach bounces back,
having little to contribute in the economic and political debates over the network
parameters. Valuable knowledge, ready to be rediscovered, recycled, and mutated in
the next round of speculative media theory, this time in a networked environment.

**< N o t e s >**

1. Arthur Kroker, lecture at InterCommunicationCentre, Tokyo, December
19, 1996 (*Mute*, no. 7, 1997: 1–2; *InterCommunication Magazine*, no.
20, 1997; posted on nettime January 13, 1997). Kroker made the remark
at the November 1995 Interface 3 conference in Hamburg.

2. From 1989 to 1994 I reviewed German media theory books for
*Mediamatic* magazine. My reviews were translated from Dutch into
English. See reviews of the following: Martin Giesecke, *Der Buchdruck
in der fruehen Neuzeit* (*Mediamatic* 8, no. 2, 1995: 145–149);
Friedrich Kittler, *Dracula's Vermächtnis* (*Mediamatic* 8, no. 1,
1994: 1942–1943); Hartmut Winkler, *Switching-Zapping* (*Mediamatic* 8,
no. 1, 1994: 1946–1947); Norbert Bolz, *Die Welt als Chaos und
Simulation*, plus Quick Reviews (*Mediamatic* 7, no. 2: 181–186). See
also "The Archeology of Computer Assemblage," an interview with Werner
Künzel plus a review of his books (*Mediamatic* 6, no. 4, 1992:
71–76); review of *Hard War/Soft War*, ed. Martin Stingelin and
Wolfgang Scherer (*Mediamatic* 6, no. 3, 1992: 282–283); review of
*Digitaler Schein*, ed. Florian Roetzer (*Mediamatic* 6, no. 3, 1992:
294–295); "Deutsches Denken: Interview with Dietmar Kamper" (6, no. 1,
1991: 21–30); "Deutsches Denken: Interview with Norbert Bolz" (6, no.
1, 1991: 31–41); review of Norbert Bolz, *Theorie der neuen Medien*
(5, no. 4, 1991: 254–255); review of *Television/Revolution, Das
Ultimatum des Bildes*, ed. Hubertus von Amelunxen and Andrei Ujica
(*Mediamatic* 5, no. 4, 1991: 255–256); review of *Philosophien der
neuen Medien*, ed. Ars Electronica (*Mediamatic* 4, no. 1, 1990, p.
73); "Media Archeology, An Introduction to the Work of Friedrich
Kittler" (*Mediamatic* 3, no. 4, 1989: 185–189); review of *Kunstforum
97 & 98*, ed. Florian Roetzer (*Mediamatic* 3, no. 3, 1989: 168–169).

# Portrait of the Virtual Intellectual

Much has been said about the changing role of the artist, the designer, and the architect in the age of cyber technologies.[1] Clearly, these professions are undergoing profound changes. However, little has been heard in this context about the figure of the intellectual. Are intellectuals condemning themselves to manage the vanishing Gutenberg galaxy? Is the whole idea of the intellectual disappearing altogether, as Russell Jacoby suggest in *The Last Intellectual* (1987)? For Joyce Carol Oates the term intellectual is a very self-conscious one. "To speak of oneself as an 'intellectual' is equivalent to arrogance and egotism, for it suggests that there is a category of persons who are 'not-intellectuals.'"[2] Gone are the days of Gramsci and his followers, who believed in the firm bond between "organic intellectuals" and the ordinary people. The condemned effete aloofness of the intellectual is in fact a sign of their isolation. "The public intellectual has become the Abominable Snowman of contemporary discourse: there are endlessly discussions about what one might look like but no one has actually seen one," notes Andrew Anthony in the English newspaper *The Observer*.[3]

Absent in the debate over the dawn of the intellectuals is the correlation between the fall of the intelligentsia and the rise of new media. Most writers and researchers are by now familiar with the computer as a tool, but this says little of the theoretical concepts they may harbor around the Internet, new media or wireless communication. It is a fashion among established intellectuals to be skeptical about the "digital revolution." Who can take those ugly screens seriously anyway? One perceives a silent wish that with the fading away of the cyber-crazes and net hypes, the technologies themselves will also somehow disappear. The intellectuals turned technocrats dream about anything non-technical: sport, food, opera, holidays, and sex.

With technology confused for "popular culture," a return of the highbrow-lowbrow distinction seems to be in the making. While "true devotees" of culture apply themselves to books, opera, and painting, the gray, uncivilized classes are to be kept busy with primitive and juvenile "new" media. The lonely online crowds are lured into a state of permanent numbness, resulting in dazed and confused packs of online consumer sitting it out in ever lasting zapping, clicking, chatting, and surfing sessions. *Digitization takes command*: electronic solitude creates a Cybernetic Waste Land. Included here is a new aristocracy harboring a deep hatred towards the online masses. To rephrase John Carey (1992): "The crowd has taken possession of media which were created by civilization for the best people." The fooling around with immature, "beta" media stands in sharp contrast with the "sensual perception of the wholeness of the artwork." The elitist, usually government-subsidized/state-sanctioned and exportable forms of expressions are slipping into open warfare with vulgar and commercial cyber-culture. Even today, few intellectuals are prepared to take the digital media seriously. While photography, film, and video are now accepted art forms, the hyper-commercial, constantly changing software landscape still lacks substantive intellectual and cultural critique. This is the case even within art and technology circles, where theorists seem to suffer from techno-ennui. Into this field one can either become like a visionary salesperson or assume the role of moaning defender of established art values. Most of the writing on new media is done by either computer experts or business journalists. The cultural sector is merely using technology as a tool and does not want its core to be effected by the binary machine logic.

Who will initiate Paul Virilio so that he can give us a more precise, nay, a more radical, interpretation of the social impacts of the new technologies? Who will critique the neo-liberal cyber-hallucinations of Pierre Lévy with his "collective intelligence"? Who will finally stop Baudrillard's tragic complaints? Bruno Latour seems to be the exception of the rule. Paris—once the intellectual capital of the world—has fallen prey to moralistic debates about "most favorite victim" status (as in the case of Bosnia and Kosovo). Here we are seeing most clearly what the current crisis of the intellectual is about. The production of attractive role models got us nowhere. The cultural climate has gone into the defensive mode. The growing anxiety is fluid and can take many forms: sometimes xenophobic, sometimes against the European Union or globalization, or just against the State in general. Both the emotional and the rational calls for political engagement are melting away, just like all other information.

The intellectual as TV personality (for example, Bernard-Henri Lévy) seems to be part of the problem, rather than part of the solution. The need for spokespeople and experts, producing opinions on a day-to-day basis has become an integral part of the current Society of the Spectacle. But the intellectual of the Media Age should not by definition be identical to the figure of the media personality. What Paris of the 1990s (as an example) is showing is not so much the need for more self-marketing of celebrities but is the absence of "techno literacy": intellectuals aware of the technicality of their profession. Instead, what traditional critics do is mix up the media question with the content issue, as Andrew Anthony does in the following: "Interest in society, especially literary interest, has been almost entirely replaced by a preoccupation with the media. Nowadays when we speak of 'Big Brother,' we refer not to George Orwell's invention, but to the reality TV show, and there are no end of media commentators to explain what it means."[4] Instead of calling for a radical upgrade of literary criticism, this genre is played out against the media, in particular by George Steiner, but also by Martin Amis in his collection of essays and reviews titled *The War Against Cliché*.[5] Confusing the medium with the message, in this case, for example, Internet with pulp television is not exactly a sign of sophistication. Over the last few decades media theory has drawn heavily from literary criticism. Perhaps it is time to reverse the intellectual exchange.

In part this is all a generation problem. The generation of the 1960s (known in France as *les quadras*) equipped with the Gramscian "organic intellectual" notion closely tied to the Party and social movements is now at the height of its power. The baby boomers conquered all possible positions and marched into all possible institutions. But there is no one leading anymore. Policy implementation has replaced avant-gardism. The Leninist question: "What is to be done?" nowadays lacks both subject and object. The 1968 generation have become parents, worried by the senseless escapism of their children.[6]

Take for example Edward Said, who still sticks to the old, well-known definition of the intellectual. In *Representations of the Intellectuals* (1994) Said insists that the intellectual is "an individual with a specific public role in society that cannot be reduced to being a faceless professional." Said warns of the dangers of specialization and professionalism and instead favors an amateurism which is "speaking truth to power." Against specific knowledge, Said highlights general concern. The intellectual should be endowed with "a faculty for representing, embodying, and articulating a message to, as well as for, a public." Arguing against rigid sociological class definitions, which define intellectuals solely through their profession, Said turns them into moral agents, defined by their attitude. The intellectual belongs on the same side with the "weak and unrepresented." This requires a "constant alertness" and "steady realism" (Said 1994).

This sounds touching and noble, and Said is right when he is stressing that the intellectual and the public are inextricably intertwined. What is missing here is an analysis of the dramatic changes of the public sphere itself. Some cultural pessimists have stated that the public itself has already vanished altogether. The daily reality is that the so-called public domain in the urban realm (for example, streets, squares, and parks) is under permanent surveillance and control. More and more of it being privatized. This holds not only true in real, but also in virtual space. What needs to outlined is the possible role of tomorrow's intellectuals in the digital public domain, on the Internet but also within the "third-generation" wireless phone spectrum, satellites, and terrestrial digital radio and television bands.

In *Electronic Civil Disobedience*, Critical Art Ensemble states that, as far as power is concerned, the streets are dead capital. Even though the brick monuments of power still stand, the agency that maintains dominance is neither visible nor stable. According to CAE, the only groups that will successfully confront this new form of power are "those that locate the arena of contestation in cyberspace." The methods of civil disobedience, like picket lines, demonstrations, and petitions, are largely ineffective and empty rituals. With neither spite nor disdain towards the remaining traditional attempts to question the current world system of global capitalism, it should be stated, in public, and as clearly as possible, that "contemporary activism has had very little impact on military and corporate policy" (Critical Art Ensemble 1996).

The same could be said of the intellectual still living in the paper world. The days of Foucault's discursive power are over. The system without alternative does not need the magical power of words anymore in order to rule. In need are those capable of transforming concepts into workable models. We are witnessing the much-vaunted "end of ideology." The realm of "ideas" as such is not dangerous or subversive anymore. Ideas do matter but there are no longer by definition "weapons." It is tempting for the critical intelligentsia to think otherwise and continue to debunk the media lies. The overall increase of skepticism, the daily cynical distrust against all transmitted information has led to an overall loss in faith about the influence and impact of ideas. Ideology has migrated into the sphere of techno-culture. Ideas that matter are hard-wired into software and network architectures. Rationality successfully besieged religions and all other metaphysical expressions and turned them into pure, cold functionalities. A renaissance of ideas can only happen after the defeat of the literary establishment is a fact. It is of no use to dream up a return to the days gone by of Parisian existentialism, the Bloomsbury set, LA exile intellectuals or the New York Partisan Review crowd. Today's challenge lies in orchestrating radical intercultural exchanges not in closed monocultures.

The return of fundamentalisms, nationalisms, regionalisms, etc. is not a serious threat to the New World Order. Benjamin Barber's endless variations on the dynamics between "McWorld" and "Jihad" (see Barber 1995) only express temporary conflicts in the margins of global capitalism. These conflicts may be bloody and affect the lives of millions of people, but the current catastrophe zones don't have any impact on the Capitalist Condition. A Black Monday on Wall Street might. The war in Bosnia did not disrupt Western economies though it proved nearly fatal to Bosnia. This time, Sarajevo wasn't allowed to throw the world into a world war. It is no longer 1914.

Alain Finkelkraut's ode to the Croatian state, Bernard-Henry Levy's use of the siege of Sarajevo as a stage for his media appearances, or Peter Handke's late and profoundly touristic discovery of the Serbian countryside marked the end of the intellectual as a public figure with any significant impact. The cynical competition for the "most favorite victim status" among the different ethnic groups made all known methods of outrage and engagement irrelevant overnight. Unlike the days of the Vietnam War, it has become more and more difficult to choose sides. This again is drawing us deeper into a status of passive consumers, bored by the overkill of undistinguishable strains of infotainment. Intellectuals who only express opinions, in the belief that the media industry (particularly television) still produces common sense content which shapes public opinion, should simply desist, boycott all talk shows and instead engage in fundamental research on the "state of the media."

In his book *The Clash of Civilizations* Samuel Huntington overstresses the role of culture within today's global capitalism. This reflects, in my opinion, wishful thinking about the return of the old style intellectual (or priest) who will have the last say in entire societies. Their will to power is of a highly resentful nature. These conservatives are defending a model of the West which no longer exists. The "clashes" they predict might in fact take place in some decades, when, for example, China will have reached the level of the Western economic powers. Within the current situation, we can only interpret these scenarios as a collective, deeply nostalgic rehash of ideological, Cold War-like conflicts that will not return.

The fact is that the intellectual as opinion leader is losing ground. In its fading shadow we see the rise of the VI, the Virtual Intellectual. These "knowledge workers" are thoroughly familiar with the "virtual condition." They have also come to terms with the declining power of book culture and the public sphere as we have known it. Before we try to outline the shape and task of this figure as a social category, it might be useful to make a distinction between "theory fiction" and the (scientific) description of new sociological phenomena. In theory fiction terms, the virtual intellectual might very well be an "Unidentified Theoretical Object," a UTO, like the ones described on page 10 of Adilkno 1998. We could then compare the VI with literary avatar categories such as the data dandy, or classification of the human body as "wetware." Just as the cyberpunk, or the Generation X slacker, or the geek/computer nerd, the VI role model might even leave the realm of literature or theory and enter popular culture in order to vanish again after a while. The power of the VI is a potential one: s/he might turn up as a virtual creature, but could as well remain elusive and never leave the conceptual, beta stage.

We need to examine the context of the emerging VI—the relationship between the computer-literate intellectual and the hardware and software industry. Arthur Kroker and Michael Weinstein did so in their remarkable description of the "virtual class" (1994). This emerging class, with its own *Wired* ideology, might also have its own "organic" intellectuals. However, the VI described here is more than just a cool spokesperson for the new media industry and the battalions of "digital artisans" attached to it. The virtual intellectual is first of all equipped with technical skills and can freely move around within online databases, list cultures, search engines, and hypertext environments. A lively and critical online intellectual life requires the transfer of crucial heritage into the digital public domain. While underway, this process has in no way really kicked off. The interests of established offline Gutenberg power within the publishing industry and universities in the early millennium years are still considerable. Despite heavy use by a considerable part of the population, Internet credibility remains low. This is the main reason why the figure of the virtual intellectual, as proposed here, can only be a draft.

The playful, ironic, and imaginary categories and the critical socio-political analysis of new class formations are two different ways of theory production. In my ICC lecture "From Speculative Media Theory towards Net Criticism" I contextualized both by putting them in a personal and at the same time historical perspective. Here I just want to point out that the virtual intellectual has elements of both: a will to design, to construct the public part of cyberspace, to be "radically modern" (beyond the melancholy of postmodernism), combined with the ability to reflect and criticize the (new) media from all possible perspectives. In both cases, design and critique, it is important to overcome the widespread resentments, cynicism, and elitism such a position attracts, on the one hand, and over-hyped sales talk on the other. This implies that all forms of technological determinism should be condemned. Technology is not inevitability; it is designed, it can be criticized, altered, undermined, mutated and, at times, ignored in order to subvert its limiting, totalitarian tendencies caused by either states or markets.

What is it that makes this type of intellectual "virtual"? Needless to say that s/he will no longer accept the editorial tyranny of the Gutenberg bosses. The virtual intellectual of my dreams would freely move around on the net, having its own web site and attached revenue string of micro payments, establishing alternative reputation systems, wary of the reintroduction of scarcity and proprietary models. Like other professions migrating into cyberspace, this new figure will be constituted through their specific mixture of local and global cultures, digitized and non-digitized source material, and real and screen-only experiences. The VI is conscious of the limitations of today's texts, without at the same time becoming a servant of the "empire of images." Since s/he has been educated in the heritage of the (sacred) text, the VI will now be confronted with the challenge of the growing visualization of ideas. Text-only systems can no longer be auto-poetic power systems. The self-referential tendency of all singular media needs to be corrected and expanded with cross-links to imagery, audio files, and hyperlinks embedded in online databases.

Here, virtual also has the meaning of open, ever changing, in constant contact with other e-writers (and readers), no longer focused on the closed, hermetic Magnus Opus that defined the "age of the author." On the whole, we may state that the nature of the virtual intellectual is first and foremost technical. Unlike its predecessors, s/he is no longer defined through the relation to the political sphere in a classical sense. The public sphere itself will more and more be a product of technical media and lead a true virtual life of its own, no longer connected to places like the coffeehouse, the salon, the boulevard or even the more abstract realm of the newspaper and television discourse. The global "(wo)man of e-letters" is part of the online masses, but does not feel a need to speak on behalf of the Internet-at-large or even a specific virtual community. The VI also lacks any sentimental drive to represent unprivileged offline groups. Future media politics is about empowerment, not about representing the Other. The goal of the democratization of the media is the elimination of all forms of mediated representation and artificial scarcity of channels. There are now the technical possibilities to let people speak for themselves, even if they have little or no bandwidth. Public access to a variety of communication tools and the worldwide support of independent, tactical media might ultimately make the political intellectual redundant.

Thus, in this theory design the virtual intellectual is located in the sphere of the negative. Even in the pragmatic work of programming, interface design, or the planning of network architecture, the negative should be the starting point. Utilizing all utopian machines available, the specific task of the virtual intellectual will be to explore negative thinking. The main threat to a critical praxis nowadays comes from the positive, "humanistic" intentions, or what Calin Dan calls "the dictatorship of good will."[7] Intellectuals might not so easily commit "treason" again, if we may refer to Julian Benda's *Treason of the Intellectuals* (1927). They might not be attracted so easily by totalitarian ideologies. But will they resist the current free-market way of thinking, as described in Ignacio Ramonet's "One Idea System"?[8]

The majority of the knowledge workers are no longer state employees, nor are they members of the Party. Today's VI could be located in the growing sector of the NGOs and their tendency towards anti-intellectual direct action pragmatism in the name of the Good (do first, think later), locked in a unholy alliance with mainstream media—or, worse, as marginalized freelance workers, *freischwebende Intelligenz*, free-floating intellectuals, not out of choice for a bohemian lifestyle, but as the only option left. The answer to escape such an impoverished ghetto in my opinion lies in a radical techno-engagement, expressed in festive forms of data nihilism, joyous negativism that resists reductive and essentialist strategies, connecting streams of data from either side of the old and new media, in both real and virtual spaces. Media freedom ultimately means leaving the media question behind. It means mixing and sampling the local and the global while flying through self-made hybrid data landscapes. The virtual intellectual: always under construction.

## < Notes >

1. "Portrait of the Virtual Intellectual, On the design of the public cybersphere," lecture at 100 days program of Documenta X Kassel, July 13, 1997. Posted on nettime July 20, 1997; responses from Frank Hartmann, July 23, 1997 and Peter Lunenfeld, July 23 and 26, 1997.

2. In *What Good Are Intellectuals?* ed. Bernard-Henri Lévy (Algora, 2000); quoted from Andrew Anthony's review in *The Observer*, July 8, 2001.

3. Anthony, *The Observer*, July 8, 2001.

4. Ibid.

5. For an analysis of George Steiner's loathing for media, see Adilkno 1998, pp. 159—164.

6. The Melbourne critic Mark Davis has written a book about culture wars: *Gangland* (1997). An interview I did with Mark Davis was published by Telepolis (www.heise.de/tp) and posted on nettime (October 14, 2000).

7. Calin Dan, "Soros—The Dictatorship of Goodwill," posted to nettime May 10, 1997.

8. Ignacio Ramonet, "One Idea System" (translated by Patrice Riemens), in "Ctheory" (http://www.ctheory.com/event/e012.html). Originally published in *Le Monde Diplomatique*, January 1995.

# The Digital City—Metaphor and Community

The Amsterdam Digital City, founded in 1993, is one of Europe's largest and best-known independent community Internet projects. It was a "freenet," made up of free dial-up access, free email, and web space, within which many online communities formed. As one of its founders I have lectured and written about de digitale Stad (DDS) on numerous occasions.[1] Not being involved in its daily operations, but still dedicated to certain aspects, this relative distance gave me the freedom to report and theorize about the inner workings of such a large system with tens of thousands of users.

Over a period of eight years the Digital City (www.dds.nl) went through many phases of growth and change, anticipating and responding to Internet developments at large. Reflecting its actual and symbolic significance, research about DDS communities and the history of DDS also expanded.[2] The privatization of its online community services in late 2000 sparked a fierce debate among active users. Attempts were made to keep the public domain community parts of DDS out of the hands of commercial interests.[3] By mid 2001 the turbulent history came to an end with the closure of the free access services. As of August 1, 2001, DDS was transformed into a regular commercial Internet provider offering broadband DSL services to a largely reduced customer base.

Considerations presented here are to be understood within the specific Dutch context of the 1990s, a period of fierce neo-liberalism in a country once known for its opulent welfare state. Dutch independent Internet culture, driven by a demand for public media access, grew up in the economically fragile post-recession years of the

1990s in a climate of permanent budget cuts in the state funded cultural sector. Non-profit Internet initiatives therefore had to find new ways to operate in between the state and the market. The Digital City story tells of the difficulties in building up a broad and diverse Internet culture within a Zeitgeist of the "absent state" and the triumph of market liberalism.

By the early 1990s the (in)famous Amsterdam squatters' movement, which had dominated the social and cultural (and law-and-order) agenda of the previous decade, had petered out in the city's streets, but its autonomous yet pragmatic mode of operation had infiltrated the workings of the more progressive cultural institutions.[4] The autonomous movement of the 1980s had successfully occupied both urban spaces and the electronic spectrum (free radio and even a brief chapter of pirate television). The movement had built a sustainable alternative infrastructure beyond street riots and political conflicts. It was the time that the cultural centers *Paradiso* and *De Balie*,[5] which were both at the vanguard of local cultural politics, embraced the "technological culture" theme in their programming.[6] In the beginning, this took the shape of a critical, if somewhat passive observation of the technologies surrounding us and of their risks, but it quickly evolved into a do-it-yourself approach. Technology was no longer seen as the preserve of science, big business, or the government. It could also become the handiwork of average groups or individuals. Mass availability of electronic hardware and components had created a broad user base for "low-tech" applications, something that in its turn spawned feasts of video art, robotics and other forms of "industrial culture," free radio and public access television, and well-attended cultural events where technology was rearranged and playfully dealt with.

The late 1980s also witnessed the emergence of electronic networks. These were of course already in use with the military, banking and finance, and academia. A cluster of grassroots computer enthusiasts had also been building up a patchwork of "bulletin board systems" for some time, but it was the hackers' repeated and much-publicized intrusions in the big network, known as the Internet, that bought electronic communications for the masses onto the political agenda. Thus was the demand for public access born. What made the Amsterdam situation special, however, was the

degree of organization among the hackers and their willingness to structure themselves as an open social movement. This enabled them to communicate with a wide
audience and to negotiate their acceptance into society at large through journalists,
cultural mediators, some politicians, and even a few enlightened members of the
police force. After a whirlwind performance in *Paradiso* by the notorious German
Chaos Computer Club (www.ccc.de) in the fall of 1988, the stage was set for the
Galactic Hackers Party, the first open, public international convention of hackers in
Europe, which took place in August 1989, produced by Caroline Nevejan, with
*Paradiso* as venue.[7] From then on, hackers had deftly positioned themselves between
(media) artists, militants, and cultural workers.

The concept of public access media in Amsterdam was already largely in place
thanks to the remarkably deep penetration of cable broadcasting (radio and television,
with more than 90 percent of households reached by the mid 1980s). This cable system had been set up and was owned by the municipality. It was run as a public service, and its bill of fare and tariff rates were set by the city council. The council had
also legislated that one or two channels were to be made available to minorities and
artists groups—also as a way to curb the wild experiments of TV pirates—and so
various initiatives sprung up whose offerings, to say the least, were far removed from
mainstream TV programming. This peculiar brand of community television did not go
for an amateurish remake of professional journalism, but took a typically Amsterdam
street-level (mostly "live") approach, on both the artistic and the political plane.
Whereas the now co-opted TV pirates were thus successfully taken out, the presence
on the airwaves of three non-profit "cultural pirate" radio stations remained tolerated. All this resulted in a politically (self-) conscious, technically fearless, and above
all financially affordable media ambiance, something that was also very much fostered by the proliferation of small, specialized, non-commercial outfits in the realm of
electronic music such as STEIM, Montevideo/Time Based Arts for both general and
more political video art, and the new media arts magazine *Mediamatic*.

These developments contributed to a media culture in Amsterdam which was nei-ther shaped by market-oriented populism nor informed by highbrow cultural elitism. The various players and the institutions in the field did get subsidies from the usual funding bodies and government agencies, but they have managed to retain their inde-pendence thanks to a mostly voluntary-based mode of operation and a low-tech (or rather "in-house tech") and low-budget approach. Also the shifts in funding practice, moving away from recurrent subsidies to one of project-linked disbursements, in keep-ing with the ruling market populism of the time, left their marks on the format of these activities. Many small-scale productions have thus seen the light, but the estab-lishment of more permanent structures has been constrained. This in turn has led to the prevalence of a hands-on, innovative attitude, an ingrained spirit of temporality, and the deployment of "quick-and-dirty aesthetics" by groups such as TV 3000, De Hoeksteen, Park TV, Rabotnik, and Bellissima (all active in the "public broadcasting space" provided by the cable channel SALTO). [8] And not to forget the Digital City's own innovations in the realm of streaming media and Internet radio and television (http://live.dds.nl), which took place with the grudging approval of its own manage-ment. This "edgy" climate also was the result in the relative absence of direct links between the new media culture and the political establishment. The emerging new media culture was seen by decision makers as a buffer, an employment scheme for the creative surplus mobs, an in-between zone of sorts, far removed from the concerns of parliamentary democracy, "significant" shapers of "public opinion" and "real" cul-ture. However, if public access media in Amsterdam were not an instrument in the hands of the political class, this did not mean that they were non-political per se. It simply meant that there was no intervention from above and, more particularly, no censorship or even surveillance.

Electronic activists were meanwhile poised for the next phase: the opening up of the Internet for general use. The hackers movement, operating under the banner of the HackTic group (which was also publishing a magazine with the same name, whose technical "disclosures" annoyed the telecom to no end), threw up a coup by obtaining from the Dutch academic network permission to hook up officially to the Internet and resell the connectivity. What no one had anticipated, least of all the budding hackers "entrepreneurs" themselves, was that all the 500 accounts which formed the starting base of the HackTic Network would be snapped up on the very first day. Not for profit access to the Internet was henceforth established early on as a norm of sorts in the Netherlands. Combined with the technological savvy of the hackers, this created a situation in which commercial enterprise would follow and benefit from the existing creative diversity rather than riding the waves of the Internet hype and making quick money without any incentive to innovate or concern for public participation. In less than two years the hackers venture morphed into a profitable business, renamed Xs4all (access for all).[9]

These developments did not escape the smarter elements of the government who were on the lookout for ways of modernizing the economic infrastructure of the country in the wake of the globalization process. Since electronic communication was also at the same time perceived to pose all sorts of possible threats on the law-and-order front, a two-pronged approach was necessary, meant to contain the "menace" and to co-opt the "whiz kids." Comprehensive and fairly harsh "computer crime" laws were approved by parliament in 1993. The second big hackers convention in the Netherlands, Hacking at the End of the Universe (HEU), in the summer of 1993, responded to this potentially repressive climate with a PR offensive. By stressing the public liberties aspect, a coalition was formed between "computer activists" and other media, culture, and business players who did not want to be reduced to mere consumers of the content and context agenda set by big corporations. The idea being that programmers, artists, and other interested parties, can, if they are moving early enough, shape, or at least influence, the architecture of the networks. This happens also to be the favorite move of early adopters, and it enables one to gain ideological ascendance when influential projects are taking shape—a move suitably if somewhat cryptically called in German "die Definition der Lage in die Hand nehmen" ("to take the definition of the situation in one's own hands") and a form of DIY citizens' activism that in the late 1990s would have been identified and re-labeled as "entre-preneurial leadership."

Elected politicians meanwhile were struggling with another "situational" problem: that of their very own position amidst fast-dwindling public support and sagging cred-ibility. This was—not surprisingly—blamed on a "communication deficit" for which a substantial application of "new media" suddenly appeared to be an instant antidote. The clue was not lost on De Balie cultural center which approached City Hall with a freenet based proposal to link up the town's inhabitants through the Internet so that they could "engage in dialogue" with their representatives and with the policy makers. The system itself was to be installed by the people at HackTic Network, the only group of techies at that time that was readily available—or affordable. The Digital City was launched in January 1994 as a ten-week experiment in electronic democracy. The response from the public was overwhelming. And in no time, "everybody" was commu-nicating with everybody else. With one exception though: the local politicians never made it to the new medium.

The Digital City was an initiative of Marleen Stikker, the later director of the Society for Old and New Media (www.waag.org), then a staff member of De Balie. Before 1993 Marleen had organized projects on the crossroads of theater, new media arts, and public debate in which technology always played a key role. In the festivals she got artists to work with interactive television, voicemail games, live radio, and video-conferencing systems. During 1993 Marleen shared her room in De Balie with Press Now, a newly founded support campaign for independent media in Former Yugoslavia. Email proved to be an important tool for keeping in contact with peace groups and media initiatives on either side of the conflict.

Marleen Stikker: "Through the use of email I got fascinated by the use of other possibilities the Internet at that time offered such as irc (chat), muds and moos (games), gopher (document directory), telnet, and freenets. During the hackers gathering Hacking at the End of the Universe in August 1993 I began to look for people which could do the technical support for such a project. Those running the hackers camp were way too busy so I got to talk with a guy, a system operator working for Albert Heyn (the Dutch Wal-Mart) who ran a bulletin board system. I was very charmed by him but we unfortunately lost contact. Then two artists, Paul Perry and David Garcia, pushed me at the crucial moment to simply start, so I went to the bookstore and passionately jumped into the Unix manuals."[10] How did she come up with the name? Marleen: "When I was looking for a name David Garcia suggested The Invisible City after Italo Calvino's novel. I didn't find 'invisible' the right term so I changed it into Digital City. I was intrigued by the city concept, not in order to build a bridge to the geographic reality, as to metaphorically use the dynamics and diversity of a city. I was interested in the presence of both private and public spaces, the exchange between people and the way in which different cultures and domains meet. In a city science, politics and culture intersect."

Felipe Rodriquez and Rop Gronggrijp (founders of the first Dutch ISP, xs4all ) got involved in the discussion about Digital City at an early stage. Felipe: "It was Marleen who came up with the name. The reason we chose the city as metaphor was to make the functionality of the city easy to express. It allowed us to let our imagination run, and make connections with the available technology, and things one can find in any city. I was one of the persons that had to make the translation from the metaphor to the technology, and this was not always an easy job. It is easy enough to translate between a post office and email, and between a café and a chat room. But how does one translate a park into Internet technology?"[11]

The freenet model was imported from the United States, where early citizens' networks such as the Cleveland were already operational.[12] The independent or tactical media element of freenets, run as non-profit initiative was combined with another rumor which had blown over the Atlantic, the "electronic town hall."[13] The idea was that only an independent public domain could guarantee "electronic democracy" (comparable to the role of the print media). It was not up to the state or local governments alone to decide how the political decision making mechanism was going to be transformed in the future network society. In order to get there the citizens themselves had to be empowered to use technology in their own often weird and seemingly irrelevant ways. What had to prevented, in the eyes of the Digital City founders was a 1:1 copy-paste from the "old" days of mass democracy with its political parties, television, and the power of media moguls into the new electronic era. In order to prevent this from happening the Amsterdam group decided not to write manifestoes or reports with recommendations but to take the avant-garde stand and move into the terrain as soon as possible: establish a beachhead, land as many troops as possible and occupy the entire territory.[14]

The Digital City started as a temporary and local experiment. In the first half-year, DDS was not perceived as a non-profit organization or a business. The limitations of being a temporary project which was only going to last a few months (and therefore not in need of a legal title) determined both the early success and its failure in the end, eight years later. As a project, run out of De Balie, temporary funding could relatively easily be found. In the early days of DDS De Balie took care of the administrative side and provided the initiative with first a desk and then a small office space. It was almost a year after Marleen Stikker, the main force behind the Digital City project had come up with the basic concept, that office space outside of De Balie was found. Around mid 1994 a legal structure was formed: a non-profit foundation with a board consisting of experienced administrators, all of them neutral outsiders. The foundation had no legal ties to the users, and the employees were not represented either. The Digital City freenet was founded as a cultural organization, not as a business. In 1994 the dotcom years were still a way off, despite *Wired* magazine giving a glimpse of what was about to happen. The Digital City had other ambitions, political ones. It was important was to get normal citizens involved in shaping the medium which until then had only been used by academics and hackers. The commercial tidal wave was about to happen, that much was clear. But would commerce really empower average users? No. With the history of radio and television in their minds, the fight over a public domain within cyberspace couldn't start early enough.

The prime cause of the Digital City's success was the freedom it granted to its users from the very beginning. This may sound trivial, but it is not, surely if you take the increasing control over net use in universities and corporations into account (especially outside the Netherlands). Awareness of privacy issues, corporate media control, and censorship was high, and the need to use cryptography was felt early, as was the right to anonymity while communicating via the Internet. The Digital City did not turn into a propaganda mouthpiece for the City Hall, under the guise of "bringing politics closer to the common people thanks to information technology." The DDS system was not the property of the Municipal corporation, even though many people assume this to be the case. In fact, DDS never received substantial subsidy from the municipality (the city council was one its biggest customers, though). In the end the "netizens" were far more interested in dialoguing among themselves than to engage in arcane discussions with closed-minded politicians.

In 1996 Nina Meilof, who had a background in local television, was hired by DDS to organize discussions about local political issues, such as the—failed—attempt to restructure the municipality into a "urban province," the controversial house-building drive into the Y-lake at IJburg, the even more controversial North-South underground railway project, and the extension of Schiphol Airport (which had the whole environmental community up in arms). The techno-savvy aspect aside, the main goal of DDS was to look at how to transcend immobile political rituals into new forms of online participatory democracy. To achieve this, the limits and limitations of the political game had to be well understood. Nina: "A major advantage of DDS remained its anarchic character. There were a lot of secret nooks and crannies, such as text-based cafes in out of the way places. One could look into home pages and find the history of that particular cafe, replete with the club jargon, a birthday list, and a group snap-shot. There was a Harley-Davidson meeting point for instance, that coalesce around one particular café which brought out its own newsletter. These kind of subcultures were of course far more thrilling than the mainstream sites maintained by big corporate or institutional players. No way those sites would ever swing."[15]

DDS looked for a balance whereby subcultures grew optimally without politics being discarded altogether. Precondition for this was the community system's independence. But that was costing money, and quite a lot. By 1998, DDS had grown into a business with 25 employees and 70,000 regular users that still wanted to retain its not-for-profit character. The management under Joost Flint was pursuing a policy of courting a handful of major customers who brought some serious money in. It was all about attracting projects which would fit into the DDS set-up, but that wasn't a totally friction-less process. DDS was divided into three components: a commercial department that hunted for the hard cash, an innovation wing which developed applications for corporate customers and the community aspect.

The "virtual community" image was never really appropriate in this case. After a few years of hyper-growth DDS had turned into a multi-faceted amalgam of small communities who shared the intention of perpetrating the DDS system as an "open city." If anything DDS was a facilitator for communities, not a community itself. It is there that the central interface of the DDS played a key role. The graphic user interface (designed mainly by Marjolein Ruyg) was so made in such a way as to provide an overview of the mass of information on offer. In keeping with the name of the system, the DDS web interface was build around the notions of "squares," "buildings/homes," and "(side) streets," but it did not show pictures or simulations of the actual (Amsterdam) city-scape, as many people expected. There were, for instances, "squares" devoted to environmental issues, sports, books, tourism, European affairs, women, gay and lesbian issues, information on drug use, social activism, and both local and national government. In between the squares there were tiny house icons pointing at the thousands of home pages. DDS also had its own cemetery, a web memorial for those who had passed away. Unlike Yahoo-type web directories, the interface was not pretending to give a full representation of the underlying activities. The central interface worked more like a guidance to give the vast project a look and identity without presenting itself as a portal.

Nina Meilof: "I was getting the statistics of the most popular "houses" (= home pages), so I went to look into them from time to time. Now we had a network of male homosexual "houses" springing up. They showed pictures of attractive gentlemen. Those were popular sites. All this was fairly down to earth. Cars, drugs, how to grow your own weed, music sites with extensive libraries. There was also a massive circuit where you can obtain or exchange software, and some of these "warehouses" were up for one or two days and vanished again. You had Internet games, that's an evergreen. But there was also a home page dedicated to some very rare bird which turned out to be an internationally famous site attracting ornithologists from all over the planet. Yet other people freaked out on design or Java scripts. And you had the links samplers. And don't forget the jokes sites."

This was a gigantic alternative and "underground" world. In contrast there was also the official "city" on the surface. The subject matter there was, in one way or another, "democracy and the Internet." For example for 6 months in 1996–97 there was an experiment on one of the "digital squares" on "traffic and transport issues," sponsored by the Dutch Ministry of Public Works and Roads. Registered DDS "inhabitants" with an email address could react to such propositions as "If we don't pull together to do something about congestion, traffic jams will never subside" or "Aggressive driving pays: it gets you there faster," or "The automobile is the most marvelous invention of the previous century." The experiment even boasted the luxury of a professional moderator, journalist Kees van den Bosch, who was inviting every month another high-profile politician to stir up the discussion. And the government was footing the bill. In the evaluation of the project van den Bosch said he was satisfied about the degree of participation. Yet it was easy to fall prey to an over optimistic estimate. Just a handful of participants generated an impressive amount of statements. Genuinely new ideas and arguments had been few and far between. The evaluation report also stated that little use had been made of the opportunity to obtain background data on the issues at stake. A large majority (say 75 percent) of the participants made one contribution and disappeared from view; the remainder soldiered on and went deeper into the discussion.

Technology-wise, DDS was not exactly a low-tech enterprise. There was an over-riding ambition to be on the cutting edge in innovative technology. Nina Meilof: "We got heavily involved into streaming media combinations of Internet with radio and TV. The aim was to provide streaming facilities for all our users. We had to be well aware of the latest technical developments and nurtured a good relationship with the bandwidth owners. We wanted to prevent the situation in which people have to go to big corporate players if they want to put television on the net. We felt that these things too should be readily available to the greatest number, so that any private person could start a WebTV station at home."

The technical innovation push did not always square well with a large number of users' growing expectations regarding content, and the quality of public discussions. In the beginning phase of DDS there was that idea that the (digital) city was some kind of empty shell that would be filled up by users and customers, without very much intervention from the DDS staff. But that formula turned out to result in a very static system. Yet not very much changed in the DDS content-structure over the years. It remained unclear whether the net really was such a good place to conduct a meaningful, in depth discussion. The first hurdle was of course the issue of moderation. Or to put it differently: was DDS a medium like others with editors who organized and edited (and hence censored) the discussion, or was it some kind of digital remake of the Hyde Park Corner soapbox? Within technical media there was never going to be absolute freedom. In the end there was always an owner (the one with the password) and someone who had to pay the bills. Those who cried "censorship" clearly did not run an Internet forum themselves. But in the DDS case this wasn't so much of an issue as long as the users had the right to be left alone to do their thing.

Another question pertained to the much-vaunted urban metaphor of the Digital City. What about its strictly local role, would that dwindle into insignificance? As a free community service provider DDS was faced the paradox that the local signifi-cance and the global "non-located" online components were both growing exponen-tially. A few years after its launch no more than a quarter of the "inhabitants" actually lived in Amsterdam yet DDS remained a Dutch-language site. The manage-ment for a long time maintained that upholding the Dutch language was a legitimate aim. For many users it was difficult to express themselves in English. The Internet was increasingly used in a very local or regional context, for example one could go on line to check out the program of the nightclub next door, or when the movies would start, etc. At the same time DDS never tried to impose its own (local) metaphor onto users. Nina Meilof: "The city metaphor stood for diversity, not for Amsterdam in par-ticular. People settled in on the net then went to look for "neighbors." These turned out to be living in the United States; however, they might as well be living nearby, ready to meet in a local bar, and that happened all the time. And so you could be get-ting of the train in Groningen (200 km to the north of Amsterdam) one day, and the platform was crowded with people sporting "DDS Metro Meeting" buttons, ready to have a MOO gathering in real life."

By the late 1990s, Amsterdam, long known for its large and diverse alternative social movements, faced some major shifts in its cultural landscape. The once solidly unconventional activists had in large numbers relocated themselves as creators and managers in the so-called new media culture, which was largely (though not exclu-sively) ITC-driven. For quite a time after it started to come into its own, this new cultural landscape had remained remarkably free of influence by mainstream or com-mercial interests. The new media scene morphed into something very different from what the Amsterdam model of public digital culture with Digital City as one among many projects had become famous for.

In itself the notion of a public sphere within the media has already been solidly entrenched, thanks to the policy of the municipality to cable nearly every household by the early 1980s, and to manage the system as a public utility like the water or electricity supply. So this approach was expanded into the realm of Internet access provision and associated new media facilities without much difficulty. However, the ongoing onslaught of "the market," and of its attendant ideology of commercialism and privatization proved increasingly difficult to resist. Like in many other global cities, Amsterdam in the late 1990s got into the firm grip of "dotcom mania." With hindsight, what was actually amazing was how long the new media culture had remained nearly immune to the dictates of the corporate sector. Partially, this had been due to the fact that the traditional elite took a fairly lenient and sometimes even supportive view of this state of affairs. But at the same time they kept resolutely clear of any involvement into it, this according to the hallowed Dutch "polder model," which established a delicate consensus between the state, business, and trade unions on the basis of non-regulation.

Five years after its founding the Digital City had evolved from an amateur, low-tech, non-budget grassroots initiative into a fully professionalized technology and business driven organization. And this culminated recently in its transformation from a non-profit foundation into a private sector ICT venture. Come December 1999, the astonished "inhabitants" learned that the directorate of the DDS had opted for a corporate framework, and that community building and support were no longer paramount objectives. By 1998–99 the free DDS facilities were available everywhere. Scores of new commercial providers and services had popped up all over the place (such as Hotmail, Geocities, and even free dial-up providers), offering the same services (often more extensive, better ones) than the DDS was able to provide. The free Internet services advertised massively and attracted a customers pool far removed from the idealistic concerns that used to inform the original Digital City. This resulted in a substantial quantitative, but more importantly, qualitative erosion of the DDS user base. Even if the absolute number of accounts had risen to reach an all-time high of 160,000 in early 2000, an analysis of the use patterns showed that these could no longer be considered conducive to community building or even to socio-politically relevant information exchange—home page building and upkeep for instance, no longer attracted much interest. The once so valuable web space had turned into empty lots. Despite an overall growth of Internet use the Digital City began losing its attractiveness for common users.[16]

As a platform for discussion of local issues, the DDS receded in importance, despite various efforts to trigger debates around important political events. Because of this, by 1999 the DDS had basically been turned into a facilitation structure providing the usual ICT services to its "clients," most of which see it as a convenient funnel for one-to-many, Dutch language interchange, and with little care for the "community" as a whole. The decline in the quality and the social usefulness as a whole had been unmistakable. Keeping the Dutch language on the outside layers of the interface and as the principal medium of transaction was indeed said to be the sole remaining distinguishing feature of the DDS as a community network. But inside its wall DDS was as intercultural as the Internet itself.

Another constraining aspect of DDS's operations, and the one which ultimately resulted in its corporatization, laid in the structurally weak and insecure nature of the early days when the DDS was conceived as a temporary experiment. However, when the (somewhat ad hoc) decision was made for a permanent status, investments in hardware and bandwidth together with increasing (underpaid) staff numbers, necessitated ever larger disbursements. This capital was not easy to get within a structure characterized by a hybrid and often somewhat uncomfortable mix of community service, technology R&D, and (first tentative, then ever increasing) commercial activities. Meanwhile, neither the Amsterdam municipality nor the Dutch state were prepared for various reasons to provide for recurrent subsidies after their initial disbursements and also the European Union, which was approached later, declined to do so. Europe's arguably biggest and best-known non-profit Internet community project was left in the cold and, thanks to merciless Third Way policies, forced into the market.

This left contract work for, and sponsorship by, the corporate sector as the only remaining avenue for resources mobilization, together with a not-inconsiderable amount of more or less obscurely tendered consultancy and hosting jobs for various public and semi-public bodies. Advertisement revenues from web banners were modest but not enough. This crisis mode of operation, besides not sitting very well with community building and community service in general also gave rise to an increasingly obfuscating rhetoric of public-private partnership masquerading as policy. As could be expected the hybrid business model (having to do a bit of everything at the same time) proved elusive in the end and this lack of direction left the DDS fatally underfunded. Surrounded by a booming IT sector the DDS management were both forced and lured to go the dotcom way.

Last but not least something needs to be said here about the management culture and choices that, either by design or by default, presided over the unhappy evolution of the DDS fortunes. Very early on, the opportunity to turn the Digital City in a truly self-governed networked community were put aside in favor of an allegedly more efficient, but in the end messy and contentious "executive" model of governance. Users were absent on the foundation board. Before long, the "inhabitants" grew tired of the paltry instruments of participation given to them, and DDS coordinator, later self-appointed director, and finally co-owner Joost Flint could exercise his authority unchallenged, which he chose to do in the opaque issues-and-debate-dodging style that is the hallmark of the stubborn and rigid Dutch regent class. The original co-initiator of the Digital City, "mayor" Marleen Stikker had left DDS already around 1995, to co-found the Society for Old and New Media, together with the *Paradiso* staff member Caroline Nevejan.

As far as the decision to go corporate was concerned and in parallel to similar developments such as the sale of Hotmail to Microsoft, it was obvious that the DDS management, besides other considerations, must have had individual account value and brand visibility firmly in mind. While the latter aspects were quite firmly evident in the Netherlands—and even world-wide, the former had reached absurd multiples of thousands of dollars per unit at the height of the dotcom/IPO/convergence craze that characterized the last months of 1999. The actual realization of these wet dreams, however, remained somewhat clouded as long as the complex issues pertaining to the new ownership structure had not been sorted out. The former DDS foundation was split in three autonomous branches, consolidated in a holding.

Hapee de Groot worked at DDS as a content manager in the years 1997–1999. Like Joost Flint, the director, Hapee had a background as a radical squatter activist. According to Hapee there have always been two sides to DDS: the outside and the inside. "In the beginning there was no difference between the two. The whole of DDS was a collective, everybody was doing everything. No bosses or dedicated persons. It was a tight group of interested people working for a good cause, a feeling that I recognize being activist. The inside DDS slowly changed but the outside picture did not."[17] When Hapee joined DDS there was already a division of labor in place with a sales department, programming department, one for the techies, the public domain department and administration. Hapee: "The head of the organization was Joost Flint. At the time it was still a foundation, not supposed to make profit, but internally it had grown into a top-down organization. Nothing could be done without permission of Joost. The board of the foundation received its information from Joost. It was the board, in collaboration with Joost which developed the future of DDS. The internal structure concerning the division of labor may have been inevitable. Combined with an open internal structure it could have worked perfectly. But there was no open structure. Access to the board was monopolized by Joost Flint." The lack of transparency was the reason why Hapee de Groot left in 1999 to work for the One World development portal.

Digital City, like most of new media initiatives described here, lacked basic forms of internal democracy. In a backlash against the democracy overkill of previous decades with its collectives and workers' councils, these NGO-type organizations were ruled in a pragmatic autocratic fashion. Because of the lack of money in the cultural sector, the general interest in building up a democratic structure remained absent both on the side of management and employees. Hapee: "After a decade of activism a lot of people, having a lot of energy, were looking for new opportunities. Some of them joined the NGO communities as subsidized unemployed workers. Others worked in media projects such as DDS. They became so involved, almost obsessed, in their jobs that they completely identified themselves with work, thereby closing down the possibility for others to unfold their ideas." Back in the exciting pioneer years when everyone participated in the construction of the Big Internet, it was just not done in the Dutch cultural sector to ask questions about ownership, power relations and working conditions. Demands to participate in ownership and power structures, if at all expressed, were categorized as "old economy" remnants coming from losers, cultural pessimists, and other negative forces aiming at undermining the constructive and positive atmosphere inside the new media organizations and companies.

This is how Hapee described the management takeover inside DDS: "At some point Joost started to put 'coordinator' signatures underneath his email messages. Some time later, with the commitment of the board, he was assigned director. In that time there were no staff meetings and Joost only talked to one staff member at a time. He has tremendous capability to play individuals and even groups off against each other. He monopolized the information for the board, thereby preventing team discussions. This made it possible for him to continue to work on his hidden agenda and preventing others from having one. Later on a kind of management team came into existence. All the team members had to achieve their targets, except Joost, because he had his responsibilities towards the board. If one questioned this publicly you were invited for a job audit. In such one to one conversations one would always lose the discussion."

To go back to the wider context, the fundamental problem which remained untouched was the outline of an open, public domain within cyberspace. In fact the digital public domain had not even been precisely defined, despite numerous and sometimes outlandish fantasies and speculations. The question was which instance was going to take responsibility for non-commercial culture in cyberspace. More importantly even: who was going to "own" the concept, the content, and finally "public" cyberspace itself? It was clear—in the Netherlands at least—that political parties had withdrawn from this debate. They were prepared to put money and energy into making their own viewpoints available online, but that did not make for a public independent platform. Bringing government services online was unrelated to the question of how electronic democratic decision making should be take place. Nor were financial injections into the IT sector a real solution. The "knowledge nation," a favorite concept toy of politicians, bureaucrats, and their consultants, was too vague a term to provide a precise and critical analysis of who was going to own and manage the public information infrastructure. In this age of convergence between "platforms" what was in fact called for was a successor to the public broadcasting system. But only a few regents were willing to put this question on the table. With national telecoms in the process of privatization the question of who was going to define, design, finance, roll out—and manage—the digital public infrastructure couldn't have been less palatable.

As a result of the Digital City board having only neutral members not involved in the daily operations, Joost Flint and his partner Chris Göbel convinced the board to hand over the ownership to the two of them. Joost and Chris were to become co-directors and the only shareholders. The chief asset was their ownership of the domain name dds.nl. The web design and hosting business had only been modest and had to operate in a highly competitive market. The value of the user database was uncertain as no one really knew the accuracy of the figures. Also it was highly uncertain how many users were in fact willing to continue their online activities within a privatized Digital City.

During the year 2000 Joost Flint and co-director Chris Göbel spent most of their time implementing their privatization plans. In according with the old board four LTDs were founded: a Services Ltd., DDS Projects Ltd., DDS City Ltd. and DDS Venture Ltd. Then, in late 2000 the public domain section (DDS city) was closed. This was the signal for many to take action. In January 2001 a group of DDS users decided to put the sales of the public domain part of DDS on hold. 400 people joined ranks of a DDS users' association, whose goal it was to take over the Digital City of Amsterdam from its present "owner," the DDS holding, and preserve, if not its entirety, then at least substantial parts of this public domain in cyberspace. Provisional statutes of the future association were posted on the site after due consultation of the constituency on the mailing list. Various areas of "governance" (legal, financial, technical, political, public relations, etc.) were identified and tasks apportioned among the ad interim "councilors."

Beside subjects pertaining to the (self-) organization of the users' association, a lot of discussion was devoted to the future of the DDS, presumed that it was going to be taken over. Consensus had in any case inside the users' association been reached on scuttling the principle of free services as a holy cow, though it may be retained if practicable. For the remainder, there is still a lot of discussion about "what to salvage" from the "old" DDS, subsumed under the header "historic monument," and whether large numbers of (by necessity, "passive") accounts should be retained at all costs, or if on the contrary the "new" DDS would be firmly geared towards the active participation "networked community" format. However, neither the general assembly of the users association, nor the interim council of the association had very much influence on the ultimate decision-making process within the current structure of the Digital City, the DDS holding, its two shareholders. Negotiations between the association and the holding did not go anywhere and within a few months the initial energy among DDS users vaporized. In the end the conflict boiled down to the primal question who owned the actual dds.nl domain name. DDS founder Marleen Stikker: "The social, cultural and democratic potential of the Internet has yet to be realized. All the more sad, therefore, that the commercialization of DDS resulted in the relegation of the organization's public mission to a secondary priority. The name Digital City should in my opinion never have been privatized."[18]

Felipe Rodriquez regrets that DDS by mid 2001 had become an ordinary Internet provider (ISP). "ISPs are providing a product whereas a freenet intends to create a community of people. DDS became an ISP in the end, because there was no other way to fund its activities in any other way. As a community the DDS was a very interesting experiment. When it was forced to become a business much of the focus on the community aspect was lost." Felipe doesn't believe the Freenet model to be applicable in 2001. "Today the Freenet model would not work, because Internet access and services have become a commodity. They are available to almost anyone in the western world. Today other communities exist on the Internet such as slashdot or nettime." The choice to become a business has destroyed the DDS community. But according to Felipe there was also another reason for the decline. "In order to maintain a community an organization needs leadership that knows how to communicate online, how to resolve conflict and how to create a pleasant environment. People from HackTic had quite a lot of experience with online communication. I had run a bulletin board for a number of years and had been involved in many online discussions. When DDS started the HackTic people already had the ability to communicate online and maintain the peace. When HackTic after a while pulled out of the project, communications from the DDS to its community became more formal and distant. Flame wars in its discussion groups were poorly dealt with, creating an image in the community of a shy and incompetent management."

It was this inability to communicate, both within the more or less random group of users which had formed the users' association to save DDS, and between the users' association and DDS holding which let to tragic ending of Digital City as a public domain initiative. Reinder Rustema had taken up the initiative to save DDS in

December 2000. He wrote to me about the lesson he learned from half a year organizing, negotiations and internal fights within the users' association of which Rustema was a president of the board until he stepped down. "What is the digital public domain? It used to refer to a certain place where people could meet and gather. It is difficult to talk in terms of places on the Internet. Hence the metaphor of the Digital City to make this clear. The dispute with DDS holding in the end was only over the use of the domain name. Owning the physical machine is less relevant as long as the domain is yours. You can make the domain name refer to any machine you wish, the machine does not even have to be your property, just one which you have enough control will do."

Reinder doesn't see much future for shared communal domains like DDS. "Never again would I want to be dependent on an organization for my domain name. For some years now there is this trend to buy your own domain name. I have now also made this step. Just like a cell phone number I see everyone ending up with their own personal domain name. You will be able to find public spaces in USENET, mailing lists, chats, MUDs and other virtual places. These "places" have been there when we first discovered the Internet and also happened to be the interesting parts of DDS. They won't go away. Interesting projects will just adopt another name and move away from systems such as DDS."[19]

The strategic issue raised here relates to the problem of local and global. Net activists and artists are confronted with the dilemma between the presumably friction-free machinic globality and the experience that social networks, in order to be successful, need to be rooted in local structures. Internet culture pops up in places where crystals of (media) freedom have been found before. At the same time the net is constantly subverting the very same local ties it grows out of while creating new forms of "glocality." The choice global or local is a false one. Even though urban and spatial metaphors in general may have exhausted themselves there is little to be found in the mathematical emptiness of "pure" disembodied virtuality. Discontent within the

Digital City project in the spatial metaphor existed right from the start. Due to Dutch pragmatism no "metaphor police" was established to look into identity, language and nationality.[20] In that sense DDS was, more than anything, a social experiment in Internet freedom with only a few hints of what political liberty in the technological future could look like. The lesson of the Amsterdam Digital City, now simply a regular commercial provider offering DSL broadband services, is, if any lesson, an economic and legal one and deals with the high art of staying independent in an increasingly commercial environment, and of no longer being able to rely on government support in matters of public interest.

## <Notes>

1.   Research presented here draws from my ongoing collaboration with Patrice Riemens. This article has been partially based on material from the following (English) publications: "Creating a Virtual Public, The Digital City Amsterdam," in *Mythos Information, Welcome to the Wired World*, ed. K. Gerber and P, Weibel (Springer-Verlag, 1995); "The Monkey's Tail: The Amsterdam Digital City Three and a Half Years Later," in *Possible Urban Worlds, Urban Strategies at the End of the 20th Century*, ed. INURA (Birkhäuser) (earlier version posted on nettime June 16, 1997); "Amsterdam Public Digital Culture: Contradictions among User Profiles" (with Patrice Riemens), posted on nettime July 20, 1998; "Amsterdam Public Digital Culture 2000" (with Patrice Riemens), in RiskVoice, 002, Stiftung Risiko-Dialog, St. Gallen, posted on nettime August 19, 2000. Another version, in German, appeared in the web magazine Telepolis (http://www.heise.de/tp/deutsch/special/sam/6970/1.html). Much of my thinking about DDS goes back to an unrealized hypertext project from early 1995 in which I mapped the (critical) DDS discourse. Other related material in the interview I did with Michael van Eeden, DDS sysop and founder of the Metro MOO (in Dutch), was posted to nettime-nl November 29, 1996.

2.   For an overview of DDS research papers in English, see http://rrr.dds.nl/dds/index.html. The official DDS history page is at www.dds.nl/archeo. For a critical analysis from an outsider's perspec-

tive, written in mid 1998, see Stefan Wray, "Paris Salon or Boston Tea Party? Recasting Electronic Democracy, A View from Amsterdam" (http://www.nyu.edu/projects/wray/teaparty.html).

3. Debates about the privatization of DDS, mainly in Dutch, can be found on the server of the DDS users' association (www.opendomein.nl). In April and May of 2001, Zenon Panoussis made an online archive of 6,248 home pages he managed to trace (on public-domain DDS servers) and download (http://dds.provocation.net/rst/). For insiders' reports see Patrice Riemens, "Last Update on the 'Refoundation' of the Amsterdam Digital City (DDS)," nettime, March 22, 2001; Patrice Riemens, "Michael ('Mieg') Van Eeden on the Current Situation with DDS," nettime, February 19, 2001; Patrice Riemens, "'Refoundation' of the Amsterdam Digital City Update: 1st General Assembly of the DDS Users Association," nettime, February 16, 2001; Patrice Riemens, "'Refoundation' of the Amsterdam Digital City (vioDDS): Update," nettime, January 31, 2001.

4. For more on the relation between urban strategies and media tactics of Amsterdam's 1980s squatters movement, see Adilkno 1994 (online version: http://www.desk.org/bilwet). More information on recent squatters' movements worldwide can be found at www.squat.net.

5. URLs: www.paradiso.nl and www.balie.nl, two buildings situated almost next to each other on the Amsterdam Leidseplein square.

6. The term "technological culture" was introduced by Michiel Schwarz, a researcher and editor who worked at the De Balie cultural center in the late 1980s and the early 1990s. Schwartz organized numerous debates, conferences and publications on technology and society in the Netherlands and also worked as a consultant for the Dutch government. URL: http://www.doorsofperception.com/doors/who/schwarz/.

7. The Galactic Hacker Party was going to be the first in a series of international hackers' gatherings held in The Netherlands every four years in August: Hacking at the End of the Universe (HEU) in 1993, then Hacking in Progress (www.hip97.nl) in 1997 and Hackers at Large (www.hal2001.org) in 2001.

8. URLs of some of the media-related cultural organizations in Amsterdam: http://www.desk.nl (cultural/commercial content provider) http://www.tv3000.nl (cultural/commercial service provider)

http://www.montevideo.nl (Dutch Institute for New Media Arts),
http://www.steim.nl (Laboratory for Electronic Music),
http://www.bellisima.net (experimental cable TV group),
http://www.hoeksteen.nl (live cable program on politics and arts),
http://www.desk.nl/100 (free radio station), http://www.mediamatic.nl
(design company, plus (former paper now) online magazine for new media
arts and theory), http://www.anma.nl (Amsterdam New Media Association),
http://www.dds.nl/~virtplat (Dutch Virtual Platform),
www.doorsofperception.com (design conference and web site).

9.   In December 1998 the Internet provider was sold to the Dutch telecom KPN by its two founders, Rop Gronggrijp and Felipe Rodriquez. For
more on the history and context of xs4all, see the following:
http://www.xs4all.nl/uk/absoluut/history/overname_e.html,
http://www.xs4all.nl/~evel/beat.htm and www.hacktic.nl (online archive
of *HackTic* magazine).

10.   Email interview with Marleen Stikker, August 2, 2001.

11.   Email interview with Felipe Rodriquez, July 28, 2001.

12.   The Cleveland Freenet Initiative goes back to 1984. One definition
of a freenet is "a public network that gives you free access to community news and information, as well as basic entry to the Internet.
Think of a freenet as an electronic town since it has a post office
for your email, a library for research, and bulletin boards for community events." (www.maran.com). On October 1 1999, at the height of the
dotcom craze, America's oldest community computer system had to close
because of a lack of funding (see nettime, October 4, 1999). There is
an attempt underway to restart the Cleveland initiative
(http://new.cleveland-freenet.org/). For more on the community network
movement, see Schuler 1996. Recommended reading is Howard Rheingold's
interview with Doug Schuler
(http://www.salon.com/11/departments/rheingold.html).

13.   The electronic town hall concept is usually traced back to a proposal Ross Perot made during the 1992 US presidential elections and
the use of email by Bill Clinton as a part of his campaign strategy.

14.   This was Louis Rosetto's strategy for *Wired* (as Howard Rheingold
once described it to me). It later became known as the "first movers"
strategy for dotcoms.

15.  Interview (in Dutch) conducted in early 1997; see nettime posting, June 16, 1997.

16.  Over the years, Peter van den Besselaar and a group of students at University of Amsterdam have done a few surveys about the shifts in the DDS user base. URL: http://swi.psy.uva.nl/usr/peter/publications. See also the research of Els Rommes, who has written a Ph.D. thesis on gender issues inside DDS (publication forthcoming). See also E. Rommes, E. van Oost, and N. Oudshoorn, "Gender in the Design of the Digital City of Amsterdam," in Green and Adam 2001 (http://www.infosoc.co.uk/00108/ab4.htm).

17.  Interview with Hapee de Groot, posted on nettime January 14, 2001.

18.  Marleen Stikker, "The Internet as Public Domain," in Waag Society 2001 (based on an interview with Geert Lovink, in Dutch, posted on nettime-nl March 7, 2001).

19.  Email interview with Reinder Rustema, July 30, 2001. Reinder's DDS research, done for his M.A. thesis, can be accessed via http://reinder.rustema.nl.

20.  For a general debate on the spatial metaphor, see individual contributions of Brian Carroll and Pit Schultz and the debate between these two "electromagnetic"scholars on the nettime list: Schultz, "there is no space in cyberspace," September 9, 2000; Carroll, "Redux: 'Spatial Discursions' by Robert Nirre" (responding to Pit forwarding Robert Nirre's Ctheory article to nettime on February 13, 2001); Schultz, "re: 'Spatial Discursions'—no space," February 14, 2001; Schultz, "no space III," March 13, 2001; Carroll, "No Space Like Cyberspace," April 20, 2001; Carroll, "Seeing Cyberspace, The Electrical Infrastructure is Architecture," July 15, 2001. Brian Carroll's research can be accessed through www.electronetwork.org.

# The Moderation Question: Nettime and the Boundaries of Mailing List Culture

Nettime has been widely recognized as one of the leading forums for the discussion and practice of innovative Internet culture and Internet-based art. Its aim has been to bring together different disciplines and practices such as electronic arts, computer science, media theory, IT journalism, and media activism. Topics have been the canon of net.art, foundations of media aesthetics, tactical media aspects of protests against corporate globalization, the fight against censorship, politics of Internet domain names.

This essay is a case study of the nettime mailing list, a cross disciplinary, international exchange for the "cultural politics of the net," founded in 1995. An analysis of nettime postings can be written by anyone as its web archive is publicly accessible (www.nettime.org). Such a reconstruction will, most likely, look into the dynamics of the postings and the content of the numerous threads. Different from most lists, nettime developed a dynamic beyond the Internet itself. This chapter describes the conditions under which nettime was formed and emphasizes its first years of existence. It is by no means a comprehensive history.

I am not a fan of disclaimers. However, this case study has to be read as a subjective version of nettime's turbulent history. With Pit Schultz, I am the nettime founder. I have been one of the rotating moderators (1998–99) and am an ongoing contributor, in particular working on the steadily growing non-English nettime lists. This account should provide the reader with an insider's perspective on the workings of the list, how it dealt with rapid growth, conflicts, phases of information overload and diversification. I do not pretend to cover the entire period from 1995 to 2001.

After a number of years of intense conditions, nettime became more mature—others would say less interesting. In the period 1999–2000 it found a balance between over-load and "censorship," resisting the immanent pressures of institutionalization and exhaustion to which most non-profit Internet projects were subjected.[1] Ceasing to organize meetings and publications around 1999, nettime became more of a mailing list like others. At present, nettime is still in search of a sustainable model, faced with constant external changes in technology and Internet business models. It now looks for ways to generate provocative and productive reflections on net culture from a range of inter-cultural, trans-political and hyper-individual perspectives.

Electronic mailing lists are described as "Internet based discussion groups (as opposed to one-directional distribution lists)."[2] On the server side they are adminis-tered by a list program (e.g. listserv, listproc, majordomo, mailbase, lyris, mailman), for the participants they are accessible via simple electronic mail. Unlike electronic newsletters subscribers can freely post. Going back to the mid 1960s,[3] electronic lists are considered a low-tech, cheap and open way to exchange information and argu-ments. They often result into a (virtual) community. Josephine Berry describes lists as one of the most important significant materials and theatres of operation. "These often long running lists, generating dozens of mails each day, produce an informative, critical and sociable "virtual community" against which and through which artworks are made, circulated and discussed." List cultures results in "group authorship, hyperlinked structures and high level of mutual quotation and/or plagiarism are but a few."[4]

According to the Serbian video maker and list enthusiast Aleksander Gubas, elec-tronic networks must have a vision, a groove and a direction. Networking must come out from true need. In a piece called "Flocks of Netgulls" he writes: "A mailing list should always ask itself what is its sense, purpose and vision. Otherwise, the network-ing becomes just another empty and prostituted phrase like multiculturalism, toler-ance, democracy, open society, etc." Lists give a sense of community and belonging. "Maybe you'll never meet the other members of your mailing list—but it's good to know they exist. It makes you feel less alone. Subscribing to a mailing list means the definition of your flock; it means that you recognized some other gulls to cry together on line."[5]

On mailing lists the moderation issue is the most sensitive topic. Lists, news groups and chat rooms create an illusion among users of a technical freedom without human interference. However, these Internet communication forums are as man-made as anything else. In most cases the "moderator" is also the "list owner," the person who owns the password to change the list configuration. This list owner can switch the list from open-unmoderated to closed-filtered, let email go through with or without attachments, let people from outside the list have the possibility to post, etc. The term "moderation" is also used for the encouraging and entertaining aspect of running a list. A good moderator is first of all a facilitator, inviting people off list to post their material or opinion on certain topics. List facilitators are always on the look for relevant, new content, spurring up debates and cooling them down if they end up in flame wars.

List culture is all about the degrees of freedom set by the moderator/list owner, thereby creating a sense of democracy. Do moderators need to be appointed, even if they are the initiators or volunteer to do hard work in the background, cleaning up In boxes full of error messages, reformatting texts, day by day? Much of the work to keep lists running in a smooth way is invisible. How do users reach agreement on what is noise and what is useful information? How much noise and meaningless one-liners can subscribers bear? What happens if there is a sudden influx of newcomers? Who will instruct them and will they introduce themselves? At what point does the list community becomes an audience? These are some of the issues lists have to deal with. The nettime case went beyond issues of internal democracy. It tested the boundaries of list culture as such by putting real-life meetings and print publications on top of its Internet activities.

Let's zap through the events first before going into detail. The center of nettime is the international mailing list, in English, nettime-l. It grew from 500 subscribers in mid 1997 to 850 in late 1998 and reached 2000 in mid 2001. An increasing number of users read the list via the archive on the web site www.nettime.org. Then there is a growing number of lists in other languages with an average of 200–400 subscribers in Dutch (established in late 1996), French (1999), Romanian and Spanish/Portuguese (2000). The lists are not related content-wise, run on the same server, use the same name and together with "neighboring" lists and web sites, create a common context, a net culture, in contrast to the portal model of centralizing and then customizing content and/or software.

For the back cover of the Readme! anthology, filtered by nettime in 1998, a collective effort was made to come up with a brief description: "What is nettime? A wild East-West saloon? A journal? A bulletin? A bulletin board? A soapbox? An endless open-mike night? A typing pool? A mailing list on the Internet? No one really knows, let alone agrees. But the result is clear: a vigorous international discourse that neither promotes cash-cow euphoria nor propagates cynical generalizations about the cultural possibilities of new media. Whether the boom gurus or doom gurus like it or not, the net is becoming the medium of the multitudes." Nettime presents itself here as "the other side of the net" (Nettime 1999).

The focus of nettime has always been to be more than just an Internet forum, to actively connect different disciplines (arts, theory, activism, journalism) and break out of the digital realm through paper publications and real-life meetings. During the phase of the *Wired*-Netscape hype (1995–1997), the nettime group brought out several publications, among others a free newspaper with a circulation of 10,000 which was mainly distributed during the Kassel Documenta X and through media labs and media arts organizations around Europe. Nettime was represented at several events and held its own first meeting in Ljubljana in May 1997 where 120 members discussed strategies for critical discourses in electronic arts and (new) media activism.

In the next period of consolidation (1998–99) nettime became a more structured (and moderated) forum where political and cultural aspects of technology and Internet development were discussed. Most of the contributions to the list were peer review articles. The efforts to gather critical writings on net culture resulted, among others, in the book publication Readme!, also known as the Nettime Bible. A weekly compiler for announcements was set up to inform the readership of the many conferences and new web sites. In order to master the growing amount of postings, discussion digests were introduced, postings bundled together by topic, a system which proved of particular use during the Kosovo war (March–June 1999) in which the community was deeply divided over the NATO bombings of Serbia.

Since early 1998 moderators have been rotating. By 2001, Nettime is being moderated by a group of four, located on three continents (Europe, North America, Australia).[6] However, the content and the life of nettime is provided by its growing and changing subscriber base, using the many-to-many capabilities of Internet-based communication. The problem of "lurkers" (read only members) is virtually absent. Having started as a European-North American dialogue on the premises of cyberculture, the list has broadened its view and readership over the last years. The process of "collaborative text filtering" creates a pool of texts and discussions which are gradually translated and end up in the non-English speaking world.

One of the many roots of nettime could be described as discontent after the death of critical theory. What might Internet criticism in the digital age look like? A fight over the definition of a new arena was at hand. In the early 1990s, neither the apocalyptic postmodernism nor the speculative theory fiction seemed to reflect the rapidly changing techno configurations. Postmodernists seem to be trapped into a self imposed melancholy deliberating never ending endings, whereas leftovers of critical theory had bitterly withdrawn into historical reference systems, negating the world altogether. The question was posed: can theory still intervene in emerging phenomena such as the Internet? Adilkno, the Foundation for the Advancement of Illegal Knowledge (a group of which I am a member) in a piece written in the morning twilight of net culture called "What is data criticism?" stated: "Data criticism is the denial of all that exists, it starts where cynicism ends; it does not put down the world, but responds to the challenge posed by the unpredictable. There is no alternative to data. Like a Medusa, the only option is to meet them face-to-face." (Adilkno 1998, p. 59) This meant making dirty hands. Intellectual involvement could no longer be meta-critique from the safe position of the outsider. Activism was required. The business jargon for this attitude was "creating opportunities."

In late 1993, half a year after I had gotten my first email address (geert@hack-tic.nl), I came in contact with a Berlin artist named Pit Schultz. Back then, exchanges via email were sporadic, sudden and filled with the excitement of the new. Pit was the organizer of the last gig of Adilkno's *Media Archive* book release tour through German-speaking countries (including Budapest). These were the heydays of speculative media theory and the trip, doing 15 cities in 15 days, had the style of a DJ tour.[7] Pit was the only local organizer with email. The first version of Mosaic, the first World Wide Web browser had just been released. Huge "radical chic" crowds showed up, night after night, filling the air with an exciting, yet undefined sense of the coming. Of what? The Dutch datadandies actually only tempered the illusions, using the ironic strategy of radical pragmatism in order to master the utopian prom-ises of the "virtual reality" and "cyberspace" people had vaguely heard about. The textual tactic of Adilkno was one of pushing the imaginative boundaries way beyond the introductory phase of digital media. Condemning the computer worlds as mere simulation, invented by the military-entertainment complex, had become a cynical worn-out remark. The atmosphere had turned Deleuzean. The playful, productive schizo pole blossomed.[8]

The first real collaboration with Pit Schultz was a commissioned television inter-view with *Wired* editor and *Out of Control* author Kevin Kelly.[9] Shot during a Berlin telco conference in December 1994, it gave us both a direct encounter of what Richard Barbook and Andy Cameron not much later coined as the "Californian Ideology." What struck us was Kelly's routine professionalism, his unshakable belief in the religious quality of technology, and his passion for techno-Darwinism. He loved all biological metaphors as long as they could denounce and deny complex social and economic relationships. Portraying computer users as a beehive, as Kelly did in *Out of Control*, Pit and I both considered a setback in the understanding of computer networks. Why would users, faced with the tremendous empowerment the net could give, suddenly have be labeled as ants or bees? Considering the popularity of Kelly and *Wired*, how had these notions become the centerpiece of the Internet ideology?[10]

The takeover of the Internet by corporate power, way beyond the naïve bravery of dotcom enterpreneurialism, was already visible in Kelly's historical grandeur. This was a humble man who not only sensed the titanic magnitude of the network imperative, but truly understood its metaphysical nature. Unlike his teachers such as George Gilder and Tom Peters, Kelly was not a heroic revolutionary. He is more like a modest strategic thinker. His point of departure lay beyond the omega point of the digital. From there he looked back on the late 20th century with an iron logic. A true visionary, Kelly presupposed short-term harsh changes the global business world had to go through. Corporations were only transitory vehicles of trans-historical things to come. Technological determinism and a biblical drive towards the final apocalyptic chapter were bound to meet. As Kelly said, when humans were about to become gods, it wasn't long before they would meet God. Technology was going to assist humankind in this eschatological enterprise.

Kelly's libertarian blessings were not targeted at a young audience who thought of starting up a business, despite his strong belief in the bottom-up approach. Kelly, and with him most of the digerati were most of all focused on the CEO level of the world's most powerful corporations. What was so interesting about these telecom suits, hidden in a West Berlin hotel near Bahnhof Zoo? It was in the (monopolist) interest to get rid of state regulation, privatizing as much as possible. Didn't the environmentalist Kelly promote decentralization? Why then did this *Wired* editor want to convince the old economy establishment? Shouldn't it crumble by itself? Why talk to them? Our questions to Kelly during the interviews however lacked precision. There had been much talk about making machines more like us, nature never being in balance, grow-ing complicated software, and a new economy not based on scarcity but on sharing. It was hard to pinpoint our discontent towards this unfamiliar form of hippie capitalism. A much more thorough deconstruction of this set of ideas was necessary before the attractive side of the *Wired* agenda could be publicly addressed. There was more to this than the male adolescent dream of disembodied collective intelligence. A net cri-tique should go further then body politics. Where to start?

A few months later Andreas Kallfelz invited Pit Schultz and I to organize a small event as part of the celebrations of 10 years of Verein 707, Kallfelz's Frankfurt-based art society. A concept was developed to do a weekend of discussions on media strate-gies in the forest outside of Frankfurt. From March 16 to March 19, 1995, the "Media ZK" (ZK stands for Central Committee) was held near Spessart with a sub-title "terminal theory for the 1990s—secret knowledge for all." Around 30 mainly German video artists, activists and critics attended. Some of them brought their com-puters.[11] The aim was to discuss possibilities of building up critical net practices and discourses. The invitation had a ironic undertone. The reference to a secret organiza-tion, deciding over the direction of the net, was prompted by the fact that this was the moment to act. Internet was about to kick off in Germany, as it already had in the United Kingdom, the Netherlands, and Scandinavia. The rest would soon follow, with Eastern Europe using its strategic advantage of having to reform its economies any-way. Some of the ZK participants were already involved in initiatives such as Handshake, connecting Berlin techno clubs via terminals to chat. Amsterdam had a whole range of models on offer: the hackers provider xs4all.nl; the digital city free net; and a content provider specially for Internet-based art projects, named desk.nl. There were various nodes of the art BBS system The Thing, all about to get connected to the net. In Berlin the Internationale Stadt project had just taken off, a mix of art-based content provider, ISP and freenet. The energy was there but the concepts some-how seemed confused.

How could sustainable Internet projects outside of the commercial realm be developed? The ZK also had theory on the agenda. How did the real existing body's desires relate to the cleanness of the cyberspaces? What to do about the poverty of new metaphors such as the "digital city"? How do real and virtual relate? What happens with the crisis of politics and the presumed decline of the public in the digital city? Would the body be neglected with the net becoming the new "clean" drug? A lecture by Hans-Christian Dany stressed the relation between Microsoft Windows and multiple personality disorders, whereas Jochem Becker pointed at quasi-subversive marketing strategies, taken from pop culture, already in use in the music video industry.

There were no immediate outcomes to the ZK Spessart meeting. The discussion within Germany was to be continued at the (first) Interfiction meeting in Kassel, in early December 1995, under the title "net criticism—perspectives and myths of counter-public in data-nets."[12] The German context was mix of skepticism and slack-erdom. There was a great devotion to software tinkering, mixed with a disbelief that networks could be set up for a broader public. The German population was presumed to be critical about technology. Perhaps the state should provide its citizens with general net access. But there was no indication in that direction. Confronted with huge debts and an economic recession, all the German state would do is send its prosecutors to its Internet pioneers over censorship cases. The attitude after the fall of Berlin Wall was anything but German diligence. The festive, ecstatic rave culture refrained from fanatic activism. The political atmosphere in the outgoing Kohl era was defensive, if not lame. The sudden reunification had not brought much except racism and neo-nazis. So wasn't the Internet just another imperial trick to seduce and diffuse resistance, critical artists and activists asked themselves? Or, to put in continental-postmodern terms, a gadget invented by the US military to further intensify the simulacrum of all the good thing past such as politics, arts and . . . the media. In short: the Internet could not be embraced uncritically. Theory was needed, if not to master, then at least to circumvent aggressive commercialism without falling pray to the postmodern disease of cultural pessimism. The question on the table was how to turn the potentially immobilizing dilemmas into a productive setup, encouraging rather than dismissing radical critique.[13]

The next opportunity occurred with the newly established Berlin Biennale intending to "exhibit" the vibrant Berlin club culture at the Venice Biennale (June 1995), with the hope of importing "techno" into the art context.[14] For this purpose, the 18th century Theatro Malibran had been hired. A room on the first floor could be used as a conference space. Pit Schultz arranged to have a three day net theory workshop where the "ZK" topics could be further discussed, this time within an international context.[15] The idea was to do workshops and debates, not a conference with lectures. Through Nils Röller, Italian philosophers and others working on urban and electronic spaces would be invited. During the preparation in May, via email, Pit, Nils, and I worked on three topics. The ideas were somewhat finished, written down. The name of the meeting: <net.time>.[16]

The first day was called "hi-low" and dealt with a discourse analysis of the *Wired* world: "euphoria/phobia," analysis of the hype and the conceptual politics of magazines such as *Wired, Mondo 2000*, and *Virtual* (Italy). "What is the relevance and impact these cult movements will have on the art world. The desire to be wired is the myth to have more power." The second day was going to deal with net theory, politics and the city metaphor. Venice, Amsterdam, Berlin and the old European net culture. Is a city defined by the market, the agora, its canals and roads or by technologies such as defense walls and resource management? What defines a city anyway? Its image, walls or rules? What is public domain in the age of Internet (Habermas, Negt/Kluge). Who will become the Camillo Sitte of the net, defining the aesthetic of the digital public layout? Is there any similarity between the gated (Mike Davis) and virtual (Howard Rheingold) community? And what to think of Paul Virilio's chrono-politics, suggesting that time, not space is becoming the central topos of power. Also it became important to question the whole idea of "home": "Why is the home page such a common term, surfing from home page to home page instead of wandering through semiotic deserts?" (Nils Röller). The third day would deal with Kevin Kelly's neo-vitalist ideology, life on the net, read through Deleuze and Guattari's *Mille Plateaux*: "digital dynamics and millennial romanticism, critique of the Californian artificial life ideology."

"The desire to be wired" was going to become the central Venice phrase. A desire which the later nettime list was going to take apart—and reconstruct, out of a common desire not to be like *Wired*. What was the agenda behind the Will to Network? How does the wired desire get written down into social and economic structure? Which desire does the Internet address? Slavoj Zizek and a few other theorists had raised these issues. But these psychoanalysts and cultural studies academics were repeatedly making the mistake of mixing up 3D virtual reality models (which were not only offline but also inaccessible for the general audience) with the rapid expanding, slowly performing computer networks. Internet was not about losing ones body in an immersive environment. Its potential to network was real, not virtual. The net was not a simulator for this or that experience. If it appealed to a sexual desire, it must have been one based on code, not on images—distributed, abstract delusion, not a (photo)graphic illusion. 1990s media theorists had been fooled by Hollywood and the game industry, what Peter Lunenfeld (2000, p. xix) calls "media of attractions."[17] This was to become a general problem. Demo design got easily mixed up with the real existing excitement over the World Wide Web, in all its infancy. The simplicity of the early web was in fact anything but sexy. In need of constant maintenance, restarting and rebooting, losing packages, with web sites under construction, not getting through ("404 not found"), the net was home for sophisticated tinkers. "The lower the bandwidth, the higher the imagination." References were the historical parallels between the Internet and the establishment of electricity as described by Thomas P. Hughes in *Networks of Power*, a book that deals with market shares, mergers, monopolies, and the war on electricity standards in the United States in the period 1880–1930. Was the layout of the

Internet infrastructure going to be repetition of the electricity episode, resulting in a few monopolies, such as Microsoft, AOL, and MCI/WorldCom?

Back in Berlin, Pit Schultz set up a preliminary nettime list on the server of the Internationale Stadt in Berlin. He wrote the following introduction: "It should be an temporary experiment to continue the process of a collective construction of a sound and rhythm—the songlines—of something which we hardly worked on, to inform each other about ongoing or future events, local activities, certain commentaries, distributing and filtering texts, manifestos, hotlists, bits and blitzmails related to cultural politics on the net. It's also an experiment in collaborative writing and developing strategies of group work. Therefore and because of the different native languages of the participants it's a multilingual forum. Every new subscriber should introduce himself with a brief description of her projects, where she comes from etc. The list is not moderated. Take care." With this mail came a proposal for a *Wired* critique, including a prize, called "Why Worried" (which didn't go anywhere). *Wired* wasn't the perfect enemy. As a common denominator, the magazine developed into a boxing ball, the reason to formulate the discontent over the state of arts in cyberculture. *Wired*, as the discourse leader, was accused of reterritorializing "new songlines and substreams of fresh desire, formatting and decoding the public face of fringe scientists, strange artists, visionary authors, young movements." It channeled a small, emerging culture to wider audiences, and by doing so, built up cultural capital for all those involved." Offending were "the clean and bright candy surfaces of Californian postmodernism. Where is the dirt?"

The outcome of the <net.time> meeting wasn't what you would expect from a Central Committee. Culture in Europe in the age of the Internet hype pretty much looked liked a wandering circus, a traveling net band, swelling from city to city. There was a springtime atmosphere, connections were made, some even turning into love affairs, along with passionate debates about Netscape on street corners, with someone you just met. Everyone seemed ready to unroll yet another creative-subversive media place, preferably with a poetic manifesto—and without ideology. This is post-1989

Europe, with the Bosnian War coming to a close. What remained are a few phrases and a mailing list. "One needs ironic sites, impossible cities, useless archives, introverted communication channels, cyber criticism, VR humor, ambiguous keyboards." A mix of demands for citizens' access to the networks and ironical comments to dampen overheated expectations of technology sparking social revolts. "Internet is a possibility to change consumer attitudes by creating places of strategic silence."[18]

Next stop Budapest, mid October 1995, where the second Metaforum conference took place. One of the many cultural events, debating new media culture within the Eastern European context, to come.[19] The first Metaforum in 1994 had dealt with multi-media, now it was time to talk Internet. Hungary had jumped on the bandwagon. ISPs were kicking off and Internet use started spreading beyond academic and NGO networks. A public access initiative, Koz Hely, was formed. There was curiosity, mixed with suspicion. One of the Metaforum organizers was Diana McCarty: "As a conference, MetaForum was one in its own chain of three, but also directly related to several other international events, meetings and festivals. The atmosphere was incredible, on the one hand, there was the general, public hype, the wired view of the future, and on the other, a whole group of critically minded people were no less euphoric, though for totally different reasons. This was built on in Venice, and reemerged in Budapest. It was like being on the brink of a revolution you believe in. And that generated a huge amount of interest and excitement, both in Hungary (not only Budapest) and the rest of networked world."[20]

The centerpiece of the Budapest meeting was an debate between two Americans of the hippie generation, Peter Lamborn Wilson and John Perry Barlow, representing the Luddite-anarcho and the entrepreneurial side of techno libertarianism, united in their interest in everything psychoactive. Peter Lamborn Wilson (a.k.a. Hakim Bey) spoke about "Islam and the Internet." Barlow's topic was "Cyberspace and Sovereignty." Diana McCarty: "The whole audience was transfixed in the magic of Peter's talk, even if he was basically tearing apart the notion of virtuality. At least in

terms of living it through computers, he created a unique virtual space for the duration of his talk. This was only broken by Barlow's magnificent entrance. They should
have arrived together in the morning, but Barlow's flight was delayed due to bad
weather and he was just lost for most of the day. When he entered the room, he was
so physically present—it just brought the gravity back. I find this hilarious in the
sense that Peter was arguing for physicality, and Barlow is somehow on the side of
virtuality (in the 1995 sense), but they were so opposite in terms of their presence and
the substance of their talks."[21] The disembodiment controversy spurred heated debates
at the time. Arthur and Marilouise Kroker, listed but not present at Metaforum II,
had made "virtual bodies" a topic, but their position was more ambivalent. Postmodern discourse was not ready to answer the pressing questions around virtuality.
Was technology going to liberate humankind or bring yet another world war scale
disaster? These, and other topics were discussed on the informal nettime meeting,
held on the Monday after the conference weekend.

Nettime didn't start until late October. Pit's setup hadn't worked out so a cc: list
was used in between. The actual nettime mailing list started on October 31, 1995
with understated material by Matthew Fuller (London), Konrad Becker (Vienna) and
Pit posting texts from Hakim Bey and Slavoj Zizek. A regular contributor was Mark
Tribe, then living in Berlin, before he set up his own Rhizome list out of desk.nl. John
Perry Barlow was the first to reply, responding to the call for "net criticism": "A
decentralized medium offers but few choices—and they are very personal ones: jack
in, jack out, or jack off. In the end, as Gandhi proposed, 'You must be the change you
wish to see in the world.' There's little else you can do." The debate between techno-
libertarians and net critics was going to dominate nettime. It gave the list the reputation being one of few places of exchange between the European and American
intelligentsia, a role which *Wired* magazine had refused to take. It was en vogue,
among digerati, to dump on the old continent and its socialist states whose only aim it
was to censor the freedom on the net. In particular *Wired* editor Louis Rosetto was

wary of any debate with critical theorists and artists. The Amsterdam-based print magazine *Mediamatic* could have taken up this task. Its speculative approach, however, made it an unlikely host for online critical debates.[22]

From its genesis, nettime was to embody the project of "net criticism" in order to counter the unbearable lightness of *Wired* magazine, which was considered the most influential organ of the virtual class. Pit Schultz: "Everything which *Wired* wrote was for us Pure Propaganda and provoked the quest for Unofficial Data. As the Pravda of the net, *Wired* forced the emergence of dissident thought."[23] The uncontested hegemony of *Wired* in the mid 1990s cannot be underestimated here. For opinion makers, politicians and young entrepreneurs there wasn't much else with such a positive-seductive appeal. The usual PC magazines lacked a comprehensive world vision. Old media, such as print and television had no idea anyway. *Wired* was heaven's gate to a new world, a sign on the horizon which fellow passionate believers in the Digital Cause immediately recognized. *Wired* came straight from the future, and, while bouncing back, took us with it, thereby sharing the endless accumulation of technological potentialities. "The Internet needs you!" In a text from early 1996 the aim was followed as such: "Our Net Criticism has nothing to do with a monolithic or dialectic dogma, like 'neo-Luddism' or 'digital Marxism'. It is more a behavior than a project, more a parasite then a strategic position, more based on a diffuse corpus of works than an academic knowledge, it is heavily interfered by contradictions and techno-pleasure, and it keeps vivid in this way."[24] Net criticism was an empty signifier, waiting to be filled with wildly paradoxical meaning. As a concept it was supposed to function as a strange attractor. To some extend the term had been random. It could as well had been called "digital studies" (Alex Galloway), "data critique" (Frank Hartmann) or Internet science (Reinhold Grether). The term "criticism" was not supposed to be taken too literally; as long as it blossomed, it carried the promise of an altogether different life.

Net criticism, the label for nettime's "dirty little practice," was designed as a collective undertaking to deconstruct the utopian *Wired* agenda. Not directly, in word or academic texts, but by doing. There was an immediate danger that net criticism would die a premature death by reducing it to mere text critique. Pit Schultz: "It is funny to use a medium without trusting it. It is even more funny to use a medium and then criticize it. Some say it is impossible to criticize a system from within. They say you have to have a distance to it to be able to interpret it, but then they don't find an end of interpretation." The trick with net criticism, this empty signifier, was to reverse the position of complaining outsider into one of an active, subversive production of discourse, software, interfaces, social networks. This was no longer part of a grand leftist project, nor was it micro politics in the margins. Pit Schultz: "If 'communication creates conflict' (Bunting) or 'subjectivity must get produced' (Guattari), it was never a goal of this project to dominate discourse, missionate you, or tell the pure truth." How could one change the course of a late modernist project of a global scale, run by science and technologies giants, increasingly dominated by finance and business interests—and still have fun? "Beyond the dualism of the philoes and phobies, driven by 'the desire not to get wired in such a way' there are still some hidden opportunities to disturb the networks of power with pure pleasure. Desiring machines are not made to function."[25]

"We are only in it for the content." A few month after the start of the list, on the occasion of the second Next Five Minutes conference a reader was hastily put together, called *ZK Proceedings 95 Net Criticism*. 200 pages, in 250 copies which sold out in a day. It contained a mixed bag of voices from the cyber underground, "almost-manifestoes" from Italy, Germany and Hungary dealing with "access," "scanned philosophies," texts on "the tragic end of net.art" and "the comeback of the Enemy (Telekom, Scientology, Netscape)," most of them essays written for previous gatherings. The introduction calls for "political directness." The need is expressed for a "production of collective subjectivity from within the nets in order to counter its oppressive and alienating effects."

A primary obstacle to a free exchange among intellectuals and artists on the net is fear of copyright. In the search for high quality content and debates, authors are faced with concern that material produced for magazines, newspapers and books is not supposed to be republished on the net. Yet, mailing lists operate in a gray zone. Contributions are being forwarded, cc:ed, but not published in the strict sense. A mailing list is not a web site, even though it may have a searchable archive with a web interface. In order to build up a community with interesting participants, writers have to be persuaded to post some old material from their hard drive, pre-publish a not finished essay, or ideally write something exclusively for the list. For "collaborative text filtering" (nettime's main aim) to happen, people have to overcome copyright concerns. ZKP Proceedings 95: "Copyright is not the most urgent issue here, but the buildup of trust between the subscribers. This bond is based on face to face contacts and mutual friendship."

The creation of a critical discourse is understood to happen in the act of "editing." What does this mean? "The goal is a non-hierarchical selection which does not end in entropic noise but results in a self-organizing editing. Nettime operates as a semi-closed mailing list based on the principle of responsible data, and the right to trash one another's mbox." Editing is not just another way of saying that lists, with their inherent tendency to overload and abundance of meaning, should be closed in order to pick and chose the desirable content. Editing here is positively loaded, not as an act of mean old censorship, but as an effort to create a common context, getting rid of the postmodern-liberal "anything goes" mentality. Here lists are not seen a neutral forum where everyone can give his or her opinion. They are tools, potentially powerful common context creators. It is not the randomness but the rarity of the not-understood which facilitates a possible emergence of the new: "In the current content business there is only one language, that of the market. Nettime speaks many tongues, risking that not every text will be understood. Paramount is the goal to preserve the original contexts."[26]

After the Next Five Minutes conference, a nettime ZK meeting was held in the then still empty offices of the Society for Old and New Media in Amsterdam.[27] With

John Perry Barlow as the only visible, well-known representative of the "*Wired* ideology" it was inevitable that the debate would be centered around his person. Barlow's surprising presence at the Next Five Minutes conference caused some commotion but did not trigger the perhaps expected debate about the ideological premises of cyberspace.[28] Instead it turned into a euphoric global gathering of media activists, sharing their amazement about the opening of so many new communication spaces. A few weeks later Barlow attended the World Economic Forum and on hearing that the US Senate had just signed the Telecom Reform Act, he sat down and wrote the "Declaration of the Independence of Cyberspace." It opens with the heroic indignation: "Governments of the Industrial World, you weary giants of flesh and steel, I come from Cyberspace, the new home of Mind. On behalf of the future, I ask you of the past to leave us alone. You are not welcome among us. You have no sovereignty where we gather."[29]

Debate about the declaration did not pick up immediately. There were holes in the communication, filled up by sudden bursts of online activity from Pit Schultz, who kept on forwarding key texts to create new contexts for an alternative cyber discourse. Nettime was still in the trial and error period. In early February 1996 the list moved to desk.nl, a recently founded content provider for arts and culture in Amsterdam which attracted a lot of artists for a while to work in media lab environment, sharing knowledge with each other, making optimal use of the dedicated line to the net, sponsored by xs4all.nl, this was a luxury in 1995–96. It is in this period that Heath Bunting started posting his "conflict creating" messages, one of the many beginnings of "net.art." The well-documented emergence of the net.art phenomena and debate ("Netart vs. Art on the Net") is closely tied to the first period of nettime.[30] It was also Heath Bunting, making fun of nettime's seriousness, who had graffittied "John Perry Barbrook" on the facade of the Hungarian art academy.

Frequency of postings increased, and by mid 1996 the list had become fully operational. A next reader, *ZKP 2 Reinventing Net Critique*, produced for the Fifth Cyberconf in Madrid, June 1996, was going to direct and systematize the nettime project considerably. The aim of the paper and online publication was to "infiltrate the wired discourse machine, trying to modulate myth building processes with external noise, Euro-negativity and illegal knowledge . . . , not pluralistic but heterogeneous, not interdisciplinary but intensive, based on near-life experiences and almost finished work." Efforts were made to compile online discussions into readable threads thereby bringing into being what "collaborative text filtering" could look like. The introduction denies that there is such a thing as 'the position' of net critique. There is no strategy, a 'new order' or unified movement attached to the concept of net criticism. "The net is not the world. There are a lot of battles to win, but there is no holy war." *Kritik* is defined as a method to "Bind information back to subjectivity and collective strata, to localize desires, to express alienation and the pain of being digital, find narratives which make sense without abusing unquestionable collective myths."[31] As the performance artist Guillermo Gómez-Peña said to Barlow, during a debate at 5CyberConf in Madrid: "Perhaps you feel like a misunderstood hero, like some kind of Kevin Costner, and you feel the natives are ungrateful." *Netzkritik*, at its best, was an ungrateful gesture.

Consciously, nettime had not been conceived as a European platform. There was no desire to appeal to Brussels for funding, providing Euro politicians with a counter ideology.[32] Eurocrats were anyway not interested in a specific European bottom-up approach. Most of the EU IT funding disappeared into consortiums of the electronics and telco industries. Remember Phillips's disastrous CD-I, which ran on a TV, failing to compete with the desktop PC CD-ROM standard. The necessity of an open European net culture was not understood in the first place. The task of governments and the EU was to regulate, not to stimulate. Euro citizens were supposed to be consumers, not innovators. The Bangemann Report and the Information Society concepts all had rather backward looking ideas on culture in which historical content, presented as Europe's rich cultural heritage would be brought online, not contemporary forms of expression.[33] As it proved to be next to impossible to compete with transnational corporations for research money, serious collaborative software and interface developments did not get off the ground, at least not within the wider nettime context.

Instead, nettime was set up as a working dialogue and collaboration between individuals and small institutions from Europe and the United States and, increasingly, elsewhere. The hegemony of the United States was well understood, and not resented, in line with the way in which Michael Hardt and Antonio Negri described the workings of Empire, the book they wrote during the Internet hype years, "well after the Persian War, well before the beginning of the war in Kosovo." Following their terminology, we could describe the Internet as an Imperial system, not by definition a tool in the hands of US imperialism. In contrast to imperialism, "Empire establishes no territorial center of power and does not rely on fixed boundaries or barriers. It is a decentered and deterritorializing apparatus of rule that progressively incorporates the entire global realm within its open, expanding frontiers. Empire manages hybrid identities, flexible hierarchies, and plural exchanges through modulating networks of commands."[34] (Hardt and Negri 2000, p. xii) Many will read this as a definition of the Internet. The "multitude" resistance, as Hardt and Negri indicate, has to be located inside "Empire," inside the computer networks for that matter, "linked to a new world, a world that knows no outside. It knows only an inside, a vital and ineluctable participation in the set of social structures, with no possibility of transcending them." This is not as a representational but as a constituent activity. "Militancy today is a positive, constructive, and innovative activity." (Hardt and Negri 2000, p. 412) The *ZKP2* intro claims the nettime "textual interpretation as a kind of heresy against the ruling symbolic orders," with one big difference compared to the older critiques: "*Netzkritik* operates from within the borders, from inside the system," using "infiltration, guerrilla semiotics, humor, excluded knowledge, local ontologies, tactical negativity and certain degree of over-exaggerated subjectivity."

Another nettime topic from early on is the economics and politics of domain names, associated with the Name.Space initiative of New York artist/activist Paul Garrin. He was one of the attendees of the Venice meeting. His www.mediafilter.org had been arguably one of the first media activist sites on the World Wide Web. In his manifesto "The Disappearance of Public Space on the Net" (early 1996), Garrin warns that "the race toward 'privatization' is taking place behind closed doors and in corporate boardrooms, well outside the sphere of public debate, and threatens the very existence of free speech over electronic networks. Just as shopping malls are private property, where 'freedom of speech' means that the owners of the property have the right to silence those with whom they disagree, often using their own private security personnel (rent-a-cops), the private spaces on the Internet will follow the same model."[35] Garrin called to "participate in and support the growing number of independent sites on the World Wide Web. Create sites and link to other independent sites. Take control of the web and create content—independent worldwide distribution is now in our hands." During the nettime meeting after Next Five Minutes 2 he elaborated these ideas to form a PAN, a "permanent autonomous network" (in contrast to the festive eventism of Hakim Bey's Temporary Autonomous Zone), which would not only share content but also infrastructure. This proposal, which in fact meant starting an alternative telco was perhaps a bit too ambitious. In the course of 1996 Garrin boiled down PAN to one concrete issue, the fight for the liberation of domain name space. The aim was to challenge the monopoly of Network Solutions Inc., the only company entitled to sell .com, .org and .net domain names. In October 1996 Paul Garrin launched Name.Space, an initiative which in the beginning would be closely tied to the nettime community. "The 'organizational' nature of net names reflect the bureaucratic, militaristic mindset of the centralized agency, InterNIC, now operating as a private, highly profitable monopoly called Network Solutions, Inc."[36] Alternative root name servers had been set up in New York (MediaFilter, Zero Tolerance), Helsinki (muuMediaBase), Amsterdam (desk.nl), Berlin (Internationale Stadt) and

Ljubljana (Lois/Ljudmila). By creating as many top level domains (such as .com) as possible, Name.Space aimed "to de-militarize the mindset of the net and open it up to more democratic models. By freeing the constraints of naming conventions imposed by the central authority, the NIC, the artificial shortages created by the command economy of names will disappear, and take along with it the name speculators who bought up thousands of names (for $100 each) in hopes of auctioning them off to the highest bidder."

It is impossible here to summarize and discuss all the nettime postings related to Name.Space and the domain name/ICANN issue. Arguably it is the most frequently and bitterly debated topic. I will here only touch on some highlights where Name.Space and the domain name issue influenced the course of the nettime project. Things turned strange early December with a posting of Paul Garrin saying "the Name War on the net began last night with a mysterious caller at 1 A.M., trawling for information, you could say, 'socially engineering' me, about Name.Space." Name.Space got surrounded with paranoia. The network of test servers did not grow further and constantly had to overcome technical troubles which, according to some were the results of the deep conceptual flaws. The unclear status of Name.Space was another reason for its early stagnation. Was it an art project, a proposal developed by the video artist/media activist Garrin, more effective in the symbolic/conceptual space than in a technical sense? There was careful support within the community, but Garrin didn't quite know how to turn the sympathy into a working consortium of partners which would be ready to push the proposal into a next stage of a business plan, as other Internet startups were about to do around 1996–97. Garrin's main support was in Europe, which was still a few years behind the United States and without broad support in the United States Name.Space was destined to get stuck in a void.[37]

By the end of 1996 the diversity of topics and threads had grown. The Budapest Metaforum 3 conference had seen a debate on the political economy of the net, between Manuel Delanda and Richard Barbrook which continued on the list.[38] The attention shifted from *Wired* to the question of content production in general. Regional diversity began to set in, with posting not just from Italy, Germany, Holland, the United Kingdom, Australia, and the United States. The question of the "Englishes" was discussed . Another thread dealt with the *Wired* 5.03 cover story on "push media," an almost imaginary media concept that had to pushed because the web wasn't going fast enough, not generating any value, not revolutionizing at the highest speed.

Beside frequent net.art postings by Vuk Cosic, Heath Bunting, Alexei Shulgin and Josephine Bosma, the "net.radio" phenomena came on the radar screen with the temporary closure of the independent Belgrade radio station B92 and its migration to the net as a first, major case how streaming media (using real audio software) could be used in a tactical way to circumvent censorship.[39] Simultaneously a debate sparked off around a text of the H. G. Wells-inspired "open conspiracy" IT investor Mark Stahlman, "The English Ideology and *Wired* Magazine." Written in reference to Barbrook and Cameron's "The Californian Ideology," Stahlman traces the intellectual genealogy of *Wired's* techno-utopianism back to England. "*Wired* is a house organ for the modern political expression of British radical liberalism and its philosophical partner British radical empiricism." *Wired* is here characterized as the organ of a new elite behind the "World State" with the aim to establish a "New Dark Age." Mark Stahlman had been one of the speakers in Budapest at Metaforum 3 where he debated his view points with Richard Barbrook and *TechGnosis* author Erik Davis and would become a long-term contributor to nettime, provoking animated exchanges of arguments."[40]

In retrospect, the year 1997 turned out to become a turning point of the nettime list community. The end of the utopian chapter of the Internet hype, at least in countries such as the United States, the United Kingdom, Canada, Australia and Northern Europe was in sight. With the list operational, regular meetings and a growing publication practice, the question was what the actual critical potential of nettime was going to look like, beyond the already successful task as a cross-cultural debating club on the "cultural politics of the net." By the end of 1996 the first non-English nettime list, in Dutch, had been launched, with a German one in the making. A German anthology of critical Internet texts was edited, to be published under the name of net-time (Nettime 1997).

The opportunity arose to host a nettime meeting in Ljubljana, the capital of Slovenia, the prosperous part of Former Yugoslavia, not effected by the war, yet within reach, visa-wise, for East European participants. The three days meeting was sponsored by different branches of the Open Society Institute, financed by the Hungarian-American philanthropist George Soros.[41]

Through the previous Club Berlin contacts (KunstWerke, Berlin Biennale), another, even bigger possibility popped up to do a project during the Documenta X, the world's biggest contemporary art exhibition, taking place every five years in Kassel, Germany. A still empty architectural environment, full of "urban fluidity," had to be filled up with content. In order to get there, the "workspace" concept was developed, a temporary media lab set-up, a response to the growing discontent with conferences and short, informal meetings. There was (net)work(ing) to be done, the phase of debating and socializing was getting to a close, at least within this particular stage of critical net culture.

All the options were put together in a letter to the list.[42] The "zk-plan for 1997" contained a sheer endless list of possible projects and problems the virtual, non-institutionalized nettime tribe could run into, while increasing its engagements with the real world of arts and media, money and power. In the plan nettime was divided in three layers: the social galaxy (meetings), the Gutenberg galaxy (paper publications) and Turing galaxy (online initiatives). Traffic in this period started to grow seriously, with, for example, part one of the Name.Space debate between its founder Paul Garrin and Graham Cook, editor of the Cook Report. Was the domain name terrain still open for decentralized approach or would it fall praise to corporatization? And was the radical opening of the top level domain names, as Garrin suggested, technically possible anyway? Periods of overheating and noise increase. With 400 participants on an open, unmoderated list nettime was testing its borders.[43]

In the first mailing on the character of nettime itself, Pauline van Mourik Broekman and Josephine Bosma describe the list as a social entity, an "island of humanity in a mediated world of the net and its periphery." However, they point at the tension between professional intellectuals (most of them male Anglo-Saxon academics) and "illiterate" media workers. Without wanting to lose the credibility of net criticism they call for "an awareness of how textual critical authority, maybe invisible to its producer, can simultaneously encourage and suppress the introduction of new voices/communications." This is not only a reference to the inequality between native speaking writers and those for whom English is their second or third language, but also to the growing anxiety between precisely formulated critiques and casual remarks, and even more fundamental: between the beauty of raw code (ascii art) and the usage of text in its conventional semantic meaning (theory).[44] The fragile global mix of critics, artists, academics and other workers on the electronic forefront could easily fall apart.

In preparation for the nettime meeting, a fourth ZKP was produced in Ljubljana, this time not a Xerox publication of a few hundred copies but a free tabloid-size newspaper of 64 pages with a circulation of 10,000. ZKP4 contained nettime material from a good half a year of text production, including new texts specially commissioned for this occasion, as had been the case in the case of previous ZKPs.[45] The main part of the paper piles, content-wise comparable to a medium size book, was distributed at Hybrid Workspace during the long summer of Documenta X and at other conferences such as Ars Electronica.

On May 21–23, 1997, 120 nettimers (out of 400 subscribers) gathered for the "Beauty and the East" event, with a public part consisting of lectures and club events, and the actual nettime meeting taking place in an old school building somewhat out of town where the Soros-sponsored digital media lab Ljudmila had just started its operations. A patchwork of small grants had made it possible for many participants to come.[46] The atmosphere was one of great excitement about this virtual listserv entity with so many different personalities, backgrounds and intentions on it, capable of gathering IRL (in real life). On the other hand, many members had already met elsewhere, and Beauty and the East was just another stop for the conference hoppers. Not quite so, perhaps. There was something in the air. This was not just a meeting of friends. There was something at stake, namely what nettime was going to be about. Would the fragile coalition between net.artist and theorists last? The debates were raw, sometimes even hostile. There was a sense of mistrust in the air. Would there be enough space for everyone to expand his or her digital desires under the roof called nettime?

The meeting started with an update of the numerous upcoming projects within the arts context such as Documenta X (Hybrid Workspace) and the plan to do a week long "OpenX" lab at Ars Electronica. A discussion kicked off how the emerging net.art would relate to mainstream art institutions. Would it perhaps be better to drop the net.art label and instead use the broader term digital artisans? But why drop a brand name that was filling so quickly with meaning, generating so much public attention? Was net.art going to limit itself, involuntarily even, to the visual arts system? A repeat of the classic visual arts/applied arts distinction? The proposed term digital artisan had an economic, entrepreneurial connotation whereas net.art, perhaps comparable to mail art and video art, would have the (unlucky?) historical task to talk itself into the museum and arts market, carefully guarded by curators, critics and gallery owners. The creation of a separate net.art genre could lead to a split in which some were and other were not seen as true net.artists, thereby creating yet another star system. But the split was already there. The inevitable net.art meme was already out.

A week before "Beauty and the East" an anonymous Digital Artisans Manifesto had been posted on nettime.[47] The artisan label would be an inclusive one, involving designers, programmers and text editors into its definition. "We celebrate the

Promethean power of our labor and imagination to shape the virtual world. By hacking, coding, designing and mixing, we build the wired future through our own efforts." The manifesto looked for coalition partners to build a sustainable economic model for the mainly freelance digital work force in an attempt to avoid a situation in which recognition from within the arts world would become the only possible source of income. Soon after Ljubljana, some of the attending net.artists such as Heath Bunting, Vuk Cosic (one of the organizers of Beauty and the East), Jodi, Olia Lialina, Alexei Shulgin and Rachel Baker were to get involved in specific net.art channels such as the 7-11 list. In part, the net.art debate moved on to the Rhizome list. A potential clash of two strategies, code and ascii text as an aesthetic object versus text as carrier of critical discourse was on the rise.[48] Subversive art strategies were increasingly going to be tested upon the nettime community itself, putting the level of mutual trust under pressure.

Besides net.art, the other central debate was on "Virtual Europe, mini-state thinking and the construction of a Data East." It dealt with topics such as the rise of NGOs, the myths of civil society, a critique of the Soros Internet program and absent EU policies.[49] Paul Stubbs from Zagreb delivered a lecture on the topic. The discussion soon focused on George Soros and the dependency in the East within the new media arts and culture scenes on the network of institutions, lead by the New York Open Society Institute, in short "Soros." Even this meeting would not have been possible without money from "Uncle George." To what extend was critique possible, thereby risking vital support in a situation of straight-out poverty? And where would alternative funding come from?[50] This was not an abstract issue. Participants from a variety of localities such as Novi Sad (Absolutno), Tirana (Edi Muka), Sarajevo, Riga (E-lab), and Belgrade (B-92/Opennet) came up with detailed reports. Concrete proposals were discussed how to solve acute bandwidth problems.

Another topic was on/offline publishing on the question of content and the abolishment of the many-to-many model in favor of the temptation to make money through funky business schemes.[51] At times the meeting had a conference character with lectures of, for example, David Bennahum ("How computers came to be cool") and David Hudson from Rewired who, with his insider knowledge from the Californian digerati world, already sensed where the "new economy" was heading. In addition to the critical journalism perspective, Peter Lamborn Wilson came up for an evening filling meta-historical analysis of the cyber dreams and money "gone to heaven." Another highlight was the lecture-performance of Critical Art Ensemble on politics of cyber bodies. Later on at night the crowd moved to an 1980s underground club, K4.

On day three, with half of the participants left, a practical nettime meeting was held outside KUD without much result. The prestigious project to bring out a comprehensive anthology was discussed (code word: nettime bible) as well as the pressing question of moderation. So far the list had not gone out of control and complaints about information overload/noise remained few. But with the current growth rate of both subscribers and postings the end of the innocent phase was in sight and at some stage Pit Schultz would "push the red button," as he called switching the majordomo list software into moderation mode. This not only meant that someone would start looking into noise/signal ratios but also that this person, or a group of people who have to be on line at least once a day, if not more, an unlikely situation in the nomadic European slacker world. Who was going to take up the responsibility to decide what was right and wrong? What to do with silly one-liners? How to curb the growing amount of announcements? They could only be filtered after someone had "pushed the red button."

The next day, a Sunday, the caravan went out on a day drive to Piran, a picturesque Venetian port town at the Slovenian Adriatic coast. A smaller group continued to Vienna where a nettime press conference at the new media access center Public Netbase took place. At this occasion the "Piran Nettime Manifesto" was presented, signed by nettime, Vienna ad hoc committee. "Last week Nettimers frolicked in the real space/time continuum on the Slovenian coast in the town of Piran where the following bulletin were established: Nettime declares Information War. We denounce pan-capitalism and demand reparations. Cyberspace is where your bankruptcy takes place. · Nettime launches crusade against data barbarism in the virtual holy land. · We celebrate the re-mapping of the Ex-East/Ex-West and the return to geography. · We respect the return to "alt.cultures" and pagan software structures ("It's normal!"). · Deprivatize corporate content, liberate the virtual enclosures and storm the content castles! · Refuse the institutionalization of net processes. · We reject pornography on the net unless well made. · We are still, until this day, rejecting make-work schemes and libertarian declarations of independence. · NGOs are the future oppressive post-governments of the world. · We support experimental data transfer technology. · Participate in the Nettime retirement plan, zero work by age 40. · The critique of the image is the defense of the imagination. · Nettime could be Dreamtime."[52]

The manifest was meant to give the amorphous structure a direction and provoke a debate about common goals. The Beauty and the East had ended without conclusions. The mixed responses to the Piran Manifesto on the list indicated that nettime was neither a group nor a movement. It was no going to transcend its character as a list community, despite the efforts to turn it into something more. There was no consensus about this "more," and Ljubljana had proved that there was no desire to come up with a decision making procedure (voting, legal structures, a board, etc.). Power remained delegated to the Central Committee, the ZK, a small and half-way open group of founders that had pushed things this far and had to sort out where to go next. As long as the list was groovy the power issue was not of real concern to most contributors.

It proved hard to push such a heterogeneous mailing list community into an a more traditional—and transparent—form of organization, with a program and internal democracy. The topics discussed in Ljubljana; net.art, Eastern Europe and the political economy of the net, were there to stay as the main nettime threads for the years to come. The issues were perhaps even the essence of the whole undertaking, if not nettime itself. Attempts to push the nettime agenda beyond its list character were bound to fail.

It was time for potlatch and burnout. A few weeks after Ljubljana the Hybrid Workspace at Documenta X in Kassel opened, providing nettime with daily content for a good 100 days to come. This temporary media lab aimed to push network culture forward, bringing together 15 groups in a total of 220 participants, each working for a ten days period both on (digital) media projects while presenting their work at the same time to the 600,000 visitors. The German "No One Is Illegal" campaign kicked off here, the syndicate list did its Deep Europe meeting, there was talk of tactical media, the Berlin convex TV built micro radio transmitters, attempts got under way to connect the net.radio initiatives (a topic also discussed in Ljubljana), resulting in the net.radio Xchange list, ran from Riga by the E-lab group. The We Want Bandwidth! Campaign mapped access inequalities and economic interest behind the Internet infrastructure boom. The last and largest group was the Old Boys Network, a meeting on cyber feminism, linked to two mailing lists for women working with new technologies, faces and obn.[53] Series of reports and interviews flooded nettime. The Ljubljana meeting had a long echo on the list. In terms of content and new connections the meeting had proved successful.[54]

What are the economics of list culture? Even with a web archive, email lists hardly generate traffic. While running at virtually no cost, like most virtual communities building up and maintaining a list is time consuming work, done by volunteers. However, in the case of nettime it became clear that scores of media professionals were benefiting from the high level postings and debates. Within the model of the gift economy the netiquette said that those who take were supposed to give back. But were they? By mid 1997, running nettime, with its expanding what-to-do list curbing the highly interested yet out of control traffic, had become an almost full-time job for the core group. With a move towards professionalism out of the question the only option left was to slow down the list expansion. A sustainable model had to be found. One way to go was list diversification into topics such as Eastern Europe, net.art, cyberfeminism, net.radio and specific regional and language-based discussion platforms. What is the "immanent" strategy in such a case? Celebrating the complexity of the moment was of little use. The initial drive of nettime, critiquing *Wired*, was fading out. The baroque multi-media *Wired* empire—with its own net.radio station, search engine, publishing arm, online magazine, and plans for a TV satellite channel—was growing obese, and was on the verge of collapse. An IPO had failed twice. On the political front, the fall of Newt Gingrich in September 1997 cut off cyber-libertarianism from Washington inner circles and resources, returning to its original state of hegemonic sub-culture. With the Internet hype turning from metaphysics to Wall Street, the project of net criticism became economic, perhaps to the dislike of artists, postmodern critics and cultural critics who would interpret this move as a step back to Marxism (or liberalism). Perhaps because the presumed discontent in economics never openly expressed itself. It was more a sense of unfamiliarity after decades of French postmodernist thinking and Anglo-Saxon Cultural Studies which had their preoccupation in common with ideology, signs and language. The necessity of getting a better understanding of where the net was heading had already been expressed on numerous occasions. The traditional distrust in business felt in circles of artists, activists and academics didn't really help. Nettime had a hard time to make the jump and get stuck into the next metamorphosis.

During August 1997 the second round of the Name.Space debate between Paul Garrin and Gordon Cook had gone out of control and turned into nettime's first true flame war, causing a near collapse of the list. Pushing the red button looked inevitable. Regulating the flow endangered the "dirtiness," an essential element which Pit Schultz explained to *Mute Magazine* in the following passage: "Dirtiness is a concept, especially for the digital realm, which produces its own clean dirtiness, take the sound of digital distortion of a CD compared to analogue distortion of Vinyl. Take all kinds of digital effects imitating the analogue dirtiness, which means in the end, a higher resolution, a recursive, deeper, infinite structure. It means here to affirm the noise aspect, but only to generate a more complex pattern out of it. It does not mean "anything goes" or a self-sufficient ethic of productivity. It is slackerish in a way, slows down, speeds up, doesn't care at certain places, just to come back to the ones which are tactically more effective. . . . There is a whole empirical science behind it, how to bring the nettime ship through dark waters . . . how to compress and expand, how to follow the lines of noise/pattern instead of absence/presence. . . ."[55] The wish to avoid dialogues, without forbidding them came out of a disgust against the formalistic approach of democracy, a Habermasian rationale in which argument and counter argument struggle towards a synthesis in order to end in a numbing consensus. "Nettime is not a list of dialogues of quote and requote, but more of a discursive flow of text, of different types, differentializing, contextualizing each other."[56]

The art of moderation concerns virtual diplomacy of the highest rank. List aesthetics is about the creation of a text-only social sculpture. It is meta-visual process art. The work of finding and shifting texts is, in itself, comparable to editing a magazine or running a publishing house. However, the gatekeeper also has to be a connoisseur of art of conversation. The public controversies among participants have an aspect of staging open conspiracies. Lists are contemporary version of salons. There is a "deep opportunism" in the mediators position, having to negotiate with all players in a confidential manner. This is why lists can't grow too fast, reaching their critical mass before the antagonists get to know each other. Anonymity remains for the lurker. Subscribers must have the feeling of being in an open, yet protected environment in which their contributions are properly valued. They are honored guests and equal members at the same time, not in need of a leader, telling them what to think or post. Moderation is about the "politics of antagonism"(Chantal Mouffe).[57] The online struggle between adversaries accommodates a plurality of differences—breaking down consensus, without blowing up the list itself.

The post-1989 ambiance of nettime (the ideology of not having an ideology) was showing itself off. There was a void between the manic drive of activists and its counter image of the entrepreneurial nervosity of the Internet startups. The "spirit of resistance without a specific goal to strive for" was the atmosphere David Hudson had found in Ljubljana, a meeting which had seen "little solutions." Nettime did not consist of "goofy leftists" (sniping at *Wired*) as Bruce Sterling had once described the nettimers.[58] It was much more laid back. Fuzzy. The question was much more, admits all the opportunity, to refrain, and withdraw, a typical Euro-continental built-in default settings, tending towards self destruction of something previously created. Letting it go. Slowing down during a time of growing expectations. Stepping back, not immediately responding to the built-in relentless requests on the screen. "There is the chance that new media creates channels to redirect the flow of power. That's what nettime is made for. An experimental place for (re)mixes. . . . Never perfect and always 'in becoming,' but not explicit, not descriptive but performative, and pragmatic."[59]

An ecstatic "summer of content" drew to a close. On August 22, 1997, Pit Schultz sent out an alarming message to the list concerning moderation, including a list of technical wishes and project update.[60] The scores of questions raised remained unanswered. Pit's call for more democracy was not followed up by concrete proposals for a preferable democratic structure. The unclear, vague structures of the founding ZK period were to be replaced by a rotating group of moderators. But who would appoint them? The silent majority of the 500 subscribers did not really bother with the moderation issue. Two weeks later, a small nettime meeting took place during Ars Electronica to discuss practical matters concerning moderation, a separate weekly announcement digest and progress in the making of "the nettime bible," the ambitious plan to capture the nettime discourse galaxy in a book. Following from this, a working meeting of an editorial team which would put together a concept and preliminary table of content for the bible at Hybrid Workspace took place.[61] By mid September nettime was effectively closed and filtering of messages started, resulting in the first announcer going out on the list. The "Kassel Ad Hoc Committee" reassured that nettime would remain an open list. "However, moderator(s) will intervene and delete spams, local announcements, self-aggrandizing advertisements, flames, personal conversations, and any other posts clearly lacking content relevant to the general readership. The moderator(s) will also write any necessary backchannel correspondence." Days later the start of the net.art list 7-11, initiated by Vuk Cosic, was announced. "Rules: no moderation."[62] A fragile coalition had fallen apart. And nettime could further expand, in a more controlled manner.

A few quiet months followed in which not much happened. After having done the approving of messages on his own, the role of daily moderation was handed over from Pit Schultz to Matthew Fuller and Geert Lovink with Ted Byfield joining later on in 1998. Sandra Fouconnier took up the task of compiling weekly announcer. In order to curb the danger of becoming an academic cultural studies list, an active approach to find other content was proposed: "rants—25 percent increase 12.8 percent more manifestos a full 50 percent more fiction, software reviews—23.8 percent increase nasty weird shit—100 percent."[63] A response: "Who needs soap if we've got net art critics and no net art. . . ."[64] Still, no major objections to moderation occurred and the list stabilized. Mid February a small nettime meeting had taken place at The Thing in New York, arranged by Pit Schultz and Diana McCarty. In the spring, activities intensified to get the book project up and in early June Diana sent an overview of the production schedule, sponsorship and distribution to the list.[65] The bible was to be finished by early November in order to be presented at V2, during their Dutch Electronic Arts Festival. Autonomedia was going to be the publisher, but the editing, design and print were going to be done in The Netherlands in order to keep the deadline. Work on the table of contents was done in July during a session in Amsterdam. Serious editing of the 500 page anthology did not start until September. During the summer, a smaller version of Hybrid Workspace was held in Manchester, UK, at Revolting, a temporary media lab ran by Micz Flor.[66] Questions of scaling and building up small, sustainable networks was what counted in the age of "techno realism" in which projects of the first hours were already on the way out such the New York art site ada'web and the Berlin provider Internationale Stadt. The selling of *Wired* to Condé Nast in May 1998 wasn't even noticed on nettime.

Another debate on nettime during the summer turned away from the moderation issue and focused on "net criticism," a term which had not yet been discussed. As a concept net criticism was potentially still a strange attractor, but in fact remained empty, stiff, tending towards academism. No comparison to the much more imaginative, controversial net.art label, a particular net attitude which had grown into a school or movement of sorts. The net criticism project, started in 1995, needed an update, a 2.0 version and in a conversation between nettime moderators this possibility was examined.[67] Frank Hartmann responded with a text on "data critique." "While net criticism as an activity indicates the limits of the Internet with all its disappointed hopes from the 60s ideology, data critique deals with the philosophical and social assessments of digital technology." For Hartmann the net is all about creating cultural context as form, not as content. "While deconstructing illusions, the age of enlightenment produced some illusions of their own. What is needed is not a New Enlightenment through technically enhanced individuals but a renewed epistemological agnosticism of sorts, an anti-dualism."[68]

Facing the next hype around e-commerce Jordan Crandall questioned the position of the vanguard. "I don't think there can be a 2.0 of net criticism without a thoroughgoing overhaul of many of its basic assumptions, beginning with the very nature of what it means to engage in critical work today, in a landscape that has changed drastically even in a period of one year. We are beginning to understand how fraught critical positions are now—how contradictory, how hypocritical, how implicated." Rather than opposing the market altogether from an outside position, as Thomas Frank suggests in *One Market Under God*,[69] Crandall refers to Bruno Latour's notion that there is no outside, only extension. "The extension is what does the work of critique. One doesn't adopt a position against, or in relation to, some exteriority—rather, one extends the network further. When you extend the network further, you bring in more elements, more processes, and prompt further understanding of its pervasiveness and omni-directionality. It is informing, coloring, detailing—tracing threads and processes, making them visible. Maybe we need to EXTEND the market as a network, rather than resist it, developing ways of speaking through it."[70]

During September/October 1998 traffic on nettime sharply increased with commissioned content for the bible pouring in. On October 10, in the middle of an exhausting editing marathon, the following message showed up: " Hello All, Welcome to NETTIME.FREE, the renewed, UNMODERATED AND OPEN Revival of the Nettime Community! Once again, there is an OPEN LIST for Nettime, free of any unwanted censorship, hidden agendas, personal tastes, anal-retentive book editors/librarians, respiratory diseases, and other information-hostile elements that have corrupted the initial mission of the nettime list as established by the founders of Nettime in Venice, June, 1995. No more digestion/indigestion . . . just free flow of information!"[71] Immediate responses to this initiative came from the "net.art" side (Vuk Cosic, Ventsislav Zankov, Valery Grancher) with Sandra Fouconnier expressing her anger about the way in which an inner circle made decisions: "A deep sigh of relief . . . and many thanks to those who took this initiative." Her proposal is to no longer bring out any printed matter ("NETtime, remember?"). And "*nettime*-free shall not organize physical meetings (Ljubljana-style) and shall radically avoid offline decision making. Why? Because this kind of stuff automatically creates 'inner circles' of people who are more involved than others, and automatically deprives a considerable amount of subscribers from important information. . . . Let's try to get things done with the instruments that are to *every* subscriber's disposal—in this case: email. Openness vs. less overloaded mailboxes. What do you want?"

Others reacted confused, even furious because they had been subscribed to a new list against their will, a violation of netiquette. David Bennahum: "Nettime.free is hereby renamed nettime.assholes. I hereby submit this post gratefully to moderation. Oh ye nettime gods, kill or forward this post as ye see fit. Your will is law, and I accept it gratefully, for a list without law is a list of nettime.assholes." It turned quickly out that Paul Garrin, due to growing skepticism on the nettime over Name.Space and the dwindling participation of nettime-related art servers in his alternative domain name undertaken, had copied the nettime subscribers list (using the then still open "who" command of majordomo) and pasted it into a parallel net-time mailing list. [72] Some agreed with filtering out ascii art messages, the "communi-cation without words," from notorious posters such as Antiorp, Nmherman, or Brad Brace. Stefan Wray: "Filtering out Antiorp nonsense is fine with me. I don't have time for jibberish from anonymous sources. If people think this is against free speech, now they can read as much nonsensical Antiorp jibberish as they want on the other nettime list." The tension between the self-importance of content and self-proclaimed subversity of net.art had come on the surface.

Moderate voices condemned Garrin but indicated that something had gone wrong with the moderation, during that time done by me, Ted Byfield, and Felix Stalder. Armin Medosch asked: "Can nettime really afford to keep going in this mode of clandestine inner circle politics, which does not just affect the list but also real world matters where nettime inner circle freemasons are involved?" The early days of brain-storms concerning *Wired* and net.art had gone. Medosch: "Where are all the people now, who made the list interesting in the first place and now stay so silent? Is their silence not more discomforting then the loud protest of the list hijackers? Probably the saddest thing is how people get so up in arms about these issues and somehow have lost the passion to debate more broadly political and non-personal stuff." Former *nettime* moderator Matthew Fuller comes up with a list of question and choices nettime-free is facing. "Perhaps what is needed first is for people wanting a strictly unfiltered mailing list for critical writing on the net and related areas to decide what they actually want, and what relationship, if any, it should have to the current nettime." Josephine Berry posts a declaration on behalf of "Lurkers Anonymous": "Lurkers shouldn't be admonished but encouraged. They help form the community within which this all happens and because they give an n-dimensionality to events which means that poseurs can't be sure of their audience and what they're thinking. Uncertainty is useful, it makes us sharpen our wits and back up our arguments. It means we never know which conversations are being held where beyond all of Nettime's eight circles. It means that what can't be measured can't be instrumentalized."

While postings of contributions to the nettime book kept coming, with people unsuccessfully attempting to unsubscribe from nettime-free, it turned out that nettime-free was not open in the first place. Several messages did not come through, indicating that Paul Garrin was reading incoming messages first, before they went on "nettime-free." Nettime's system operator Michael van Eeden: "I find it very rude of you to put me and 850 other people on a list without asking us. Of course, it is possible to see the list as a Work of Art, but the amount of shit (and most of all your personal propaganda) is getting more and more. I have tried to unsubscribe, it doesn't work. I have tried to send a message about this to the list, it doesn't get through. My conclusion is that you didn't even set up a real mail list—you're 'playing' majordomo yourself."

After five nerve-racking days, nettime-free ceased to exist. In an explanation to nettime Paul Garrin gave his motives for "re-routing" nettime declaring it "an exercise in electronic disturbance." He apologized to those who felt offended or inconvenienced. Faced with massive discontent over his action the "comedic parody" was subsequently revealed as an exercise in information warfare, a "psychological operation" aiming to "polarize the group" (a goal which Garrin achieved). A. Hicks, in a response to Garrin coming out as an infowar artist: "The whole nettime.free stunt (if indeed that's even what it was) has been the moral equivalent of shooting someone in the head and saying, 'See, as a friend I just wanted to show you how your enemies might shoot you in the head if you're not ready.'"

The nettime-free "experiment," launched in the midst of a stressful and exhausting exercise in "collaborative text filtering" did test the boundaries of net culture, as did the Readme! project, a way too large undertaking (of volunteers) in summarizing and superseding the rich and diverse content and contexts, translating it back into print. The constellation of efforts bringing together Internet exchanges with meetings in real life and independently produced printed matter, all aimed to have an instantaneous, yet cool and laid back impact on net culture at large had proved a hard job. However, nettime didn't fall asleep, it changed as the net itself constantly did and also survived the dotcom craze in a healthy manner.

This by no means official nettime history stops here. I can only briefly summarize what happened in the period 1999–2001. In early 1999, another test came to independent list culture (and in particular syndicate and nettime): the Kosovo conflict. Already over 1998 there had been regular postings on the nature of the Kosovo Liberation Army being "NATO backed terrorists," with reports on atrocities and deportations by the Milosevic army, "cyberwars," and numerous cases of media repression in Serbia and Kosovo. The traffic at the height of the Kosovo war in April 1999 reached 3.8 Mb, double the amount of the 1.85 Mb during September 1998 with Readme! in production. The average monthly postings over the year 2000, despite the continuous growth of the list, remained around 2 Mb. A critical analysis of the different positions within the net cultures discussed here would take an entire chapter. A free newspaper (*Bastard*) was produced in Zagreb by Arkzin which summarized the controversies and critical work done by artists, activists and theorists from Europe, the United States, and elsewhere such as Japan, Australia and Taiwan, in which nettime was just one node of many. The contexts and networks had shifted. The NATO debate and globalization issues ("Seattle") were much larger than net criticism and surpassed nettime, even though strategies of net activism ("hacktivism") remained of importance.

At this point in time, mid 2001, nettime is still very much alive, having doubled in size compared to a few years before. A few more non-English lists were added to the growing collection, indicating that English no longer is the majority net language. The moderation issues kept coming back but not with the fierceness as before. Something fundamentally had to happen in order to turn nettime into more than just an extraordinary mailing list. If it wasn't going to be a thread-based web interface along the www.slashdot.org model, as the activist portal www.indymedia.org had done, what then? A return to the 1996–97 days of publications and meetings seemed unlikely. Unwilling to professionalize the project, unable to mobilize new waves of voluntary labor, nettime had settled itself down in a more or less manageable niche. Limiting itself to the email plus web archive formula nettime did not take up the challenges of turning itself into an open postings web portal. Nonetheless, working with a low-tech and low-intensity labor setup, on a no-budget basis, the nettime list family had developed an effective and sustainable way of letting thousands of artists, scholars, and activists worldwide exchange their critical data.

## < N o t e s >

1. Jonathan Peizer, head of the Internet department of the Open Society Institute, is one of the few doing research into the dynamics of difference between the dotcom IT-company model and the non-profit NGO sector. See Jonathan Peizer, "Venture Philanthropy—Developing the Standards for Success," nettime, December 12, 2000: "The Trusted Source Relationship," nettime, May 29, 2001.

2. For a general description, see Irene Langner, An Introduction to Internet Mailinglist Research (http://www.gmd.de/People/Irene.Langner/docs/19990917/trier199909.html) and her paper at the GMD Doktorandentag 1999, "An Introduction to Mailinglist Research in the Social Sciences" (http://www.gmd.de/People/Irene.Langner/docs/19991122/). Another mailing list study can be found at www.netzservice.de/Home/maro. See also Lunenfeld 2000, pp. 38–41.

3. David S. Bennahum, "The Hot New Medium Is . . . Email," *Wired* 6, no. 4. "The first lists existed on local networks, what people then

called time-shared systems. One of the earliest systems to employ distribution lists was the CTSS computer system at MIT. Developed in 1965, MIT's MAIL was set up to send administrative messages to network users." (http://www.wired.com/wired/archive/6.04/es_lists_pr.html)

4.  Josephine Berry, Introduction-Site-Specificity in the Non-Places of the Net, Ph.D. thesis, London, 2001.

5.  Aleksander Gubas, "The Flock of Netgulls," nettime, May 23, 2001.

6.  Moderators Anno 2001: Ted Byfield (New York), Felix Stalder (Toronto), Scott McPhee (Sydney), Andrea Fischer (Vienna).

7.  The book *Medien Archiv*, by Agentur Bilwet (German for Adilkno), published by Bollmann Verlag, had come out at the Frankfurt book fair in October 1993, presented at a special book launch party, including as speakers Arthur and Marilouise Kroker, organized by Andreas Kallfelz and his Frankfurt art society, Verein 707. After this successful event, Andreas took on the job to organize a book tour. Besides Geert Lovink and Arjen Mulder (on behalf of the Adilkno group), Dietmar Dath, a German SF critic, joined the crew.

8.  In an interview with *Mute* magazine editor Pauline van Mourik Broekman, posted on nettime February 3, 1997, Pit Schultz described his biography as follows: "I was involved with The Thing BBS network from 92–94, the high time of ascii and text based internet like MUDs and MOOs, before the web. At the same time I was working with the group, Botschaft. There were also some exhibitions of low media art, a communication performance in the TV tower in Berlin, meetings, long term projects in the public sphere like an installation with Daniel Pflumm in a subway tunnel, a collaboration with the group 'Handshake' which later became Internationale Stadt, or Chaos Computer Club which Botschaft shared office space with. After an Agentur Bilwet/Adilkno event we organized, I started to work with Geert Lovink, which was a truly new phase of work." A German translation appeared on Telepolis (http://www.heise.de/tp/deutsch/inhalt/te/1108/1.html).

9.  Commissioned by Stefaan Decostere, then still working for the Belgian state television BRT, and recorded for his documentary "Lessons in Modesty" (1995). Arthur and Marilouise Kroker were initially involved in discussions over the concept of this film but later left the team.

10. Only few critics have analyzed the biological preoccupation of the *Wired* avant-garde. By far the best is the inside account is Pauline Borsook's *Cyberselfish*, a critical romp through the terribly libertarian world of high tech. Borsook traces libertarian biologism back to Michael Rothschild's *Bionomics*: "Bionomics borrows from biology as opposed to Newtonian mechanics to explain economic behavior. It favors decentralization and trial and error and local control and simple rules and letting things be. Reduced to a bumper sticker Bionomics states that the economy is a rain forest."

11. Among the participants were Hans-Christian Dany, Andreas Kallfelz, Jochen Becker, Florian Schneider, Verena Kuni, Pit Schultz, Felicia Herrschaft, Stefan Beck, Barbara Strebel, Geert Lovink, Florian Zeyfang, Ed van Megen, Gereon Schmitz, Joachim Blank, Armin Haase, Ute Süßbrich, Janos Sugar, Dietmar Dath, Barbara Kirchner, Christoph Blase, Wolfgang Neuhaus, Ludwig Seyfarth and Mona Sarkis.

12. See Herbert A. Meyer (the organizer of the first Interfiction), "ZKP Interfiction," nettime, January 12, 1996 with a report, most of it in German, of the Kassel meeting, December 9, 1995.

13. Typical European questions of the early and mid 1990s would go like this: "Is technological development bringing us to self-destruction or to a new Renaissance? Are we experiencing the last phase of Western civilization, or the dawn of the digital era? Does computer revolution favor alienation or communication? Does computer simulated closeness increase actual solitude? . . . Scientific progress offers infinite possibilities, previously unknown or even imaginable. But there is something that must be safeguarded, and that is the value or unique, unrepeatable, irrevocable personal and collective history." (Symposium Art + Technology, Venice, June 1995)

14. Pit Schultz, one year later: "While having good food and bright talks during the day, the 'co-optation' of 'techno-underground' during the night became an imprinting birth experience for this project. Since then nettime remained what one can call independent and extremely cautious towards processes of converting cultural capital. This is not happening because of dogmatism but because of the will for maximum freedom, freedom money cannot buy." From "Panic Content, Intro to ZKP 3, Berlin, October 9, 1996," never-published draft posted on nettime list, April 8, 1998. Refraining to advertise for nettime remained a policy through the years. "Semi-closed" referred to a

subscription policy of getting the right mix of participants, not just lurkers. What counted was the quality of postings in a common effort to contextualize each others material. Essential texts would anyway find their way out of nettime to other lists, sites and media. Multiplication happened elsewhere, hence no need for marketing.

15. The <net.time> meeting was organized by Pit Schultz, Nils Röller, and Geert Lovink. Involved in the organization of Club Berlin were, among others, Mercedes Bunz, Daniel Pflumm, and Micz Flor. One of the curators was Klaus Biesenbach. On the participant list were David Garcia, Heath Bunting, David D'Heilly, Paolo Azuri, Claudia Cataldi, Vuk Cosic, Hans-Christian Dany, Camillo De Marco, Paul Garrin, Carlos Leite de Souza, Alessandro Ludovico, Siegfried Zielinski, Diana McCarty, Suzana Milevska, Roberto Paci Dalo, Katja Reinert, Gereon Schmitz, and Tommazo Tozzi. The email invitation and some of the correspondence related to the Venice meeting were posted on the nettime list a few years later for archival purposes. A one-hour radio program produced by Geert Lovink for the Dutch VPRO radio and containing interviews with Garrin, Dany, Cosic, Bunting, Schmitz, and Schultz can be found at http://www.ljudmila.org/nettime/jukebox.htm.

16. The name <net.time> was chosen by Pit Schultz, who, known for his critique of the space metaphor within electronic media, was drawn to the idea of a network-specific time as a possible common experience. "The time of nettime is a social time, it is subjective and intensive, with condensation and extractions, segmented by social events like conferences and little meetings, and text gatherings for export into the paper world. Most people still like to read a text printed on wooden paper, more then transmitted via waves of light. Nettime is not the same time like geotime, or the time clocks go. Everyone who programs or often sits in front of a screen knows about the phenomena of being out of time, time on the net consists of different speeds, computers, humans, software, bandwidth, the only way to see a continuity of time on the net is to see it as a asynchronous network of synchronized time zones." From the Archives: Introduction to nettime (draft by Pit Schultz for ZKP 3), nettime, April 8, 1998 (original from October 9, 1996).

17. Lunenfeld's "user's guide to digital arts, media and cultures" has a chapter on the role of the never-finished prototype, "which has become an intrinsic part of artistic practice." Demo or die.

18.  Nils Röller in his Venice report, emailed to Pit Schultz and Geert Lovink, June 12, 1995.

19.  The conference series Metafofum I—III (1994—1996) was organized by János Sugár, Diana McCarty, and Geert Lovink and held at the National Art Academy, a mix of Hungarian and international topics and Speakers. From the Program: "MetaForum II / NO BORDERS / HATAROK HELKUL / critically examines the role that the internet plays now and what is possible in the guture. How and where do geographic borders render cyberspace mythical? How is democracy defined and enforced in the fourth dimension? What role do economics play in the colonization of the last frontier? How is identity altered by new communication technology?" An early net.art debate was the Art Discourse on the Net panel discussion, chaired by Miklós Peternák. Participants: Lászlo Tölgyes, Pit Schultz, Heath Bunting, Walter Van Der Cruijsen, Konrad Becker, Matt Fuller, The Thing.

20.  Quoted from private email correspondence, May 10, 2001.

21.  Ibid.

22.  In the early 1990s *Mediamatic* magazine had the potential to become a sophisticated European counterpart of *Wired*. The founders of *Wired* had left Amsterdam for San Francisco in 1992, dissolving the magazine *Electric Word*. One of its editors, Jules Marshall, had decided to remain in Amsterdam and joined the *Mediamatic* board. Instead of expanding the magazine on line, *Mediamatic* founder Willem Velthoven decided to take up CD-ROM production and later also corporate web design, leaving both the paper and the online magazine in limbo. The alliance with the business-geared design conferences Doors of Perception, jointly produced with the Dutch Design Institute under John Thackara, was another indication that a critical net discourse was unlike to come from *Mediamatic*. The Australian magazine *21C* could have stepped in. Both lacked editorial consistency, frequency, global distribution and adequate marketing strategy. Like many cultural magazines at the time, *Mediamatic* and *21C* had weak online presence.

23.  From Archives: Introduction to nettime (draft by Pit Schultz for ZKP 3), nettime, April 8, 1998 (original from October 9, 1996).

24.  Geert Lovink and Pit Schultz, text for a lecture at Groningen University, February 11, 1996. Translated quote from the first

collaborative text in a series of four, written in German, in 1995–1997, attempting to map Netzkritik (net criticism): "Grundrisse einer Netzkritik," in *Interface 3*, ed. K. Dencker (Hans-Bredow-Institut, 1997); "Anmerkungen zur Netzkritik," in *Mythos Internet*, ed. S. Münker and A. Roesler (Suhrkamp, 1997); "Aus den Schatzkammern der Netzkritik," in *Kommunikation Medien Macht*, ed. Rudolf Maresch und Niels Werber (Suhrkamp, 1999). The fourth text, a lecture during an international media theory conference held in Kassel in September 1997, remained unfinished and was not published.

25. Short Notes, from: pit@contrib.de date: December 1995, preface to ZK Proceedings 95, Net Criticism, Amsterdam, January 1996.

26. Three quotes from Pit Schultz and Geert Lovink, "Go Paper," introduction to ZK Proceedings 95, Net Criticism, Amsterdam, January 1996.

27. For the list of participants, see ZK Amsterdam participants, posted by Pit Schultz, nettime, February 12, 1996.

28. David Garcia, one of the N5M organizers and an early nettime participant, in a private email correspondence dated May 19, 2001, recalls: "Barlow offered to come to the event and said that he would do anything from dish washing to door keeping just so long as he could contribute. He was carelessly rebuffed or ignored, and sent progressively more angry mails. I took the initiative to neutralize the situation and sent him a 'great; come; you're welcome' message. But he was given no official place in the program of the conference. Nevertheless he was an energetic contributor. The role he played was very much that of *last of the cold warriors*. I remember him sniffing the air melodramatically and declaring that he could detect 'the stench of incipient Marxism.' He hovered about on the fringes of the event dressed in black like an angry bat. I think his role at N5M was a mirror of the role he played on the nettime list. Scourge of the Euro lefties. As for the wider relationship between N5M2 and nettime, paradoxically considering Nettime's European v. America dialectic of those days, many of the key links between Nettime and conference were based around the contribution of American personalities and practice. Peter Lamborn Wilson, Critical Art Ensemble, and, lets face it, Barlow."

29. Nettime, February 13, 1996, forwarded by Marleen Stikker.

30.  For an introduction to net.art and the role net.artists played within the nettime contexts, see Tilman Baumgärtel, "net.art, Verlag für moderne Kunst, 1999"(in German) and "net.art 2.0, Verlag für moderne Kunst, Nürnberg 2001 (German and English)," in *Netzkunst*, Jahrbuch 98–99, ed. V. Kuni (Institut für moderne Kunst, Nürnberg, 1999). A compilation of the 1997 net.art debate on nettime can be found in ZKP4, available on the www.nettime.org site. Tilman Baumgärtel put together a remix of his interviews on net.art for the nettime anthology *Readme!* Another source are the numerous interviews with net artists conducted by Josephine Bosma and posted on nettime.

31.  "Toward a portable net critique," Introduction to ZKP2 @5Cyberconf, Madrid, June 1996 (English and Spanish), p. 4.

32.  Other initiatives such as the Syndicate list, founded at the second N5M conference in January 1996, did have a more explicit European agenda (goto: www.v2.nl/syndicate). Syndicate's intention was to intensify the growing exchange between East European and West European new media cultures. A more formal structure for this was going to be the European Cultural Backbone, a research exchange program between a limited number of European cultural media labs. In some instances nettime was listed as a partner in these networks, for example at the P2P From Practice to Policy Conference in Amsterdam (www.waag.org/p2p), November 1997.

33.  For a critical analysis of Europe's Internet policy and anxiety, and a comparison with that of the United States, see Korinna Patelis, The Political Economy of the Internet, Ph.D. thesis, Department of Media and Communications, Goldsmiths College, London, 2000, pp. 113–141.

34.  Regrettably, Hardt and Negri's (2000) understanding of Internet-related issues is rather rudimentary. Comparable, and, in my opinion related, to the surprising absence in this study of an analysis of the fall of the Berlin Wall in 1989, the following "transitions" in Eastern Europe and the disintegration of the Soviet Union. In the one passage the Internet is compared with the Roman roads and the 19th-century railways and 20th-century telephone networks, with the difference that now production is taking place within the computer networks. "The novelty of the new information infrastructure is the fact that it is embedded within and completely immanent to the new production processes." Hardt and Negri describe the information highways as a

hybrid of the rhizomatic-democratic and oligopolistic-tree model. "There is already a massive centralization of control through the (de facto or de jure) unification of the major elements of the information and communication power structure. The new communication technologies, which hold out the promise of a new democracy and a new social equality, have in fact created new lines of inequality and exclusion, both within the dominant countries and especially outside them." (p. 300)

35. Paul Garrin, "The Disappearance of Public Space on the Net," nettime, January 6, 1996.

36. Quotes from "Liberation of NameSpace" by MediaFilter, nettime, October 12, 1996. Other related nettime postings in that same period: "Your.Name.Here" by Douglas Rushkoff (NYT Wire Service), November 12, 1996; "Networking with Spooks" by John Dillon, November 29, 1996; "Expanding the Internet Namespace" by MediaFilter, November 29, 1996.

37. I had been a critical supporter of Garrin's Name.Space until late 1999, interpreting it as a very serious social sculpture in the Beuys tradition, not as a business or technology but as an art project that takes itself bloody serious in its attempt to invade and interrupt the corporatization of the net. The temporary highjack of nettime by Garrin in October 1998 (see nettime archive) was a real test in loyalty. The final break came in February 2000 with accusations of Garrin sniffing into correspondence between nettime moderators and a proposed "Reclaim the Net" campaign going nowhere. Garrin's paranoia conspiracy culture bearded bitter fruits. For others the Name.Space disputes and nettime-free had been reasons to uphold affiliation with Name.Space.

38. The Barbrook-Delanda controversy on the nature of markets took place during the Metaforum 3. For the program, see nettime, October 1, 1996. Manuel Delanda's essay "Markets, Antimarkets and Network Economics" was posted on October 6, 1996, together with Richard Barbrook's text "Hi-Tech Neo-Liberals." A transcript of Richard Barbrook's talk, "Markets as Work," can be found under the date November 14, 1996. Delanda's response was posted on November 17, 1996. On November 21, 1996, Delanda posted another contribution, "Some Background on the Debate Barbook/Delanda." See also the transcript of the closing debate of Metaforum 3, "The Best Content Money Can Buy," November 7, 1996.

39.  Radio B92 Press Release and Drazen Pantic, "Time for Justice!, nettime, November 28, 1996." Also: Andreas Broeckmann, "Belgrade Radio B92 off the air—on the net," forwarding a report from Roger Kenbeek and the translated report by Bart Rijs from the Dutch daily *De Volkskrant* ("Revolution in Serbia Begins with a Homepage"), December 4, 1996. An earlier, informal report from Adrienne van Heteren (October 11, 1996) explained the background and activities of B92's Internet department www.opennet.org.

40.  Mark Stahlman, "The English Ideology and *Wired* Magazine," posted in three parts, nettime, November 18, 21, and 27, 1996. In response, on November 27, 1996 an email exchange between Mark Stahlman and Erik Davis was published.

41.  During the mid and late 1990s discussions concerning George Soros and his network policies took place on both the nettime and syndicate lists. For example: Mark Stahlman, "The Capitalist Threat, NGOs and Soros," nettime, February 5, 1997 (see also other of his later post-ings); John Horvath, "The Soros Network," nettime, February 7, 1997; Ivo Skoric, "Uncle Soros, The First Capitalist Dissident," nettime, April 4, 1997; Calin Dan, "The Dictatorship of Good Will," nettime, May 10, 1997; Geert Lovink, "The Art of Being Independent, on NGOs and the Soros Debate," nettime, May 13, 1997; Inke Arns and Andreas Broeckmann, "Small Media Normality in the East," nettime, May 16, 1997; Paul Stubbs on NGOs, nettime, May 23, 1997; Paul Treanor, "Why NGOs are wrong," nettime, May 30, 1997. The debate continued, respond-ing to accusations on George Soros's involvement in the Asian currency crisis. See "Blaming Soros," Burmese currency crisis thread, nettime, July 29, 1997.

42.  Geert Lovink and Pit Schultz, "To All Nettime Members, Request for Comments—Call for Collaboration The Central Committee Plan for 1997, Some Small and Big Nettime Reforms,"nettime, February 7, 1997.

43.  A graphic visualization of the posting statistics can be found in Readme!, filtered by nettime, pp. 22—23. It notes that within the period of 12.95 and 10.98 the average of postings was 2.8 per day, with a one-time maximum of 26.

44.  Pauline van Mourik Broekman and Josephine Bosma, "Het Stuk," net-time, January 27, 1997, also in Nettime 1999.

45.   The call for contributions, written by Pit Schultz, posted on
nettime April 20, 1997 gives a good idea about the rising tensions—and
feelings of excitement—where nettime as a collection of projects was
heading: "Instead of stating a long list of what is good and bad, med-
itating with you about the categorical imperative of spamming, complaining about the social effects of egoland, measuring the productive
difference between The Well dialogues and nettime monologues, seeking
for social context as content control, do simply get a life off the
screen, seek for the seasonal highs and lows of an 'esprit de la
liste,' installing a semi-automatic bozo filter, establishing a god's
eye of correct jargon, fighting a holy war against ideological ghosts,
trying hard to really communicate and come together, trying even
harder to follow the subterranean threads or even the main vectors of
argumentation, trying to understand the Tao of email or dreaming about
pushing the big red moderator button—instead of all these tasks for
the electronic Sisyphus, i think that the golden path runs just next
to us." The making of ZKP4 in Ljubljana, in the week before the meeting was accompanied with production problems. The social costs of
stressful voluntary work under deadline had reached a peak and the
publication series ZKP came to an end. The monumental production of
the readme! anthology, one and half years later at De Waag in
Amsterdam, with collaborative remote and local editorial and design
work going on for weeks and weeks, proved to be even more stressful.
Up to this day, readme! has been the last nettime print publication.

46.   A list of participants in Beauty and the East can be found at
http://www.ljudmila.org/nettime/all.htm. A more extensive list was
posted on nettime by Vuk Cosic, May 19, 1997. For the announcement text
plus program, see http://www.ljudmila.org/nettime/announce.htm. On the
same site you can find a sound archive of the radio programs related to
Beauty and the East, the "Net Criticism Juke Box"
(http://www.ljudmila.org/nettime/jukebox.htm). The URL of the photo
gallery, made by Marie Ringler is
http://www.t0.or.at/foto/nettime/down2.html. For a few reports, see the
following: Marina Grzinic, An Insider's Report from the Nettime Squad
Meeting in Ljubljana, Telepolis
(http://www.heise.de/tp/english/pop/event_1/4071/1.html); David Hudson,
"Alptraum Wunscherfüllung" (in German)
(http://www.spiegel.de/netzwelt/netzkultur/0,1518,13422,00.html); anonymous report on the Ars Electronica site (www.aec.at/lounge/nettime);
Tilman Baumgärtel, in Telepolis (in German)
(http://www.heise.de/tp/deutsch/inhalt/konf/3086/1.html).

47.   Anonymous, "The Digital Artisans Manifesto," nettime, May 19, 1997.

48.   <AREA SHAPE=RECT COORDS="954,262,1047,293" HREF="
<USEMAP="#xy"><!—NETTIME> </MAP>, Jodi, map, nettime, 20 May 1997. For
a summary of the debate in the period leading to the Beauty and the
East meeting, see Robert Adrian, net.art on nettime, May 11, 1997.

49.   Inke Arns, Beauty and the East, Day Two, threads to prepare the
debate, nettime, May 18, 1997.

50.   For the full text of Paul Stubbs's lecture, see
http://www.moneynations.ch/topics/euroland/text/paulblitz.htm.

51.   Pit Schultz, Beauty and the East, First Day Debate, nettime, May
19, 1997. The final program was posted on nettime May 20, 1997.

52.   Marie Ringler, "The Piran Nettime Manifesto," nettime May 26,
1997, with responses van John Perry Barlow, Mark Stahlman, Ted
Byfield, Matthew Smith, and Luchezar Boyadjiev. After the response of
Richard Barbrook the thread changed into a discussion on "zero work"
and pan-capitalism.

53.   Old Boys Network (www.obn.org), info on the faces mailing list
for women in new media: http://faces.vis-med.ac.at/.

54.   The producer of Hybrid Workspace was Thorsten Schilling. The editors were Geert Lovink and Pit Schultz. The documentation of the
Hybrid Workspace project was edited and published (with the support of
the Society for Old and New Media) on the www.medialounge.net web
site/CD-ROM and launched at the Next Five Minutes 3 conference in
Amsterdam, March 1999. The URL of the archive is
http://www.medialounge.net/lounge/workspace/index.html. For more on
Hybrid WorkSpace and the temporary media lab concept, see "The
Importance of Meetspace" in this volume.

55.   Interview with Pit Schultz by Pauline van Mourik Broekman,
available in the nettime section of the Hybrid Workspace archive
(http://www.medialounge.net/lounge/workspace/main/projects.html).In
this interview there are a few more paragraphs dealing with possible
alternative approaches towards economics related to nettime. Another
text in this section is a first nettime history written by Diana
McCarty for an Italian publication and dated July 20, 1997.

56. Interview with Pit Schultz (see preceding note).

57. See Chantal Mouffe, *The Democratic Paradox* (Verso, 2000).

58. Quoted from the English original of David Hudson's Beauty and the East report (in German) "Alptraum Wunscherfüllung" (http://www.spiegel.de/netzwelt/netzkultur/0,1518,13422,00.html).

59. Pit Schultz, in *Mute* interview (see above).

60. Pit Schultz, "the we of nettime," August 22, 1997. This postings also contains postings of David Bennahum, Tapio Makela, Steven Carlson, Patrice Riemens, and Tilman Baumgärtel, some expressing their disagreement with the Garrin-Cook flame war, others calling for moderation in the light of the decrease in quality.

61. The Ad Hoc Kassel Committee consisted of Janos Sugar, Matt Fuller, Critical Art Ensemble, Patrice Riemens, The Nettime Brothers, and Michael van Eeden. Their first report dealing with the issue of moderation was posted on nettime September 14, 1997. The second report, on the making of the bible, was posted on September 18, 1997.

62. Vuk Cosic, 7-11 list, in "!more new announcements," nettime, September 20, 1997. List archive: www.7-11.org. One week later Vuk downloaded and republished the entire Documenta X web site, thereby saving its content which ignorant bureaucrats in Kassel had decided to take down because they did not want to pay for the Internet traffic in between the art shows (http://www.ljudmila.org/~vuk/dx). The awareness of the importance of an ungoing presence of works, including web site conservation still lacked. Years later "Documenta Done" got exhibited at the Slovenian Pavilion during the 2001 Venice Bienale. The Slovenian pavilion was curated by Aurora Fonda, besides Vuk Cosic, she invited 0100101110101101.ORG and Tadej Pogacar (http://absoluteone.ljudmila.org/). Vuk: "The choice of old stuff is meant to direct the focus on the way of displaying net.art contents in a gallery environment. We still have to see how this will work." (nettime, June 2, 2001). A part of the catalogue was dedicated to nettime content, "NKPVI—Network Komitee Protocols VI," ed. Vuk Cosic and the nettime moderators Ted Byfield, Felix Stalder, Andrea Mayr and Scott McPhee, thereby continuing the relation between nettime and the Venice Biennial—and net.art. Vuk, in the introduction: "I have decided to present one more collection of Nettime postings because of this Venice

spiral, and also because of the historically non-negotiable fact that net.art owes its communications spine to it. I sincerely hope that the series of clever and humorous writings in this book will seriously stimulate the curious reader in the way nettime has stimulated net.art."

63.  Matthew Fuller and Geert Lovink, nettime moderation, nettime, February 1, 1998. Moderation was done twice a day, with a morning and evening delivery (GMT). Later on in 1998 Ted Byfield and Felix Stalder took up moderation work. A general re-assessment from Pit Schultz after the rotating moderation system had been introduced can be found in his contribution to Jordan Crandall's Eyebeam list (http://www.thing.net/eyebeam/), forwarded to nettime, media, art, economy? April 7, 1998. The analysis dealt with the urgent question of how a sustainable critical net culture could be financed, taking the burn out of individual members into account, and set within the larger context of the Internet economy. " The paradigm of becoming your own little entrepreneur and organizing your little life like a business got already a dimension which can be called totalitarian, in the same irrational sense one had to become a good communist in socialist areas and times."

64.  Stefaan Van Ryssen, nettime, February 3, 1998

65.  Diana McCarty, "ZKP5 (AKA The Nettime Bible) coming soon!," nettime, June 5, 1998. A next invitation to send in material: Pit Schultz, ZKP5—the book—call for content 002, August 18, 1998.

66.  The URL of Revolting is www.yourserver.co.uk/revolting.

67.  "Net Criticism 2.0, A Fast Conversation of Two Moderators with Ted Byfield and Geert Lovink," written in preparation for the nettime bible, nettime, July 21, 1998. With responses from Jordan Crandall, Brad Brace, John Hopkins, Andreas Broeckmann, and Alex Galloway.

68.  Frank Hartmann, "Towards a Data Critique," nettime, July 21, 1998; reprinted in nettime 1999. See also Hartmann 2000, pp. 318—321 (in German) and the interview with Frank Hartmann by Geert Lovink, "Beyond the dualism of image and text," nettime, June 14, 2000. Here Hartmann raised the question of why nettime had not gone beyond the mailing list format: "I think [nettime] is just too full of academic lurkers who are keen not to miss some trendy things. Knowing that a lot of the

interesting stuff happens outside academia anyway, why did <nettime>
not take the chance to develop a cool web interface, name it something
like E-THEORY, and become the virtual center for media theory?"

69.  "I believe that the key to reining in markets is to confront them
from outside. . . . What we must have are not more focus groups or a
new space where people can express themselves or etiquette lessons for
executives but some countervailing power, some force that resists the
imperatives in the name of economic democracy." (Frank 2000, p. xvii)

70.  Jordan Crandall, net criticism 2.0/network extension, nettime,
July 28, 1998.

71.  Eon@autono.net, Welcome to Nettime.Free, nettime, October 10,
1998. Quoted responses from Sandra Fouconnier, October 11, 1998, A.
Cinque Hicks, October 12, 1998, Stefan Wray, October 12, 1998, Michael
van Eeden, Armin Medosch, Matthew Fuller and Josephine Berry, October
13, 1998.

72.  Pit Schultz, explaining the background: "paul garrin is in a very
bad situation since the decision made with network solution and the
reorganization of the top level domains getting postponed again to
2003. it is a sad moment for his project and the concept of 'tactical
media' in general. he invested a lot of money in lawsuits against
Network Solutions and the US Administration itself. maintaining the
technical infrastructure needed for Name.Space and his employees is
expensive too. Yet his last possibility is to sue Network Solutions
who is actually having a monopoly on the administration on the biggest
top level domains and access to the root files (".") of the DNS system, to pay him back his investments. His aim was a non-regulated
model of DNS where thousands of top level domains would be possible.
Clearly he is fighting against the big guys here, and there is little
chance he can win this Don Quixote fight. In this moment of extreme
frustration nettime-free appears." (brief piece on nettime free, nettime, October 13, 1998)

# Crystals of Net Criticism

# Language? No Problem.

Debates over the future of the Internet are increasingly held by global citizens. The public no longer has to respond to governmental officials, business representatives or celebrity experts and launches its own public forums on line. However, the knowledge exchange of how to set up such a digital public sphere is still performed in English, a fact which native English speakers may not even notice. For non-native English theorists and artists however, language is very much a topic. Not everyone involved is willing to go through the painstakingly slow process of writing down one's own thoughts in a correctly spelled, precisely formulated, witty English, necessary to be taken serious. Participation in international discourse is therefore limited to those who want to make the extra effort, do a creative writing course or get help from native speaking friends. While debating on Internet time there is no use in waiting for a translation. With automatic translation software still at an unacceptable publication level, it sometimes take years before a key text is translated from French, Japanese, Italian, or German into English. Publishers who paid for expensive translators are reluctant to make these translations available on line, thereby further increasing the time lag in what I see as vital cultural exchanges about rapidly changing global issues.

The language hurdle in print media and global policy making are not that high in informal channels such as lists, news groups, and chat rooms. Basic mongrel forms of English are springing up. In an article on "Englishes," posted on the nettime mailing list in December 1996, the Australian media theorist and critic McKenzie Wark points at the variety of Englishes (African-American, Japlish, Euro-English) and combines this with the roughness of quickly typed Internet messages. "I'm typing this live into a mail message. If I was writing for my newspaper, I'd polish it a lot more. And in the process, the raw jazz of writing would disappear. On the net, one sees the shape of language through the little mistakes and fissures that in printed texts gets edited out."[1] Wark argues that English always has been a bastard language. "It's a bastard to learn—for every rule there seems to be a swarm of exceptions. All those tenses and verb forms. All those synonyms. But there's a reason why it is so: its a Creole language, with mixing from everything, from Pict to Pakistani. Its prehistory in the British isles is a small scale model of what's happening to it now on a global scale." However, there is a growing gap between the informality of Internet conversations and the official expert discourse. I wrote the following response to McKenzie Wark and sent it to nettime. As part of the process, I asked McKenzie Wark to copy edit my text before sending it out to the list.[2]

McKenzie Wark's contribution on the ever changing role of the English language in the age of the net was being posted in the dark days before Christmas of 1996. But then people rushed to do the shopping, and gathered with friends and family. In most of Europe it started to freeze and snow. Life slowed down and so did nettime too, at least for some days. I and many others might have forgotten the computer for a while, but the "language problem" remained. Have you also tried to discuss recipes with friends, feeling socially disabled because you never learned the English names for all those kitchen garnishes, deluxe herbs and flamboyant birds? For gourmets, language can be a true obstacle in the enjoyment of the self-made haute cuisine. The careful pronunciation of the names is a crucial part of the dining pleasure. Naming is the social counterpart of tasting and a failed attempt to find the precise name of the ambitious appetizer can easily temper the mood.

McKenzie Wark used the term "Euro-English," being one of the many "Englishes" currently spoken and written. It's a funny term, only an outsider (from Australia, in this case) could come up with it. Of course, it does not exist and Wark should have used the term in the plural, "Euro-Englishes." The term is highly political. If you put it in the perspective of current Euro-politics in Great Britain. Is the

UK part of Europe, and if so, is their rich collection of "Englishes" (Irish, Scottish etc.) then also part of the bigger family of Euro-English "dialects"? That would be a truly radical, utopian European perspective. Is "Englishes" perhaps the 21st century Latin, spoken on the "continent"? Continentals only hear accents, like the extraordinary French-English, the deep, slow Russian-English or the smooth, almost British accent of the Scandinavians. It seems hard to hear and admit one's own version. One friend of mine speaks English with a heavy Cockney accent (not the Dutch one) and I never dared ask him why this was the case. Should he be disciplined and pretend to speak the Dutch accent? I don't think so. What is right and wrong in such cases? Should he attempt to speak BBC English? Switching to other Englishes is a strange thing to do, but sometimes necessary. If you want to communicate successfully in Japan you have to adjust your English, speak slowly and constantly check if your message gets through. Mimicking Japlish is a stupid thing to do, but you have to come near to that if you want to achieve anything.

BBC World Service radio service, either on AM, FM or short-wave is my point of reference, I must admit. The BBC seems to be one of the few stable factors in my life. It's always there, even more so than the Internet. In bed, I am listening carefully to the way they are building sentences, and guess the meaning of the countless synonyms with which I am not familiar. A while ago BBC World Service started Europe Today where you can hear all the variations of "Euro-English," even from the moderator. Sometimes it's amusing, but most of the time it is just informative, like any other good radio program. Would the sum of the dialects spoken at Europe Today be the "Euro-English" McKenzie speaks about, beyond all accents and apparent mistakes, a still not yet conscious "Gesamtsprachwerk"? According to McKenzie, within this "bastard language" one can "sometimes see the shadows of another way of thinking." This might be true. We all agree that we should not be annoyed by mistakes, but instead look for the new forms of English that the net is now generating. But for me, most of these shadows are like the shadows in Plato's cave story. They are weak, distorted references to a point somebody is desperately trying to make. We will never know whether the "charming" and "strange" outcomes are intentional, or not. Non-native English writers (not sanctioned by editors) might have more freedom to play with the language.

Finding the right expression even makes more fun, at least for me. At this moment, I am writing three times as slow as I would do in Dutch or German. Not having dictionaries where I am at the moment, nor the sophisticated software to do spell checking, one feels that the libidinous streams are getting interrupted here and there. Online text is full of such holes. At sudden moments, I feel the language barrier rising up and I am not anymore able to express myself. This is a violent, bodily experience, a very frustrating one that Wark is perhaps not aware of. He could trace those holes and ruptures later, in the text. But then again we move on and the desire to communicate removes the temporary obstacles. How should the Euro-English e-texts be edited? At least they should go through a spell checker. Obvious grammar mistakes should be taken out, at least they should not be rewritten by an English or American editor. If one is in favor of "language diversification," this should also be implemented on the level of the printed word. "Euro-Englishes" or "net-Englishes" are very much alive, but do they need to be formalized or even codified? I don't care, to be honest. At the moment, I am more afraid of an anthropological approach, an exotic view on net-English, that would like to document this odd language before it disappears again. But our way of expression is not cute (or rare). It is born out of a specific historical and technological circumstance: the Pax Americana, pop culture, global capitalism, Europe after 1989, and the rise of the Internet.

Globalization will further unify the English languages and will treat local variations as minor, subcultural deviations. As long as they are alive, I don't have much problem with that, but should we transform these e-texts onto paper, only to show the outsiders that the net is so different and exciting? I would propose that the Book as a medium should not be used to make propaganda for the idea of "hypertext" or "multi-media." A discussion in a news group, on a list or just through personal email exchange is nothing more than building a "discourse" and not by definition a case for sophisticated graphic design to show all the (un)necessary cross references. McKenzie Wark didn't speak about the right to express yourself in your own language. He would, I suppose. His native language is English, the lucky boy. But the topic has to be raised. Americans seem not to be bothered by the topic. I haven't heard a single cyber-visionary mentioning the fact that the net is becoming multilingual. It is not in their interest to develop multi-lingual networks, nor would it greatly effect them.

Despite the common belief I do not think that the bulk of the content will be in English. An increasing amount of users will not write in English and will have only basic English skills. Marketing departments of the software houses do bring out versions in other languages. But this is only done for commercial reasons. And the Internet is not going to change so quickly. Right now, less than half of its users are living in the USA. Rebuilding Babylon within the net will be primarily the task of the non-natives. Of course, many have found a way in dealing with the dominance of the English language and think that newbies should do likewise. But this attitude seems shortsighted, even a bit cynical. If the net is about to grow, to be open and democratic, to have its free, public access & content zones, than sooner rather than later the language issue will be on the table. Until now, this has been merely one's own private problem. It depends on your cultural background, education and commitment whether you are able and willing to communicate freely in English. This "individual" quality goes together with the emphasis on the user-as-an-individual in the slogan of cyber-visionaries about the "many to many" communication. It's really up to you in this world of borderless opportunities. But the language used in "all 2 all" communication remains unmentioned. "Translation bots will solve that problem," the eternal optimist will tell you. Everything has been taken care of in the Fantasy World called Internet. But so far nothing happened. The amount of languages used on the net is increasing rapidly. But they exist mainly separately. It can happen that a user in Japan or Spain will never (have to) leave his or her language sphere, or is not able to.

Languages are neither global nor local. Unlike the proclaimed qualities of the net, they are bound to the nation state and its borders, or perhaps shared by several nations or spoken in a certain region, depending on the course history took in the 19th and the 20th century. Countless small languages have disappeared in this process of nation building, migration and genocide. In Europe there are at least 20 or 30 existing languages and they are not likely to disappear. So communicating effectively within Europe through the net will need a serious effort to build a "many to many" languages translation interface. A first step will be the implementation of Unicode. Automatic translation programs will only then become more reliable. At this moment, French and Hungarian users, for example, seriously feel their language mutilated if they have to express themselves in ascii. But let's not complain too much. Once I saw a small paper in a shop window in Amsterdam, saying "English? No problem." Rebuilding the Babel Tower together should be big fun.

To overcome the situation that translation is everyone's own business, it would be great if we could socialize this problem and create a kind of "virtual translation desk." A place on the net where authors, translators and editors could meet. This could even be a company with a strong component for mutual, non-profit projects. Many people think that this already exists, but this is not the case. Yes, professional translators are there. They work for big companies, like the simultaneous translators and only big and expensive conferences can effort them. And there are the professionals doing literary translations. But none of those are on the net (why should they be?). For many-to-many languages translations we need the model of the gift economy (and some help of future bots). Anyone using this awful phrase "global communications" without mentioning the multi-lingual aspect of it, seems implausible for me. Let's change this and put the translation on the agenda. Separated, bilingual systems, though, remind me of "apartheid." The linguistic Islands on the net should not become closed and isolated universes. Our own cute bastardized Englishes has no future either. There will never be one planet, with one people, speaking one language. "Das Ganze ist immer das Unwahre" (Adorno) and this specially counts for all dreams about English becoming the one and only world language for the New Dark Age. Still many netizens unconsciously do make suggestions in the direction of "One language or no language" (in parallel with the eco-blackmail speech "One planet or no planet"). The pretension to go global can be a cheap escape not to be confronted anymore with the stagnation and boredom of the local (and specially national) levels. Working together on language solutions can be one way to avoid this trap.

## < Notes >

1. McKenzie Wark, "Englishes," nettime, December 23, 1996. See also "Two Letters on Language," January 7, 8, and 10, 1997.

2. "Language? No Problem," nettime, January 5, 1997. Printed in nettime ZKP4, Ljubljana, 1997. From McKenzie Wark's editor's note: "I was tempted to change 'flamboyant birds' in the first paragraph, by substituting in its place either 'exotic birds' or 'exotic fowl'. Flamboyant connotes showy and ornate—its something one would say of a Las Vegas stage show. Exotic connotes rarity of occurrence, as well as a less specific quality of unusual appearance. The justification for making the change would be that, as the editor, I am getting closer to the 'author's intention'. Its worth noting that 'bird' is also unusual in this context. Its used colloquially in Australia for a fowl meant for the table—but I don't know if the expression is so used anywhere else. The OED is not enlightening on this subject. 'Fowl' is more correct, as the term fowl includes chicken, duck, geese, turkey and pheasant—but not quail. But 'fowl' sounds no more natural. So while 'exotic fowl' seems to me to be both a correct expression and closest to the author's intention, it isn't something that looks quite natural—hence I see no net gain in such a change. I've left 'flamboyant birds' because, quite simply, there's nothing *grammatically* wrong with it. Its just an unusual usage. But this often happens in Euro-Englishes: neglected areas of connotation for particular words get

reactivated, or extensions of connotation that don't yet quite exist
in English-English come into being. I think that is, historically, how
English develops and changes—just look at the remarkable richness that
has crept into standard English-English through Irish-English." The
text in its current version has again slightly been edited. The original, if there is one, can of course be found in the www.nettime.org
archive.

# A Push Media Critique

The March 1997 issue of *Wired* has an unusual cover.[1] No digirati this time. Just a big blue hand on a red background, designed like a warning signal, saying "PUSH!" The hand tries to hold us. Or is it pushing something into our faces? The slogan says: "We interrupt this magazine for a special bulletin." The breaking news is about "the radical future of media beyond the web." The intro is signed by "the editors of *Wired*."[2] Will they declare a state of emergency for cyberspace?

Why should *Wired* have to interrupt itself? It is not television, CNN-style. *Wired* always pretended to be different from the old top-down media. Is it because of some new audio and video software that is hitting the market? Is the "shock of the new" indeed so overwhelming that it forced the editors to write a common statement about the rise of "push media"? There must be something else going on. *Wired* seems to be going through a crisis and needs to reinvent itself. Due to the commercialization of the net, big publishing houses, cable giants, telecoms and software companies have moved in and are now pushing the web in the direction of old-style broadcasting technologies. *Wired* calls this the "Revenge of TV." But this is only the logical consequence of *Wired's* own strategy. For years, the magazine has been reporting euphorically about the coming symbiosis of TV and the net as the ultimate killer app. At this moment, web browsers are being surrounded by other applications. The WaitWaitWait is about to lose its hegemonic position. The static, book-based idea of "web pages" will be taken over by much more dynamic audio and video. If the net has to become a mass medium then it has to merge with the industries of film, television, cable, etc. . . . And if the market says so, it has to happen. That is what the ideology of the free market says. So sit down and watch the next paradigm shift going by on your screen.

Still, there is a certain discontent, a sense of betrayal in this odd document. The Wired generation has to wake up from the dream called the web. Suddenly, HTML is described as the language of an "archive medium. Archive as in stacks of old books in a library." That's different from what we have heard before. "The web is a wonderful library, but a library nonetheless." This is a slap in the face of all the followers, pixel pushers and HTML slaves, useful web idiots, and other digital fellow travelers that have devoted all their energy towards . . . building a library. This was not what they promised us.

*Wired's* own destiny is closely connected to the rise (and fall?) of the World Wide Web. The magazine (founded in late 1992) is not about the old Internet nor does it deal with hackers' issues. It eventually became big because of the commercial interest in the WWW (and multi-media). The title, "Kiss your browser goodbye," could there-fore easily be read as an indication that *Wired* itself "is about to croak," or at least needs to go through a tough phase of rebirth rituals (downsizing, restructuring, sell-out, take-over, etc.). There are several indications for this, which are all publicly known. First the German edition was canceled and then the company failed (twice) to go to Wall Street. Now, Wired TV seems to produce programs but is not (yet) able to broadcast them. The UK edition ceased to exist from March 1, 1997. For the first time there were rumors about an internal fight between the techno-libertarian man-agement and a few critical and progressive individuals.

The *Wired* enterprise must have desperately needed a new ideology (or "vision") that they tried to find in the catch phrase "push media." But this pushing does not fit exactly within the previous ideology. Just read what George Gilder is writing about television and why it ought to decline. The techno-determinists are angry. Television has to die, history is on our side! But the reality is, again, resisting Big Ideas. Economically, the web is still tiny in comparison to, for example, the advertisement revenues of television. This was one of the reasons why *Wired* could not grow any longer. The profit of the magazine had reached its limit. The company was forced to diversify and became a small-media conglomerate. Besides the magazine, *Hotwired* and the book publishing division *Hard Wired*, there is now (ironically) Wired TV. This may sound like Lenin's dialectics: one step forward, two steps back. But it is only with a television division that Wired Inc. might be able to make the next quantum leap. The company needed to go to the stock market. Venture capital alone was not enough to ensure the financing of all these different ventures. At least that's what I think, but I am not a professional *Wired* watcher.

At this point, the *Wired* story stumbles, hesitates and comes up with a curious manifesto that above all reflects the uncertainty about the future of the magazine. For net critics it might be amusing to see how *Wired* is being ruled over by true media capitalism. But let's be honest: these are questions that we will all have to face sooner or later. For example: can we preserve some of the old net values and standards, encourage technical and social innovation and public access, without falling back into the patterns of mass media and the existing culture industries? It can be satisfying to see *Wired* struggling. But "*Wired* bashing" can only have positive results if we use it as a mirror, not just see it as an imaginary enemy. Even in times of trouble there exists a real "desire to be wired."

*Wired* wants to "move seamlessly between media you steer (interactive) and media that steer you (passive)." These push media "work with existing media" and create an "emerging universe of networked media." We have to read between the lines here. It simply means that the web will have to give up the ideological hegemony it had in the last three years as the "medium to end all media." The web is just one channel, among many others. "The web is one," as *Wired* puts it now. A fairly realistic point of view, but not fitting into the original net religion that the Wired visionaries have been preaching. The web had to replace all other media and integrate them or, as the "special bulletin" continues: "As everything gets wired, media of all kinds are moving to the decentralized matrix known as the net." In reality, it is going the other way around. The net is moving to the centralized business known as the Broadcasting

Media. "What is about to disappear is the defining role of the old web." Irritated and somehow disappointed, the editors have to admit that "the traditional forms—broadcast, print—show few signs of vanishing." How unfair, they should have disappeared by now. What went wrong?

It is also the fault of the netizens themselves. "The subterranean instincts of couch potatoes rise again!" In secret, many continued watching TV. The editors thought it was time to face this bitter reality. "True, there's a little couch potato in all of us. The human desire to sit back and be told a completely ridiculous story is as dependable as the plot of a soap." Unfortunately, only a few of us have been able to get away from the "45 years of addiction to passive media. Only a handful of us turn out to be up for the rigorous activity of reaching out to engage the world. Bummer."

In order not to lose its role as the *Pravda* of Silicon Valley, *Wired* must take the lead and incorporate the latest developments. But this time their enthusiasm does not sound very convincing. "The new networked media borrow ideas from television, but the new media landscape will look nothing like TV as we know it. And indeed, it will transform TV in the process." What is lacking here is a clear economic analysis. Television is not just a screen or an interface. The introduction of (some sort of) interactivity is most of all a money/profit question decided by a few companies in an ongoing war on standards.

Cybernauts, net heads, web surfers, wake up. The boredom will be over soon. "Push media are always on, mobile, customizable." These total media arrive automatically and "always assume you are available." They are begging for your attention. It will therefore be important to know how to switch them off. The Push Manifesto is indeed warning us of possible misuse, like government regulation of networked push media and privacy violations ("it finds you rather than you finding it"). Neither old nor new (in the utopian sense), push media are rapidly "closing the gaps between existing media, towards one seamless media continuum." The totality of the 'unification' seems to worry the editors. "All we can say is, Let a thousand media types bloom. Soon." But this presumes a deeper knowledge of both new and old realities, for example television.

"Each cycle of extend/unify notches up the ratchet of media complexity. Ontogeny recapitulates phylogeny, in interactive media as in biological media." This must be Kevin Kelly speaking. We are getting to a conclusion. He has seen it all and stays calm, like a good techno-Darwinist. For Kelly it is just a stage that *Wired* and all of us have to go through: "All media recapitulate the evolution of former media. So online media have evolved from smoke signals (email) to books and magazines (the web). We are now about to arrive at television (push media)." It is touching to read how carefully naive the Special Bulletin is when trying to describe the zapping behavior of the viewer. It is obviously a topic *Wired* has not written about thus far. Perhaps it is time to include the 50-year-old theories of mass communications, audience studies on the behavior of the viewer, computer history and studies about the economic (monopolistic) forces dominating the converging media of the telco and IT industries.

### <Notes>

1. Originally published as "A Push Media Critique, On the rebirth strategies of Wired magazine," nettime, March 2, 1997. The piece sparked a debate on nettime and lists about *Wired*, which was on the lookout for a new ideology. The lively Push Media nettime debate moved on and discussed the Goofy Leftist Sniping at Wired thread, simultaneously going on at the Well. Postings from Dave Mandl, McKenzie Wark, Tillman Baumgärtel (pointing out that Wired itself was in the push media business), Mecedes Bunz, Felix Stalder, Mark Stahlman, Matthew Smith, Matthew Fuller, David Hudson, Steve Cisler, Bruce Sterling (reposting the Well thread) and Gordon Cook, nettime, March 3—13, 1997. For the business aspect behind Wired's push media story, see "Wired dreams of 500 channels," CNET news.com, February 11, 1997 (http://news.cnet.com/news/0-1005-200-316517.html): "How can a media company 'push' its content on the Internet Wired Ventures is counting the ways. At the Demo 97 Conference here today, the company debuted a Wired Desktop, a new program that splashes news headlines, along with Wired's trademark fluorescent graphics, onto a user's computer screen

through Marimba's Castanet software." Gary Wolf, interviewed for Telepolis on push media (http://www.heise.de/tp/english/inhalt/sa/3107/1.html). For more push media critique from the German media theorist Hartmut Winkler (in German), see http://www.uni-paderborn.de/~winkler/push_2.html.

2.   Kevin Kelly and Gary Wolf. "Push! Kiss Your Browser Goodbye: The Radical Future of Media beyond the Web," *Wired* 5.03, March 1997 (http://www.wired.com/wired/5.03/freatures/ff_push.html). All quotes in the article, unless mentioned otherwise, are from this article.

# Mass Psychology of the Net: A Proposal

There is an ever-growing list of Internet-related branches of learning: digital studies, techno-cultural studies (UC Davis), usability research (the Jacob Nielsen circus), the emerging discipline of visual culture (which surprisingly includes audio!), Intermedia (a term used from Budapest to Osaka), Reinhold Grether's *Netzwissenschaften* (net science), Internet studies (as pioneered in Perth at Curtin University), media philosophy (the term Vienna-based media theorist Frank Hartmann proposed), net criticism (my passion), hyper media (Richard Barbrook's label used at Westminster University), and digital media (COFA, Sydney). These are just random examples of another Babylon under construction. At the same time existing university departments are starting their own new media investigations in order to incorporate "new media" within the existing structures such as film departments, theater schools or design departments. There are efforts within "journalistic" communication studies programs, which are slightly different from cultural studies, which itself has little to do with the anthropological study of culture, or the unrelated continental European hermeneutic approach. All these areas study media, all have computer labs and spin off their own uniquely labeled activities. So, what's in a name? The establishment of an independent branch of knowledge, with its own concept and curricula, staff, buildings, faculties, international conferences, quality journals and research funds easily takes decades. But the object of study is not as patient as that. New media won't be new forever. Once all devices produce a digital output, the more interesting question becomes what "meta digital studies" are all about. The ironic term "mono media" has already been proposed to mark the exhaustion of the "multi-media" concept. Perhaps in a few years there won't anymore be Internet, simply because the technology has moved on. Indeed, catchy terms can grow into a comprehensive discourse, becoming brand names, taking over neighboring weaker areas, eventually reaching the highest possible level of "discipline," if there is enough institutional backing. But which one will get that far?

Instead of establishing a new discipline it may as be interesting to look into old, forgotten ones. I won't go into the rich history of cybernetics here, although it would be fascinating to see Institutes of Cybernetics re-open. What I am concerned with here is a very specific field of study, mass psychology, re-vitalized and applied to the Internet. Unlike theorizing virtual communities, the research into open online crowd behavior is much more fuzzy, not to say dystopian. My proposed new field of studies, mass psychology of the net, would deal with large-scale systems, filled with amorphous, more or less anonymous user masses. Before I go into detail it might be necessary to explain why I am proposing to rethink the term "mass." Recent audience theory in media studies had rendered "mass" unfashionable. Instead of looking down on the gray mass, pop culture theorists started to praise ordinary people for their inventive and subversive methodologies to zap away any sort of ideology. Growing out of the belief in an increased differentiation and fragmentation of the once so homogenous society, the decentralized many-to-many poly-channel Internet was proudly presented as the crown on the effort to break up mass media.

In its first, hidden phase, the Internet was developed by universities, the military and large computer companies. Hackers, working within the institutions laid the ground work for the open distributed architecture. In the mid to late 1980s the net got discovered by non-academic hackers and small entrepreneurs. This is was became to be known as the second Internet phase: the golden age of cyberculture. The second generation was a mixture of yuppies and hippies, characterized by an individualistic libertarian anti-state attitude. However, they supported the "netiquette" rules and worshipped the same Unix code cult of the founders. The youngsters were still committed to the ethic and long-term research focus of academia.

In the third phase we witness the coming of the online masses. The return of the masses is an unavoidable result of two reinforcing tendencies: the ongoing growth of the number of users combined with a further concentration of web content in the hands of a few media companies, resulting in a (relative) decrease of user skills. Both the first generation informatics engineers and the new, freedom-loving visionaries of cyberspace were not equipped to deal with the mass-scale implementation of computer networks into society. The idea of serving customers was alien to them. Users ought to grow into their role of self-empowered actors. They were not clients, even if they had paid money for a service. After the "warm" phase of speculation, with its "irrational exuberance," and hidden disdain for the user, a next period requires a critical under-standing of the "mass psychology" of the netizens. The wild clicking hordes, going all over the place, have to be tamed into controllable flows of customers, properly sur-veilled and researched like the shopping mall and television audiences.

The second Internet phase was determined by the individual psychology of the user, situated in small groups. Brenda Laurel, Sandy Stone and Sherry Turkle used post-modern notions and psychoanalysis to describe the emancipatory desire to change gender, identity and personality. Mass psychology on the other hand takes the economic-statistic web reality into account. The user-as-consumer becomes a special effect of the portal it inhabits, swapping from subject to object status. Surfing behavior is constantly being tracked and this knowledge is then filtered back into the interface design and content, creating a constantly changing feedback loop. The user flocks are creating patterns, instrumentalized by usability departments to further drag "customers" deeper into the portal. Richard Rogers, in the introduction to *Preferred Placement*: "The network will not be opposed to the surfer, and become network dictator, binding the surfer to browse and read only material the network software chooses to provide. Rather, the network and the software created for the surfer to access media provide interaction constraints." A question for today's mass psychologist puts it this way: "How are search engines, portals, default settings and collaborative filtering formatting the surfer and offering passage to the media?" (Richard Rogers, "Introduction, Towards the Practice of Web Epistemology," in Rogers 2000, p. 12)

For a better understanding of the behavior of "cyber masses" we could go back in history to the Golden Age of Mass Psychology, the period between the two world wars. The discipline was established by Gustav LeBon with his famous *Psychology of the Masses* (1895). Sigmund Freud's *Group Psychology and Analysis of the Ego* (1921) was a next highlight, reworking the First World War experiences. A continuation of LeBon's fear-driven conservative agenda is Ortega y Gasset's *Revolt of the Masses* (1930). Mass psychology is not only an elitist class science on how to deal with the rise of the violent (proletarian) mobs. There is an equally large and interesting progressive mass psychology. Take Siegfried Kracauer's *The Mass Ornament* (1926), Alfred Adler's *On Mass Psychology* (1934), Hermann Broch's *Massenwahntheorie*, a study which he started in 1939, or Hendrik de Man's *Psychology of Socialism* (1927). And not to forget Wilhelm Reich's *Mass Psychology of Fascism* study (1933) in which he, as one of the first, pointed to the importance of understanding the "attractive" sides of Hitler's tactics. The highlight of post-World War II period is Elias Canetti's *Crowds and Power* (1961), a book which had a profound influence on a diverse range of authors from Klaus Theweleit with his study *Male Fantasies* (1977), to Jean Baudrillard and Adilkno, the theory group I am a member of.

Under the influence of David Riesman, Daniel Bell, Alvin Toffler, and Alain Tourraine, "masses" became associated with the declining "second wave" Fordist production and the outgoing Cold War. From the 1970s on, it became fashionable to celebrate the "disappearance of the masses." With millions standing in daily traffic jams, filling up sport stadiums, beaches, airports, train stations and malls, bringing the infrastructures of the world's metropolitan areas to a collapse, the humanities could no longer deal with this numbed reality and started to look for alternative, individual tastes in consumer patterns. Against the forces of globalization, with its unified markets for the same television programs, films and news items worldwide, utopian conservatives started selling the idea that the world was actually diversifying. Postmodern theory spread the rumor that there were no longer crowds, only micro units, communities and most of all, scattered individuals, trying to define their own uniqueness, each of them dealing with their own psycho specialties. The social sciences and humanities followed the "lonely crowd" in their spasmodic attempts to differentiate themselves. Masses had "imploded" into the thousand and one media and the "silent majority" happily fractured into a multitude of minor identities, unable—and unwilling—to express themselves in traditional forms of political representation.

As a field of study, mass psychology was abandoned in the 1970s and 1980s. The discipline broke up into social psychology, anthropology, sociology, cultural studies, etc. Soon after I finished my M.A. degree at the Baschwitz Institute for Mass Psychology of the University of Amsterdam in 1984, the department was closed. It was forced to merge into the newly founded department of communication studies. The library was stored and remains inaccessible to the general public. By the 1990s, mass psychology had vanished. To such an extend that a bull market newsletter author called Mr. Dines could relaunch the discipline by selling his *Mass Psychology: A Guide to Your Relationship with Money (1995)* as a "brand new field." A critical mass psychology approach could counter balance the Usability school of Jacob Nielsen aimed at the maximization of portal profitability in the name of user convenience.

Hannah Arendt wrote in her study *The Origins of Totalitarianism* (1951): "masses are not held together by a consciousness of common interest and they lack that specific class articulateness which is expressed in determined, limited, and obtainable goals. The term masses applies only where we deal with people who either because of their sheer number, or indifference, or a combination of both, cannot be integrated into any organization based on common interest, into political parties or municipal governments or professional organizations or trade unions." This could be a precise description of today's Internet. In a period defined by distrust in political parties, advanced forms of vagueness (xness) and an social apathy, the Internet is facing the comeback of the masses, not on the "real" squares or in the streets, but within large computer systems. AOL servers are housing millions of users, believed to demand entertainment, beyond the dead information of the static web page. Large-scale virtual environments are filled up with crowds and tribes on the search for their flip into the real. Hacks, crashes, sex, riots, virtual panic.

Take the following description of the once so promising "Castanet" channels, developed by Marimba and promoted by *Wired* as "push media": "The Knowledge Media Institute is busy building the Roman Coliseum of the net, a virtual stadium capable of housing 100,000 participants tuned in to everything from rock concerts to university lectures with video, sound, animation and text chats. With Castanet an attendee will download the stadium and the means for video and sound broadcasting just once. Take your favorite web site and envision it as a TV show. 'All we now need is the killer channel.'" (*Wired* 4.11) Castanet didn't go anywhere, but the promise is still there. No more scattered users. Watch out for the swelling online masses and their counterparts, the elitist virtual class, hiding behind exclusive, password-protected firewalls.

# Net.Times, Not Swatch Time:
# 21st-Century Global Time Wars

**For the** first time, history is going to unfold within a one-time system: global time. Up to now, history has taken place within local times, local frames, regions and nations. But now, in a certain way, globalization and virtualization are inaugurating a global time that prefigures a new form of tyranny. If history is so rich, it is because it was local, it was thanks to the existence of spatially bounded times which overrode something that up to now occurred only in astronomy: universal time. But in the very near future, our history will happen in universal time, itself the outcome of instantaneity—and there only."
—Paul Virilio[1]

As we enter the third millennium, there has been an implosion of time into real time, and an emergent global consciousness that is reshaping the ways we have come to think about time.[2] The legacy of our inherited 19th-century temporal model segmenting the planet into 24 separate time zones (and two simultaneous dates) increasingly no longer fits well with our nascent third-millennium global temporal perceptions. New technologies of instant global communication and global mass transport are continuing to squeeze the world to grow smaller still. Wading more deeply into a post-wired world and the digitally networked future, 24 time zones are increasingly being seen by many as being 23 too many. But what are the currents and forces that are driving and shaping this new time awareness? How do they differ from the undercurrents and engines of the previous era of time redesign, and what are some examples of new time systems recently proposed that illuminate the new choices we are now faced with. If we blindly swallow everything served up to us under the rubric of an inevitable globalism, we might rapidly find ourselves subject to a rapacious new global tyranny. Alternatively, this new epoch of change presents an opportunity to right some historical wrongs and free ourselves from the legacy of inherited time constraints imposed by empires of the past. Y2K turned out to be a bust, but what about 3MT, Third Millennium Time?

The new axis mundi, or transcendental bridge as Dutch architecture theorist Wim Nijenhuis calls it (discussing the work of French philosopher of speed Paul Virilio) is an indifferent time, no longer the vectoral time of chronology. We are encapsulated in a time environment, a time sphere, not knowing if the time is going backwards or forwards, without future or past. Jean Baudrillard describes the same phenomena using a spatial metaphor: time's desert (the desert within this time of history).[3] Submerged in the mediascape we can easily forget time—watching a film, emerged in the audioscapes of a CD, hooked on television, lost in cyberspace. The technological extensions are taking us elsewhere, away from the world. An overdose of news or reality TV doesn't change the basic media experience. Because of the interactive illusion of being online, "going virtual" is all the more intense . . . it is getting lost, experienced as a spiritual transcendence.

Manuel Castells (1996) talks about a "timeless time," belonging to the space of flows, a global time characterized by the "breaking down of rhythmicity, either biological or social, associated with the notion of a life cycle." It is time, not space or natural resources, which is becoming the key source of value in the age of global casino capitalism. Castells relates the "edge of forever" with the denial of death, instant wars and the concept of "virtual time." How might this inform new ideas of global time? Castells does not mention the possible rise of spaceless, virtual time standards, located within networks, no longer referring to the geographic Greenwich Mean Time (GMT). The coming tyranny of one global time is already visible in such sectors as banking, transportation, and telecom. Call centers, airlines, and the service industry in general, already work around the clock. The revolt against the global time regime is about to start: net.strikes, computer sabotage, simulation of work, actions against surveillance or avatars pretending actual presence.

Everyone who has ever been involved in intercontinental chats, video conferencing or webcasts will understand the importance of a clear global time standard. In order to move forward, many who've examined this issue strongly feel that there is a need for a new global standard, as the existing standards we have inherited from the 19th century are rife with problematic aspects. On the purely practical level, too many mistakes have been made with the GMT-based Universal Time Coordinated (UTC) system that we now use. The format is identical to the commonly used local time formats, and this causes much confusion. It is not readily apparent UTC is actually different from any other local time since it is expressed in the same format. Then there is the summer and wintertime "springing forward and falling back" and the fact that GMT (local time in London) and the European continental time (CET) are constantly changing in relation to each other.

There is also the difference between northern and southern hemispheres: "down under" in Australia and New Zealand it is winter during the northern summer; half the world's days are longer while in the other half it is the nighttime that endures. Likewise in different latitudes, the rate at which the length of night and day change in relation to each other varies tremendously—toward the poles one moves through six months of light and six months of darkness . . . close to the equator, the length of the local daylight period hardly varies by more than 5 percent on any day of the year. There are also political objections: the use of the colonial GMT (now UTC) standard, first set by the British Empire, and ratified by 18 other colonial powers in 1884 with Greenwich as the "center" of their world. In fact, GMT based UTC is nothing more than a local London time, no matter that it is called "Universal." Why should the rest of the planet continue to adhere to a time standard created to administer a now dead naval empire? 120 years after the Prime Meridian Convention of 1884, people are starting to ask questions, and create alternatives, embedded in code, to liberate their personal temporal desires.

In this sense proposals for a new global time standard do make sense. Early adopters in the online community have already begun looking. Within the context of collaborative use of audio, video and text channels via the web in real time by individuals working from highly geographically separate places on the globe, new independent time standards are already proving useful. Additionally, affluent cyber-youngsters seem to think it an attractive idea that it is neither day nor night in cyberspace (as is the case inside casinos). It is cool to stay up all night, hang out in one of your favorite chat rooms, do some net.radio jamming together, surf, hack, and have a bit of cyber sex here and there. But that's all lifestyle, cleverly used by corporate marketing departments anticipating and working hard to engender a further spreading of the global/timeless attitudes. The seductive sex appeal to transcend the messy world and start all over again runs strongly through many global time redesigns. The instantaneous communication opportunities available via the Internet certainly make apparent the foolishness of assigning a multitude of numerical expressions for time to a single moment of shared "now." During the ascendance of "market populism" (Thomas Frank) in the 1990s, it was up to the corporations to such a standard, not some Greenwich Royal Observatory, run by an obsolete nation state. It belongs to every self-respecting revolutionary to abolish the previous time/date standard and start all over again, as was traditionally the case with each new Chinese Emperor, and our modern revolutionary forebears, the French revolution, and the beginnings of the Soviet State. Smashing the clocks is a sign to start the uprising. But many different revolutions are in the process of unfolding right now, and whose clocks most need smashing?

To gain historical perspective and insight on our present temporal conundrum, we can look to the past and the epoch that preceded the creation of the standards that have been in place for the last 120 years. Through careful examination we can see what the drivers of that situation were, and search for contemporary analogies in our present day to better understand why we are again re-inventing time.

In 1884 new technologies of the emergent Industrial Age brought about a collapsing of the thousands of local times into a globally coordinated series of 24 standard time zones and two simultaneous dates. However, none of this was smooth, inevitable, or welcomed. The imposition of "company time" by railroads literally cut right though and ignored the local times of the places through which they passed. Being relatively industrially advanced as well as geographically compact East/West, but elongated North/South Great Britain's railroads began standardized their time in the 1830s and the nation followed suit in 1848 by adopting the time from the Greenwich observatory as transmitted by telegraph line. Previously, the pace of life and the ability to communicate over distance was limited so that even towns 10 kilometers apart could and did have independently derived local solar times, and many were quite content with this long-standing modus vivendi, and saw no compelling reason to change. However, the introduction of the then new technologies of speed and communication—trains and telegraphs—brought these minute differences into harsh contrast, and radically altered society's experience of time and space with the ruthless imposition of regional temporal monocultures wiping out the rich diversity that had been local time. The old patchwork of local times was swept away and replaced with a new sense of the now larger "here"—Industrial Empire Time.

> The application of science to the means of locomotion and to the instantaneous transmission of thought and speech have gradually contracted space and annihilated distance. The whole world is drawn into immediate neighborhood and near relationship, and we have now become sensible to inconveniences and to many disturbing influences in our reckoning of time utterly unknown and even unthought of a few generations back." —Sir Sanford Fleming 1884 (Blaise 2000)

With the creation of 24 standard world time zones, larger scaled coordination of activity could take place, and did. After much fighting over whose standards would prevail, an Anglo-American axis emerged, and all minutes in each "time zone" around the world were harmonized to match the local time of the British Naval Observatory in Greenwich, England and the Greenwich meridian was declared "prime." All hours were set forward or behind accordingly, creating a new zone centered on a north/south meridian every 15 degrees longitude away from the newly declared zero, one for each hour of the day. To facilitate commerce, navigation and science, Anglo-American Industrial Imperialists created the Standard Times Zones and the world time system we are still saddled with today, along with all of the associated problems of their colonial imperial designs on time.

With the close of the 20th century, in the fin de millennium temporal/technology culture angst that manifested itself in industrialized western societies as the Y2K panic, time is again in the air. Already we are knee-deep into the Information Age's assault on the mechanistic Industrial Time models of the 19th century. One hundred and twenty years of "progress" and technological acceleration have increasingly built greater pressures on fault lines inside the 19th-century Industrial Time model. What were felt to be huge sectors of time 120 years ago are now beginning to seem too small to contain our inflating sense of the new "global here and now." Each new revolution of the Earth about the Sun sees new pressures to collapse time further from 24 zones to one, as layer after layer of new global networks entwine the planet, and more corporations globalize their scale of operation. In our contemporary epoch of globalization, how can we best navigate the perils of temporal re-design and not repeat the mistakes of the past? How can we seize this opportunity to liberate ourselves from the constraints of Industrial Imperial standard time zones and achieve an organic and shared sense of the "global now" without finding ourselves subjected to new temporal tyranny even more mendacious than that of the past? The Third Millennium Global Time Wars have already begun. Enter the global time fray now, and help shape this process before it shapes you. We are teetering on the brink of either time chaos, time tyranny, or time nirvana. For centuries the hands of our clocks have turn clockwise. Now we are in need of clock wisdom.

Anticipating this disorienting loss of temporal perspective, and striving to create a new cartography of global time to navigate the third millennium are three 20th-century fin-de-siècle time re-designs. XTime, a base-10 open source collaborative global time system, TIMEZONE, an irreverent Art Terrorist offering from the media artist group Etoy and InternetTime, either a harmless new marketing gimmick from Swiss multinational SWATCH, or perhaps a corporately branded time effort with sinister implications. Time is, as they say, what you make of it. Who are these aspiring Time Lords and what worlds are they trying to lay the framework for? After nearly three years of development, XTime was alpha released in the spring of 1998. Later in October Etoy unveiled their TIMEZONE. In November of the same year, the Swatch Watch Corporation released its InternetTime product. You don't need to be a weather man to see that time is in the air, but which way are the winds blowing?

XTime was named for X (chi), the first letter of the Greek word 'chronos' (meaning *time*). That X is also the Roman numeral for 10, and the 24th letter of the alphabet combine together suggest a decimal (base-10) time system to function as an alternative to the legacy of the 24 hours of Babylonian time. XTime is an inspiring example of non-corporate innovation, challenging the 19th-century empires of time, and continuing to challenge the 20th-century power of corporate appropriator Swatch. Seattle-based designer jonathan jay ("i am an anti-capitalist," he jokingly explains of his name) is one of developers of XTime, an open source, global metric time standard. According to jonathan, "With XTime you can de-synchronize from standard time, and create a free timespace for your own endeavors." XTime was designed to confront the imperial and colonial designs from previous eras, and unite the world in a non-Eurocentric postcolonial version of a global "now." That is why 00:000.XT (the "zero moment" of XTime) occurs at midnight in the middle of the Pacific Ocean (near the International Date Line) on the Anti-Prime Meridian of 180 longitude instead of some seat of global power. The IDL belongs to no one and is intrinsically international in character, de-centering the 19th-century imperial time schemes. Since XTime is decimal, just like the metric system and our contemporary mathematics, it is de-mystifying and a boon to help folks better see how time flows and where it goes. "And it's handy for space-time manipulation," quips jay.

Rather than create yet another time system that centers itself on profit or elevates an imperial capital or corporate headquarters over the rest of the planet, XTime was re-designed from the bottom up with elements that engender social leveling like de-centering nearly everyone equally. A fine-grade global decimal time system like XTime helps erode the time zones that divide us from each other, allowing people the planet round to return to their own solar times. Rather than maximizing civic homogeniza-tion or corporate hierarchical empowerment, efficiency and profit, XTime promotes thinking outside of the clock. Just as learning another language allows you to better understand your mother tongue, learning decimal XTime gives you another perspective into time itself, and stereo vision definitely improves depth perception. Realizing that corporate globalization was a threat we sought to create an alternative time standard to the looming 24/7 tyranny of the global corporate office and the global 24/7 sweat-shop. Tired of your 40 hour a week job? Quit it with XTime!"

Rather than chopping time up into 24 separate pieces or zones of shared "now," XTime is a single time zone, a "global now" for our entire world. However, unlike the 12 × 2/60/60 structure of our Babylonian legacy time of 12 hours twice, with 60 minutes and 60 seconds, XTime is a base-10 or decimal expression of time. Since the Arabic numeral system we use today is a base-10 or decimal system, it makes com-mon sense for us today to divide time into decimal pieces. In fact, this is exactly the same reasoning ancient Babylon astronomer priests used 5,000 years ago when they set about to divide the day and night into understandable pieces of time to them. The ancient Babylonians had a base-60 or sexagesimal math system. After they divided the day and night into 12 houses or hours to match the 12 constellations of the zodiac year, they sub-divided each hour into 60 minutes and each minute further into 60 sec-onds. Nothing could have been more natural to a sexigesimal mind.

XTime was developed over a period of several years, starting in 1995, working collaboratively with about 25 folks over the web. XTime is based entirely on the deci-mal part of the day equal to 1/100,000 of the mean solar day of 24 hours. As there are 84,600 seconds in 24 hours of Babylonian legacy time, so too are there 100,000 ticks of XTime in each day. This duration of .00001 ($10^{-5}$) of the mean solar day or 0.864 seconds is called the "Chi Duration" or the Xsecond. With this new tempo of time, roughly 70 chi/minute, in classical musical terminology this chi tempo would be Adagio. This new tempo of XTime has been used to drawn new decimal longitude meridians around the globe from pole to pole. Starting with an XTime (Xprime) Meridian of 00:000.XTM on the Anti-Prime 180th meridian and moving westerly with the perceived motion of the sun, XTime wraps the planet in a new cartography of time. 25:000.XTM overlays directly on 90 degrees East in Bangladesh, bisecting the Eastern Hemisphere. 50:000.XTM runs right through the moribund millennium dome in the UK and the old "Prime Meridian." 75:000.XTM divides the western hemisphere in half running through Chicago and the Galapagos Islands along 90 degrees West.

Interestingly enough, there are several historical precedents for decimal time. Over 2,000 years ago, the ancient Chinese had a decimal time system, as did the ancient Egyptians. In some respects, XTime is a kind of global archaic revival. In 1783 the French revolutionaries also created a decimal time. Perhaps because the metric system was still very new, at that time they created a kind of proto-metric decimal analog of Babylonian legacy time using 100 chi for each metric minute (86.4 seconds long, or 1.44 minutes), and metric hours comprised 100 of these metric minutes. However, this revolution was short-lived, and their decimal time failed to take hold, falling out of use even before the ascendancy of Napoleon. XTime does not use an hour and minute analog for its internal structure. Instead, XTime follows the example of the successful and now standard metric conventions for distance and mass. Utilizing the now standard prefixes of the SI system to derive larger and smaller units of time, XTime typically uses chi (X), and kilochi (kX) to express time inside the human scale of perception. Chi are roughly equal to seconds, and kilochi are roughly equal to a quarter-hour.[4] To find out more on the inner workings of XTime, visit www.xtime.org. So much for the neo-rational approach.

Swiss media art group Etoy, who are simulating their own corporate identity, has also claimed authorship over the idea of global time, launching the TIMEZONE project 8 months after XTime, and six weeks before Swatch. "The international etoy.CORPORATION operates its own surreal time zone. October 5th 1998 / Gottlieb Duttweiler Institut Rueschlikon / Zürich, research / development & coding at Blasthaus gallery in San Francisco. TIMEZONE is about time in the digital age: about traveling the web within milliseconds . . . jumping between time zones without moving flesh. About permanent access / availability of 24 hours working power around the globe (this is an important topic for the globally active etoy. CREW, operating from etoy. OFFICE-TANKS (corporate cargo containers) in Zurich, Vienna, San Diego and Manchester. Etoy.TIMEZONE is the solution to the insanity of continuous physical traveling through international time zones, for time shifts in international markets and to the problem of getting older (psychological / image problem). etoy.TIMEZONE raises the amount of available working hours per day, keeps the etoy.CREW younger and makes the etoy.UNIVERSE even more enigmatic. . . ."[5] Whether etoy "sold" its original idea as consultants to Swatch via the hip Swiss cultural consultancy inter-mediates of the Duttweiler Institute remains unknown. The fact is that the artist group glorified technology without reflecting the ramifications of global time. Neither did etoy talk about non-proprietary alternative time standards. Let's say it was etoy in its premature, ecstatic phase. Not much later etoy clashed with the online toy retailer eToys. During the well publicized "toywar" eToys claimed ownership over the domain name of the much older artist group. eToys lost the court case and soon after filed for bankruptcy, as did many overvalued dotcoms.[6]

In October 1998, the Swiss watchmaker and lifestyle multinational Swatch announced its latest product, InternetTime. In spite of overwhelming evidence to the contrary, SWATCH (inaugurated by Nicholas Negroponte of the MIT Media Lab) went on to claim that InternetTime "represents a completely new global concept of time: No Time Zones. No Geographical Borders. Swatch has divided the virtual and real day into 1000 "beats." One Swatch beat is the equivalent of 1 minute 26.4 seconds. That means that 12 noon in the old time system is the equivalent of @500 Swatch beats." Swatch is "not just creating a new way of measuring time, we are also creating a new meridian in Biel, Switzerland, home of Swatch. Biel Mean Time (BMT) is the universal reference for InternetTime. A day in InternetTime begins at midnight BMT (@000 Swatch .beats—Central European Wintertime). The meridian is marked for all to see on the façade of the Swatch International Headquarters on Jakob Staempfli Street, Biel, Switzerland. So, it is the same time all over the world, be it night or day, the era of time zones has disappeared." In spite of their claims to the contrary, BMT is not based on the meridian running through Biel (which is located on longitude 7.16 east). In fact BMT is nothing else than a decimal Central European Time (CET). So much for corporate marketing hype. No one is paying particularly close attention, but that is really the problem.

The gnostic origins of InternetTime seems obvious. John Perry Barlow's Declaration of the Independence of Cyberspace, written in Davos, Switzerland in February 1996 must have had an impact on the corporate world, with the Swatch claim on InternetTime as one of the outcomes. Barlow called on governments not to interfere and let the Internet alone, thereby opening the door for corporate rule. "We will create a civilization of the Mind in Cyberspace. May it be more humane and fair than the world your governments have made before."[7] Swatch's unilateral declaration of Internet Time fits into the late 1990s corporate takeover of the net. Swatch Time potentially endangers time diversity. With software from Microsoft, access facilities and infotainment from AOL-TimeWarner, bandwidth from MCI/WorldCom, domain names from VeriSign, the proprietary time standard belongs to a Swiss multinational. In an April 1999 *New York Times* article, Amy Harmon reported: "The company has made software that displays Internet time on a computer screen available free from its site on the World Wide Web. Perhaps it is not surprising the notion of a world without time zones strikes a chord even among some of the more gimmick-weary

Internet users. With its capacity to collapse distance, the computer network has already managed to alter the physics of space." As the Swatch web site puts it in pop talk: "Okay, so how can a surfer in New York, or a passenger on a transatlantic flight know when it is @500 Swatch .beats in Central Europe for example? How can the New York surfer make a date for a chat with his cyber friend in Rome? Easy, Internet Time is the same all over the world."

"There is a revolution taking place eliminating time zones and geographical borders. It's called Internet Time, it's measured in .beats." (www.swatch.com) There wasn't much protest in the aftermath of the Swatch Internet Time launch against the abolition of time difference and the corporate appropriation of the Internet time standard. CNN installed the clock on its home page, as did a few other corporately controlled sites. One could dismiss the Swatch InternetTime as a marketing ploy, aiming to sell even more of its flashy lifestyle watches. With InternetTime Swatch entered the market of cyber consumer electronics. As a watch manufacturer it positioned itself as a "converter." Watches can display both the old, local and new, global time. There is a danger of a new monopoly. At some stage in the development of the medium, users will ask for the right "net time," electronic micro payments might flow towards Biel. Swatch watches, still a gadget, are quickly dematerializing into software. The Y2K panic showed that "computer time" (and its standards) has long been ignored, and this neglected aspect is now taking its revenge. And this neglect may as well also be the case with Swatch time.

The suggestion of generous Swatch managers, now having joined the gift economy by giving away their time standard for free, should be regarded with suspicion. The Swatch name and logo, attached to the Internet Time, is a clear indication of what this operation is all about. It would be up to ISOC, the Internet Society to develop and propose a publicly owned, neutral Internet time standard. The ISOC could at least have come up with a statement that no single company can simply claim to set such an important standard as Internet time. But they didn't. Nor did the Electronic Frontier

Foundation. By protesting, the EFF could be rid of its one-sided libertarian agenda, showing that a potential danger for the Internet is not merely coming from governments, increasing also from non-accountable corporations, such as Swatch. But it didn't.

The cool "avant-garde" character of the Swatch strategy was suddenly shaken when the company announced in early April 1999 it was planning to broadcast a series of voice and HTML text messages from space using a Russian satellite, renamed "Beatnik," originally built for amateur radio communications. According to Wired News, many ham operators were outraged that amateur airspace will be used for advertising. "The leaders of both the French and Russian satellite amateurs deny any knowledge of plans to use the satellite for marketing purposes, according to documents published on a Swatch boycott site. In the letters, "AMSAT leaders" distanced themselves from the project and apologize to the ham radio community as amateur bands are prohibited from commercial use by an international amateur radio treaty.[8] On Thursday April 15, 1999, thanks to the protests of amateur radio operators worldwide, Swatch canceled the illegal mission.

Rob Carlson reported on his "Swatch Protest and Boycott" web page. "I'm pleased to relay the message of French astronaut Jean-Pierre Haigneri here: "Due to noncompliance to amateur regulations, instructions were received by the Mir crew to cancel the active launch of the rogue satellite and release it in the off position." Haigneri, an amateur radio operator himself, spoke directly to amateur radio operators from the Mir station this Sunday to alleviate concerns about the satellite's status," Carlson continues. "Swatch indicated on April 16, 1999 in a full-page ad in the *New York Times* that they had decided to assist the Spaceflight Control Center and donate the batteries supporting the beatnik satellite to the Mir cosmonauts. This move indicates that noncompliance with the rules and regulations of the amateur radio service was indeed an issue, in spite of Swatch's attempts to sidestep that fact."[9] Rob Carlson and others did not refer to the agenda of the Swatch Time project itself, but their protest was a legitimate one, and effective as well.

Universal time is the logic of the corporate "world state." Mark Stahlman would say it is an open conspiracy of the World Government.[10] The tyranny of Global Time stands for the 24/7 economy, in which workers' rights have been abolished, having to work flexible hours, in night shifts, without benefits. The rise of global time can be read as victory of finance over other economic sectors and parts of life. Financial markets have been operating on global time for a while, especially since the Big Bang of the 1980s in which computer trading systems worldwide got connected. Wall Street is not yet open 24 hours a day but we'll soon get there. An impoverished, free-lance labor force is employed day and night, disrupting biological rhythms and social time. Global time not only stands for the liberation from the geographic time zone system. It also expresses the abolition of the difference between working hours and free time. On global time everyone is available 24 hours a day.

Alternative time standards like XTime are about something else. To many, the cold hard fact remains that the Internet is firmly grounded in real places in the real world, because of the people the web is connecting. Rather than global and timeless, we would be well served by new standards that are global and time-full. Since the dawn of time, exactly 50 percent of the planet is always in shadow and 50 percent fully illuminated by the sun. It is only just recently that *Homo sapiens* has figured out this small fact and begun to wrap our monkey-minds all the way around this little blue watery world on which we spin. We need a new conceptualization of the "here and now," but we should be careful for what we wish. The history of time is one filled with long standing battles over the millennia as those in power continually seek to control the systems for reckoning time, and thereby extend their hold over the time dynamics of society (Rifkin 1987). A global time imposed by a multinational profit-driven corporation might presage corporate control over global society. A global time constructed by networks of collaboration in resistance to Empire might instead serve us, unifying and accelerating a global resistance to hegemonic corporate control. A stitch in time might save more than just nine.

Perhaps the idea of global time remains too abstract for most people, but just give them some time. New ideas typically take quite a while to circulate and allow examination by a critical mass of people. Swatch, with its plastic light-and-bright 1980s style, might be too flashy and playful to be considered serious. Perhaps their offering of InternetTime was nothing but a marketing idea in the first place, in order to fire up the Swatch brand name. InternetTime has proved not cool enough for computer geeks. It's not free software, stupid. The marketing strategy has been too obvious, too dumbed down. The claim from Biel to own InternetTime did not seem to bother many, but perhaps this is because it is still (at this time) voluntary in nature. Swatch is not yet in the position to enforce its time regime on parts of the world population which are actually already subjected to "global" working conditions. However, an alliance with Microsoft or AOL could change the picture rapidly.

In late 1999 yet another time standard was introduced, Greenwich Electronic Time, "the electronic time standard for global e-Business." (www.get-time.org). GeT is a joint initiative of industry and the government of the United Kingdom. According to the web site, "GeT will provide the standards, tools and infrastructure to facilitate time in the Digital Age. GeT's atomic clocks, based on the Greenwich Meridian, together with a developing world-wide network of "trusted" time sources will ensure accuracy in the world of e-commerce. GeT will become the "Time Portal"—with educational material, time-tools and advice enabling us all to better manage our time." GeT can clearly be read as the UK answer to XTime and other initiatives that challenge British 19th-century imperial rule, which can be read in Tony Blair's opening words during the launch of GeT: "Because of the Greenwich connection, it will be clearly branded as a UK service to global business, underlining the leading role UK companies are playing in the online marketplace." The timewar is about to begin.

Etoy's TIMEZONE, now long forgotten and taken off the web, might be too surreal and too farcical for serious consideration, and too unwieldy for practical application. Since it is art, maybe Etoy's goal was only to loosen fixed ideas about time, and to raise the specter of a globally scaled corporate vision of time. However, the vast majority of the world's population still lives under the spell of seasonal agricultural time cycles. Of the exploding urbanized work force most are subjected to the 20th-century industrial time frame. Only a tiny part works under global time. But that is rapidly changing.

Apart from the desire for one global time, there is also a deeper revolt against time as such, one that stretches back not 120 years, but hundreds of years, to the first timewars and the struggle against the imposition of first mechanical and then factory time. Perhaps this present historical node offers us yet another opportunity to achieve time freedom—the chance to right some for the historical wrongs that occurred in a past where a right turn was made instead of a left, and brilliant egalitarian temporal innovations were passed by. It is possible to become polymorphous again for there are many times, not one time.[11] Look at the many times: cosmic, astrological, dream times. Global time is just one of them. So too, there are many cyberspaces, not just the Internet. It is been proved easy to route around the eschatological time of the dot-coms. Let the net.times roll, spread open and free standards that belong to all and no one. While fighting the corporate takeover of the World Wide Web, a growing group of Internet users is celebrating time diversity: the ecstatic time of the never-ending rave, the time of fate, celebrating the black light while enjoying the time stretch of never ending media mixes. There is the extensive time of boredom and reflection, and intense times of experience and flashes of pleasure and enlightenment. Let's ignore all clocks, especially those from Swatch, whether real or virtual . . . an engaged form of gnosis, unwilling to let corporations control vital pre-conditions of being. Living in this world without being from this world, as Peter Sloterdijk would say.

## <Notes>

1.  Paul Virilio, "Speed and Information: Cyberspace Alarm!," Ctheory mailinglist, article 30, posted August 27, 1995.

2.  A first version, posted on nettime in December of 1998, drew a response from Michael van Eeden, who mentioned a Swatch watch called "nettime" (December 15, 1998), a response from Nicolas Scharnagl and Joost Rekveld (December 16), and two responses from Hellekin O. Wolf (December 17). Wim Nijenhuis and jonathan jay were of big help in the writing of this draft. Another round of discussion on nettime about Swatch Internet time occurred August 7–9, 2001.

3.  See Patricia Leavy, "Femigraphing Frankenstein," http://www.ctheory.com/flesh/tf011.html. On the desert concept, see Jean Baudrillard, *Simulacra and Simulation* (University of Michigan Press, 1994) and USA 80, *Tumult 3* (Merve, 1982).

4.  In fact, 1 kX = 14.4 minutes, or 1% of the day. There are exactly 100 kX in every 24-hour period.

5.  Taken from http://www.etoy.com/timezone. By mid 2001 this page had been taken off the etoy site.

6.  For more on the court case, see www.toywar.com. eToys lost the court case in February 2000 and went broke in March 2001 in the wave of dotcom closures.

7.  For John Perry Barlow's original posting of February 8, 1996, see www.eff.org/barlow. For the final version, see www.eff.org/~barlow/declaration-final.html.

8.  Leander Kahney, "Spam That's Out of This World," April 6, 1999 (http://www.wired.com/news/technology/0,1282,18968,00.html).

9.  See "A radio amateur satellite kidnapped by a big commercial company," AMSAT France press release, April 13, 1999 (http://www.epistolary.org/rob/swatch-protest/amsat-fr-bulletin.shtml). For more on Rob Carlson's site, see http://epistolary.org/rob/swatch-protest/.

10.  Mark Stahlman is the president of New Media Associates.  Many of his articles and ideas can be found in the  www.nettime.org archive.

11.  The link collection at http://www.panaga.com/clocks/clocks.htm features a long list of time definitions and clocks. There are alter-

nate time systems such as 28 hour a day, information from the Decimal Time Society, reference to a home page of the Universal Time Organization, dozens of metric time clocks, reverse time, and WRLD.time ("a common-sense time standard"), doomsday clocks, abortion counters, sidereal clocks, national debt clocks, population clocks, sun clocks, Christmas countdown clocks, and time zone maps, just to mention a few.

# Fragments of Network Criticism

**What is** good is what is new, in both form and content. A product of the eye, not
of mind and habit. What is good forgets whatever form it might have had, and is
unexpected.
—V. S. Naipaul

The supposedly neutral and scientific "meme" concept, as developed by Richard
Dawkins, poses the question how "information" travels trough time.[1] Within the
meme-as-cultural-gene context there is the presumption of an imaginative future,
which will no longer be able to cope with the output of all the data, produced in our
present. In this vitalist information theory, "memes" are urged to compete with each
other in a dramatized struggle over life and death to win the favor of the attention of
the coming race of superior info-navigators/post humans. Apparently, the Future can
not decide itself what to remember and what to forget. But it is the task of careful
curators and archivists to decide over the "past of the future" and not let neo-
Darwinist programmed automatons do the selection. Who will set the rules and
parameters for the "survival of the fittest information" competition in an age of
seamless storage capacities?

Media culture at the fin de millennium is obsessed with the Storage Question.
That is, cultural storage and not technical. Soon computers will have enough capacity
to store everything we like. But that's only going to make matters worse. Which information will we, planet Earth, take with us into the next centuries? The storage-and-
selection panic is even overshadowed by an even greater fear for "information

overload." Today's fight over the hearts of the people (and tomorrow's history) can only be won with a deep knowledge of the "attention span" of the user masses out there. Mediocre home pages, outmoded advertisements, boring databases and third class imagery are considered "dead information." What makes slumbering "content" interesting and "alive" is the amount of "visitors," their communication inside the particular context and their actual interaction within a specific cloud of data. All other stored materials, online or not, with or without fancy design or the latest software, are presumed non-existent, and will be so in the future. That's the hard-core logic of this digital age: attract users, or become toast.

The first generation computer engineers considered the computer as a logical, mathematical "number crunching machine." The computation tool, seen as a product of both World War II and the Cold War and its military pre-history, is still present in current machines. Storage and retrieval in this context are merely commands not social processes with possible historical implications. The architecture of the hardware is determining the software. Autonomous processes and the appearance of large numbers of users inside computer networks therefore do not exist as such for these pioneer programmers. Dr. Frankenstein and T-1000 (from Terminator 2) remain what they are, popular myths, produced by the entertainment business. The same can be said about New Age cyberculture with its spiritual "meta body" stories. Computer knowledge that matters is still shared by a relatively small amount of programmers and so is its philosophy (Turing) and history, going back to late medieval times (Lullus).

Over the past decades the owners of engineering knowledge have learned to deal with the inherent "instrumental rationality" of the computer and related automation processes. The academic community focused on topics like privacy, social responsibility in labor/capital relations and links with the military-industrial complex for example, but not with the computer as a potential medium. The self-evident, almost unconscious relation we make nowadays between the computer and its unavoidable merger with television and "the media" seems alien to the engineers, hackers, and programmers of Internet's first generation. Virtual Reality remains a technology used for scientific visualization, not for entertainment. The gap between computer research and development and the "networks for the masses" is as big as always and despite the "digital revolution."

The media memory concept poses the question of how the connection between "collective memory" and new media is going to be made. More than fifty years after the victory over fascism in 1945, the Holocaust still is the prime test case about how media and memory should relate to each other (historically, of course, Auschwitz, Hiroshima, and the invention of the computer are deeply interwoven). James Young, in his book on the history and meaning of Holocaust memorials, *The Texture of Memory* (1993), prefers to call it "collected memory." He says that "the society's memory might be regarded as an aggregate collection of its members" many, often competing memories. If societies remember, it is only insofar as their institutions and rituals organize, shape, even inspire their constituents' memories. For a society's memory cannot exist outside of those people who do the remembering—even if such memory happens to be at the society's bidding, in its name."

Media memory, in this context, could be the way in which society actively uses the stored information about the past. With Young, we could speak of an "art of public memory" in which large interactive archives play an important role in the future, as extensions of the existing sites of memory. Media memory is embedded in the way people are using machines, it is an active process of constructing the past, not merely technical one, which can be reduced to "storage" and "retrieval." For James Young the sites of memory range from "archive to museums, parades to moments of silence, memorial gardens to resistance monuments, ruins to commemorative fast days, national malls to a family's *Jahrzeit* candle."

How will the memory of the Holocaust appear within cyberspace, how will it relate to the existing museums, archives, films and TV programs, libraries, education in schools and the huge variety of artworks, described in James Young's book? The organization of "collected memory" goes beyond the now often discussed ways the brain functions and the myths about "uploading" the brain into a computer, as Hans

Moravec proposed. Media memory asks about the role of the machines in the social process of remembering and the contribution of technology in the everyday life dialogue with the past, how to combine the passive aspect of "storage" with active ways of "memory." This even goes beyond designs of a "virtual architecture" and large online databases which will give us access to historical information. Especially in relation to fascism, media memory, being self-reflexive, should also deal with "instrumental rationality" and the quasi-neutral scientific role of ordinary, task-oriented Internet engineers.

Media are about archiving. Endless life "reality" castings are soon becoming unbearably boring. Nothing happens if one cuts the feedback to history files. Media are about the art of editing stored data. During the entire 20th century the techno-modernist movements have been obsessed with revolutionizing the standards, the computing and storage capacities of the technical media. Engineers were not focused on how to conserve the cultural heritage these media carry. Technical media are, in essence, self-referential, especially in their early stages of development. The fight over standards and ownership is a passionate one, quite different from other industries. Why would you identify with a commercial standard in the first place? If you cannot stand its emptiness, stupidity, if you don't like gambling and debating, tinkering and waiting, then stay away from the computer topic. Only very few manage to treat computers as tools. One never knows if an idea or concept will ever be further implemented. So do not even start looking for sustainable communication standards. Hardware and software are not made for eternity. Only in fifty years or so will we be able to evaluate the premises and promises of new media, then sunken into the sediments of popular culture. Future generations will look back on our time and think: why, in the 1990s, did they all use these secondary Microsoft products? Why did not they revolt against the ugly stupidity of its interface and the corporate take over of this once so public and open Internet platform? Will anyone understand the holy wars between PC and Mac? Next generations will be full of nostalgia about the utopian glory attached to the "universal" machines and the primal net.

Media, these days, are still partial media, with a promise to reach an ultimate moment of synergy, the medium to end all media. That utopian moment, to invade and connect all senses, has a particularly strong, irrational, mythical drive. WebTV is a current buzzword for this. Multimedia is a more general term, referring to a general device to see movies, watch TV, listen radio, read books and newspapers, make telephone calls and send emails. Will the data reach us via telephone cable, the TV cable, via the ether, via satellites? Will the digital customers have seamless band-width, eternal conversations? This digital *Gesamtkunstwerk* is creating bizarre struc-tures, hilarious failures, crippling interfaces, tragic bankruptcies, brilliant monsters, invisible eyes that will watch over us. It is actually all existing and already history, driven by ordinary commercial interests. Nothing special about this e-goldrush. What is the driving force behind this Inclination to Synergy? Is it the good old "claim on an absolute totality" (I. Kant)? Why this obsession with standards? Who could care less about Windows against Mac? It is perhaps just curiosity, a desire to look into the future, beside the all too human hunger for power and profit. Where is the totalitarian aspect hidden in the architecture of these *Gesamtmedia*? And what could be its possible negation? Little is yet known of its radical opposition to the dig-ital utopia except for some forms of fundamentalism, from George Gilder to the Luddites. The attitude of indecision has lost its supreme position long ago. Consumer choice rules, the option to reject and boycott certain products is presented as the far more powerful follow-up of voting, the only remaining weapon of "civil society" to influence global markets.

Why there is such a lack of ironical distance in new media? Few can afford to look down on this pumping techno engagement, not being obsessed, overworked, without ruined bodies—and free of ignorance. Show us your joyful pessimism, supreme neglect, your spiritual wisdom over all this hollow data trash! Today's neo-Luddites are unable to disdainfully detest technology. Forget them. Their scientific ecology lacks outrage. The Rage against the Machine will be ignited by proletarianized "knowledge workers." A meta-techno intelligentsia is on the rise, transcending the primitive social Darwinism with its winner-loser and adapt-or-die logic. The organized stupidity of e-commerce will be challenged. Being a "virtual intellectual," understanding today's tools, working within the net is not enough. "The concept of intelligentsia must not be confused with the notion of intellectuals. Its members think of themselves as united by something more than mere interest in ideas; they conceive themselves as being a dedicated order, almost a secular priesthood, devoted to the spreading of a specific attitude to life, something like a gospel." (Berlin 1984)

Sociological categories, such as the intellectual, are dull and static, lacking style, direction or sense of conspiracy—not cool, that is, not "brandable." Active social vectors are essential components otherwise all network(ed) efforts deteriorate into lifestyle design and internal fights. Activists will come up with a new elegance and comfort which is openly hostile to the global managerial class and its New Age cults, necessary to compensate the massive damages caused by their commodity fetish culture. The cultural studies strategy to embrace ambivalent feelings towards pop culture fulfilled its role and liberated many from rigid and dogmatic anti-positions. But this creative impulse was still operating from within new social movements which have long gone, while its principles got buried inside institutional politics. It crossed borders, to return safely. Today's customized luxury is cheap and predictable, no matter its price—and thrives without alternatives.

The autopoiesis of the new media is exhausting itself in total self-glorification. Regression into an aristocratic *laissez faire, laissez passer* gesture of the outsider has its dramatic qualities, but even the snobbish rich and famous can no longer afford non-involvement. The logic of the new has to be abandoned altogether. A first step could be the acceptance of technology being in a phase of permanent revolution (not "out of control"). The second would be to build in feedback loops on social, political, and cultural levels, short-cutting the endless repetition of the R&D-introduction-resistance-hype-acceptance loop. One day "the new" itself will be a worn-out concept. Marginalization into normality is a more likely scenario for the "fate" of technology than constant taming or delays in the implementation. Techno-scientific knowledge could fade away as alchemy did a few centuries ago.

There is an ultimate moment of synergy: the medium to end all media. In these serious dreams, senses are shortcut, having become suspicious about the eye, ear, nose. They fail to register modern invisible phenomena such as the psyche, electricity, radiation, radio waves, computer data. It is from this real existing discontent that the desire arises to directly connect to the body's nervous system. Today's interfaces are too slow, too clumsy, too rational. An example of this common discontent is David Cronenberg's *eXistenZ*, where a slimy bio-pod gets plugged into the bio-port, positioned at the low spinal column. Nothing in this classic VR-genre film is reminiscent of the gray plastic office machines, or their opposites, the decayed, open cyber-punkish gadgets. In *eXistenZ*, the clean modernity of high-rises has disappeared altogether. What is left is a freaky universe, a return of medieval environments where US West Coast subcultures have gained all but world primacy. Foucault's bio power has finally triumphed over the cold and dead, metallic mechanisms. Kevin Kelly's rules have been followed up: "Move technology to invisibility." His vision to "mimic biology" has literary whipped out the current computer hardware and software culture. As a result of this, relations between the realms of the Real and the Virtual have altered. In the *eXistenZ* computer game, Virtuality no longer is an archaic or futuristic setting. Instead, the Real gets sub-versed, implanted by animated game characters, almost indistinguishable from nominal participants. Hyper reality is sold here as the ultimate drug: social, interactive, intelligent. Reality as playground seems to be most addictive, compared to all secondary, escapist fantasies. We don't need no Disney-lands, our existential Reality™ is weird enough. Where are the de Beauvoirs, Sartres, and Camus of the Digital Age now that we need them?

They discuss why new money doesn't give to charity. There are nine new-moneyed men sitting in this room, trying to tell why they'd rather invest in start-ups than donate to modern art museums or UNICEF. Technology is modern art. Technology will save the world, they say. —*Wired* 7.07

Are the venture capitalists, young entrepreneurs, lonely coders of Silicon Valley, obsessed with their first $20 million (which are always the hardest), the only role model for the Network Society? The opening sentence of Kevin Kelly's book *New Rules for the New Economy* (1998) says it all: "No one can escape the transforming fire of machines." Technological determinism claims to have history on its side. "The mighty tumble, the once confident are left desperate for guidance, and the nimble are given a chance to prevail." According to *Wired* 7.07, one in thousand business plans will finally get enough money to be further developed. It's a "digital gold rush," like the heroic episode at the close of the 19th century. Sudden wealth for a few, based on luck more than anything else, is today's business plan lottery. This migration was based on the gold standard, which started to tumble a few decades later. But this historical analogy, or prediction, is not what "Generation Equity" is eager to hear. It is not encouraging to face the fact that all their tiny software applications, after the hype has faded away, profits have been taken and profits been made, will just be a cog in the machine of the Third Order.

Corporate America digested the "revolutionary" preachings of Kelly, Peters, and Gilder. It installed its intranets, web servers and e-commerce software and geared up for the next phase after e-commerce: e-business (if you can't sell your Internet scheme to customers perhaps some ignorant company will buy the idea). Concepts, models and technical features have been incorporated, while stripping off redundant libertarian selling labels. *Wired* is still brilliant at catching this ideology: "Markets should be fair by design, so they don't need regulation or monitoring, democratic (the more participants, the better), and rational. Usage fees should be reasonable and encourage participants to behave in ways that are good for everyone." But then the sad part.

Josh Levine, a programmer of online stock trading software, "remains unimpressed by the progress toward this ideal marketplace. "So far I haven't seen anyone do anything strikingly bold or brave," he says. "Most are just reacting to the changes that technology forces upon them. Myself included." (*Wired* 7.07, July 1999) A pragmatic confession of the Digital Situation from Brooklyn (that is, not Wall Street).

Facing the actual situation is not *Wired*'s strongest point. It had to cut all ties to "European" ways of thinking such as negation, critique, deconstruction, skepticism, etc. until they passed all exits. From that point on, only one discourse was left: the "how-to" management sales talk. The road ahead, leading straight into paradise. Or we might all be struck by the Apocalypse. . . . In the early days, it was enough to project some trends into the future, without any solid analysis of the present. But these days, with the digital revolution well under way, the future is becoming much harder to predict. There is a much more dynamic, complex image, with culture, economics and politics interfering in a simplistic, linear out-of-control creed which merely states that "iron and lumber will obey the laws of software."

In Kelly's *New Rules for the New Economies* basic reality checks fail. Writing the book in late 1997 and early 1998, he manages to keep out all references to the financial crises in Southeast Asia, Russia, and Brazil. In this childlike vision of the fiction-free world there is only a deterministic and violent "change," with some "creative destruction" of old institutions here and there. Reckless, early victories have not resulted into a more sophisticated knowledge of the workings of the global economy. No collapse of Barings Bank, no hedge funds crisis, no Japanese recession, no law of diminishing returns. Instead, fountains of wealth for those who get the message straight. A prosperity for all (despite all statistics proving otherwise). A globalized world economy no unexpected side effects. While preaching self regulating, self optimizing chaos, the digital salvation models themselves are pretty much straight lines heading northeast: up, up, up. The global, intangible, inter-linked networks lack any awareness of their dynamic systems.

It could be useful to write a heretic psychology of the virtual class. The lack of "techno realism" is turning the 1960s generation of computer visionaries into tragic, even schizophrenic figures. On stage and in their publications and on their web sites they have got to praise the non-existing economy at all costs. They are performing in front of an ever- growing hoi polloi of "baby suits," switching to auto-pilot, having lost their own direction, following the directions of the business gurus. Do not express even the slightest doubt—it might influence the portfolios of you and your friends. The obsessive belief system makes it hard to drop out. There are few renegades when it comes of the New Economy of Silicon Valley, and its spasmodic turnover of start-ups. Microsoft can be happy about the absence of cultural dissidents. It only has to deal with lawyers.

Sloganomics: "In individuals insanity is rare; on the Internet it is the rule." (almost Nietzsche); "One Planet, One Network, One Leader"; Job Opportunity: Mobile Phone Assistant; Virtual movement: Reclaim the Net; "In cyberspace no one knows you are an artist."; Nobody Comes Close (Firm slogan); *A tale of Two Internets* (book title); "Virtual companies are paper tigers. In appearance they are fascinating, but in reality they are not so powerful. From a long term point of view, it is not the New Economy but the users who are really powerful" (Genc Greva); "Kybernetik der Tat"; "We Want Your Ideas!"; Know Your Wired Enemy; "You mail too much."; Bouncing Modernity; A book: *Complex Society and its Enemies*; Passwords of Perception; "A Good Internet is a Dead Internet" (after Kierkegaard).


It is being said by system theorists that self-referentiality is a sign of emancipation. Discourse growth within the media context would then be the ability to transform an applied set of ideas taken from other disciplines into a higher set of complex concepts and references. Can we already speak of a tendency towards a General Media Theory? Or have we passed the media age, without proper theory?

Perhaps history could answer. Detailed, critical historical studies, going back to the birth time of "new" media, the period between the two world wars, modernism, the heyday of film, and then the period straight after WW II. We can't have enough media archaeology. And there is still too little known about the early history of the Internet. For many this remains a mythological, pre-historical period, dominated by this one image of the behemoth of the Pentagon (ARPA), mixed with some Kittlerian premises of military techno-determinism, including its cult of secrecy and paranoia. Since the 1991 Gulf War, the Paul Virilio meme has entered popular culture. Kittler4all: media are of military origin and nature. But with this theory myth, one will never understand where today's drive towards a synergy of text, sound and (moving) images into one streaming medium is coming from.

The dark world of the conspiracy thinkers, such as Thomas Pynchon and his followers, is primarily text-based. It can only interpret the mystical world of imagery (of film, TV, etc.) as a secondary distraction. It may therefore be important to develop a civic "post history of media" to balance the hermeneutic reading of media, which can only "lay out" the essence of phenomenon (software, interface, etc.) through its roots. Popular use of technology has the power (or ignorance?) to neglect the military logic and twist its given formats, still remaining conscious about the titanic forces residing within the technologies, which may return one day as an accident. A deep and widespread knowledge of this accidental nature can help to take the magic away from casting [*Sendung*], the authoritarian power which attempts to dominate the subject, either through seduction or repression. One day, origins and basic structures will no longer be dominant. Media can grow, and transform into something different, more playful, open, with modular architectures. Breaking the magic spell of meaning and casting will create democratic structures in which truly flat channels prevail.

This leaves us to the strategies of "futile resistance" in the age of hyper growth. Everything flourishes, and so does protest. Conservative libertarians like to portray NGOs, protesting against multinational corporations and their inter-governmental bodies such as WTO, GATT, IWF, World Bank, and EU as "enemies of the future" as hard-core libertarian Virginia Postrel states. The war over the very concept of "future" has broken out. While on the scale of the Internet as a whole, activists and communities are playing an ever decreasing role, due to the dominating discourse of e-commerce and e-business, however their significance on the symbolic media level is steadily rising. Counter-information from social movements, direct action groups and loose coalitions of ravers and Reclaim the Street activists are circulating with the speed of light around the globe. And online journalists are all the more willing to report on the micro-ruptures such actions are causing. Some random examples: the presence of the Zapatista movement (Mexico) on the net, the world-wide protests against the Western surveillance system Echelon, June 18, 1999 (protest day against global capitalism), the world-wide campaigns against Nike, McDonalds, Monsanto and Shell, the support for the independent radio B92 in Belgrade.

In today's popular belief systems, it is being said that media have replaced, or at least overruled, politics. On the opposite spectrum, we see the naive idea that politics can be renewed by the active use of (new) media. But if we just look a bit closer to the relation between specific policies of the nation states, or particular parties regarding the development of cyberspace over the last ten years, we can see a remarkable influence of the state on the media sector. It is obvious that politicians need to pay a lot of attention towards their mediated image. Who doesn't? There is no need to redefine politics for that reason. The culture jamming media activists and their concept of "image pollution" are just reacting to this tendency. With the spin doctor comes the net.activist.

But relations between the political hackers, corporations and the state differ from country to country. Specific techno-politics generate different media (or net) cultures. In some places, for example in Eastern Europe, there is very direct media control focusing on content and ownership, resulting in a flourishing independent media scene. In Nordic countries there is a more subtle, structural approach, whereby the state is influencing cultural parameters, using indirect financing to secure a limited number of "open" channels.

Deregulation of media access has not resulted in enhancing actual public access. Nor did it boost innovation. Most IT companies are not into research. They just install and implement, and make only minor adjustments to existing software. The so-called innovative and creative technology sector often is nothing more than a branch economy, repackaging products of a few global players. The corporate world in fact would never have invented the Internet. The time span to develop such a centennial project is simply too long. The growing drive to get an immediate return on investment might even slow down the digital revolution in the long term. Today's inventions of Internet start-ups are fake applications. There is no time for research in the agendas of hasty entrepreneurs. What is needed are new spaces for reflection and critique, free zones where researchers of all kinds can work without the pressure of sponsors and administrators, free from short-term commercial pressure. The same can be said of the "digital Bauhaus" concepts, which lack any negation of mainstream digital utopia and are hardly different from average photoshop plus HTML courses.

It is said that visual arts are playing a creative role in the R&D of the visual languages for human-machine interfaces, shortly before they leave the high tech laboratories. For decades now the paradigm of the interdisciplinary approach, mainly between engineers and electronic artists, has been promoted yet remains unfulfilled. The fusion of the engineer-artist into a techno-renaissance movement is the actual idealism of the media arts system. It dreams of bringing together all relevant disciplines, contributing to the fundamental research and development of new technologies. A second Manhattan Project with the aim of nothing less than shaping the final future of mankind, presuming that the quality of communication is determined by the functionality of the bio-adapter. Within the electronic arts paradigm, on display in places such as ZKM in Karlsruhe, ICC in Tokyo, V2 in Rotterdam and the Ars Electronica Center in Linz, the human-machine interface is presented as the key vehicle which will cause the next revolution. The exhibited utopian interfaces are holistic environments in which the body-machine synthesis has reached the highest state of perfection, disposed of all clumsy mechanic and graphic fittings. The electronic artist is seen as a Leonardo-type genius, envisaging ways to "capture" the spiritual world in a meta-physical attempt to overcome the rather sub-human model of the cyborg with all its heavy glasses, data suits, touch screens, implants, track balls, etc. The monumental demos shown in the electronic art galleries have a rather baroque look and miss the coolness of science fiction gadgets. Whereas technology is getting smaller in order to maintain its speed, electronic art installations seem to be in need a lot of space, filled with monitors, terminals, screens and tracking devices.

For the time being, even to get rid of keyboard and screen seems not such an easy task. R&D teams of IT giants remain reluctant to have any outside involvement. The only labs which operate explicitly outside of arts and culture, such as MIT's Media Lab and Xerox PARC, manage to gain some significance. Most of the high end in new media arts is being done outside of industry and remains invisible, except for some art shows. They sustainable funding to really push an idea into the market. The logical consequence would be to take off the "art" label altogether and sell it as theme park entertainment machinery—but that would question the sources of funding and there-fore its legitimization.

One thing is sure though: the price of hardware is going down. Within the develop-ment of technology electronic installation artists no longer have a special status (if they ever had one). Access to technology is less and less exclusive. Consequently artists can easily slip back into the role of decorators, with the "digital artisan" figure as the maximum achievable option. So where are the electronic art guilds? An online, trans-local trade union for digital art workers could be an option. There will be a steady rise of loose networks for temporary collaborations in which resources are shared, aimed at running web sites, streaming media servers, TV programs and online publications.

Institutional electronic installation arts, incapable of taking a real avant-garde stand, has maneuvered itself in an impossible position. It is neither participating in fundamental research, nor does it have content to speak of, compared to "regular" web sites, videos or audio pieces. At best they are prototypes of unlike futures, aesthetic explorations into possible media worlds in search for an alternative visual language. Research and commerce have been the exception. With the rise of commercialism, installation artists these days are no longer needed. Web design has democratized the landscape rapidly, creating a new class of electronic artists exhibiting their work in their own virtual spaces outside of institutional control. As a consequence human-machine interface design has been stagnating, despite all brilliant concepts.

## < Note >

1.   An earlier version was posted on nettime August 23, 1999. The first section was written for the Ars Electronica Festival catalogue Memesis (Springer-Verlag, 1996).

# Sweet Erosions of Email

**NORTH FALMOUTH,** Mass.—(BUSINESS WIRE)—June 8, 2000—(NAS-
DAQ:BTHS) Benthos, Inc. In an historic breakthrough in underwater communications made possible by the use of a Benthos ATM 885 Telesonar Acoustic
Modem, the US Navy has completed its latest series of tests in which the subma-
rine USS Dolphin, while cruising at a depth of 400 feet, was able to successfully
send several email messages via the Internet to facilities located ashore.

It is a popular saying that email is the ultimate killer application of the Internet.[1]
No matter how opinions may divide over the possible economic, social, or cultural
impact of new technologies, there seems to be a next to global consensus about the
blessings of electronic mail. Unlike the bandwidth consuming multi-media content on
the web, email, as a medium, has well positioned itself beyond any criticism. It is
being said that streaming media are for the happy few, with their T1, DSL, or cable
modems, whereas email is regarded as the big equalizer. With broadband technology
widening the "digital divide," low-tech email has the historical task to empower
those with less access to technology. Lately I have started feeling increasing uncomfortable about this almighty, unquestioned assumption which is not addressing what
is actually happening.

> In Greek mythology, Sisyphus, an evil king, was condemned to Hades to forever roll a
> big rock to the top of a mountain, and then the rock always rolled back down again.
> Similar version of Hell is suffered every day by people with forever full e-email boxes.
> —Nikolai Bezroukov[2]

Ever since its invention, there has been a well known list of complaints about email. Spam is certainly one of them. The use of email by telemarketers is still on the increase, despite the filter software which is constantly being upgraded and developed further. Like other biological and electronic viruses, spam is gaining intelligence and keeps breaking through the immune systems. Porn, ads for financial services and business proposal from Africa are well known genres. But that's still old school. What is new are good willed individuals and organizations, who, without any sense of right or wrong subscribe thousands of email addresses out of some database, without having consulted their niche market beforehand. These are the merits of direct marketing. In most cases it is not even possible to unsubscribe, and if one starts complaining, the conversation easily turns into a flame war. You are supposed to be happy to be informed. Friends and colleges are not sending anonymous spam, they are actually doing a great service for you. So why make trouble? You have been chosen as an ideal target audience for this or that service or opinion. There is little to do against the growing tide of electronic goodwill. The right not to be informed is a yet unknown phenomena, but one with a strong growth potential.

NEW YORK—(BUSINESS WIRE)—June 8, 2000—Despite nationwide firings that resulted from improper email use at the workplace, fifty eight percent of the 1,004 employees recently surveyed by Vault.com are "not worried" about their employers monitoring their email accounts.

Unwanted mail is part of the growing anxiety over information overload, an ancient disease associated with email ever since its introduction in the 1970s. The amount of email per day, in some circles still proudly mentioned as a status symbol, was once associated with the ability to master the new medium, but has turned into a nuisance for most IT workers. Folders are being created in order not be confronted with the bulk of email. Online web archives are on the increase, used by those with enough connectivity. We can expect a growth in the use of customized personal filters.

With the democratization of the Internet and its default dissemination into all social spheres, the diversity of usage of email is growing too. It is tempting at this point to start complaining about a loss of values. The invasion of the common folks is lowering the quality of the conversations, so they say. I don't take that line. What is interesting to observe is how new users are responding to email communication in a diverse way. All I can do here is present some of my subjective observations:

- The more users online, the more unpredictable it is how fast people are responding to incoming email. Three weeks is not unusual. Most of the email is not dealt with within the same working day. If you work on a global level, time differences have to be taken into account as well. All in all, a response in the next day seems very unlikely. So, instead of the popular mythology that we are communicating at the speed of light on a 24-7 basis, the average speed of computer mediated communication is slowing down, getting remarkable close to the times when overland postal systems were fast and reliable (assuming that this is not a myth either). If you really want to reach someone it is better to grab the phone. This is a clear sign of the dirty reality invading the terrain of the virtual, messing up the perfection of technology. Instead of having to be afraid of the loss of identity, locality and global standards, we can look forward to a much more carnivalesque Internet full of unpredictable ruptures and reversals of meaning.

- More and more emails remain unanswered. This is a fascinating phenomenon. Apparently email has lost its aura, if it had any in the first place. It is tempting but dangerous to interpret the fact that someone is not responding as a bad sign. People are busy, or lazy, and the Internet is just a tiny aspect of their lives (which cannot be said of the IT professionals and those reporting about tendencies in the net). The immaterial, fluid character of the e-messages only adds to the growing indifference towards the virtual in times of its almighty economic and imaginative presence. It has never been easier to ignore, and delete, incoming messages.

- As a response to the erosion of speed and efficiency of email people will do anything to grab attention on the other side of the screen. One can use CAPITALS, write "Important" or "Urgent" in the subject line and attach a red flag onto the mail, indicating its "high priority" status. Alternatively you can also send someone a fax saying that you have just send them an email, or you can leave a text message on someone's mobile phone. Results of these desperate attempts vary, though the tendency is clear: for the overworked, email has turned into a stress channel instead of a relief.

• Regional and local cultural aspects obviously have to be taken into account. National and private holidays are interrupting exchanges constantly. So does language. Limited knowledge and an uncertainty about the ability to write in English is one of the main reasons why international communication is hampered. In some cultures it seems to be less embarrassing not to answer than to end up with a badly written letter, which will most likely fuel global misunderstanding. The reason could be shyness or politeness, or is the act of non-communication an even more sophisticated one? Some cultures protect themselves from (post-colonial) co-option by active forms of disconnection. This act should not be read as technophobia or as a symptom of unfamiliarity with new media. Internet use will never be universal. Policies concerned with bridging the "digital divide" should aim at empowering regional and local use and development of technologies rather than importing global recipes.

• Breakdown of connectivity on a technical level is another fact most email users still have to get used to. Servers are going down all the time, everywhere, not just in the so-called developing world. Systems are attacked by viruses and hackers. Mailboxes easily get deleted, or simply disappear, especially of those using free web mail services such as hotmail.

With the next hundred million email users entering the Internet over the next year, one should not get angry or be disappointed about the expected disfunctionalities. The net is as good as its users which, in many places, in demographic terms is getting nearer to the average citizen. The rapid spreading of the technology is something people have dreamed of, and anticipated throughout the last decades. In no way will the Internet alter, lift, or cool down human nature so there is a lot we can still expect to happen, beyond good or evil, from jubilees, charities, parties and other types of celebrations to rape, murders, genocide, and other known or not yet known e-crimes.

The quality of the email communication ranges from deep friendships, fierce debates, significant periods of silence, sudden flame wars and touching miscommunications, resulting in all too human activities such as love affairs, marriage, e-business, and everything between rumors, gossip, casual talk, propaganda, discourse, and noise. At best, the net will be a mirror of the societies, countries, and cultures which use it— not the sweet and innocent, sleepy global village but a vibrant crawling and crashing bunch of complexities, as chaotic and unfinished as the world we live in.

## Related URLs

Junk email and spam: http://www.sni.net/ecofuture/jmemail.html

Email in organizations:
http://firstmonday.org/issues/issue3_9/williams/index.html

On the problem of archiving:
http://www.firstmonday.dk/issues/issue4_9/lukesh/

Desktop Critic: Attack of the Living Email:
http://macworld.zdnet.com/1999/05/opinion/desktopcritic.html

Old email never dies: http://www.wired.com/wired/archive/7.05/email.html

US Army advises on how to avoid information overload:
http://www-cgsc.army.mil/milrev/English/JulAug98/bateman.htm

## <Notes>

1. Originally written for *Billedkunst* magazine (Oslo) during Communication Front, Plovdiv, Bulgaria, June 2000 (www.cfront.org). Posted on nettime June 13, 2000.

2. See the Information/Workload Annotated Webliography, maintained by Nikolai Bezroukov (http://www.softpanorama.org/Social/overload.shtml).

# Travelogues

# Culture after the Final Breakdown:
# Tirana, Albania, May 1998

As expected, Tirana offers much more reality than one can cope with. The dust storms through Tirana's streets have the sweet-bitter smell of poverty.[1] My first encounter is overwhelming and confronting. Albania, Europe's poorest country, has been the most isolated communist regime in the region. Rhythm must have been slow in this former outpost of the Ottoman empire. Ismail Kadare, Albania's best-known writer, now in exile, is trying to find excuses for this historical inertia. For Kadare slowness does not equal backwardness. As he writes in *Printemps Albanais*, his report of the 1990 events, "slowness can reveal, as under an impenetrable armor, ripeness and the inner light" (Kadare 1991). This insight must be for the Deep Europe connoisseurs. Tirana in late spring of 1998 gives a rather different impression—a steamy, grimy intensely Balkanesque "summer in the city" feeling combined with the sense that the entire country is struggling to get back to or move on to normal. Is this Palermo or Skopje in the late 1940s? The country is visibly recovering from the total breakdown of March 1997, its *Pointe Omega*, the year zero. Kadare is right: Albania's "1989" is just over one year old and the world should take this delay into account.

Did Jean Baudrillard ever witness the violent aspects of a massive, sudden, social implosion? I wonder. Baudrillard, who so stylishly played with the model of the implosion, must have sensed something in this direction, but his style is too linear, one-dimensional to describe the multi-layered realities of the Balkans. What is the sublime object of poverty? French language games are fading out in the case of Albania because history in the making can easily do without such concepts (and intellectuals all together). It is not even about media. In Albania, the slow decay from within, even more disastrous than elsewhere in Eastern Europe, combined with a collective frustration over missing the historical wave of 1989, finally turned into an explosion of violent disinterest and gloom. It is tempting to speak of "post apocalyptic zones."[2] But that's again postmodern rhetoric. Which contemporary theorists have been studying the Albanian condition? Not Zizek, not Hardt and Negri. No multitudes resisting Empire to be found on Tirana's streets. There has hardly been trade with Albania or tourism along its Adriatic coast. The country is hardly ever mentioned by journalists, and the 1999 Kosovo drama did not change its image of no-go area.

Robert Kaplan's widely acknowledged *Balkan Ghosts* (1993) and *The End of the Earth* (1996), 1990s travel guides through the world's abandoned places, rust belts and war zones provides a useful starting point for a theory about abandoned regions. Yet Kaplan (1994, 1996) lacks a theoretical framework that could match the conservative agenda of culturalists like Samuel P. Huntington.[3] In what shape are the territories outside Fortress Europe? Can we only speak them in terms of "exclusion"? Do we unavoidably end up with an "exotic" view on the picturesque Balkan, served up for tomorrow's travelers once they know how to read this wretched place? And then, what's wrong with tourism? If done in a sustainable way, it could bring prosperity to this godforsaken place, where one seems to be ready to migrate overnight.

What puzzled me most about Albania is its delayed, primal drive to (self-) destruction. Roads are in the worst possible condition, at times non-existing. Places lack electricity and running water, not to mention destroyed schools, dilapidated out of anger. What is this hatred towards anything infrastructural? There is still no comprehensive analysis of the "events" of March 1997 when the country got into a stage of chaos, a confused form of civil war. The rule of law was absent for almost a week. The dry overview by Miranda Vickers and James Pettifer, *Albania* (1997), stops in late 1996 and carries a now ironical, perhaps then optimistic subtitle: *From Anarchy to a Balkan Identity*. We should now read it backwards. That's dialectics these days. The old one step forward, two steps back—with no synthesis in sight. What we can see is tragic, ultra-modern history in the making, monitored by brand new Euro-cops of the West European Union, half-hearted Italian neo-colonialism to prevent mass escape from the ruined country mixed with plenty of wild electronic media, pirated software and even a tiny bit of Internet, provided by the UN and Soros via satellites and radio links.

In the office of the Soros Internet Program, Ilir Zenku shows me the big satellite disk on the roof, the lifeline to the world for many of the NGOs. He tells me of the plundering of a warehouse during the lawless days in March 1997 where the Internet Program had stored dozens of PCs and monitors which had just arrived from overseas. A few days later some of the computers could be bought back on the streets for a few US dollars. A good year later a small Internet access room is set up. Still, bandwidth is low. Dialing in from inside Tirana is a painfully slow process, let alone from outside of town. But there is progress, Ilir assured me. There is the 64-Kbps satellite connection, dial-up phone lines, and some ham radio modems and special spectrum radio modems. The collaboration with the computer science department of Tirana University sounds promising. Jonathan Peizer, director of the Soros Internet Program explains: "we managed to create an Internet link through affiliations with the United Nations which allowed us to avoid commercial restrictions. We then created a public access center and linked the program to our education and other initiatives. This provided access to NGOs, media, and students. Internet growth in Albania will be limited until the situation changes, but the important thing is that it exists now, and Albania is linked to the rest of the world instead of totally isolated from it. Aside from domestic usage, we are using the Internet links in Albania to assist an unrelated project focusing on Kosovar refugees—had Internet not existed in Albania however, we could not have addressed this issue effectively."[4]

Seen from the dirty, crowded streets of Tirana, filled with its notorious stolen Mercedes cars from all over Europe, Kosovo seems a distant place, despite all the refugees flooding into Northern Albania. The Nole government is concerned with the worsening situation in Kosovo, as are all Albanians. The Albanians lack military options: their army is a joke compared to the well-armed and experienced Yugoslav army with its paramilitary units. Albania can only call for foreign involvement, not just in Kosovo, but also for itself. It is time of reconstruction and "development." There is a crying need for capital, infrastructure and human resources from NATO, EU, Soros and other NGOs from Rome, Athens, Istanbul and Saudi Arabia. It actually does not matter where the aid comes from. At least, that's the impression. Cars are carrying German and Americans flags, but they may as well be Islamic symbols, though they would not speak to the imagination, as much with the promise of prosperity.

On a day to day level life goes on in this café society. Thousands of Albanians lounge around terraces of hastily and illegally erected cafés. So here we are—the first ever new media arts event held in Albania (May 1998) called Pyramedia, organized by the Syndicate network, a mailing list of small institutions and individuals from both ex Western and Eastern Europe.[5] A small group of 10–20 dedicated Albanian artists, teachers and students have shown up to attend the three days of screenings and presentations. Edi Muka, who is teaching contemporary arts (video, installations, etc.) at the Tirana Arts Academy is the driving force behind many of these events. I interviewed him twice, once at the V2-DEAF festival in September 1996 in Rotterdam where we first met and after the (violent) fall of the Berisha government, in July 1997 during the Deep Europe project in Hybrid Workspace at Documenta X.[6]

This time, we spoke on the terrace of Donika Bardha's Gallery XXI, Tirana's first commercial modern art gallery which opened in March 1998, a green (and clean) oasis close to the central Skanderbeg square and surrounded by a decent café and restaurant. This quasi-privatized corner of the pavement has palm trees and a fountain. Edi Muka is cool; his dress, sunglasses, the way he's got things under control. Edi Muka is well informed, not only about arts and culture, but about politics and media as well. After he returned from Italy, where he fled in the early 1990s, he worked with foreign journalists and in the field of "independent media" and their Western support organizations.

According to Muka, Tirana will sooner or later feel the impact of the influx of Kosovo refugees in the North. But for the time being it is still recovering from the "anarchy" of March 1997, the few days when the state lost its monopoly on violence.

Shortly after these events, a commission of all the political parties represented in Parliament was formed to reconstruct and study the events. But within a few months controversy between the members broke out and the final report is still pending. So the cause of all the destruction remains vague. Can it be reduced to a plot or conspiracy? At a certain point Berisha decided to let everything go when he found out that he could not use the army to attack the city of Vlora.

Edi Muka: "Berisha defends himself now by saying that he had to arm the members of his party in order to defend them. Maybe I am wrong. No one knows how reliable the data of this commission is. But the fact is that most of the town halls were set on fire. There was a lot of corruption under the Berisha government, illegal deals regarding privatization and real estate. A lot of them were done in favor of Berisha's Democratic Party members. So this was a good chance to wipe out the evidence. In Vlora people initially burned the police office and the secret police headquarters. The burning of town halls came later." Culture lost too. Museums were looted, even worse than in 1992. Churches too. Most of all, the looting stalled the process of gradual progress. For example, after March 1997 students did not go to school anymore. It was impossible to get them back to the classroom. Muka: "if you see such a destruction happening around you, after seven years of supposed 'democracy,' the already strong desire of Albanians to leave the country grew ten times."

Since December 1997, things have apparently changed for the better. Edi's students returned to their classes and a number of cultural events took place. In October 1997, eleven artists participated in Reorientation, an exhibit in a ruined factory outside of town, curated by Muka. The show was mainly installations, referring to the state of ruin and was considered a turning point. Gezim Qendro, now the director of the National Gallery participated, along with Edi Hila, one of Albania's modern post-1990 painters as well as younger artists.

Edi Muka: "Despite the fact that it took place in a part of town which is full of guns, a lot of people showed up. They were eager to see something different." Another landmark was Albania's participation in Ostranenie, the ex-East media arts festival which took place for the third time in Dessau in November of 1997. Albanian video artworks were screened there for the first time. Also, the annual visual arts competition took place in Tirana. Muka: "in the past, everybody just hung some artworks on the wall of the National Gallery, no curatorial work, no critics, just a big chaos. This time there was some selection. But there was still a lack of the ability to experience things. There were only a few who reflected on what had happened in 1997. I don't think this is normal.

There is the tendency to escape, the young generation leaves the country and the old ones continue to do business in their way. I concentrated my work on a group of young artists, students who do reflect on the situation. In February 1998, a first show with them followed in the renovated gallery of the Academy of Art. It was really good and a large audience showed up. I gave some lectures about ready-mades and abstraction, which is still not very known here. Students have difficulties understanding what happened historically and epistemologically." And then Galeria XXI opened, which is trying to promote the art market in Albania because there is no such thing. The early revival is evident in other fields as well. The Days of New Music program a few months ago tried to open up traditional Albanian folk music and elaborate it in a "modern" way. A proposal to build and staff a new National Theater was approved. But there is still no decision on the future of the International Cultural Center, the enormous white pyramid once the Enver Hoxha Memorial Museum. In its most recent reincarnation, it was used for the Italian "Levante" trade fair, displaying trash consumer goods.

All this is now in the hands of Edi Rama, the new Minister of Culture. Rama, 34, is an experimental artist who played an important role in the student movement of 1990 and worked and exhibited abroad. His story is telling: 1996, he was beaten up by Berisha supporters and he then moved to Paris where he lived in exile. This spring, when he returned to Tirana for his father's funeral, he was invited to replace Arta Dade, then Minister of Culture, who lacked any vision on revitalizing a culture in ruins with little or no budget. Rama immediately agreed. His first action was a radical reorganization of the ministry, the first one ever in fifty years. Edi Muka has known Rama for years. "He is a charismatic person with a lot of ideas, even though he might not have much experience with administration. He has already left some marks."[7]

I managed to get an appointment with Rama on the fourth floor of the former Central Committee building. Edi Rama: "I inherited an institution still based in the old structures. It is also important to change the physical aspect of the building. It was not functional and there was a lot of dust that needed to be cleaned." Rama would not say how much money he can freely spend. Rama: "the budget is low, but even that is misused. So the first step is to create projects that will make a decent use of the budget possible. Only after that, we can increase pressure on the Ministry of Finance and start to approach NGOs."

I asked him about his priorities, in film, visual arts and media. Edi Rama: "Until now, the ministry worked as a sponsor of cultural ghettoization. It supported our self-complimentary attitude towards history and the related institutions that we inherited from the past. The Writers Union, in fact all cultural institutions—these old structures are not anymore a threat towards democracy, but they are a obstacle."

Do you see a growing divide between the lowbrow media culture and the elite high culture? Rama: "If I can make a comparison. During the Communist period we were living in a Jurassic Park. Now the dinosaurs have disappeared, but we are still in a park where anything can happen. You never know from where the danger is coming from. In that respect, things are very disordered. The new media situation is like a jungle. But I am convinced that the only support we can give to these newcomers is freedom. With the possibility to express yourself in a free space will also come a need to learn and how to deal with this space. Nowadays, here, people are convinced that freedom is much more difficult than isolation. To administrate freedom means to administrate yourself. During the time that you had to pass on the shelf of totalitarianism, you were administrated by someone else. You were not an individual. There was no responsibility and no anxiety. In freedom, all these elements become part of you."

When asked about all those leaving the country, Edi Rama is sending out a permanent invitation to all Albanians to do something for this country. "But it is pretty hard to make invitations because you cannot offer any guarantees. The problem with this community has been that it always worked against its own future. The most paralyzed were the young generations. They were marginalized by the gods of politics and culture. The big challenge now is to listen more careful to their needs in order to make them feel at home in their own country. To a certain age every Albanian is a refugee in his own country. It is felt as a transit station."

Since Rama is not member of a political party, I wondered whether it is more or less difficult than expected? Edi Rama: "I do not need to operate in a political field because my power is not of a political power but a cultural power." Until now, local Soros Foundation officials have not felt the urgency to open a Soros Center for Contemporary Art. This might change soon. Like in other countries, the leading "civil society" intellectuals, mainly writers, were not so sensitive to contemporary art forms let alone "electronic art." But there is another, underlying reason for the low priority status of new culture. Understandably, human rights violations, food aid and the basic restoration of law and order take highest priority with Western governments and NGOs. But with this comes a very specific, subconscious, definition of "democratic culture," a formalistic, instrumental and legalistic approach which defines democracy according to its institutional structures, not to its actual lively elements. We can see a similar problem in the field of "independent media." What counts is the primacy of frameworks, not initiatives or individual modes of mediated expression.

Edi Muka says of this: "We can see a standardized way of thinking within these NGOs. They are working according to pre-established models, without paying too much attention to the local requests. It is definitely important what they are doing, to promote NGOs that develop democracy. But what is desperately needed in Albania is a "cultural revolution." A large program to reach all generations, not only the young. Let's take one example. The main support for translations comes of course from the Soros foundation. They are now mainly doing philosophical books from the 1950s and 1960s (Nietzsche, Sartre, Camus, . . . ) and literature."

Contemporary books on visual arts, media and cultural politics are a first requirement in order to spread a comprehensive understanding of the new (media) technologies, their internal logic, history and potential. And this counts for many fields in culture. Otherwise, the existing divide between Western commercial media trash and post-communistic and nationalistic state-sponsored folklorism will establish itself, leaving little or no room for contemporary forms of expression.

According to Edi Muka, staying in cafés all day long is nonsense—artists' spaces should be created, giving people the possibility to prove themselves. Step by step this will bring attention to back to Albania and will take away the desire to leave the country. International exchange also plays an important role in this. Soon, Soros won't be the only source of money. Pro Helvetia (Swiss) is coming, a French Institute will be established and perhaps also a German Goethe Institute. Regional exchange should also increase to avoid ethnic tensions like those experienced with neighboring Macedonia. Muka: "The tendency should be to find common points, as citizens of the world, not as ethnic Albanians."

What is striking is the absence of discourse. There is no Albanian art magazine. Before 1990, art critics were politicized. Then, in the early 1990s, they could not speak up because they were compromised. Within the discipline of art history, political aims had taken precedence over professional standards. The National Gallery has taken the initiative to start an art magazine and the first issue is due to come out soon. A rare exception is *Perpjekja* [*Endeavor*], a quarterly cultural journal, edited by Fatos Lubonja. An English anthology appeared in 1997, edited by Fatos Lubonja and John Hodgson.[8] It takes a critical approach to developments in Albania and runs translations that deal with issues common to other former Eastern European countries. A structure needs to be created to train art historians, critics and curators. Muka: "what I am doing now is teaching students to write down their ideas, to arrange a creative space. But that is not enough. Now it is time to build the educational programs."

## <Notes>

1. Posted on nettime June 10, 1998. For a print version, see *Junction Skopje*, ed. Inke Arns (SCCA Skopje, 1998), pp. 40—44.

2. According to a recent apocalyptic report (Paul Brown, *The Guardian*, May 7, 2001; http://www.gu.com/Print/0,3858,4181986,00.html): "There are more Mercedes on the streets of Tirana than any other capital city in Europe but 90% of them are stolen. This illustrates the anarchy that has reigned in Albania since its peculiar brand of Chinese communism lost its iron grip 10 years ago. Freedom simply got out of hand, the mayor, Edi Rama, says. 'Even Mrs. Thatcher would have been astonished at our success in embracing capitalism. There is no society. Private property is the only thing that matters. Everything else is not our concern.' The stolen Mercedes arrive daily on a special car ferry from Italy run by the mafia. Since Albania has no method of disposing of old cars, its roads are littered with wrecks."

3. Even after the publication of Kaplan's book *The Coming Anarchy* (Vintage, 2001), there is no theoretical vocabulary to be found in his work.

4. "Ins and Outs of the Soros Internet Program in Former Eastern Europe, An E-Mail Exchange with Jonathan Peizer By Geert Lovink," nettime, January 4, 1999. For m on the OSI Albania Internet program, see http://www.soros.org/inetpages/country_projects.html.

5. For a short report of the Pyramedia meeting, see Andreas Broeckmann, syndicate, June 2, 1998. URL: http://www.v2.nl/mail/v2east/.

6. Geert Lovink, interviews with Edi Muka, nettime, September 29, 1996, August 2, 1997, September 25, 1998, June 7, 1999, and August 6, 2000.

7.   In the meantime Edi Rama stepped down as minister of culture to run for the post of Tirana's major—which he won in October 2000. On November 9, 2000, there was a failed attempt to assassinate Rama (see Edi Muka, syndicate, November 10, 2000).

8.   For more information on Perpjekja/Endeavor, see http://www.v2.nl/mail/v2east/1998/second/0042.html. "The cultural review Perpjekja/Endeavour was founded in the autumn of 1994 by a group of intellectuals who felt the need to introduce a critical split into Albanian culture. This culture has been dominated by what Perpjekja has often called the ideology of national-communism. Under the influence of this ideology, the Albanians have been more inclined to escape from reality into an imagined glorious past, or into a future happy state, than to look at  themselves and reality in the eye." Email: perpjekja@openmedia.org.al

# The 9/21 Aftershocks: Taiwan, December 1999

Wall Street IT stocks spasmed on the morning of September 21, 1999 after the news broke of an earthquake hitting central Taiwan.[1] International rescue teams rushed to the site. The 25 million Taiwanese were in shock. Over 2,000 people had died under the rubble. It turned out that the chip production in the "science parks" had remained largely undamaged. Hard disk factories had anyway been relocated before, to the other side of the Strait, in China.[2] After a dip in production, hardware manufacturing continued to soar again, wiping away the last signs of the 1997 Asian financial crisis which had also hit Taiwan. Presidential elections were due to happen in a few months. When I arrived at Chiang Kai-Shek airport in late November 1999, coinciding with the protests against the WTO meeting in Seattle, two and a half months after 9/21, the quake zone was no longer on the front pages.

Two years earlier, in December 1997, I had met Ilya Eric Lee, a lively and gifted student in the humanities, nettime contributor and one of Taiwan's Internet activists. Tokyo scholar/raver Toshiya Ueno had a weekend trip arranged for me to visit Taipei and meet the Inter-Asian cultural studies activist Kuan-Hsing Chen.[3] In a back room of a cafe, during a small meeting, it was Ilya who showed most interest in critical issues of new media. Most of the participants were into gay and lesbian gender bending using BBS multi-user environments. At that time Ilya was involved in a rural area "digital divide" project, training NGOs in remote mountain areas and coastal villages in setting up web sites.

Ilya and I maintained contact ever since and I managed to organize for him to attend the tactical media conference Next Five Minutes in March 1999. There Ilya heard of the Belgrade radio B92. Immediately after returning to Taiwan, in the first weeks of the NATO bombings, he opened the Chinese version of the Help B92 campaign. What at first seemed an exotic, let's say futuristic gesture, turned out to be one of the few independent, non-commercial, non-governmental web sources in Chinese, when the bombing of the Chinese Embassy in Belgrade fueled another propaganda war, between Beijing and the West. Though critical of the NATO bombing, B92 had collaborated with Albanian independent news organizations until the very end, when channels on both sides were shut down. The fatal, (auto)destructive policies of the Milosevic regime was the cause of all this mystery. The mysterious bombing of the Chinese Embassy was distracting the audience, both in China and in the West, from the war crimes committed by the Milosevic forces. The anti-Americanism, demonstrated by the Beijing students in front of the American Embassy did not address any of the actual causes of the Kosovo conflict. B92 and other independent media in Serbia did so, and were in great need of international support, voiced through the Internet which Ilya and other media activists also for example in Japan did organize.

Arriving in Taipei airport in late 1999, I was met this time by Ilya and the art critic and curator Manray Hsu. Manray is a fellow pragmatist and collaborator of Cities on the Move, an exhibition series dealing with the Asian metropolitan condition. Together with a few others, Ilya and Manray had hastily set up the "Aftershock" group and were about to establish the www.restoration.org.tw server, meant to coordinate the communication between the numerous NGOs in the widespread zone of destruction. The aim of Restoration is to build both a social-cultural and technical network. 250 copies of a Xerox reader with translations of texts on tactical media, starting from the B92 case, had been produced. My coming to Taiwan, planned before the catastrophe struck the island, spontaneously turned into a promotion tour for the "Restoration" server. I found myself in the middle of a dense 8 day tour throughout the island, with seven public lectures, each time with different topics and audiences, and meetings with activists on the structure of Restoration.[4]

First stop after driving south of Taipei was Shihgang, a village in an agricultural area which suffered substantial damage. Abandoned, crashed high-rises along the road were first sign of what had happened. A two story school had survived and was now used as office and meeting place, and storage for shrines and personal belongings. For the first time some 15 NGOs from the quake region came together here and presented their work and structure. The meeting was hosted by the New Homeland Foundation. Some of the groups dealt with social issues such as the sudden rise of unemployment and the need for community work, while others worked on long term environmental problems, for example a broken dam. An oral history group had started recording personal witnesses in order to create a collective memory, in the form of a web site, a video library, or a monument. Although the Taiwanese army had by now withdrawn, civic support was still there, from, for example, Kobe, Japan, which was seriously hit by an earthquake in 1995.[5]

Where is the money, people started wondering. Who is accountable for decisions now being made over the architecture of schools and other public buildings? Will small farmers survive, what could be their take on modernization, or even selling through the Internet, as has already happened in some cases? It seemed that these NGOs, with some having web pages, all using email, were now in the process of building up their own social and technical network, a loose decentralized civic net which would allow a variety of opinions, proposals and forms of expression, unlike the model of a hierarchical national organization. Perhaps Ilya's presentation of the Restoration project here in Shihkang was going to make a difference. New social movements in Taiwan, originating in the late 1980s, were now at a crossroads. Will the earthquake with the help of computer networks, generate new forms or fall back into familiar top-down forms of organization?

Next stop Puli, the town in the mountainous center of Taiwan most seriously hit, with 50 percent of housing now having to be taken down, a figure which could grow to 80 percent. At the offices of the New Homeland Foundation, where Ilya had been busy in previous weeks installing a Linux network, we discussed possible telecommunication (and media) infrastructures. Some web space on the popular Taiwanese

Yahoo! server seemed a nice offer, but the problems here, concerning education, urban planning, work, care for the elderly, were so big that seemed more appropriate to think a whole different scale. A fiber-optic network for Puli, together with community media, did not seem to contradict the primary need for housing. The tent villages in the parks were now about to be closed, and with it was coming a growing fear of isolation in remote metal barracks, away from the neighborhood. You cannot live in a cable, but then, what could be a debate about the future of Puli without a digital public domain?

Full Shot Studio is one of late 1980s video activist collectives, producing documentary films about social topics, memory and pain, ecology and Taiwan's culture of aboriginals and other minorities.[6] Full Shot specializes in regional video training programs. Their work was presented at the 1999 Yamagata Festival of Documentary Film in Japan. One week before our arrival, the entire Full Shot crew had moved to a temporary house/studio in Taichung, the biggest city near the quake zone. From there, eleven video workers, in four teams, had started to document the process of reconstruction—for a least one or perhaps two years. Looking at their promo, Full Shot has a straight forward, old school approach. This became even more apparent after the presentation of an ambitious project of four women designers and a photographer, called "So Studio" who are bringing out a well designed, four color magazine, produced for a mountain village.[7] Their particular interest was in recording people's stories, printing their pictures, and recording landslide sites, to find out what the possible impact of the coming rainy season on the "shaven" mountain sites will be. A discussion broke out over the question of representation and the need of locals for such a glossy magazine. The So Studio group emphasized that solidarity does not imply that NGOs should present themselves to the local population as "mister total solution." Full Shot insisted on speaking for the people, whereas So Studio were more interested in developing their own aesthetics, with the aim to hand over production to the villagers as soon as possible.

Next day we left the quake zone and drove further south into the mountains to Meinung, a town of 50,000 inhabitants, mainly members of the Hakka minority. It is an area of tobacco plantations, mango, banana and bin-lang, the stimulus chewing gum sold along the highways by "spice girls." In 1993 a campaign started here to rescue the Yellow Butterfly Valley, just outside of the town. The government was intending to build a dam, which would have destroyed one of the last pockets of nature, now symbolically preserved in a park, run by environmental groups. The dam is meant to provide water to chemical plants and steel works on the industrialized west coast. Throughout the years the Meinung People's Association has proved to be a successful social movement, with substantial support within the local population. The topic of the meeting that Thursday night was Internet activism. The campaign has a web site and is associated with various groups and networks, worldwide, which fight against dams as well. How can new media be used, starting from this advanced level, with such a motivated and experienced group of activists? The crucial, perhaps final media campaign starts any time soon.[8]

The second part of the Restoration tour took place in Taipei and started with a press conference a meeting with representatives of twenty "new" social movements, of which most made active use of email, mailing lists and web sites. Taiwan, known for its computer hardware manufacture, is hardly visible on the Internet map mainly because of a language problem on the Western side (namely, not understanding Mandarin). Needless to say, that Internet is growing at high speed rate, with e-commerce, in its American form as the dominant rhetoric. Dotcom business hype dominates the overall impression Taiwanese get of what Internet is all about. Many at this meeting felt that in this climate, with a relative weak net culture, media companies with old one-to-many models can easily dominate the new medium. Some examples: a list called South, an electronic newsletter focusing on culture and minorities issues is run by two editors and has a readership of 35,000. Run with the support of a company, South has little or no back channels. One business newsletter even has over 300,000 email subscribers. Like in Japan, the more intimate communication happens through (telnet) bulletin board systems. Web sites and even mailing lists are considered too public. Feeling the need to change identity, being able to communicate anonymously, Taiwanese net culture seems to be better able to express itself.

At the end of the meeting I screened a video, full of hard-core European realities (war, drugs, pop), *Victims of Geography*, which caused a healthy dose of cultural confusion.[9] What is this Balkan nihilism, fighting for independent media without any social or political agenda? Digital existentialism, made in Yugoland, seems hard to crack. Attention shifts from contemporary media activism to convergence, mergers of telcos and the media industry, IPOs and the e-goldrush—global trends also happening in Taiwan. The island seems to have become more international, even compared to a few years ago. Speakers, curators and artists are coming over for a visit, and to work. Electronic art is shown, sponsored by the Taiwanese PC manufacturer Acer. On the weekend we attended a lecture by the French theorist of new social movements Alain Touraine, and a lecture in front of a huge audience by the somewhat sad, melancholic, yet extremely successful Peter Eisenman, who is building a museum in Hsinchu.

While giving a lecture, Ilya, Manray, and I discovered an unused new media arts lab at the National Arts Institute on a hill overlooking Taipei. The lab, packed with high-tech including video and audio studios, without any students, hidden away amidst traditional and classical modern arts, indicates the problems and hopefully potentials of new media here. In the view of the Institute's leaders, technology is treated as equipment, tools to serve other disciplines such as graphic design, theatre and performance, music and film. In an over-politicized climate where the arts have been instrumentalized for ideological causes, the computer user is seen as an engineer, assisting and programming other people's concepts. The artist him or herself is trained in a traditional manner, using old media, from calligraphy to sculpture. In some cases the artist can call in the help of the new forms of expression, for example to document or amplify the work. In this traditionalist view, the computer does not have to develop its own language. It is enough to learn the software manual. This instrumental approach of new media culture ignores the issue of aesthetics because neither the computer operator nor the artist seriously engage with the possibilities and limits of the machines. Technology is used in the way manufacturers have configured them, which in this case for example results in disastrous 3D computer graphics and "fractal art."

It could be useful to make a comparison in this context between Taiwan and China. In Taiwan computers are predominantly supposed to be good for making money. They ship chunks of data from here to there and everywhere, but do not automatically produce distributed, democratic structures, nor interesting art. The next years will see a further, spectacular rise of Internet use and Taiwan will play a very interesting role in this, obviously because of the overwhelming, yet not always explicit presence of China. The staged state propaganda war between Taipei and Beijing will be fought via the Internet, that much is sure. There will be infowars, in one way or another. What China obviously can't produce, is an open, lively and diverse net culture. The paranoia is simply too high. A (not so) subtle system of self-censorship is in place: surf and shut up. The fear of being jailed one day, under different, yet unknown circumstances is always there. So why bother to express your opinion on a public forum, using your own name? An anonymous chat might do. Web surveillance and repressive laws are on the rise. Cybercafés, important places as few people have PCs at home, are monitored and closed down. This results in an apparently chaotic, and wild Internet development, which can be cracked down at any given time. American models of e-commerce and infotainment are the ones who will profit from this silenced net culture, with "happy" consumerism as the only option left.

It is an illusion to think that Chinese citizens can route around the "market Leninism" of Communist Party officials. Liberty comes with a price, and the few taking risks may have to pay for it. Having only controlled portal sites, "mainlanders" are condemned to "watch" the Internet, and not use it, let alone further develop—and defend—open standards and software. The production of new media art in China still happens in a condition of joyful cocooning. There are serious limits to these private, informal uses of technology. The presence of machines by itself is not generating a culture. Contemporary arts in China therefor remains slightly innocent and immature, despite its own distinct and vibrant cosmopolitan style. What has to be necessarily neglected under these circumstances is the collaborative nature of technology, in which multi-disciplinary approaches are not just a good idea but an absolute necessity. A technological culture is as complex as all other forms of creative or industrial work. It therefore needs media labs, schools, festivals, exhibitions, public debates on its substance and direction, funding bodies and above all a critical discourse which tries to make sense of why we all need these media.

Unlike China, Taiwan is about to develop a public new media sector, also on the Internet, and 9/21, the quake, has certainly been a catalyst. But networks are not build overnight. They grow, sometimes fast, at times in unpredictable directions. And their immediate impact remains invisible, as this is their very nature. So do not wonder if networks in Taiwan are forgotten about for a while.[10]

## <Notes>

1.  Posted on nettime December 19, 1999.

2.  A report about the impact of the 9/21 quake on the global IT industry by Michael DePrenda can be found at http://www4.tomshardware.com/column/99q4/991009/.

3.  Politics and Cultural Studies in Interasia Interview with Kuan-Hsing Chen by Geert Lovink, Taipei, December 20, 1997, posted on nettime March 1, 1998. Kuan-Hsing Chen is the initiator and co-editor of *Inter-Asia Cultural Studies Journal*, published by Routledge.

4.  For information on the tour in Mandarin, see http://www.etat.com/aftershock/DM1201.htm.

5.   The name of the Kobe group is Response. See
www.1.meshnet.or.jp/~response/index.htm.

6.   Fullshot Studio: http://www.fullshot.org.tw/.

7.   So Studio: http://voice.abbeyroad.com.tw.

8.   Meinung People's Association's URL: http://mpa.ngo.org.tw/. After
many years of struggle the association achieved from the DPP government
the promise not to build the dam. They have turned their attention to
education and actively participate in the discussion over the WTO and
Taiwan's future.

9.   *Victims of Geography*, video documentary by Pictural Heroes,
Glasgow, 1999.

10.   On July 24, 2001, I posted an update of independent Internet culture in Taiwan and the people featured in this travelogue to nettime.
In this email exchange with Ilya Eric Lee we talked about his experience in the Taiwanese army, the "infowar" between Chinese and
Taiwanese hackers, media art initiatives and the activist server
www.elixus.org.

# At the Opening of New Media Center
# Sarai: Delhi, February 2001

During the last weekend of February, Sarai, arguably the first new media center in South Asia of its kind, opened its premises with a three days conference on the Public Domain.[1] Sarai, a word which means in various South Asian and Middle Eastern languages an enclosed space, tavern or public house in a city, or, beside a highway, where travelers and caravans can find shelter, is located in the basement of a newly erected building in Delhi (India). The Sarai initiative describes itself as an alternative, non-commercial space for an imaginative reconstitution of urban public culture, new and old media practice and research and critical cultural intervention.[2]

Sarai receives key additional support from the Dutch Ministry of Foreign Affairs (Research Division of the Development Aid Section), the Daniel Langlois Foundation for Art, Science and Technology and the Dutch aid organization HIVOS. The inception of Sarai coincides with a three year long exchange and collaboration program with the Society for Old and New Media (www.waag.org), Amsterdam. The Dutch Foreign Affairs Ministry also supported this partnership. It also received a grant from the Rockefeller Foundation for specific projects. Sarai is in the process of developing local links with initiatives in Delhi and India and international links with partners in South Asia and elsewhere. Significant among these is an effort towards the setting up of an informal South Asian New Media Network to collaborate with like-minded initiatives in the region as well as an emerging relationship of partnership and cooperation with the Australian Network for Art and Technology (ANAT).

Sarai is a unique blend of people and disciplines. The main background of the initiators of Sarai is in documentary filmmaking, media theory and research. Historians, programmers, urbanists and political theorists have subsequently joined them. One of the founders, Jeebesh Bagchi, describes Sarai as a "unique combination of people practices, machines and free-floating fragments of socially available code ready for creative re-purposing. Here the documentary filmmaker can engage with the urbanist, the video artist jam with the street photographer, the film theorist enter into conversations with the graphic designer and the historian play conceptual games with the hacker."

Sarai is a program of the Center for the Study of Developing Societies (CSDS), an independent research center founded in 1964. CSDS is funded by the Indian state and a range of international donors. The center has welcomed dissenting voices in South Asia and it is well known for its skepticism towards received models of development. Sarai is a pilot project for the Dutch Ministry of Foreign Affairs. So far most of that money was spent on building water pumps in rural areas. For decades Dutch policy had been to only support the poorest of the poor. However, recently more and more NGOs in the field started using Internet. There is a growing awareness of the importance of IT use within development projects—and society as whole. New media are becoming an important part of the rapid growing and diverting process of urbanization.

With a public access space full of terminals and a cafe, Sarai neither has the feel of an isolated research facility, nor does it have the claustrophobic agenda of many new media arts institutions. Let alone does it equal an IT company, even though the place is flocked with young computer hackers. Monica Narula (another founder of Sarai, member of the Raqs Media Collective) is a filmmaker, photographer, and in charge of design at Sarai. She is responsible for the look of both the web site and the internal network interface. She says: "Delhi is a polarized space. Young people and students have nowhere to go. Either places are too expensive for them or nothing happens. So, the idea here is that people can come to Sarai, use the internal network interface via one of the terminals in the public space, and also have coffee and interact. In principle and execution the internal Sarai interface is much more sophisticated compared to the web site. This is because in India download time means money; people often can't be bothered to have plug-ins installed. After a fierce internal debate we decided to develop the heavier, creative interface for the public terminals and keep the web site really light."

The atmosphere during the opening was one of an exceptionally high intellectual level, the air filled with lively debates. The Sarai community, now employing 13 staff members, is open for everything, ready to question anything. Jeebesh, himself a filmmaker and another member of Raqs Media Collective says: "I was not happy with the way in which classic research feeds back into society. I don't like being specialized. The idea is to proliferate and multiply, creating a new hybrid model in order to discover something and not get stuck with the form in which we are producing it."

Sarai has a number of research areas: ethnographies of the new media, the city and social justice, film and consciousness, mapping the city, free software and "language and new media" to do with the role of Hindi. The Internet provides an occasion for a new form of Hindi language expression, different from the culture of the Hindi literary establishment. The "CyberMohalla" free software project is under construction. It will focus on tactical, low cost hard and software solutions for web authorization, scanning, streaming of audio and visual material. Sarai will provide schools and NGOs with solutions that are resulting from this project. From early on, Sarai has been collaborating with the Delhi Linux user group which led to the Garage Free Software project whose aim it is to set up a gift economy, working on alternatives to expensive proprietary software. It will also develop user-friendly interfaces and develop Linux based applications in Hindi.

Over the last half year all those working at Sarai have been busy creating the space, installing computers on an entirely open-source network, designing and uploading the web site (www.sarai.net), doing basic construction work in order to prevent the monsoon storm water from entering, and setting up the groundwork for the Sarai archive so as to enable it to hold a variety of platforms, from books to DVDs, and connect it to a database with material accessible to visitors of the public access area. The Sarai database is best accessed via Sarai's internal network interface.

Monica Narula says: "We have worked on three versions of the site. The first was basic, the second one visually interesting but slow and somewhat linear. The newest and present version is faster and more complex. In our design, what we start working with was the idea of multi-perspectives. We wanted to combine elements from traditional work with contemporary street feel and its bright colors. Here in Delhi we experience simultaneous time zones. 'Old' representations show up in the most unexpected places. Therefore also the urge to work with a multi-perspective approach to representation."

Already before Sarai started, Monica had the idea of the computer taking you on a journey through the city. Monica: "The experience would be interactive but would also give you a path. Icons representing concepts would lead you through a narrative space around a concept using image both still and moving, text and sound. That idea is fairly ambitious. We realized that such a difficult design was all about coding, and we are working on it. In such an experience a sense of discovery remains important. You click on a certain motive and reach somewhere else. You think you know the city, but you discover you don't. By looking at it you start seeing new elements. That's the basic motivation behind the Sarai interface, even the form it has now."

For the handful of international guests visiting the opening, the quality of the Internet connection was a surprisingly stable 128K ISDN leased line, supported by back-up battery systems in case of "load shedding" which indeed frequently happens. At one occasion, last year, North Delhi had a 36 hours electricity power cut. The batteries for the Sarai servers are worth more than the servers themselves and can hold for up to 4½ hours. Apart from that each PC has its individual UPS system.

Using both old and new media is a key element in Sarai's design program. Monica Narula: "It's about being interpretive and subjective. Our 'Mapping the City' project is not meant to present a demographic or ethnographic account. For us the question is: how does the city feel to us? Questions of class and gender are involved in this. There are so many untold stories, from people that usually do not matter. And we want to tap into the oral world of telling and listening to stories as well. Even me—I like reading but I also like talking and listening. We will focus on the dialogue aspects, looking into storytelling and oral traditions. For example, using film, photography and sound we would like to do an anatomy of one specific location, a little zone, making a cross section from the rich trader to the man who is pulling the street car, all within a square kilometer. Such as an area in Old Delhi, where at one place someone once registered twenty-one different ways of transport."

The city of Delhi, with its approximate 10 million inhabitants, is an endless source of inspiration for the Sarai members, lacking the disgust for poverty, pollution and noise of the elite and innocent Western tourists. The setting is post-apocalyptic. Shuddha Sengupta, also a member of the Raqs Media Collective and one of the Sarai founders: "In Delhi we are in some ways living in the future. In a situation of urban chaos and retreat of the public and the state initiatives. Tendencies that are currently happening in Europe. The young generation in Europe will face some of the realities that many of us are accustomed with in India, whereas we may leave some of these realities behind. The difference between a contemporary moment in India and Europe is one of scale rather then of an essential nature. There is more of everything here. More people, more complexities, and also more possibilities."

I asked Shuddha whether he would therefore say that Delhi is a global city as Saskia Sassen defined it in her book "Global Cities" as Delhi looks more like a national metropolis rather then a node for global finance. Shuddha replied: "Earlier Delhi was not considered a global city because it did not have a harbor, unlike Calcutta and Bombay. In global capitalism that doesn't count any longer. What's important is the capacity of a city to act as a network with other cities. Delhi is a center of the extended working day, providing the global market with back office accounting and call center services. There is an emerging digital proletarian class which is connected to the world."

Ravi Sundaram, a Sarai founder and now a co-director, and fellow at CSDS added: "Saskia Sassen's book *Global Cities* came out right after the rise of finance capital in the late 1980s. I think we have to rework that notion. The new phase of globalization in the 1990s does not only depend on financial nodes anymore. They are complex network of flows. Delhi is a new global city and there are many of them. In the new economy people are trading in global commodities, using global technologies, increasingly using the net, surrounded by an empire of signs. Delhi used to be like Washington DC. That was 15 years ago. Now it is a mixture more reminiscent of LA South Central with its urban chaos, migration, and uncontrolled growth of suburbs, informal networks and capital flowing everywhere. In that sense I would not limit global cities to financial nodes and labor flows. The narrow definition of global cities borders the sociological. We should move to a more cultural, political and engaged form."

I met Ravi Sundaram for the first time in June 1996 at the fifth Cyberconf in Madrid. He delivered a paper about the difference between the coming of cyberspace in India and previous national industrialization policies such as the building of dams. Ravi's research topic within Sarai is electronic street cultures, the gray economy of hardware assembly and the role of software piracy and cyber cafés in the spreading of PC usage and the Internet. The aim of Sundaram's investigations into the local "ethnographies of new media" is to add complexity to the view that computers are a conspiracy of the rich against the poor with only the upper class benefiting from information technology. Sarai rejects such clichés. Ravi: "The elites in the West and India share a culture of guilt. In the view of these elites, 'their' technology and creativity cannot be a property of daily life. Rather, the domain of the everyday is left to state and NGO intervention for upliftment." Sarai does not share that agenda. "We live in a highly unequal, violent society. But there are very dynamic forms of technological practice in that society. We speak to that, and not just in national terms. We speak equally, within transnational terms, which marks a difference to earlier initiatives in cinema, radio or writing. We are not the third new media (like in third cinema)."

How does Sarai look at the development sector? Jeebesh Bagchi, also from the Raqs Media Collective and a Sarai member: "Development often implies the notion of victims of culture. I don't think in those terms. People live, struggle, renew, invent. Also in poverty people have a culture. I feel a little lost in this terrain, knowing that Sarai, to a large extend, is financed through development aid programs. I would never use a term like 'digital divide.' We have a print divide in India, an education divide, a railway divide, an airplanes divide. The new economy in India is definitely not conceived as a divide. It is a rapid expansion of digital culture. The digital divide is a 'social consciousness' term, born out of guilt. We should interpret the media in different terms, not just in terms of haves and have not."

Sarai rejects the "Third World" label altogether. Jeebesh: "Within arts and culture, the human interest story usually comes from the Third World whereas formal experimentation is done in Europe and the United States. That's the international division of labor between conscience and aesthetics. It would be unfortunate if this would happen with Sarai. Working within the net, with different forms of knowledge, there are no longer discrete spaces. Working from within a so-called developing country means that you are constantly put under the techno-determinist pressure to be functional. At present there is no other domain to be creative outside of the development realm of sanitation, water and poverty. The pressure will always be there. But what worries us more is what discourse critical minds in Europe and the States will construct around Sarai."

Being the South Asian early bird on the global screen comes with certain responsibilities—and pressures. The thread of being instrumentalized, having to act within Western parameters is a real one. Sarai members are aware of the danger of exoticism. Jeebesh: "I am afraid of over-expectation and burn out. Ideally Sarai should not become representative of its country or the region it is located within. We should break with the tradition of national cinema and the national filmmaker going to international festivals, saying 'I am from India, I am from Germany, etc.' We can lose focus if that's happening. We are interested in a dialogue among equals and do not want to get caught in the curated festivals of the world."

Monica: "Showing work abroad has a good side. It gives you deadlines, to start with! But I am not interested in becoming an authentic Third World voice. The aesthetics have to be driven from here. If there are collaborations, they have to be equal and have to integrate the smell and texture of a city like Delhi. Sarai is also aware of the danger of supremacy of text. You can say a lot with images. Images can be called either highbrow art or kitsch from the street, but they are also much, much more than that."

It's not all that easy to combine the busy excitement of new media production with more reflective research activities. Demanding programming and design of new media works can easily take over from theoretical reflections. Sarai is in the first place a research facility, but the pressure will be strong, from both in and outside, to show concrete results in terms of interfaces, software and new media titles. I asked Jeebesh how he would stop a hierarchy between new media production and research from happening. "It's a deep, institutional tension. There is an academic codification of research. In India there are only a few independent researchers. The academy here is creating systematic knowledge, but it's not creating dynamic public forms. In the early 20th century most of the brilliant thinkers were independent researchers, creating a dynamism of thought which we still carry on."

According to Jeebesh, Sarai should create media forms, which the academy cannot neglect. "Feature film has been respected as an equal, artistic art form, whereas the documentary form has been patronized by the academy. We should create such a dynamic tactical media form that it becomes equal to academic knowledge." Sarai does not intend to become a production house. Jeebesh: "We are into experimenting. Still, there is certainly slackness among documentary filmmakers. We shoot and there is an equation between what has been shot and the film itself. The claim to be the makers of reality bites has created a climate which is not very self-critical. There is a crisis of representation. I do not want to represent anyone. So what then is an anti-representational documentary? With new media we would like to emphasize that intellectual crisis."

Where in Delhi does Sarai look for collaboration? Jeebesh: "Some of the intellectuals are experts, a technocracy which is being taken serious. After 1989 you can more freely say what you feel because the burden of state socialism and communism is no longer there. We will therefore see more interesting things happening. It will not only be about talking but about doing. From the beginning Sarai did not want to network with people who have already established themselves. We can collaborate with individuals, on a mutual basis. More challenging is how you engage with the popular design sensibility. What kind of dialogue with this strange and eclectic world do we want to create, not based on domination or populism. How does a programmer create software for a non-literate audience?"

So far in India popular culture has been defined by film. There is a tradition in India to interpret society through film. Jeebesh: "Film will remain an important reference. Till the mid 1980s film was looked down upon. In the 1990s different readings of film and social inequalities were created. These days film has a strange presence through television culture. The music video clip does not exist here. What we have is television relaying film songs. India is a song culture and visual sign board culture. It is deeply embedded in the stories you tell. New media are reconfiguring narration and codes of self-description. There is interesting science fiction now. The problem is that film and television may be imaginative but it is not creating a productive culture. There is a tension with new media, from which potentially something new could grow. We are still surrounded by 20th century broadcasting concepts—inform, educate and entertain. New media should not follow that rubric."

There are numerous obstacles for Sarai in building public interfaces. Will the general public find its way to Sarai and how will Sarai reach out? Jeebesh: "Let the practice speak over time. We must become a place where young people feel at home and become confident so that they will start using it. An intellectual place where different opinions can be articulated, not a ghetto where people feel they have to say correct things." The balance between dissent and power is a delicate one, constantly having to question and re-invent itself while slowly becoming an institution. Co-director Ravi Sundaram: "One has to be deeply skeptical of all institutions, including our own. Being part of an institution means being part of power, whether we like it or not. Both universities and arts institution are strong nodes of power. In India both of them are in a financial and intellectual crisis. For a long time arts institutions were a monopoly of the state. That's over now."

Jeebesh: "Recently an American media artist was visiting Sarai and at a certain point the conversation focused on the question how to map a database onto a surface, if I want to see the content of a database as an image? What is the aesthetics of a database? That's productive discussion. If people take that as an art form, and see it as an art work, that's fine, as long as it comes from an internal curiosity. In a non-visual, non-literate culture we have to somehow work out how the database relates to the surface, which is not text based."

Shuddha: "People may be interested in such arts-related issues on an individual basis. There should be an open space for the creative pursuits that people wish to follow on their own instinct without taking away the concerns that Sarai has as a collective body. We are not here to provide a platform for Indian new media artists to engage with the international community. Nor is it in our interest to stop it."

It is Sarai's explicit wish not to create a new discipline. A brave statement in times in which artists either have to buy themselves into the IT industry or, as in the case of net art, are bailing out by writing themselves into art (history) discourses and their institutions. Shuddha: "Sarai is not going to become an arts institution. There are many of us who are practitioners, working with images, text and sound. We look at those practices from different points of view. We would like to find hybrid forms, beyond the categories of the artist, activist, theorist or critic. Some of the work will take on the form of the aesthetic. Other work will engage with the realm of the political, of knowledge, and with the realm of understanding. None of these elements will have a primacy because we don't see it in those terms. Which is not to say that we will not have an engagement with the aesthetic or the realm of pleasure. We certainly will."

Jeebesh does not want identify himself with any artist specialization. "That's the problem of net art or net culture. It limits cross conversations. We will be very sensitive about that. We should not establish formal identities and disciplines. This can create structural divisions between us. That's why I like to call Sarai a post-institutional space where the public is always present, pushing you to be different."

Ravi Sundaram: "I never understood most of net art. I have always been interested in avant-garde practices but I have not yet identified net art as such. These are complicated aesthetic translations and we at Sarai still have a lot to discover. Two years ago we never imagined what and where we would be today. We have a shared language and a lot of creative disagreements and we would like to share that with outsiders too. If dialogue is a transparent, honest process, not rendered in national, Indian/Western terms, it becomes easier. It is a cruel, historical baggage that we are born into. It is marked on us that you are from the Third World. We abandon that old baggage."

Shuddha: "Working with sound, text and images over the past years we have found that the taxonomic regime of people being described as writers or film makers has been an inhibition of our work. We wanted to do more interesting work than 'filmmaking' allows. Funding wants to classify your practice and organize it in certain modes of qualifications. Having said that we do not want to enter into another regime of qualification of ourselves as net artists. One of the reasons why we entered the new media is because we felt that it allows for a certain liberation in which qualification regimes can be put aside." Ravi Sundaram adds: "All of us want to break out of disciplinary forms. I come out of formal academic institutions. Yet, Sarai is a program of an academic research institution, CSDS." Jeebesh interrupts: "I like the tradition of public intellectuals, such as Ashis Nandy of CSDS who has a disdain for academia. He says 'I don't write, I think.'" Ravi Sundaram interrupts again: "There might be an avant-garde urge to mock institutions. But the money and recognition will come from that very same place. We have to recognize that tension. If we do not recognize the tension we will become rhetorical. We want to be in both places. We are not innocent of power. We live in a highly unequal society. But it is important to render this public, straight."

Let's go back to Sarai's original drive, to develop its own language of new media. What would it be based on? Shuddha: "The communication imperative is an important one for us. Media technologies in India so far have only been one to many. That should not happen to the net. The relation between communication and power should be investigated and challenged, even only conceptually to begin with. In order to get there we need to establish a truly international sensitivity. With that I do not mean national or regional identities. New media culture is not yet international. What goes on elsewhere has to be taken into account. When I used to look at the Internet and the new politics of communication that emerged earlier, I thought: our space, our city should be able to create this. I hope it will be possible for someone living in Teheran or Rangoon, in parts of Asia and Africa to think that something like Sarai should also be possible there. At one time it was impossible for us to imagine a Sarai. For me, after coming back from the Next Five Minutes 3 conference (Amsterdam, March 99, www.n5m.org) it seemed possible. Before we were unable to bring together the energies that were necessary. There is a process of discovery of such energies."

**<Notes>**

1. A slightly different version of this report was posted on nettime March 23, 2001.

2. Sarai, The New Media Initiative, Centre for the Study of Developing Societies, 29 Rajpur Road, Delhi, 110054, India. Phone (00) 91 11 3951190; email dak@sarai.net; URL http://www.sarai.net. For the opening a reader was produced, entitled The Public Domain, with a variety of texts about new media in South Asia. For more information on how to order, please write to dak@sarai.net. There is also a Sarai list, called reader, discussing IT culture and politics in India and else-where: http://mail.sarai.net/mailman/listinfo/reader-list.

# Dynamics of Net Culture

# Radical Media Pragmatism

**You may** not be interested in the economy, but the economy is interested in you.
　　—André Simon

A state of confusion is emerging in the simultaneous condemnation and embrace of prag-
matics. Between cold cynicism and overheated optimistic theodicies, a new belief system
is on the rise: the blurry logic of communicative capitalism.[1] What are "new media"
beyond the embryonic state of their hype? What is media theory after the age of speculation? What is interaction design beyond fascinating demos? Game over, next player?
Will the developers of early media architectures slip into the mainstream, or will they
show civil courage and reinvent the exhausted notion of "underground" once again? It is
neither/nor. This is the age of cybernetic promiscuity, exploring the deep gray spaces of
the (un)productive. Innovative media cultures are connecting many to many, as long as it
works: art, design, content merging with software, with TV, the Internet, radio and music
for communities, commerce and other (non)governmental organizations. Even dramatic
failures count as instructive tenets. What counts now is quick and dirty production—not
the unique "concept" as such but, rather, serial production fueled by the hope that one
of them will be the killer application, the next big thing, the golden mean, the perfect
combination. Welcome to the expanding universe of radical pragmatism.

　　"We shape the things we build—then they shape us." The starting point here is
the ambiguity we feel towards pragmatism and its successes. This applies to the accel-
erated growth of the mediascape in particular. It comes as no surprise that the big
corporations are taking over, and that nation-states try to respond with regulatory

measures. Yet what puzzles us even more are the arrangements of our own micro-economy. How to run a media lab, a (preferably profitable) ISP, a radio station, a design studio, a cyber café, or even a web site or a mailing list? There are so many models out there, so many different traditions—some local, some national, some international or cosmopolitan. There are in fact so many of them that it is becoming less and less clear what is meant when we speak about exchanging "concepts." Recently, the cyber conference circuit spent a great deal of time—maybe too much—looking at demo design of already successful projects. Now the time has come time to look at the failures and assess them in the same way.

Take for instance the celebrated city metaphor. Whereas the Dutch "digital cities" were quite successful as public-access "freenets" (though not without their own share of trouble) similar projects in Vienna and Berlin foundered and disappeared, and other cities may have their own stories to tell.

## Vienna

In the Viennese case, the BBS (mailbox) system Black Box had started an initiative to bring together local users and content from the arts, culture, and politics. However, this construct did not work out in practice. Some people saw the project as being too closely tied to the city council (and to the ruling social-democratic party in particular). This nonetheless, did not prevent the big municipal agencies from developing their own official "virtual Vienna." In the end, the users set out to decide the future of the project. That is: they stayed away, partly also because the good old Black Box BBS system (now with an email gateway) kept on doing well. In the end it was the art content server Public Netbase that survived all the storms and still continues its public access functions.

## Berlin

The Internationale Stadt (IS) found its origin in Handshake, an art project which connected several techno-clubs over IRC (chat rooms). It later merged with the small

Internet provider contrib.de. But the concept of IS was blurry from the start. Sometimes it claimed to be a public access network freenet-style, yet, by and large, it kept presenting itself as a content provider for culture and the arts—which was closer to the truth. As an access provider, it never grew beyond 300 paying customers, but this was not perceived as a problem. Their connectivity problems, on the other hand, were legendary. In one case, they were offline for a full three weeks. Insiders may have a good laugh about this "genius dilettantism," but one should keep in mind that Berlin is not an easy place to work as a far as connectivity goes. Add to this the general atmosphere of a lack of humor, bad moods, and a sophisticated culture of complaint and, hey presto!, there you have a unique version of skeptical net culture. Its credo: technology never quite works as you were told but we make it happen anyhow—a cool and laid-back attitude not that easy to crack for outsiders. Berlin new media culture, much too small for the heavy weight size of its cultural heritage, bouncing between a manic and a melancholic production mode. Berlin found its way out in the electronic music and clubbing scene, turning the yearly Love Parade into a global tourist hit. The Internet just didn't quite fit in. In the end, IS turned out to be a true work-in-progress project, in the "hacker" sense—endlessly tweaking its interface, but never really concerned about the commitment to the customer/user implied in the idea of "service." Network flaws ("notworks"), stressful for IS users, were proclaimed art for the sake of the argument, but in the end no one bought this excuse.

When the Internet hype eventually hit Germany in 1996, IS transformed itself into a private company and took on several big clients. In a perfect world—or maybe in a just slightly better one—this commercialism might have cross-subsidized the non-commercial, public service part of the venture. But it did not work out that way. Being a collective, IS ran into severe management problems, and before long the artists began to leave. The Kassel-based international art show Documenta X played a mysterious part in these developments. IS was not awarded the Internet provision contract as had been hoped. Instead, two IS collaborators were individuals where chosen to be part of the Documenta exhibit as "net artists." The Real Audio server "Radio IS" (continued as orang.orang.org), a remarkable rich collection of samples and audio files, remained a success. Yet, at the same time, the commercial aspect became prominent (with contracts for the new Leipzig Fair, etc.), and IS as a whole lost direction. The by-then-bankrupt Berlin City Council understood little about the dynamics of the cyber economy, obsessed as it was with stolid stoneware. The IS group eventually fell apart, and the members returned to their previous occupations as artists, video makers, programmers, and so on. Internationale Stadt finally shut down on April 1, 1998, a black day for independent European cyberculture, and for everyone who collaborated with them internationally. It was an unfortunate occurrence, comparable to the closure of the Berlin alternative station Radio 100 in 1990 just as the techno club scene in the Eastern section began to flourish. If you understand how long it takes to build up the infrastructure with such lively, informal networks within which artists, musicians, activists, and critics can work, you'll understand how much was lost. What emerged from the rubble of IS was the net.art sero.org server, and the mikro.org initiative—holding monthly media lounges in the WMF nightclub and focusing on the (re)organization of the Berlin cyber scene on a grassroots level. It still remains to be seen how long an electronic culture like this one will last in such a big cultural metropolis, without its own independent technical (and economic) infrastructure.

## Amsterdam

The fancy net.capital of Europe is booming. The official reason given is the success of the post-welfare, so-called Third Way "polder model" that fostered economic growth. A bitter reward after a decade of devastating Reaganomic-Thatcherite budget cuts. Yet, Internet business in Holland is just as shaky as elsewhere with start-ups going bust as easily as anywhere else. And in Holland too, cultural capital and venture capital make strange bedfellows. Netural Objects, the business spin-off spawned by the Society for Old and New Media is a case in point. The story starts in the heady early days of the Digital City, which in 1994 commissioned custom designed furniture for public terminals. These workstations were to embody the ideal of public access in libraries, cafés, and schools. Then, in the wake of the spectacular rise of both public and commercial IT activities in Amsterdam, the Society for Old and New Media was formed by a group of activists, designers, programmers, and other media enthusiasts. They took over De Waag, a small castle right in the city center, a magic historical place where Rembrandt once painted his *Anatomy Lesson of Prof. Tulp*. One of the first achievements was the "Reading Table for Old and New Media," a revolutionary public terminal providing free Internet access. The prototype was installed in the café/restaurant downstairs in De Waag castle. The developers worked from the ground up, assembling a physical and virtual interface. They were rewarded with the prestigious Rotterdam Design Prize in 1997. Soon thereafter, the society's management decided to start serial and mass production of these "kiosks." However, not enough market research was undertaken. The business management style of the venture capitalist also proved to be too fast track. The rate of return was pegged too high, too quickly. Within half a year (February 1998), Netural Objects met its demise, chasing too few customers with a product plagued by too many flaws that was not ready for the market. Fortunately the society's commitment to the public domain didn't suffer too much from the fiasco. The bittersweet taste of realism set in.

The encounter with venture capital and its brash business methods put the limits of entrepreneurial political culture in stark relief. Was this the Waterloo of "Dutch digital imperialism" after all? Probably not. Even in the legendary Silicon Valleys and Alleys and Gulches and Glens, only a handful of start-up companies survive, let alone prosper. But for the thrifty Protestant conceptualists involved, the process—and especially the result—was a kind of shock therapy they hadn't expected.

## New York

March 1998: the ada'web site, "one of the most dynamic destinations for original web-based art," has come to an abrupt end. Co-founder Benjamin Weil announced that Digital City Inc., the site's sponsor, had withdrawn funding. Accountants of AOL, who had purchased Digital City Inc., viewed ada'web as a loss and halted funding. So, ada'web ceased producing new artistic content and disappeared overnight. In its short period of its existence ada'web presented about fifteen web-specific projects by "high-profile" contributors such as Lawrence Weiner and Jenny Holzer.

Without putting out calls for public support fiercely searching for alternative sponsors, Weil opted for the easy way and pulled the plug. At least so it seemed publicly. The ada'web content was not moved to one of the numerous independent art servers. No sooner had Weil stated his point than a fierce debate erupted on the nettime mailing list over (net)art's dependence on corporate money. The video/net activist Paul Garrin stated that corporate sponsorship necessarily results in censorship. So, "next time you get caught off guard and lose your "free" net resources or your sponsorship . . . don't be surprised! There is no free lunch. Everything has its price."[2] Weil's response was: "This reminds me of those people who keep on saying that artists have to starve in order to produce good work. It is at best romantic, at worst idiotic. Art has always been supported by wealth, may it be individual patrons, corporations, of the state. . . . The whole notion of a disinterested state that is so much better than the corporate world, in that it supposedly does not have any agenda, is again one of the most worn-out and preposterous statements that can be made at this point."

Now here is a prime example of everyday pragmatism. Are you able to pull your own weight, or will you go for sponsors or state funding? Now that the wild *Wired* years of speculation about the metaphysical essence of *le cyber* (as our French friends put it so charmingly) are over, the mean and lean years of survival have begun. So, who will survive? Will it be the long-term non-commercial projects on a small scale?

Or will it be, on the contrary, those projects which are going for economies of scale? In response to the ada'web closure, the Belgian web designer Michael Samyn has a clear answer: "Nowadays culture, society, capitalism have become our 'nature.' It's our environment. Ignoring it is not revolutionary. It's silly and there's no point in it. You can fight nature but you cannot win from it. Your best option is to try and make it more comfortable, maybe even fun. Marginality equals non-existence."

Another nettime subscriber, Keith Sanborn, disagreed: "To equate the corporation, the state, and the individual might be called "cynical or disingenuous," but I would say it is simply nonsensical. [Weil's] line about "wake up and smell the coffee, it's the 90s, not the 60s" is precisely the smug "end of history" rhetoric of a Fukuyama or a Bloom. Therefore, are we to conclude that we should all lie down and accept the "inevitable" march of history over our dead bodies towards the greater glory of capitalism in this best of all possible worlds?" Instead, Sanborn called on us to make your own web sites: "Start your own war. Or else pursue that hybrid corporate museological career and don't forget your most Bohemian tin cup." Ted Byfield (New York) found a way out. His nettime contribution stressed fluidity of networks, rather than the nodes of the cyber economy: "Just 'where' is nettime? At desk.nl? At The Thing in New York? In Ljubljana? In Berlin? In London? In Budapest? To be sure, this distribution—as much between people as between sites—is both our strength and our weakness. In the wake of our meeting in Ljubljana, I heard some grumbling about disorganization, about how there were no solid resolutions, no definitive programs or advances. And I thought to myself that this was great: it's very easy to cement social organization around Programs, but harder to preserve looser bonds—loyalties, trust, a certain faith."

The invisible, social network is what makes the Internet so different from previous broadcast media. And yet, perhaps there are not any fundamentally new aspects to the "cyber economy." After all, business is business, and the same goes for politics, culture, the arts, and so on. The magic of (shared) communication in itself remains untouched by these developments. What counts are illusion and imagination, in whatever environment. But these fluid, untamed elements are precisely what is endangered now. We cannot revert to previous pronouncements of visionary sales talks or neo-Luddite anti-technological persuasion. Now the time has come for sophisticated forms of negative media pragmatism: living paradoxes rooted in a messy praxis, unswervingly friendly to the virtual open spaces that are being closed everywhere.

**< N o t e s >**

1.  Posted on nettime April 21, 1998. Print version in Index, 2/98. URL: http://www.artnode.se/artorbit/issue2/f_index/f_index.html

2.  Nettime's Ada'web thread started on March 3, 1998 with a forwarded article by Matthew Mirapaul, Leading Art Site Suspended, taken from the *New York Times* site. Responses were posted by MediaFilter (Paul Garrin) on March 3, Michael Samyn (March 5), Keith Sanborn (March 5), and Ted Byfield (March 8).

# Network Fears and Desires

**When I** hear the word "interactive," I grab my gun. And shoot.
—André Simon

Once a social network—with its loose groupings of individuals and groups—has gone through the exciting, initial phase of meeting, discovering each other's new ideas and concepts, and staging common events, it seems boring to continue, engage with the same old personae, and read the same arguments again and again.[1] Suddenly, the limitations of online communication are being discovered. There are short, intensive periods full of ecstatic collective experience and dull years of isolated struggle and survival. In the case of independent net culture, rooted into the *Wired* years, the dense time of the small, expanding (inter)networks now seems to have reached its vanishing point. Work is being continued within smaller, more specialized global tribes which might be more sustainable in overcoming the Long Boredom. The seamless creative potential of the collective body has ended up in repetition. Certain patterns begin to reveal themselves. The Euro summer of 1998 smells like mid 1970s, late 1980s. Not dark, rather gray. No paradigm shifts ahead, just business as usual. As feared and predicted, corporate content finally dominates the web. The constant technological flow of new applications keeps users busy, creating an addiction for even more promising upgrades.

Network growth is not a linear process. Communities do change when they expand. Once the net enters the level of the economy of scale, it leaves its first movers behind and enters different levels. Even the most ugly, compromised cultural managers, former net pioneers turned exploiters, will, sooner or later, be overruled and puked out by the powers to be. These are the days of amazon.com, Yahoo!, real.com, and Netscape. Their success stories will not last forever. Don't believe the market. Widespread neo-liberal biases makes it hard to make a realistic estimation of their chances—let alone making a critical analysis (or even materialistic theory) of the cyber economy. For the time being we all are still blinded by all the promises, potentials, rumors, hypes. This especially counts for the astronomical, truly virtual stock values.

Growth no longer affects net-related initiatives in the fields of arts, culture, and politics, no matter if they are into making money or not. "The Art of the Big," *Wired* 6.07's cover story by Bruce Sterling (July 1998), deals with Hong Kong's new air-port, Shanghai's 69 skyscrapers under construction, China's large dams, and the CERN's tunnels underneath Geneva. The devotion to Mega can be read as an exotic travelogue for those who stayed behind, not simply as an appeal to the (tired) commu-nity to transcend in order to, once again, re-invent itself. There is, for example, a sat-uration point for bandwidth, beyond which, more simply does not mean faster. Against expectations of hyped-up early adapters, Big Internet is creating a new mass of "users" which just shuts up and clicks. They are "watching Internet," a phrase that would have been impossible to come up with a few years ago. This silent majority in the making, tamed to click the "Buy" button, was not envisioned by the early adapters and the visionaries of the first hour. "It is a Mall World, after all," *Wired*'s Gary Wolf has to admit, not sure whether to be disgusted or to embrace it.

Everybody is bearing guilt, with the exception of a handful scientific Marxists. They come with the perfect analysis, not having been involved in any of the micro struggles of the past decades. Their objective Truth is gaining importance as an unbearable wisdom of the fatal destinies ahead. With one eye on streaming financial data, another on the *Financial Times* at the breakfast table, Negative Marxism without Subject has reached its highest stages of alienation. It is time for a bloody cold dialectical switch, to become what Marxism always was: hard-core economic analysis, made in the United States. No, Monsieur Jospin, the Internet is not one of your *Tres Grand Projets*, unfortunately, despite the European origin of the World Wide Web, born at CERN in the French (!) speaking Swiss town Geneva. Europe is brilliant in killing its own innovations. Your "Market economy, not market society" phrase may be a useful (Euro-French) distinction. But it does not explain why you and other Eurocrats have been asleep for so long, in the hope that old electronics giants such as Philips, Siemens, Alcatel, and Olivetti in the meanwhile would build the network economy for you. Now that you have woken up, you fail the legitimization to complain about US domination. Let's not fool ourselves. Marx is at Stanford, studying the dynamics between Microsoft, Silicon Valley, and Wall Street and writing his Critique of the Global Managerial Class.

Is the permanent digital revolution in danger of becoming a reformist project? The System is effectively taking over, even sucking itself into the intimate spheres of friendships and personal aims. The objective Wheel of Net History is taking subjective tolls. Time slips away and we are caught up in something we never really wanted in the first place. Web Design for Dummies. Net anxiety over nothing. Debates with nothing at stake. Rivalries when there is plenty of loot. The general mood online flips. There is the feeling of an diffuse civil war, with people hacking each others' sites, emails sent, forging the names of other users, causing general uncertainty, pointless polemics, distrust against those winning prizes, getting all the grants and jobs, blokes with power, dumb gender wars on the rise, curators and editors, leaving out crucial contributions to the field, accusations made under obvious pseudonyms, moderators accused of censorship, a nasty attack on a personal friend mistakenly sent to a list resulting in anger and pain, apologies, unsubscribes, unanswered mails.

But wait a minute. We know all this. The so-called unavoidable process of decay is not God-given or a Law of Nature. It is about time to introduce intelligent social feedback systems. Indeed, a Collective/Connected Intelligence (thanks, Pierre Lévy and Derrick de Kerckhove!) which can overcome the now well-known 20th-century cycle of birth, rise, fame, and fall which numerous groups and movements had to go through. It should be possible to play a game with such predictable mechanisms. This is the search for a media theory in which the charming, rather fatal wetware factor fits into the larger forces of hardware and software development.

http://www.cybernetics.su, where are you, now that we need you? Big silence. Perhaps it is up to you and me this time. It is easy to write down the draft of *The Rise and Fall of the Globalization*. See the new markets fall. That's too macro. It is good to gather knowledge about economic forces that are behind the Will to Get Wired. But in the end they will not tell us much about the psychological processes within smaller networks, which the Internet still consists of, despite the current massification. That is what the marketing gold diggers are looking for: Laws of Virtual Community, whatever that may be. What is needed is a critical network psychology, not in the form of some brilliant observations by academic outsiders, but fast and proactive social wisdom which can be implemented in groups, small organizations, lists, and techno tribes. Not only to prevent conflicts over nothing, but mainly to stage real fights, if there is something at stake. First of all, there is the Media Question. The Spectacle has entered every possible domain, and its widespread power has made it virtually impossible to imagine a gesture, form of communication, or action which is not mediated, digitized, or archived. All forms of protests and politics are under its spell. But this tragic reality should not limit us if we are looking for ways out of broadcast misery. Fine, there is still the hacker ethic, models for Electronic Civil Disobedience and tactical media. Concepts, flexible enough to resist the pressures from the Forces of Simulation. But like all ideas, these memes have a limited life span. They must constantly be updated and renamed in order not to lose their magical attraction. No reason to be sad. Bolo'Bolo, TAZ, squats, and raves will show up in new configurations.

After the gold rush, the "we" form is questioned. The lightness of Being Digital get really unbearable. The community is in danger of disintegrating into a thousand and one lonely hearts club bands, captured in the commodification strategies of the Big players. Community is anyway a too harmonious, catholic term for the social dynamics within lists, newsgroups, chat rooms, and web sites. We are not One. There has never been a unity—and especially not these days. The "we" form in the age of the net is one of the few possibilities left to address groups and subnetworks and formulate common strategies (presumed people are interested in collaboration and exchange . . . ). Using the problematic "we" form is an indirect critique of the liberal-bourgeois form of debating in which opponents politely exchange arguments, just for the sake of it. Heterogeneous micro politics are always in danger of falling apart, much more than parties, trade unions, and other institutions. One of the tricks to stop people organizing themselves is to reduce their argument to their Private Opinion which is seen as a contribution to the general (democratic?) discourse. In times of consolidation, dispersion, and decay, the We is under attack, while at the same time more used than ever. It is the time of strategies. At the moment of the short highs there is only the unspoken, ecstatic We feeling. Later on, "we" do not want others to speak on behalf of us. This is symptom of a more general tension, a feeling of discontent, between hyperindividuality and solitude, on the one hand, and the closed, claustrophobic atmosphere inside (online) communities, collectives, companies, and movements on the other. This tension could be the starting point of a debate on new ways of organization.

Commodify your dissent. Certainly. And you will be commodified too. Such a disaster! The co-option fear is even more prominent and destructive these days compared to the unease over mediation. For some there is pleasure in getting to know the rules of the game, understanding the tricks of Doing Business, studying the metaphysics of making money and its ritual, sacral aspects, fooling around with The Baby Suits. For other "net slaves" commodification means creativity and subversions drying out. At a first glance, commodification feels like justice, a liberation, a chance to finally get back some of the money for all the efforts invested in tackling software. Mostly, money will only remain a promise. Having a job mostly means regulation of work hours. Embarrassing cheapness of the work, combined with strong, personal feelings of discontent, even guilt are the main reasons behind the paranoia over commodification. There is a fear of betrayal, being left alone with empty hands, in the IT outbacks, having to work with bogus strangers without a clue, surrounded by adolescent geeks, autistic game addicts, bored careerists, secretary types. One becomes infected by corporate germs. But these are easy to cure. A good book or conversation, a TV documentary, or travel will do. One has to be aware of neo-liberal rhetoric, but ideology is not the issue here. From the political, strategic perspective, fear is the greatest obstacle for the immaterial workers to organize themselves and engage with each other in serious way beyond occasional collaborations. Commitment and dedication are rare phenomena in the age of flexible work, but necessary if amorphous fear is to be surmounted.

*Consciousness Regained*. Radical media pragmatism demands from the actors to remain cool and laid back. Immediate responses are not always the best ones. Who can still proclaim to do "multi media" after the monstrous misuse of this term? It should still be possible to ignore all market forces and cheap trends and keep on doing what you have once started. There is a state of hyper-alertness, toward compulsive transformations, sudden silences, giving up terrain for no clear reason, driven by the hunger for the Next Thing. What counts is integrity. It is getting easy these days to become resigned. There are a thousand reasons to quit, or to continue on the same grocery level. The world, structured by pre-cooked events, ready to be microwaved and consumed, can be rejected. Downright reality is unbearable. "No spiritual surrender," an Amsterdam graffiti says. This also counts for the pseudo interesting office world of Internet firms. Colorless digital existence can be softened by self-made utopias, hallucinatory experiences, with or without recreational drugs and technologies. Regular switching to other channels which are outside the cyber realm is an option. There are countless universes. Negroponte's existential reductionism ("In being digital I am me") is just one of them. "You are only real with your make-up on." (Neil Young)

*Here Comes the New Desire*. Unknown, forgotten forms of negation, refusal, anger, and pleasure are there, while still encrypted against the mentality of police forces and fashion hunters. There are plenty of sadistic traps for trend researchers and their clientele: alternative radio, independent labels, French theory (from twenty years ago), interactive games, online events, and www.techno.net. Life is so cruel: see them clicking and buying, the poor consumer bastards, desperate to get an identity, any, which makes them feel alive, for a moment or two.

*Cybercynical Knowledge 98.* Their search engines and portals have to be distrusted, ignored, misled. Computers generate useless data, not contexualized information. This should be knowledge4all. The postmodern late-leftist discourse of the 1968 generation has now closed all its possible options. There is no way out for them, locked up as they are in their down-sized, optimized, professional jobs. Let it be. The same can be said of the more recent "new social movements," with the exception of sudden out-bursts of uncontrolled (and therefore unorganized) social-ethnic unrest. Do not get distracted by ideological pseudo-events such as journalist-led Culture Wars or popular xenophobia waves. Some fights are nothing more than shadow boxing, while others are real.

It is time for other options, in search for the genuine New that does not fit into known eternal return of the disappointment pattern, of being taken back into the System. Virtual Voluntarism means being able to overcome moods of melancholy, perfectly aware of all possible limits and opportunities, looking for the impossible on the side, out of reach of both futuristic and nostalgic influences. Not blind activism, replying in anger. Being able to present alternative realities, shocking the Johnsons, way out of reach of the Appropriation Machines. The market authorities will arrive too late. Yes, this is a dream, but we do cannot survive in a (digital) environment without options. In order to get at the point, we should reach a level of collective "self consciousness" to overcome the system of fear and distrust which is now spreading. No attempt to reconstruct what worked once. No glorification of the inevitable. In order not to throw away everything which has been built up, concepts could be build on top of it and not narrow all options into making the world institutionally legible. The

"Next Age," the name of a department store in Pudong/Shanghai, is hybrid: not any-more new, pseudo clean, never entirely digitized, stuck between real growth and an even more real crisis, obsessed with progress, in full despair.

<Note>

1. An earlier version, titled Network Fears and Desires, Some Strategies to Overcome the Malaise, was posted to nettime August 7, 1998. It was published in print as "A Manual of Network Fears and Desires" in *Station Rose 1st Decade* (Selene, 1998) and in *The Integrated Media Machine*, ed. Mauri Yla-Kotola et al. (University of Lapland, 1999).

# An Early History of 1990s Cyberculture

**You chose:** Internet or Capitalism. You chose: Freedom or Internet.
   —Genc Greva

During the roaring 1990s, Hakim Bey's Temporary Autonomous Zone (TAZ) concept was turned into a meme.[1] Similar to carefully designed poetic ideas, viral concepts travel far and are not easily extinguished. One of the many channels responsible for the reputation of TAZ was *Mondo 2000*, an upbeat underground cyberpunk paper from San Francisco. The full color magazine was filled with techno-fashion, drug fantasies, DIY video tips, science fiction, the most recent gadgets, and the occasional theory essay. In retrospect, *Mondo* paved the way for *Wired* (starting in 1993) which was more successful in the containment of the rebel element, critical of the corporate takeover of the net, marginalizing the early, pre-WWW cybercultures of the US West Coast. TAZ, however, was not very suitable for *Wired* business protagonists such as Louis Rosetto and Kevin Kelly. It smelled too much like outworn subcultural strategies of resistance and revolt. The Luddite, apocalyptic aspect had to be replaced and turned into a productive, optimistic cultural machinery with only one goal: to make money as fast as fast possible and then get out. It was all about timing. Questions about the Internet architecture were overruled in a gold-rush atmosphere of "moving first." The Internet paired with financial gain turned out to be the dominant image ten years after TAZ and VR. In the words of a fellow New York observer: "Making money is now an organizing principle in society in ways that we've never seen before, not even in the late 1920s or any time in the late 1800s, not even with the famous Dutch 'tulipomania.' The Pentagon can't hire good people anymore, business majors are 'dropping out,' 11-year-old CEOs being turned away from conventions. A major capital formation, like England in the mid 1800s. Pure ideology, pure bubble, pure investment, pure shattering of traditional institutions."[2]

Unlike the British culture/creative industries model, the pose of the *bohème* is virtually absent in the silicon gold-rush stories. Being underground is not seen as a productive motive. Gutenberg intellectuals, stuck in their book culture, still obsessed with the fading power of discourses, marginalized themselves into irrelevant pockets of complaints, hobbled by cultural pessimism. This is the age of the engineer-entrepreneur as hero. Business leaders are the true avant-garde, not those stuck in corporatized academia or the even more underfunded arts and culture sector. Apart from temporary gatherings such as conferences there are no cool localities to be visited. The Silicon Valley region itself is anything but visually attractive, nor is New York's Silicon Alley or Tokyo's Bitvalley. There is little to be seen on the terminal screens, neither in the local night life, nor on the actual computer screens hastily scripted together. The dotcom hype is pure speculation, exploiting the potentialities of the virtual ("justoutofbeta" forever, still "under construction"). The Internet wave does not come with a fashion or a style. There is no dotcom interface design school. The only remains of a somewhat alternative past are the fifty-somethings wearing beards and sandals, telling stories of their amazing inventions and encounters with other mythic figures back in the 1970s. Internet heroes are surprisingly uncool, average white males.

Late 1990s cyberculture, dominated by venture capital, lacks a face. It does not need to have its own look because its design has been outsourced to old media advertisement agencies, the news industry (cnn.com), video game designers (PlayStation), and television (WebTV). The days of web design are over. Innovation shifted from the development of standards and protocols toward business plans and marketing skills. Forget content, attitude, or identity. Today's motto is: Catch the youngsters, squeeze the creativity out of them, turn the team into a slavery project until you ship, float—and sell out. The electronic gold rush lacks both ethics and aesthetics. John Brockman's elitist digirati category (www.edge.org) looks more like a baby boomer hall of fame then a list of people with new ideas. There simply isn't time to play around with ideas and the mainstream can't handle experimental interfaces anyway, nor can the (baby) suits, who perhaps would like a bit of cool and bright design, but who are in reality enslaved by spreadsheets and Powerpoint-ism.

Even the spiritual aspects of the early cyberculture, also found in Bey's writing, had to be stripped of their occult freakiness and turned into something positively light and exciting. This can also be said of the entire cyberpunk genre which became incorporated into the contemporary "the future gets fun again" slogan (*Wired* 8.01). Post-industrial culture, from Survival Research Laboratories to Burning Man, is getting boiled down to positive and creative thinking—innocent commodified technotainment. Stripped of all possibly disturbing, "dark" elements, the hegemonic Californian cyberculture is turning the Internet into a medium without qualities.

*Wired* magazine itself had to be sacrificed to the irresistible drive toward the Johnsification of cyberspace. *Wired*'s search engine (hotwired.com), publishing house, net.radio station, and Wired TV endeavors repeatedly failed to get onto the stock market and were sold off by May 1998. Perhaps the Wired IPO had come too early. The digirati avant-garde had shown the way most start-ups end up: either bankrupt or re-integrated into the safe and the protected environment of corporate America. Revolutions predicted by Toffler, Gilder, and Peters all turned out to be good selling daydreams. Particular elements from the libertarian rhetoric have been adopted, but most of it is already forgotten after the fall of the Gingrich gang, back in 1997. Though one idea has gotten through: the Internet is the message. With Jeff Bezos of amazon.com being chosen *Time*'s Man of the Year 1999, no business can any longer ignore e-commerce and e-business. Why bother any longer about *Wired's* dreams of flying cars, tourist trips to Mars, immortality for all, and other forms of "organized optimism"? *Wired*'s answer would be: America is making billions on the stock markets, selling out on decade-old ideas, so why not dream away? The colonization of the "fun" future had to continue. Why stop betting? After all, maybe Mars tourism would indeed be the next new thing.

Some time soon all sectors of the economy will be hardwired and all transactions and communications will be Internet-driven. The closing of the American Internet, after the handover of all standards and principles to AOL, Microsoft, and to IBM, MCI/Worldcom, CNN, and Disney, now seems to be a God-given fact. Why bother any longer about the future of the Internet? The net might soon reach the end of its history (and turn into something else). Time to devote precious "quality time" to other more urgent, even more exciting topics?

*Wired*'s agenda back in 1993 was to preach and to convince the dull and ignorant CEO types about the advantages of the Internet Revolution, luring them into something cool. From then on capitalism was going to be "funky business." Prior to the early 1990s corporate habit, most computers were used by secretaries and the IT guys, who were the only ones who knew how to run and use computer networks. The desktop computers in homes and offices were not connected to each other. The conversion and transmission of data was still a slow and painful process. Early adopters of the Internet were not just seen as hipsters with some new alternative lifestyle: they were perceived—correctly—as those possessed with the historical mission to turn new media into a business. This task could not be done without a carefully planned cleansing of cyberculture. The geeks could continue their weird lifestyle for the time being; they were not allowed on stage anyway. Neither were the hackers most of whom had turned into security experts. For a while theorists, artists and other freelance cultural entrepreneurs played a role in mediating and visualizing this odd new world coming into being. But after a while, this subcultural pool of visionaries was replaced by more down-to-earth online IT journalists and business types. In order to gain wide acceptance, only very few ideas of the original computer culture were allowed to be propagated. All notions of the growing social inequality and critiques of the multinational corporations were carefully avoided, if not censored. Yes, the old establishment had to be criticized—but only for not being techno-savvy. The lack of understanding of computer networks within corporations and large sectors such as health care, local governments, old media etc. had be capitalized upon.

Certain aspects of the late 1980s "Californian" mindset had to be cultivated and taken out of their political and cultural context. This is what happened to Hakim Bey's TAZ. For many years to come, newcomers on the Internet had to ask themselves the question whether this parallel virtual world in the making was in essence a temporary autonomous zone, where "information wants to be free." The TAZ phrase was not in fact literally adopted from Hakim Bey. Although he does mention the concept of "the web" and speaks about the use of computer bulletin board systems, Bey stresses that the "web" he envisions does not depend on any computer technology. "The key is not the brand or level of tech involved, but the openness and horizontality of the structure. The TAZ above all desires to avoid mediation, to experience its existence as immediate." The festival aspect of TAZ, his emphasis on (data) piracy, the Islands in the Net, the flirtation with Luddism, all these elements have never played an important role, expect for Bey's "psychic nomadism" concept, used to describe the feeling induced by long hours spent surfing the web. The net might have been anarchic and uncontrolled, but was never quite a party. TAZ, as it was understood within the first phase of the hype (1993–1996), became attached to a (cyber) libertarian agenda, a geek culture to which the anarchist author of TAZ had only loose ties.

The image of the Internet as a TAZ attracted a certain type of young and creative content producers who had no secure position within the regular media industry. This diffuse group of early adopters had a strong interest in both coding and interface design. This group understood their historical mission of paving the road in the hope of cashing in somewhere later on in the process, whether for financial rewards or otherwise.. With no payment systems yet in place, little bandwidth, and no audience to speak of (everyone was an actor), the idea of "freedom" was one of the main attractions to get involved. For the early adapter of the late 1980s/early 1990s, freedom was defined as autonomy, a cross between, a post-leftist agenda of social change, criticizing the notions of revolution and its reformist version of the Long March through the institutions (in this case old broadcast media) on the one hand, and the hippie outlaw agenda of being left alone by society, the state and its laws on the other. A curious mix between Toni Negri and Ayn Rand, with elements of both J. S. Mill and Kropotkin. I hesitate to use the "colonization" metaphor because prior to commercialization (before 1993) there was little to occupy. The cyber journey was as much about exploration as it was about connecting, playing around. It would be improper to reduce 90s Internet experiences to the libertarian cowboy agenda. It was the blend of promises that formed its attraction.

At the turn of the millennium, this particular history of the 1990s only seems to provoke feelings of nostalgia for a time when Gibson, Sterling, *Mondo 2000*, and Virtual Reality were still secret passwords. The now-contained Internet is here to stay, and will transcend into an amorphous form of almightiness. As far as autonomy is concerned, the image of World Wide Web ghost towns pops up, abandoned home pages, bored avatars, broken links, switched-off servers, controlled communities, spam-flooded lists, and newsgroups. The freedom is there, but no one cares and no one will be able to find the counter-information through the corrupted portals and search engines at any rate. And the zone? The animated debates during the 1990s over the nature of virtuality and the ways in which it leaves behind the real have been tempered by the sheer speed and violence of the way in which computer networks are now pervading all aspects of life, including today's resistance movement against the rule of global corporations (www.indymedia.org). TAZ was boiled down to a late 1980s concept, associating the Internet with rave parties. Restless souls can easily jump over this tragic reading of the history of ideas and open a new chapter full of unknown, unlikely futures.

## < N o t e s >

1. A slightly different version was posted to nettime December 27, 1999. It drew responses from Alan Sondheim, McKenzie Wark, scottart, Paul Garrin, Max Herman, and Robbin Neal Murphy (December 27–29).

2. David Mandl, personal email correspondence, December 1999.

# The Importance of Meetspace: On Conferences and Temporary Media Labs

Much of the work dedicated to building up new media culture is spent on organizing and attending conferences—precious resources, perhaps better used to support actual media projects, one could say. Yet, the drive of humans to gather together in dirty "meatspace" is unstoppable.

Technologies, in the midst of unfolding, are in great need of concepts. After engineers have put technology out of beta stage and into the world, the new objects of desire first land into the hands of conference-going "conceptualists." Conferences are both cathedrals and bazaars for new ideas. Startups need to meet potential funders, journalists get their face-to-face interviews, academics researching the virtual team-up with their real-life colleagues. Theorists present their visions and artists show their latest demo designs. Having been in involved in organizing new media conferences for a decade, I would like to present my thoughts on the "art of conferencing." Not much has been written explicitly about organizing new media conferences and festivals. Here I will look into the reasons why new media culture, as a concept industry, is so focused on real-life gatherings which debating formats I encountered. The idea of how "temporary media labs" grew out of the exhaustion of the mid-1990s new media conferences and the associated celebrity system will also be discussed.

During a broadcast on Amsterdam cable, Derrick De Kerckhove, Manuel De Landa, and John Perry Barlow—speakers at the third Doors of Perception conference—proudly compared their collected frequent flyer miles, gossiped about how to upgrade and about what to do if you missed a connection. Was this "information ecology," as the original program had stated?[1] Digirati seem to fly even more than executives in other branches. At first glance, their conversation seemed scandalous, perverse. Wasn't the Internet supposed to overcome the necessity to travel? It is hard to speculate about the possible impact of future high-res tele-conferencing systems. Most likely the multicast webcams will not crush the conference industry. Breast-to-breast rendezvous will remain popular, despite the virtues of online exchanges. The overall increase of communication worldwide will only push up travel figures.

Teaming up in real life is still the most effective and fastest way to learn and exchange points of view. Physical encounters prevent us from making small but fatal mistakes, the most common cause for flame wars, which have destroyed many personal relationships on the net. A clumsy email, mistakenly sent to a list can have devastating consequences. This is a mistake easily corrected at a gathering on location. During the get-together we get a fast grasp of the context of people's work, intention and personality. Do we converge to be part of the herd? Perhaps not. Conferences are not just for genuine community, exchanging ideas on an equal basis. It is not by definition a good idea to keep concepts for yourself. In the marketplace of goods and ideas there is always plenty of time for informal talks, agreements, rumors and conspiracies. At the cultural fringes of the new media branch there is a strong need to share feelings and experiences, to "recharge batteries," and re-create a sense of direction. The participants then return home and continue with the implementation of new media which are in nature conceptual, unstable, invisible, and not understandable to outsiders. A never finished *Gesamtkunstwerk* of images, texts, sounds and meanings. This may sound blurry, but that's exactly what it is. The new media conference sector operates in the fuzzy field of irrational human needs. New media is not a clearly defined product. There is always more work that needs to be done, new software to be installed, upgrades to downloaded, code to change. Conferences function foremost to gain motivation in order to continue with the never ending patch work, requiring both creativity and persistence.

"The Concept Economy Wants You!" Besides hardware and software, the 1990s has seen the rise of conceptware, a cluster of ideas, ready to be implemented into interface design. With customers needs as its weak link, experimental conceptware has mostly been dealing with the difficult integration/synergy of the computer with the "old" media (audio, video, graphic design, intellectual discourses, theatre, etc.). Most conferences in the cultural IT sector deal with the question of how to link back to the old world through notions such as the body, the city, the museum. Take the undefined concepts such as "cyberspace," "virtual bodies," or even "WebTV." Going beyond the existing Internet—and perhaps less ambitious than the mystical "total VR"—the rising disciplines of hypermedia, digital studies, interactive research, which all incorporate elements of philosophy, art history, cultural studies and the performing arts, have to come up with attractive memes, models and metaphors. Bordering on vapor theory (Lunenfeld 2000, pp. 33–36), cyber concepts have to be capable of bridging the divide between new technologies and old powers. The "conceptual sector," consisting of visionaries, curators, artists, consultants, designers and programmers, will further develop and implement them into demo applications, web sites, or wireless test content.

Conceptual cyber work does not easily fit in the traditional cultural sector. Nor is it merely a technical skill. It's not a job for specialists, but for generalists which might have had many strange, different activities before the rise of the net. Do we deal here with "vaporware"? Not always. There is an increasing pressure on the early adopters to put up an "anarcho-business." Yet, concept developers are suspicious of commercialism. Not because they are against money (quite the opposite) but because they have seen again and again business demolishing their concepts. Magical terms become worn out within months. Neither hard-core academic nor entirely business oriented, workers at the cyber-conceptual forefront are positioning themselves as interface. They are sensible for social and political arguments, interested in critical discourses though not openly defending them, and always ahead of the "dinosaur" Other, those working in old media and cultural bureaucracies.

Conceptualists don't write business plans (as least, they ought not do so). They might be too dreamy to become CEOs or executive managers. They perhaps sit on the board but even that is a rarity. Fast companies don't have time to sit and think. There is no place in their busy schedules to be creative. The implementers therefor need to have private conceptual jokers, no matter how mad their jokes and tales.

Even if we admit the primacy of the hardware and software industry, one has to understand that the users eventually will be surrounded by conceptual cyberspace, not just by Intel, Windows, Netscape, the Mac OS, or Linux for that matter. Within the rising cyber concept business there is a constant need for visions, metaphysical constructs and metaphors. Internet "visionaries" are not only spreading the "hype" through the traditional media like television and magazines. Their main audience are young professionals, in need of leading ideas. Such people need guidance, contacts and motivation, necessary in the first, risky phase of their new existence. They also need to recharge their batteries pretty quickly in a condensed hit.

The most common way to encounter these blessings is—besides reading upbeat magazines—attending a conference. It can be a commercial one, dealing with wireless or e-commerce but that's not what I am talking about. I am more interested in with the non-profit cultural sector here, focused on arts, architecture, design, cultural policy and media. In a cyber concept atmosphere, an unspoken consensus seems necessary. There is an unwritten rule that the creative brainstorm should not be hampered by critical remarks. References to "old" discourses are perceived as disturbing. One can make historical references, reintroduce old rituals and religions, celebrate the unity of body and spirit, but negative thinking seems to be out of favor. It seems that new media conferences ought not to raise controversies. A successful event generates a cloud of expectations and good feelings. There is hardly any pro and contra and little time for discussion. The strict format is decided by the programmers of such events in an early stage. Who likes to spoil the party anyway? One keynote lecture after another, with a panel session to answer some of the questions, that's it. Experts, put in random panels, working in wildly different areas, not knowing each others' work, have little to exchange, let alone to argue about. After a while audiences stop visiting such gatherings. The new has faded away. A conceptual crisis of the conference format occurs.

The one-to-many model of the speaker at the podium addressing the auditorium seems such an outdated model. Will future conferences only have small workshops for the happy few who are able to pay the high fee, for those who are already member of the cyber elite, the famous "virtual class"? Maybe that solution is a bit too simple. Conferences are about inclusion and exclusion. Who is on the list of invited speakers, whose trip, hotel and entrance fee is paid? What happens to those on low income or young people? Established institutions tend to look first for big names. The question of whether the celebrities can contribute to the chosen theme plays a less important role. Often panels are random anyway. Famous experts bring in the "feel" and thereby raise customer satisfaction. Conference visitors often end up with a strange mix of speakers and a conference without much focus. This of course is compensated by the short period of numbness and hallucination when the charismatic Star is on stage and delivers his or her prophetic lecture-performance.

From the very start in the early 1990s, European multi-media and net-related festivals had the function to generate consensus, not controversy. This goes together with the general tendency to "stage" podium discussions and beautify boring conference halls. The result is over-organized events that, sometimes managed by hired professional laity, with knowledge limited to "cultural management," are eliminating spontaneity, serving the consumer mentality of visitors who would like to get spectacle for their money and precious time.

German audiences have the amazing discipline to discuss with 500 people, structured by *Thesenpapiere* (propositions, read by the speaker), *Rednerlisten* (list of speakers from the audience), and *Diskussionsbeiträge* (contributions). In Amsterdam, for example, people often start yelling and, having a short attention spam, walk away when they get bored. Dutch discussion culture is raw, dominated by a cynical rhetoric, responding to the often unarticulated moral consensus. Public debates must therefore have an entertainment aspect. You go to a debate like you go to a film or to the theatre. In other countries, the audience remains silent, whatever you try, because it is not common to speak in public. They prefer to express their opinion in a more informal environment, like a corridor or a café. Other cultures might have to deal with "machismo."

The ideas developed here go back to my collaboration with Caroline Nevejan and Marleen Stikker, both founders of Society for Old and New Media (De Waag) in Amsterdam. Before starting this ambitious cultural media lab in 1996 they worked at two cultural centers, De Balie (Stikker) and Paradiso (Nevejan). As program producers they organized numerous debates, meetings, public discussions, lecture series and conferences. Both were obsessed with the "art of debating." Their aim was to rearrange, and question, the relation between speakers and the audience in order to overcome the consumer culture which had killed public debate during the dark 1980s. This was the age of celebrity democracy. Audiences were supposed to be entertained. It was no longer enough to call for a public debate. What counted was the way in which a certain topic was "staged." The borders between a town hall meeting and a televised debate had faded away. Static and passive formats were out. No two hours speeches read from paper. Pro-and-contra debates had to be "directed" in order to break through the deadly consensus of the Dutch post-welfare state. Old controversies and discourses were not allowed to reappear again. Using audio-visual media, constantly changing positions of tables and chairs and a sharp, witty rhetoric of well-instructed chair(wo)men, attempts were made to cut through the routine pitches of experts, politicians and writers. Remote contributions via telephone, video conferencing, webcams and chat rooms were brought into the local debate.

What is discussion without critique? It is hard to imagine a public debate free of public relations considerations. The secrets of selling yourself are well known. The advice of the spin doctor is to never answer negative allegations. With everything publicly said becoming newspeak, conflicts are hidden and have to be unearthed. Official "issues" are to be treated with a healthy doses of suspicion. In whose interest is it that a topic suddenly becomes hot? Which public relations and marketing managers are pushing behind the screens? Which public relations firm is advising the politician or corporation in this case? Victims can only speak within the victim discourse and are not a reliable source anymore. Institutional power structures are finding their own way to make deals. And the "enemies" are hiding until violent clashes and bitter hatred suddenly occurs. The rest is dealt with in a boring, rational way, using the well known empty phrases. The rising cyberculture finds itself in the middle of this crisis of the public discourse/space, while dreaming of an electronic democracy and many-to-many communication.

The technology criticism of the 1980s has not been able to regroup itself and failed to attack the neo-liberal cyberhype in the public arena. The only well known commentators are cynical journalists who would like to eliminate Internet hype as soon as possible. No Luddites in sight (with the Unabomber as an exception). Critical media scholars such as Noam Chomsky show no interest in new media. The same counts for Neil Postman and other "media ecology" defenders of book culture. Cultural studies has so far mainly been dealing with MTV television/pop culture. This rough picture is slowly changing, but the introduction of critical cyber texts and their authors still takes a long time.

Another factor holding back a rich discussion culture is the growing language and translation problem. The globalization of public discourse is presupposing the availability of material in English. Even in Europe is it pretty unlikely that one will enter the international conference circuit if you do not speak English fluently. This has been one of the most frustrating, implicit exclusion mechanisms in the organization of conferences on critical net discourses. A range of challenging media theory from French speaking, Spanish, German, Italian, or Japanese theorists is not entering the international arena. How to organize the translation of interesting papers if the author is not speaking (enough) English? Simultaneous translation is expensive. If there are no translation booths, which is increasingly the case, they're out. The result is an English-centric discourse. Yes, there are the automatic translation programs such as Babelfish, with often hilarious outcomes. Is the solution to wait for technical solutions to improve and translations of their texts, ten or fifteen years after they have written? Within the quickly changing new media environment this seems unacceptable—but the current reality. Translation funds for (online) content will therefor become more and more important. In order to maintain "digital diversity" more texts will have to be translated into English. Trans-local exchanges, such as between Dutch and Slovenian for example, are even more desirable—and precious.

There is also the dilemma between self-organization and achieving public outcomes. A conference always has both elements. The exchange of ideas and concepts is the primary motivation for people to travel and get together. This is sometimes hard to admit for the organizers of cultural events, who are under the pressure of foundations, institutions and sponsors to come up with concrete results and statements as to where The Cyberthing is heading. Like festivals, exhibitions and publications, conferences are seen as a viable element of what constitutes the public sphere. Without visible outcomes it seems such a luxury, so in-crowd, such a waste of money and all the efforts. If results do not find their way into the general public, via the press, money might not be available next time. For new media insiders this is another story. They are building up mutual benefit societies, invisible rhizomes of new contacts and friendships, in which concepts can freely circulate. There is a fine balance for all parties involved, funders, organizers, participants and the general public, between staging an accessible yet innovative event which is not just celebrating the latest techno gadget or government policy and topics which only interest a small, increasingly isolated new media ghetto, disgusted with the commodified cyber spectacle.

The idea to do "temporary media labs" grew out of the discontent with the conference format. At conferences there is, at best, ten or twenty minutes to quickly click through a demo version. "Exhibiting" web pages does not make much sense: their lively, layered complexity gets lost. Even the interactive installation with a stand-alone monitor seems not the proper medium to express networks. In previous years much has been done to introduce new media to an ever-growing audience. But the networks themselves, their mysterious and seductive aspects, remained invisible. It is hard to represent or even visualize what is actually happening on a mailing list, a newsgroup, a chat room, or even 3D environments such as Active Worlds. Catchy flash animations can give us a clue, but mostly remain soulless and empty. Complex flows and exchanges turn into dead information. With the variety of virtual communities constantly growing it is no longer enough to merely announce their existence. Audiences demand substance—not only outsiders but, most of all, members of the cyber tribes themselves. The web is more than interface.

Jesse Hirsch, a Toronto-based net activist, part of www.tao.ca, once said at the 1999 Next Five Minutes 3 conference that while e-commerce was moving economic activity from the actual to the virtual environment, it was going to be the task of activists to bring the virtual back into the actual. The best way to speed up the process of production is to meet in real space, to confront the loose, virtual connections, to engage in the complex and messy circumstances of real time-space, to and present the audience (and possible future participants) with actual outcomes. And then go back again, in scattered places, on line.

The idea of the temporary media lab was born out of the desire to cover events, conferences, festivals, and demonstrations in search of a net-specific style of reporting. Some of the web journals which did this that I was involved in covered the Ars Electronica festival of 1996 and 1998 (www.aec.at), Next Five Minutes 2 and 3 conferences in 1996 and 1999 (www.n5m.org), the Euro-summit protests in Amsterdam (www.contrast.org/eurostop) in June 1997, an early version of the independent media center (IMC) model (www.indymedia.org), and the hackers' gathering Hacking in Progress in August 1997 (www.hip97.org). The format of the online journal is to bridge the real and virtual by building in interactive elements between online audiences and the actual site. It also allows participants on the spot to give their own impressions of the event. Web journals are exploring unusual ways of reporting, with image, sound and text, allowing remote participation before, during, and after the event.

Web journals are now a standard feature for all sorts of corporate events, inter-governmental meetings, global summits, music festivals, television programs and fairs. The web sites of such live events all have streaming media features. Usually, after the event, the announcement, lectures, list material, "live" data and reviews are brought together in one web archive.

The temporary media lab concept goes one step further. It no longer covers an ongoing event but, instead, targets the hands-on production of content in and around an already-existing group or network of groups and individuals. It is patently clear that virtual networks of people are good at discussing and preparing but not for actual pro-duction—this is done much more efficiently and creatively on the spot, face to face. In this way the tensions that so easily build up in virtual worlds can be erased while demos and concepts can be developed collectively. This of course seems like a luxury situation in a world in which increasingly online work is being done from home.

Conferences are known and respected as effective accumulators and accelerators. They offer ideal opportunities to recharge the inner batteries in the age of short-lived concepts. Temporary media labs are even more effective in this respect: they focus, speed up, intensify, and exert a longer-term effect on local initiatives and trans-local groups. Meetings in real space are becoming more and more a precious good for the way they add a crucial stage to almost any networked media project, whether in the arts, culture, or politics. Unlike conferences though, the role of the (passive) audience remains open yet undefined. As with any other concept, the broader public will be confronted with the issue anyway, sooner or later. Temporary media labs are experi-menting with social interfaces, visual languages, and cultural/political processes. Though the immediate outcomes can be presented at the end of the session, the real impacts of such small task forces, perhaps only comes later, elsewhere.

Hybrid WorkSpace (HWS), which took place during the 1997 Documenta X in the Orangerie in Kassel, went on for 3½ months; it received an impressive share of the 620,000 visitors who came to the main event. Fifteen groups stayed for 10 days each; among those groups were No One Is Illegal (which was launched there), We Want Bandwidth (www.waag.org/bandwidth), the German Innercities campaign, some audio initiatives which later turned into the Xchange real-audio/net.radio network (www.re-lab.net), loosely affiliated or unaffiliated tactical media practitioners involved in focusing on global media (www.n5m.org), the Deep Europe/Syndicate group from former Eastern Europe (www.v2.nl/east), a group preparing the nettime Readme! book (www.nettime.org), and finally the first Cyberfeminist International, which brought out its own documentation (www.obn.org).

To bind online social environments to a physical space therefore may as well make the need for space metaphors obsolete. In the hybrid space the real and the virtual gets mixed. But the connection between the realms is not going to be smooth. It is a never ending story of disruptions, bugs in the human-to-human communication, conflicting standards and cultural glitches. The virtual should not become a quasi parallel world. Nor should we return to the tactile solidity of the "real" cities, rendering a nostalgia for the social which might have existed once. The temporary workspaces and gatherings do not intend to produce a consensus. The aim is to design interesting problems and spark debates.[2]

The Revolting temporary media lab in Manchester, which took place over five weeks in August and September 1998, can be seen as a follow-up to HWS.[3] Organized by Micz Flor, Revolting took place in a social environment very different from Kassel: a run-down English inner city, away from the big art crowds (even though it had a similar mix of people, themes, and low-tech approaches). It brought together local groups and communities to focus on practical outcomes, small presentations, and debates. Revolting had a special emphasis on spreading specific content via different media, such as a regular free newspaper, local radio, and the net.

The third temporary media lab, Temp, one which I curated myself, took place in the project space on the fifth floor of Kiasma, the new Helsinki contemporary arts museum, which had opened in June 1998.[4] The media lab went on for five weeks (in October and November of 1999). Temp might also be read as a reference to the Tempolab meeting in the Kunsthalle Basel (June 1998), a closed session of a distant though neighboring tribe, the global "contemporary arts" scene, curated by Clementine Deliss. The general idea is of course also a reference, and tribute, to Hakim Bey's Temporary Autonomous Zones, a reminder that revolts of anger and desire, of passionate bodies and souls, remains an option, despite the overall victory of global capitalism.

During Temp five groups each worked on five different topics, all focused on ongoing outcomes. First came a newly formed European network of groups working on issues of refugees and "illegalized" migrant workers. The group organized and coordinated the demonstration held in Tampere during the Euro summit on this delicate political topic (see: www.contrast.org/border). In December this group again gathered in Amsterdam where this network was officially founded, with participants from even more countries. Balkania was the name of the second Temp group. Twenty media artists from Southeast Europe discussed the situation in their region after the Kosovo conflict and drew (negative) utopian images to bypass the current dramatic situation in the Balkans. The third, all Finnish group focused on the technology policies in Finland itself. "Nokia Country/ Linux Land" dealt with the growing power of this telecommunications giant on the one hand, and a free operating system on the other. It asked such questions as: What influence is Nokia have on the ever shrinking welfare state? And is power really challenged with the introduction of open source software such as Linux, which originates in Finland? During the fourth group a Nordic/Scandinavian/Baltic network of media labs and media arts institutions was created, with a special emphasis in the program on the difficult political situation in Belarus. Two events marked the closing of Temp: a one day conference on the urban condition in Asia, organized in conjunction with the opening of the Cities on the Move exhibition in the same Kiasma building, and an environmental web-based game, open for public participation. Temp finished with a small exhibition of the results of the five week project and a web site where all the projects archived their outcomes.

Some groups and individuals are making a good use of temporary media lab facilities, others do so in a lesser way. So what? The temp media lab concept is not an army setup or a content factory. It is just a name for a model, connected to similar initiatives and situations, such as Polar Circuit in Lapland, ANAT's summer schools in Australia, Communication Front meetings in Plovdiv, Bulgaria, Art Servers Unlimited (London/Labin), the Crossing Over workshops of the Virtual Revolution group throughout Europe, the Oreste space at the Venice Biennale of 1999.[5] Compared to conferences, outcomes of temporary media labs may be more invisible but what they boost is are sustainable models of an independent new media culture, beyond hype and policy of the day. Digital media arts and culture are all in a flow. Tactical media networks are unstable and the outcomes are hard to predict in the short run. But I am convinced that temp media labs are a strong motor behind the networks of digital culture. The temporary, local truth has made it worth the effort to organize such events. Time and time again, until the format runs out of energy and we all know, by intuition, how to set up networks, servers, sites, how to generate income—and most of all: how to deal with the all too human flaws in communication. There will always be disturbance on the line.

## < N o t e s >

1.   Parts of this essays were posted on nettime: New Media and the Art of Debating Second Thoughts on the Organisation of Conferences, September 26, 1996 and The Importance of Meetspace, A Manual for Temporary Media Labs, nettime, January 8, 2000.

2.  For more, see Pit Schultz and Geert Lovink, First Analysis of the temporary WorkSpaces, posted on nettime August 17, 1997.

3.  See www.yourserver.co.uk/revolting.

4.  Temp was commissioned by Kiasma's media art curator, Perttu Rastas, and was produced by Seppo Koskela. URL: http://temp.kiasma.fi. The URLs of the different group works: http://temp.kiasma.fi/eng/0.html, Cross the Border: http://www.contrast.org/borders/tampere/, Future State of Balkania: http://temp.kiasma.fi/balkania/index.html, Linux Land/Nokia Country: http://temp.kiasma.fi/ict/ Baltic Sea Media Spaces: http://temp.kiasma.fi/eng/4.html and http://nice.x-i.net/training.html, Eko.Katastro.Fi: http://eko.katastro.fi/

5.  URLs: Oreste: http://www.undo.net/oreste/ and http://www.geocities.com/Paris/Lights/7323/orestebiennale99.html; Polar Circuit, held in Tornio/Finland: program posted on nettime, July 13, 1997, for information on Polar Circuit 2 see nettime April 17, 1998. Polar Circuit 3 was held in 2000. Information about Virtual Revolution's Crossing Over workshops: http://www.ljudmila.org/co. Amanda McDonald Crowley of the Australian Network for Art & Technology (ANAT) organized, similar to temporary media labs, a series of "master classes for new media artists and curators," of which the Alchemy event in Brisbane (May/June 2000) was the biggest: http://www.anat.org.au/projects/alchemy/index.html.

# An Insider's Guide to Tactical Media

**Life means** a provoked life.
—Gottfried Benn

There is a commitment to combine radical pragmatism and media activism with pleasurable forms of nihilism.[1] Not the apocalyptic, conservative culture of complaint which postmodernism has left behind, but short heroic epics on the networked everyday, reporting from within the belly of the Beast, aware of its own futile existence, compared to the millennial powers to be. Tactical networks are all about an imaginary exchange of concepts outbidding and overlaying each other. Necessary illusions. What circulates are models and rumors, arguments and experiences of how to organize cultural and political activities, get projects financed, infrastructure up and running and create informal networks of trust which make living in Babylon bearable.

Paul Shepheard: "Strategy is the motivation, the overview. Tactics is the positioning of the parts ready for the implementation of the strategy. Operations is the carrying through. Yes, the theory has a military origin . . . but it stands as an analysis of action and is useful in any situation where intention and material have to be combined."[2] Define first, talk later. Tactical media are post-1989 formations.[3] They are a set of dirty little practices, digital micro-politics if you like. Tactical media inherit the legacy of "alternative" media without the counterculture label and ideological certainty of previous decades.[4] There is a friendly attitude towards the neutral and even more tactical term "independent media." This label is for example used in the

"Independent Media Center" formula, the temporary press centers set up during protests against a series of summits of politicians and business leaders.[5]

The term "tactical television" came up during the preparations of the first Next Five Minutes conference, held in the Amsterdam pop temple Paradiso in early 1993.[6] Although a global gathering, N5M was dominated by a large scale encounter between two distinctive cultural communities. On the one hand, Western European and North American campaigning media artists and activists and on the other hand their equivalent from the former communist countries of Central and Eastern Europe, dissident artists and samizdat activists, still basking in the after glow of the role they played in bringing down the communist dictatorships. In the excitement of discovering each other, these two communities tended to gloss over their ideological differences, understandably emphasizing only the shared practice of exploring the "tactical" possibilities of consumer electronics (in 1993 mostly the video camcorder) as a means of organization and social mobilization. Although the differences between these two groups was under-played at the time, they were nevertheless profound and illuminating.

In the United States and Western Europe, tactical media, both then and now, are overwhelmingly the media of campaigns rather than of broadly based social movements, and are rooted in local initiatives with their own agenda and vocabulary. They are not a megaphone representing the voice of the oppressed or resistance as such. Once upon a time in the West, there were movements without one specific campaign. Tactical media are into questioning every single aspect of life, with "the most radical gesture." But now there are a plethora of campaigns detached from any broadly based emancipatory movements. In contrast, central and eastern European media tacticians, or the samizdat media, had been very much part of a huge historical uprising. Sudden movements which resulted in the dismantling the Soviet Empire. Liberating moments, not to lament about.

Resistance has disassociated itself from lifestyle. Protest contains a multitude of styles, but luckily enough, and too bad for the fashion hunters, it is no longer a style in itself. It has become a sheer impossibility to judge someone according to their outer appearance. Reggae and techno styles both have meaningful, comprehensive sets of ideas, values, and sign systems but do not indicate the persons' opinion or practice. Visual representation as such seems to have become such a minefield. Literally every subversive expression can—and will—be co-opted. This is such a frustrating reality that it might be better to ignore the discourse of appropriation altogether. Although the tactical media concept includes alternative media, it is not restricted to that category. The term tactical was introduced to disrupt and go beyond the rigid dichotomies that have restricted thinking in this area for so long. Hybrid forms are always provisional. What counts are temporary connections between old and new, practice and theory, alternative and mainstream. And then to disconnect them again. This is also defined by the local circumstance, not only by a personal attitude. Amsterdam has its access to local TV, pirate radios, digital cities and fortresses for new and old media. In other places there might be theater, zines, street demonstrations, book culture, raves and clubs, experimental film, graffiti, debates, literature, and photography.

Six years after the first N5M, at the third Next Five Minutes on "tactical networks" in March 1999, on the brink of Kosovo war, the consequences of unaccountable global capital flows had bitten deeply. While refusing to leave globalism to the investment houses and multinationals, these groups were combating global capital with global campaigns. And present in these strategies was the faint hope that if a campaign generates enough velocity and resonates with enough people, it might just take on some of the qualities of a movement. Simulation vs. "real" action. The urgency of some of the questions tactical media groups are facing generate an angry skepticism around any practice that raises art and media questions. For old-school activists the equation is simple: discourse plus art equals spectacle. They insist on a distinction between real action and the merely symbolic. As Sören Kierkegaard did in 1847 when he wrote in his diary: "A revolutionary age is an age of action; ours is the age of advertisement and publicity. Nothing ever happens, but there is immediate publicity everywhere. In the present age, a rebellion is, of all things, the most unthinkable. Such an expression of strength would seem ridiculous to the calculating intelligence of our time."[7] Life may still be passionless, but the dichotomy between "real" action and mere publicity can no longer be made. The call of action is in itself a mediated statement. In our hybrid lives it has become impossible to unravel what's real and what's virtual. The category of the true "extramedial event" has become truly unthinkable, beyond the range of strategy and tactics.

Critical Art Ensemble came up with the following description of tactical media: "There has been a growing awareness that for many decades a cultural practice has existed that has avoided being named or fully categorized. Its roots are in the modern avant-garde, to the extent that its participants place a high value on experimentation and on engaging the unbreakable link between representation and political and social change. Often not artists in any traditional sense refusing to be caught in the web of metaphysical, historical and romantic signage that accompanies that designation. Nor are they simply political activists because they refuse to take a solely reactive position and often act in defiance of efficiency and necessity." It is the in-between position which characterizes being tactical, a not always easy position. It can therefore be stimulating to link up with similar minded spirits. CAE continues: "For those of us who are involved in tactical media felt a kind of relief that we could be any kind of hybrid artist, scientist, technician, craftsperson, theorist, activist, and could all be mixed together in combinations that had different weights and intensities. These many roles (becoming artist becoming activist, becoming scientist etc.) contained in each individual and group could be acknowledged and valued. Many felt liberated from having to represent themselves to the public as a specialist and therefore valued."[8]

Grown out of despair rather than conviction, tactical media are forced to operate within the parameters of global capitalism, despite their radical agendas. Tactical media emerge out of the margins, yet never fully make it into the mainstream. There is no linear career path through the world of newspapers and television channels. That fate is a different one, caused by an ongoing friction between critical engagement and professionalism. The post-millennial media industry is competitive and above all cynical. There is hardly room for investigative journalism which is after all the basis of all "tactical" output. Activist researchers have an ambivalent relationship towards their colleague editors and journalists working inside mainstream media. On the one hand, tactical researchers depend on the attention of newspapers and current affairs programs to publicize the (often shocking) findings of their investigative work. On the other hand, the numbed and servile mentality at editorial desks, taking credit for the research work of others, and the constant internal censorship, are issues addressing the core of the problem, not just bothersome obstacles.

Acting tactical is a question of scale. How does a phrase on a wall turn into a global revolt? These days a well-designed content virus can easily reach millions overnight. Tactical activists invest a lot of time to research how to design a robust "meme" which can travel through time and space, capable of operating within a variety of cultural contexts. The duality between "small is beautiful" and "subversive economies of scale" is constantly shifting. Low-tech money-free projects are charming, but in most cases lack the precision and creative power to strike at society's weakest link. Tactical media are ready to work with money. They need it for the temporary setup. But tactical networks also know the limits of networking and information dissemination. There is no aim to become an alternative CNN, a Yahoo! for the protest generation, or the grassroots version of the Borders bookstore chain. The snowball effect of branding is actively discouraged, not out of principle, but because the outcome is so well known and predictable. There is no need for globally recognizable signifiers. Instead, tactical media work with the basic but difficult recognition of difference. Essential information and ideas will spread anyway, growing against the odds while staying off the radar of the "cool interceptors" as long as possible. If discovered it's necessary to optimize publicity and metamorphose to the next level at the earliest possible opportunity. The eternal cycle from excitement to frustration and exhaustion has to be broken. That would be a truly utopian achievement.

The pathos of the outsiders' position is spared here, but not out of an ideological disagreement with the anti pose. The target of protests are well defined. Negating the confused circumstances of everyday protest is an easy stand. Radical gestures have the tendency not to address the complex dynamics of new technologies and avoid the urgent question of the lack of distribution channels of dissent and concrete issue-based campaign strategies. The tactical label can be given to any form of expression or activity, but it is media we're talking about here. Tactical is referring to the ambiguity of more or less isolated groups and individuals, caught in the liberal-democratic consensus, working outside of the safety of Party and Movement, in a multi-disciplinary environment full of mixed backgrounds and expectations. Lacking a big picture and liberated from leftist dogmatism and ghetto group psychology, their new shapes of protest take viral forms, spreading with the speed of light.

Tactical media mix old and new machinery and are not bothered by platforms or standards, resolution, or a bit of noise. The aim is not to reach purity. Nor is "polluting" the image, sound, or text by definition an interesting deconstruction exercise.[9] The sample is not the expression of a fragmented world, it is the technological a priori of all information. Nothing to worry about—or to glorify. Tactical material is more documentary than fictitious. The world is already crazy enough. There is not much reason to opt for the illusion. With history in overdrive, narratives can be picked up from every street corner. Postmodernity is no longer a strategy or style, it is the natural condition of today's network society.

What forms of organization does media activism take? While truly discouraging stories from the (media) economic forefront on the rise of mergers, censorship, etc., it is good to ask the old question again: "What is (not) to be done?" A return to negative thinking could play an important role in the development of strategies for media activism. There is plenty of good will and ruthless cynicism. What mostly lacks is playful negativism, a nihilism on the run, never self-satisfied. A gay techno-science beyond Good and Evil, questioning the political correctness rhetoric in order to get beyond innocence and anger. Not a remake of the elitist Nietzschean *Lebensphilosophie*, one century late, but an ever-changing strategy game of building infrastructures and then leaving them when the time has come to leave the self built castles and move onwards.

Exploration into the field of the negative not only imply hampering the forces of global corporate capitalism, but foremost investigate the workings of the dominant organization form of "citizens' protest," the non-governmental organization. The NGO is not just a model for aid organizations that have to correct failures of govern-ment policies. It is today's one and only option to change society: open up an office, start fund raising, lease a copy machine, send out faxes and emails and there you have your customized insurrection. "How to make the most of your rebellion." The professionalism inside the office culture of these networked organizations is said to be the only model of media-related politics if we want to have a (positive) impact, or "make a difference" (as the ads call it). It's time to question the bureaucratic and rit-ualized NGO models, with their (implicit) hierarchies, management models and so-called efficiency.

"The Revolution will not be Organized." These are not the words of some chaotic anarcho-punkers or eco-ravers calling for spontaneous revolt, right now, tonight. The crisis of the Organization is the "condition humane" of the outgoing media age. And it may as well be the starting point for a new, open conspiracy that is ready to antici-pate the very near networked future. Not anymore as a Party, a Movement, or a Business, nor as a network of branches (with or without headquarters), new forms of organization may be highly invisible, and not focused on institutionalization in the first place. These small and informal communities easily come apart and regroup in order to prevent the group from being fixed to a certain identity.

"The site less visited." Media activism after 1989 is not about Truth. This makes the strategy debate so difficult and short-term tactics so wildly diverse and attractive. It is about the art of getting access (to buildings, networks, resources), hacking the power and disappearing at the right moment. The current political and social conflicts are way too fluid and complex to be dealt with in such one-dimensional models like propaganda, "publicity," or "edutainment." It is not sufficient to put your information out on a home page, produce a video or pamphlet, etc., and then wait till something happens. The potential power of mass media has successfully been crippled. Today, reproduction alone is meaningless. Most likely, tactical data are multiplying as viruses with unexpected (negative) growth patterns. Programmed as highly resistant, long lasting memes, the new ideas are being constructed to weaken global capitalism within an unknown time limit—somewhere between Today and Next Century.

No apocalyptic or revolutionary expectations here, despite the ongoing rumors of an upcoming Big Crash of the global financial markets. Unlike the Russian communist world empire, "casino capitalism" (Robert Kurz) might not disappear overnight. There is enough deprivation and alienation ahead. But that should not be the reason to lay back and become console socialists. *Gelassenheit* (composure)—the right attitude of being-in-the-media—has to be as tactical and sophisticated as the rage. Unlike Peter Sloterdijk (1989), I don't think we need to go back to Eastern authoritarian religions or even its heretical undercurrents. But then, everyone has his or her own odd sources of inspiration. My admiration for obscure German thinkers is certainly not recommended either. It would be better to drink from future sources. In any case, tactical media are not so much in need of theories or Big Ideas but specifically in finding out the mechanics of survival within global capitalism.

There is a need for contemporary forms of organization, such as global (online) labor unions, networks of immigrants, refugee tongs, free association of digital artisans.[10] The question here is how to go beyond the exchange of information. Exchange systems could be developed ("open money") so that a peer-to-peer gift economy of "open content" can blossom. These are all conceptual art pieces to start with, realized on the spot, somewhere, for no particular reason, lacking business ambition. These models will not be envisioned by this or that visionary. They are lived experiences, before they become myths, ready to be mediated and transformed on their journey through time. Media activism constantly mediates between the real and the virtual, switches back and forth, unwilling to choose sides for the local or the global.

Tactical media are creating temporary hybrids of old school political data and the aesthetics of new media, which deal with interactivity and interface design. As a next step, this is being implemented on both the level of the social personal level where our wetware bodies meet and that of the "non-located" technical network architecture. Activists develop "negative software," (anti-)racism search engines, (temporary) public terminals, free group-ware, anti-aesthetic browsers against both Microsoft and Netscape, electronic parasites that live on corporate software and content. Recording is not enough. Reality.net, equipped with tons of web cams can be fortunate and collect evidence, but it can as well add to the spreading paranoia about the surveillance by the Corporation State. Sometimes it may be appropriate to detect and "delete" CCTV cameras. Neither eco-fundamentalist, nor techno-utopian, media activists are taking risks and act freely. This may sometimes be in a criminal way, if necessary (like computer hackers), thereby ignoring old legal standards (censorship, copyright).

A "light" and independent media infrastructure is not merely expressing diversity. It is not enough to correct the "lies" of mainstream media and facilitate communities with their own channels. Being a "difference engine" on the level of representation may put out a lot of useful public content, but it does not touch on the "media question." What is of interest are the ideological structures written into the software and network architecture. It is not enough to just subvert or abuse this powerful structure. There is an equal challenge to develop new standards by writing free software and interfaces. The same can be said of the efforts to develop databases of free content, a still marginal activity that will soon gain importance once everyone will have to pay for content to download. The virtual public sphere cannot come into being in a purely global, commercial environment, neither in places where the state has absolute control over the nation's intranet and firewalls. It is in this "third place," the public part of cyberspace, in-between state and market, that media activism flourishes.

With prices of electronic consumer goods dropping, tactical media still cost money, especially for those positioning themselves at the electronic frontier. For the time being the struggle (if there is any) is about the definition of the terms under which the "information society" will become operational. Who is defining the terms of the techno paradigm? During the mid and late 1990s the net euphoria was all about the production of cultural and political concepts, which may or may not be implemented on a larger scale later on, in some unlikely future—or may become marginal again. The galaxy of ideas rapidly imploded into a few products, standards and portals. What is going to remain, and do all the unused concepts end up in the dustbin of history?

Which network architecture will be used? Will users accept the dominant software and screen design or might they go on the lookout for alternatives to Explorer and Netscape browsers such as Opera? Will they even install Linux? Techno-determinists from the Friedrich Kittler school look behind or underneath the Intel chip architecture for imploded power structures. In contrast, media pragmatists from the Amsterdam school conversely point at the politics of user interface design. "Das Design bestimmt das Bewußtsein" (design determines consciousness). There is tactical knowledge to be found in the "Manifest for the Design Economy," reflecting on the dotcom madness of 1999–2000: "Go with the cashflow," "In cyberspace no one knows you are artist," "Information is dark, not light," "If this world isn't up to your standards just invent new ones," "The American way of designing the future is market Stalinism," "Reclaim Public Space," "DTP = Decentralize The Power," "Looking is Stealing," "Choose your future, design yourself" (NL-Design 2000).[11]

Is there still space for theory, reflection, and meaningless playing around? Is production stress overruling creativity? Terminal workers are determining future formats of the new media which will shortly become standards, ready to be commodified.

Further growth of new media products may need a phase of consolidation on the level of marketable products. The "digital revolution" could therefore soon reach the watershed, the turning point of the revolution, its Digital Thermidor. There is less and less reason to make fun of the "dinosaur behavior" of apparently outdated and "tired" multinational corporations, unaware of the mighty powers of the net. Restructuring programs are under way. Differences between the Old and New economy, if they ever existed, have quickly been erased. CEOs listened carefully to cyber-libertarian visionaries and have drawn their own conclusions.

Tactical media are opposition channels, finding their way to break out of the subcultural ghetto. This is both the source of their power ("anger is an energy," John Lydon), and their limitation. Typical heroes are the nomadic media warrior, prankster, hacker, rapper, jammer and camcorder kamikaze. They are the happy negatives, always in search of ways to deter the foe. Once the enemy has been named and vanquished it is the tactical practitioner whose turn it is to fall into a state of crisis and depression. The cycles of success and failure, burned out by media exposure are becoming shorter by the day. Then (despite their achievements) its easy to mock them with catch phrases of the right: "politically correct," "victim culture," etc. These ways of thinking are widely seen as carping and repressive remnants of an outmoded humanism.

Tactical media are never perfect, always in becoming, performative and pragmatic, involved in a continual process of questioning the premises of the channels they work with. This requires the confidence that the content can survive intact as it travels from interface to interface. But we must never forget that hybrid media has its nemesis, *das mediale Gesamtkunstwerk*. Of course it is much safer to stick to the classic rituals of the underground and alternative scene. Tactical media are based on a principle of flexible response, of working with different coalitions and being able to move between the different entities in the vast media landscape without betraying their original motivations. Tactical media may be hedonistic or zealously euphoric. Even fashion hypes have their uses. But it is above all mobility that most characterizes the tactical practitioner. The desire and capability to combine or jump from one media to another creating a continuous supply of mutants and hybrids. To cross borders, connecting and re-wiring a variety of disciplines and always taking full advantage of the free spaces in the media that are continually appearing because of the pace of technological change and regulatory uncertainty.

From the dual real-virtual perspective, media tacticians are accused of merely talking and not doing much. By focusing on the media question they are said to be creating more empty signs. And there is much in the current European political reality to support this critique. After all, the expansion of the media realm has not automatically resulted in an equivalent growth in emancipatory movements and critical practice. It has merely resulted in an accumulation of self-referential topics. Media these days are accused of fragmenting rather than unifying and mobilizing. Paradoxically, that is partly because of their discursive power to elaborate on differences and to question, rather than just voice, propaganda. Jean Baudrillard's elaborations on simulation were useful in the 1980s when the media scape exploded. Approaching the millennium everything seemed simulated and Baudrillard's elaborations started to sound conservative and out of touch with the actual Internet reality.

Meanwhile, we continue to languish in a world in which many struggles appear to have left the street and the factory floor and migrated into an ideological space of representation, constructed by and through the media. This is often characterized as a shift from public space towards virtuality or a shift from social action towards the mediated. In a time where we can see such growth in media channels where there is a tremendous expansion of various cyberspaces it is a nonsense to talk about "a return to the real." In fact one might even ask whether any meaningful politics can exist outside of the media sphere. The debate about net activist strategies is the focus of the "merely" symbolic vs. the "real action" discussion, with critics voicing skepticism about whether you really can provoke a campaign by just sending out hostile commands via the Internet or whether one can construct a movement via technical means, through mediation only.

Another level of critique addresses the problematic nature of self referential campaigns, that is campaigns that do not go beyond the media topic itself. It is easy to lose oneself and dive into an attractive and fatal media trap. Media are relative autonomous entities. Attractive because it is so vast, there is always more information, more channels, more software and sites and the political issues within that sphere of contestation, the titanic struggle within the media industry over power is a universe in itself. Tactical media are vulnerable to the accusation of being trapped in the same old safe assumption that all power struggles are being fought out in the media space. However, to believe this would be to believe that the campaigns to damage Shell, Nike, or McDonald's have just been fought on the level of pure semiotics. It is a too easy and luxurious position to disdain the media question altogether, saying it is not "real."

So far three layers of net activism appear in a still rudimentary way:

• Networking within a movement: the first level of net.activism consists of facilitating the internal communication inside the movement. It means communication on and behind mailing lists, setting up web sites which are designed as a toolbox for the activists themselves. It leads to creating a virtual community whose dynamics do not so much differ from offline communities, besides the fact that people do not necessarily need to meet physically, but very often they do.

• Networking in between movements and social groups: the second level of net activism is defined by campaigning and connecting people from different contexts. It means joining the forces of collaborative and cooperative efforts, to create inspiring and motivating surroundings in which new types of actions and activities may be elaborated.

• Virtual movements: the third level of net.activism means using the Internet vice versa as a platform for purely virtual protests which refer no longer to any kind of offline reality and which may cause incalculable and uncontrollable movements: E-protests like online demonstrations, electronic civil disobedience, or anything which might be seen as digital sabotage as a legitimate outcome of a social struggle: counter-branding, causing virtual losses, polluting the image of a corporation.

Although a shared agenda may be emerging, one should also be realistic about the differences and clashes between activist agendas. The three layers do not always work in perfect harmony. Tactical media, used on all three levels, is not a positive model for anyone to identify with, let alone follow. Alliances are still relatively loose with a tendency to fragment into an infinite number of parallel and distant gangs and subcultures. There is no "World Federation of Tactical Media" and probably there never will be. Perhaps we are just a diverse collection of weirdoes, off topic by nature. Of course there is an element of pleasure in knowing that you are with your 20 dearest friends on your own net.radio channel but this is swiftly accompanied by the realization that it will be indefinitely confined to these twenty friends and what seemed like an opportunity has quickly become a ghetto. Let's look again for new coalitions while trying to avoid falling into the traps and limits of institutionalized politics. Unfortunately, the Internet has not freed artists and activists from the necessity or perils of having to deal with institutional politics. There is no Internet without power, cable policy, money and access rights. Don't believe the hype of a disembodied, pure and unspoiled Virtual Organization. Feeling empowered by the net, while communicating from your bedroom could just mean that one is increasingly becoming unaware of the infrastructure which makes your virtual actions possible in the first place. Despite being a truly global medium, the political economy of the net is clearly bound within legal boundaries of nation states and shifting commercial infrastructures of telecom giants.

Once the strategy debate was all about the fear and paranoia of being co-opted, having to sell out, getting integrated into the System. Throughout the 1970s and 1980s activists discussed the fine borderlines where negotiation with authorities, and working for them, turned into betrayal. Which journalist could be talked to? Was it acceptable to write for a national daily, work for television? The moral policing of politically correct behavior (language, fashion). To what extend is an active defense against police violence appropriate? The media activism debate at the turn of the millennium is less moralistic, more exploratory. The challenge is to locate power. Is it be found on the street, at places where world leaders meet, in the mass media, the net, the institutions such as WTO, G8, World Bank, or the World Economic Forum? The strategy and tactics used in this search are becoming technological themselves. Less about the attitude against power, tactical media are based on long-term critical investigations into the nature of networked power.

The notion of tactical media is inclusive. It is a delicate coalition, a living experiment, not a recipe. One of the debates tactical media practitioners differ about concerns "hacktivism." The question on the table touches on the very nature of the Internet. Is the net by definition a corporate environment which, in specific circumstances should be attacked? Or is the net rather a neutral, open and, in principle, a freedom loving infrastructure? In early 1998 the Floodnet software was developed, aimed to facilitate activists to hold "virtual sit-ins." Immediately, hackers were divided over the effectiveness of the Floodnet software, developed by the Electronic Disturbance Theatre. Libertarian minded hackers suggested that the "flooding" of corporate and government servers was ending up nowhere. Massive hit attacks, directed at the enemy site were getting lost in the general net, thereby mostly harming others, in particular your local ISP. Political "hacktivists" first denied the technical problems by hackers and saw great opportunities in organizing "online demonstrations" in which thousands could participate.

The first electronic civil disobedience/hacktivism debate occurred on the Ars Electronica Infowar mailing list in July-August 1998 and continued on nettime and other lists.[12] At Next Five Minutes 3 in March 1999 a panel was organized to discuss the issue. The development of much more effective Denial of Service (DoS) software compared to the "virtual sit-ins" of Floodnet, plus the push of a "cyber terrorism" discourse in government circles made the net activism debate more serious. DoS attacks on major US news media in early 2000 by a guy named Mafiaboy turned the attention away from collective forms of net protest, back to the stereotype of isolated adolescent individual male hacker. However, for net activism the position from 1998 remained the same for a long time.[13] The "hacktivism" issue should be put in the broader context of the arsenal of net activist strategies available. The oldest and most important work on line is investigative journalism, bringing topic-related material together, informing and organizing activists and setting up campaigns. The anti-McDonald's site www.mcspotlight.org is a pioneer in this field. Then there is the news portal model, like the "anti-globalization" protest site www.indymedia.org, an editorial system, built on free software, with localized versions in dozens of countries all over the world, including a web conferencing system where activists discuss strategies. A somewhat older model is the net activist server such as www.tao.ca, running out of Toronto, organizing activists, mainly via mailing lists and providing autonomous web space on both a local and global level. Of course activists are using a mix of these models. Take for example the online demonstration against Lufthansa about the German airline's policy of deporting rejected refugees (www.deportation-alliance.com). This campaign brought together all the elements mentioned, including a visit to the annual shareholders meeting and a "virtual sit-in."

The strategies mentioned above are basic and technical in nature, though not always as innocent as they may seem as governments or sects such as Scientology who are both keen to close sites with controversial content. The debate really starts over the issue of "hacktivism." Hackers and system operators tend to condemn "virtual sit-ins" and DoS attacks for the unfocused side effects, affecting servers not involved on either side of the protest. Whereas hackers dislike to spoil bandwidth and like to see the net as a free and open neutral space, hacktivists stress the analogy between cyberspace and real space. For hacktivists the net is like an info highway and there are no reasons why the new public roads, like the old ones, could not be blocked for a protest—as long the cause is clear.

Rop Gonggrijp, a hacker and one of the founders of the Dutch ISP xs4all, warned "script kiddies" not to launch DoS attacks from the fat 1 GB intranet, set up for the HAL2001 hackers gathering. "While it may seem cool to have powerful people think of you as dangerous, you're only serving their purpose if you deface web sites from here, or perform the mother of all DoS attacks. You're helping the hard-liners that say we are no good. They don't care about the web sites you deface. They don't care about the DoS attacks. Heck, their leadership doesn't even know how to hold a mouse. They care about making us all look like a threat so they can get the public support needed to lock us all up."[14] Individual attacks provoke repressive legislation against all, so Rop believes. Hacktivists have so far not responded to this and other concerns of hackers. Traditional activists have not yet skilled up sufficiently to take up a serious debate over such technical issues. Rop warns that DoS attacks are treated by authorities as a serious crime. He himself thinks of them in terms of adolescent behavior: "The post script-kiddy existence offers many rewards: you might have the feeling you've done something useful more often, people won't look at you funny, and you might even get to meet girls. But more importantly: we as a community need you to grow up. Many privacy enhancing technologies still need to be built and a whole new generation needs to be made aware that their freedoms are being dismantled."

In the current political debate after "Seattle" about direct action there are several parallels to the situation of the late 19th century which can be made. Sabotage is radically antagonistic to the representative discourse, i.e. in the institutionalized contexts of the working class or social movements. Those representative forms have always referred to a nation state, while spontaneous, unorganized, or better-organized forms of resistance have expressed a global class consciousness. What is nowadays called direct action re-presents sabotage. From No Logo to Ruckus Society, from wild strikes in the hardware, hi-tech and service industries to the semiotic guerrilla of Indymedia, RTmark, or Adbusters, current forms of activism attempt a redefinition of sabotage as social practice, but not in the usual destructive sense, rather in a constructive, innovative and creative way. Such a constructive approach results in a movement without organs or organization, with a variety of perspectives.

To conclude: tactical media is a deliberately slippery term, a tool for creating "temporary consensus zones" based on unexpected alliances. A temporary alliance of hackers, artists, critics, journalists and activists. The desire to go tactical is based on the wish to be released from the tiredness of self-satisfied groups and communities while retaining the right, when the time has come to disconnect from the media at large and start to work on a specific mix of global and local issues. Tactical media retain mobility and velocity and avoid the paralysis induced by the essentialist questioning of everything, in which everyone is an object of suspicion and nothing is any longer possible. One of the most well trodden of tactical routes remains hybridization, blurring the old with the new, the street and the virtual.

Beyond analysis and judgment the tactical is also about reclaiming imagination and fantasy. The classical rituals of resistance are no longer reaching large parts of the population. This was the crisis of direct action in the early 1990s, which is in part a failure of imagination. A way out was found in the epidemic of pie throwing. The ritualized humiliation of power with a pie in the face.[15] A highly meditated practice, the pie does not exist without the image, its only meaning is as a media event. We could see it as a primal way of attacking power. The pie is the perfect poisonous countersign. The wisdom of the tactics of radical alienation is that the further you go into mediated spaces, the more likely you are to "fall back" into reality. Radical demands are not by default a sign of a dogmatic belief system (they can be, of course). If formulated well they are strong signs, penetrating deeply into the confused postmodern subjectivity so susceptive for catchy phrases, logos and brands. And most of all: strong images. The pied leader is one of those irresistible photo opportunities.

Becoming hybrid is not the choice of a new generation. It is a techno-cultural condition. Hybridity is neither an ideology nor a goal. It is dirty digital reality. Hybridization is often seen as per se good (and bad by purists), generative of infinite possibilities to switch between channels, mix up the signals, intentions and disciplines, naturally operating in accordance with the economic and technological shift towards synergy. Hybridization is about survival, it is not really a choice. For those who make the mistake of treating it as an ideology, there is simply no way back. Hybridity in this world is about connectivity in the sense of promiscuously connecting everything with everything, the neo-liberal idea of "anything goes as long as its connects." But at some point tactics and hybridity, and other serenades on the world and its complexity stop and choices have to be made. That's where the story of transitory post-1989 tactical media ends, and other dimensions are being opened.

## <Notes>

1. Writing this chapter I partly used and rewrote fragments from the following texts: "Strategies for Media Activism," lecture at forum event of "Code Red," The Performance Space, Sydney, November 23, 1997, posted on nettime December 2, 1997; "The ABC of Tactical Media" (with David Garcia), nettime, May 16, 1997; "The DEF of Tactical Media" (with David Garcia), nettime, February 22, 1999; "New Rules for the New Actonomy" (with Florian Schneider), in *Rough States*, Media Circus reader, Melbourne, July 2001. An extended version was posted on nettime June 26, 2001.

2. Paul Shepheard, What Is Architecture? An Essay on Landscapes, Buildings and Machines, quoted by Brian Carroll, nettime, July 24, 2001.

3. Related texts: Andreas Broeckmann, Next Five Minutes: Tactical Media, Some Points of Departure, http://www.dds.nl/~n5m/texts/abroeck.html; Peter Lamborn Wilson, Response to the Tactical Media Manifesto, nettime, posted by Pit Schultz, May 19, 1997; Hakim Bey, The Obelisk, nettime, posted by Diana McCarty, November 23, 1997; David Garcia, Old and New Dreams for Tactical Media, nettime, February 23, 1998; N5M3, Concept of Next Five Minutes 3, nettime, December 24, 1998; Hacking

Activism, An Email Dialogue Between Alex Galloway and Geert Lovink, nettime, February 19, 1999; Ralf Homann, Art of Campaigning, nettime, July 29, 1999; Josephine Berry, Tactical Art in Virtual Space, nettime, September 13, 2000; Critical Art Ensemble, *Digital Resistance* (Autonomedia, 2001). See also Ryan Griffis, Interview with Critical Art Ensemble, nettime, December 18, 2000.

4.  A group of media activists in Rome, Italy took up the term "tactical media" in 1996 and formed the Tactical Media Crew, www.tmcrew.org, a international activist web site/portal in five European languages, covering, among other topics, Chiapas and the Zapatistas, Noam Chomsky, feminism, free radio, Italian social centers. Their motto, a quote from Marshall McLuhan: "World War III will be a guerilla information war, with no division between military and civilian participation."

5.  See www.indymedia.org.

6.  For a report of the 1993 Next Five Minutes conference, see Douglas Rushkoff, *Media Virus: Hidden Agendas in Popular Culture* (Ballantine, 1994). See also David Garcia, "A Pirate Utopia for Tactical Television," nettime, May 5, 1996; Franz Feigl, "Talking about Shortcomings of Aesthetic and Political Television," speech at Next Five Minutes, January 1993 (http://feigl.com/OOIT/N5Mspeech1/); archive of N5M 1–3 videotapes (http://www.iisg.nl/visual_archives/n5m/index.html). For more on the context of "collecting new media" and tactical television initiatives, see Tjebbe van Tijen's introduction of the N5M video catalogue (http://www.iisg.nl/visual_archives/n5m/histintro.html).

7.  Sören Kierkegaard, Diaries, quoted in Julian Evans, "An Age of Passionless Power," *Australian Financial Review*, June 22, 2001.

8.  Quoted from the manuscript of Critical Art Ensemble 2001.

9.  In this sense the concept of tactical media differs from that of sovereign media as described on pp. 12–15 of Adilkno 1998. See also Eric Kluitenberg, "Media Without an Audience," nettime, October 19, 2000.

10. Hakim Bey is a key thinker when it comes to question of organization. For his adaptation of the Chinese "tong," see pp. 13–18 of Bey 1994.

11. See also NL-Design 2001.

12.  http://www.aec.at/infowar/NETSYMPOSIUM/ARCH-EN/. URL of the Electronic Disobedience Theater: http://www.thing.net/~rdom/ecd/ecd.html. Floodnet homepage: http://www.thing.net/~rdom/ecd/ZapTact.html. More on ECD was written by one of its members, Stefan Wray: http://www.nyu.edu/projects/wray/wwwhack.html; http://www.nyu.edu/projects/wray/RhizNom.html; http://cadre.sjsu.edu/web/v4n2/stefan/. For the original essay of Critical Art Ensemble on electronic civil disobedience (from 1994), see http://www.critical-art.net/ECD/Ch_1.html.

13.  N5M3 net activist forum (www.n5.org/n5m3). From the web journal report: "The artist Steve Kurtz from Pittsburgh believes floodnetting, as practiced by Electronic Disturbance Theater is not effective. "Before the Pentagon or the Mexican government feel an itch, countries with limited internet access end up clogging up the all the servers in between. If the press finds out those actions are pointless, it'll backfire very quickly." Rop Gonggrijp of Xs4all added: "Instead of flooding the target, you end up putting down you local proxy server, which regularly caches the content of the remote site." See also Luther Blissett, "The XYZ of Net Activism," nettime, March 3, 1999.

14.  Rop Gonggrijp, "COPS, CRIMES and HAL2001 or ScRiPt KiDdY MaNuAl To HaL2001" (original to hippiesfromhell list), forwarded by Patrice Riemens, nettime, July 18, 2001.

15.  See Biotic Baking Brigade, http://www.asis.com/~bbb/.

# Organized Innocence and War in the New Europe: Adilkno, Culture, and the Independent Media

Adilkno, the Dutch Foundation for the Advancement of Illegal Knowledge, founded in 1983, is an association of five non-academic theorists who bumped into each other during the early 1980s, in autonomist circles within squatters and anti-nuclear movements.[1] In 1994 the first English translation of their work appeared, *Cracking the Movement*, a book about the Amsterdam squatters' movement and its dealings with the media.[2] Although Adilkno, of which I am a member, has been writing about the media from the start, this theme has become increasingly important since 1989. A series of textual explorations was published, mainly in *Mediamatic* and the Belgian film magazine *Andere Sinema*, presented as "Unidentified Theory Objects." This series of speculative explorations resulted in the book *The Media Archive*. The original Dutch edition appeared in 1992. Throughout the 1990s translations in German, English and Croatian appeared, with new texts being added each time. The initial speculative media theory approach broadened towards a general cultural analysis. The final edition of *The Media Archive*, the Slovenian translation, appeared in 2000, double the original size and also contained essays on the 1990s wars in the former Yugoslavia, mirroring the moving Eurovision song festival ("Bosnia-Herzogovina, may we have your votes?").

Adilkno's media theory has to be read within developments in Amsterdam since the 1980s. This self-willed free state, international home and operations base of hippies, queers, the unemployed, artists and tourists, sat in the shadow of great upheavals on the European continent. Since Amsterdam has no noteworthy industry, is home to neither the government nor the national media and cannot be called a high-tech center, there was enough space to experiment without anyone breathing down one's neck. The oft-mentioned tolerance which serves as the city's hallmark, and its flip side of non-commitment and indifference, make it possible for numerous media initiatives to build up a sound tradition relatively independently of one another without deteriorating into a closed scene. In the fields of free radio, magazines, computer communication, video and (live) cable television the experiments exceed the character of one-time events.

Theory and practice in Amsterdam are only indirectly connected. The anti-intellectual attitude of the punks' and squatters' movement, which have been important breeding grounds for many media initiatives, embroiders on the general attitude that people should not chatter, but get to work. Intellectuals either are populist ministers or hide behind elitism. However, lacking discussion, criticism and self-reflection are not experienced as a deficiency. The combination of practical tinkering with a healthy dose of cockiness ensures that projects people elsewhere only dream about are set up and continued without a lot of money from authorities or businesses.

Adilkno is only one element within the new media culture in Amsterdam. What many of the media experiments have in common is their local, hybrid character, the mingling of high and low tech linking them together using records found on the street, telephones, old computers, amplifiers, camcorders and ramshackle cassette decks. There is great interest in the hype which rises from the high-tech laboratories on the US West Coast. Yet their experiments are too clean, too healthy, too spiritual. We need not lapse into anti-Americanism, but the pretense that American technoculture would lead the rest of the world is kindly refused here. The US version of virtual reality is not the only one and need not be copied. There are many cyberspaces—at least that's the premise. The European variant in its conceptual stage is polyglot, filled with a deep melancholy.

Amsterdamers enjoy polluting the concepts of others by stirring in a portion of their brilliant dilettantism. Hardware might well be global, but the connection of hardware, software and wetware, on the contrary, is always tied to the regional particularities of the culture. The techno-cultures on the various continents cannot and need not move in synchrony. In techno-culture on a global scale there is no longer talk of an edge over others. From the point of view of hybrid practice, the differences among the United States, Europe, and Asia are not so great. Differences exist only if one assumes that only media experiments done with the latest high tech are interesting. But high tech is also the waste product of the military-industrial complex and its corporations. A select group of electronic artists is allowed access only with their approval. The mixers of high and low are not bootlickers, and they accept the waste character of technology.

The figure of the data dandy falls under Adilkno's category of "potential media figures." In the Media Archive, a series of potential media and potential media figures are collected under the denominator of "Unidentified Theory Objects" (UTOs). These compact texts are purely speculative. Adilkno does not practice media archaeology, hermeneutics, media criticism, or cultural studies. The genre of Adilkno, the media text, describes no reality or ideas outside the text. Its material is the media itself—not the equipment or programs, but their possibilities. In the electro-sphere there exists a multiplicity of potential media and media figures. Their present or future existence is indefinite, though it can definitely be tested. The insight the media text yields about them is irresponsibly rash. The media text speculates with chance, danger, dream and nightmare. It challenges potential media to become real—in the first place, in the media text itself. It provokes language into taking on these forms. Potential media exist only as options, but once they are described you run across them everywhere. This also holds for the data dandy. Although Adilkno members emphatically deny being data dandies, or propagating any similar decadent, outmoded, postmodern consumerism, many people claim to have data dandies in their circles of friends and this notion is difficult to counter.

After Adilkno's first book, the psychoanalytic film analysis *The Empire of Images* (1984), *Cracking the Movement—Squatting Beyond the Media* appeared in 1990. It describes the 1980s squatters' movement in Amsterdam and shows how the many big street riots in 1980 and 1981 turned into an advanced, subtle game with the media.

The city could be read—and manipulated—as a system of signs. A radical mix-up of the urban and the virtual. *Movement Teachings*, the original Dutch title, proposed that in the beginning there were only overwhelming "events." The pattern that people discovered later was called a "movement." "In the beginning was the event. Time was compressed, space concentrated into one point—and a metamorphosis took place. Movement is born out of this first impulse. It seeks a way to consolidate the last stage of transformation, to give it substance." But a movement cannot metamorphose; it can only go on: "It lacks the mobility to easily become something else. It will endlessly branch off, get stuck, scheme, resprout, be exploited, write about itself, see itself on film."

Media are never just tools you can work with at will. The transformation of an original rage and subversion into information is a painful process. The crystallization of a movement is accompanied by fragmentation, selection and exclusion. Once taken up into the media sphere, the now virtual movement can never again return to street level, however hard it tries to force its way back via the staging of spectacles. In *Cracking the Movement* Adilkno speculatively divides the reaction to the mediatization of the squatters' movement into three strategies: the anti-media movement, the extramedial, and sovereign media.

Being "anti-media" is on the one hand a widespread phenomena, while on the other there is hardly anything written about this attitude. "There are individuals who have undergone the extramedial experience and are left upon return with an immense anger. They experience being turned into information as an assault on their lives. They go on the offensive. The anti-media movement they unleash fights hard, but wants nothing to do with powers that oppose the freedom of the press. They demand that democracy breaks its ties with the media. They do their part by literally cutting the connections. Not out of fear of contact, but for the chance to meet someone again. The antimedians wrestle with the problem of how to meet others without bringing the media into play." Riots, raves, and other temporary autonomous experiences grow out of the desire to share directly, without mediation. In certain cases media have to be literary abandoned.

In the 1990s many squatters have renounced belief in any media, their own included. The realization that all information, including one's own, is subject to media laws and is just one part of a gigantic selection, has resulted in a healthy media relativism. Autonomists no longer wish to justify or express themselves. Squatters move from one house to the next like nomads and no longer believe in defending a place with words and bricks. Information as such has no healing or subversive properties. People no longer harbor the expectation that others will be "turned around" simply by reading a pamphlet or manifesto. Although the radical refusal of new technologies as instruments of control over humanity has largely disappeared, skeptical pragmatism is widespread.

Hakim Bey writes about this in similar terms in his essay on Temporary Autonomous Zones. Opposite the net, he places the Counter-Net and the Unofficial Web, which consists of "the marginal zine network, the BBS networks, pirated software, hacking, phone phreaking, some influence in print and radio and almost none in the big media." The TAZ exists in information space as well as in the "real world." But "the web does not depend for its existence on any computer technology. Word of mouth, mail, the marginal zine network, "phone trees" and the like are sufficient to construct an information webwork. The key is not the brand or level of tech involved, but the openness and horizontality of the structure."[3]

The TAZ, according to Hakim Bey, is not out to simulate resistance or to resist spectacularly. "The TAZ desires above all to avoid mediation, to experience its existence as immediate. The very essence of the affair is 'breast-to-breast,' as the Sufis say, or face-to-face." The TAZ cannot be for or against technology; it does not wish to be utopian or nostalgic. "Because TAZ is an intensification, a surplus, an excess, a potlatch, life spending itself rather than merely surviving, it cannot be defined either by Tech or anti-Tech." Hakim Bey no longer believes in well-intentioned anti-information spread via the radical networks. "Frankly, I already had plenty of data to enrich my perception." What he wants is "marvelous secrets." "Most of all I want computers to provide me with information linked to real goods—'the good things in life.'"

Adilkno's second strategy is an enigmatic category, about which there is little to say: the extra-medial. "Extramedial figures view painful wrestling with the media issue with something like pity. When asked to participate, they don't answer. They do not wish to be spoken to. They appear to live in another universe. They are occupied with all kinds of things, but their purpose remains invisible through the media lens. They seem never to know what they want. But this dismissive attitude is not merely indifference. They are intently concentrating on 'the right thing'; their silence comes from this. They answer only unasked questions. Their attention is focused on the approach of an event. And when the time comes, they are the ones who move into action without hesitating. Then they are together in extramedial space. Metamorphosis occurs."[4]

The third alternative is that of sovereign media. Recognizing and living with the media's omnipotence does not always lead one to happy destructivism. The laborious strategy of anti-publicity or total absence can be avoided. Instead of being employed in an alternative way, the media can be raised to ecstatic heights. This, the media's supreme self-experience, has passed the stage of information absorption and transmission and left for a long journey to the bottom of the media archives. In the description of Adilkno, sovereign media seek no connection: they disconnect. "They leave the media surface and orbit the multimedia network as satellites." Not in order to silence others or shut up themselves, but to fully indulge into "becoming media." The point is to cause media effects without references to an outside world. This is achieved through sovereign media. "[Unlike the] anti media movement, which is based on a radical critique of capitalist (art) production, the sovereign media have alienated themselves from the entire business of politics and the art scene. An advanced mutual disinterest hampers any interaction. They move in parallel worlds which do not interfere with each other. No anti-information or criticism, politics, or art is produced in order to start up a dialogue with the authorities. Once sovereign, media are no longer attacked but tolerated and of course, ignored. But this lack of interest is not a result of disdain for hobbyist amateurism or political infantilism; it is the contemporary attitude towards any image or sound that is bestowed on the world." (Adilkno 1998, p. 13)

After five years of devotion—with great pleasure and abandon—to speculative media theory and potential media figures such as the data dandy, Adilkno began acting as if the media lost dynamism. The introductory phase had approached its epiphany. It was time to design exit strategies by injecting large doses of artificial pessimism into ones own discourse.[5] Negative dialectics 2.0 used as a tool for anti-cyclic thought. Instead of riding the net hype, Adilkno opted for the position of non-participation, choosing not to formulate a critique of instrumental utopianism. *Ideologiekritik* was supposed to be merely *Begleitmuzik*, softening the painful transitions necessary for the implementation of new technologies. Radical gestures remained inside the pseudo-democratic "pro and contra" dichotomy. Instead, Adilkno installed itself in a distant meta position, beyond, or rather beside the raving spectacle around cyberspace.[6]

Rapid expansion of the media universe comes with an implosion of the power of imagination. The media were once again "the others." While hordes of young businesspeople lap up the "digital revolution" and chase visions of a utopian world full of communication, the cultural situation in fact looks very different. Apart from the aggressive information elite (Arthur Kroker's "virtual class"), the intellectual climate took on a defensive character. People were preparing for "Cold War II" (or Jeltzin's "Cold Peace") and secretly looking forward to a new period of stability. They were prepared to accept its accompanying stagnation as part of the bargain. In retrospect, 1989 turns out not to have been a moment of liberation. For Westerners, Glasnost ultimately became synonymous with the deadly radioactive cloud of Chernobyl, solely out to destroy the health of Western Europeans (with actual victims out of reach from the Western radar systems in the Ukraine and Belarus).

Europeans have the greatest difficulty putting into words the current dialectic of construction and demolition which manifests itself around them. The last of public intellectuals are doing their best to characterize the post-1989 juncture, without succeeding. The amalgam of the war in former Yugoslavia, the strange new media, capitalism without an enemy, emerging Asian Tigers, grassroots neo-liberalism, the PR war around Shell's oil platform, The Brent Spar, French nuclear tests, foreigners and refugees, the devastation of Chechnya — it's all impossible to grasp anymore. Nietzsche would be laughing about Europe. He wouldn't be complaining about the impending loss of national identity or the power of the Brussels bureaucracy. He would look down disdainfully at the bumbling, pompous Euro citizens trying to side-step their own history. See here the mental state of Europe's roaring 1990s: one group believes it's arrived way into the 21st century as others are catapulted back a couple of centuries. What one sees as progress spells sheer destruction for another. They come and go on the screen. Scroll down, zap on. Developments are observed with worry but can no longer be associated with conclusions. But that's no longer necessary, for what occupies Europeans most of all is the development of one's own lifestyle. And no one is laughing at the little worries of the middle classes.

At the fall of the Berlin Wall, emotions were conspicuously scarce. Skepticism and disbelief prevailed, and the Eastern neighbors were met with a cool reception. Romanians' skeptical certainty in early 1990 that everything would stay the same could not be refuted, and is now generally accepted, even in the West. Old officers returned to the political stage with neo masks, as neo-communists, nationalists, or Thatcherite entrepreneurs. Their transformation caused decreased income, the break-down of social services, unemployment, radical privatization to the point of simple robbery, war, genocide and hatred. What is going on in the East in an extreme form (and at an increased speed) is happening on a similar scale in Western Europe too. An broad anti-war movement, as in the Vietnam era, a solidarity movement like the one for Nicaragua, or a peace movement like the one against nuclear weapons in the

early 1980s, seemed unimaginable. Western pacifism was a hopeless, uninformed gesture.[7] It proved hard in the case of Bosnia to identify with any of the communities
involved. Wars in the Balkan did not fit into the simple logic of politically correct
activists. In a strictly medial sense Western citizens remain observers, letting in complex information from the Wild East according to an ecological media diet so as not
to be further numbed. The danger of data obesity is immediate. Zappers and surfers
see themselves as victims, if not of events, of information, which has been set before
them every day for years. Everyone is in the race for the most-favored-victim status.

In Adilkno's later writings, the concept of media is no longer used as a dumpster
where all fantasies are deposited and retrieved. The media is seen as a part of broader
set of cultural industries such as tourism, shopping, sport, commerce and sex. For
Europeans, the abstract media sphere is not merely a consumable product but part of
the realm of culture. Though the ideology of the market is raging, the media remain
part of a metaphysical terrain, where Western "culture" is thought to be located.
However in contrast to the (still?) open concept of "media," which (if we follow
Friedrich Kittler) has mainly a technical connotation, the concept of "culture" plays a
crucial role in the dominant ideology of the West, one which is gaining in importance,
and in which rightist-elitist notions are mainstreamed into a collision of tele-
evangelism and tele-communion. The West German pop theorist Mark Terkessidis,
formerly of the monthly *SPEX*, shows in his book *Kulturkampf* (1995) that the oft-cited
"swing to the right" is playing out mainly in the sphere of "culture."

According to media makers and intellectuals, social conflicts are no longer economical or ideological, but cultural. As in American conservative Samuel Huntington's
*The Clash of Civilizations* (1993), the West must defend itself as a "minority." The supposed "cultural hegemony" of the left-liberal 1968 generation in the media, in schools
and in universities must be broken, especially in the area of (national) culture. There is
a harkening back, says Terkessidis, to the late 18th century German romantic Herder,
who defined culture in defensive terms, as an ethnic identity which only really fulfills

itself in the exclusion of others. As black rappers rediscover their own culture, Europeans must rediscover their "Eurocentrism." "The ideology of culture, with its blend of symbolization, lifestyle and ethnicity, offers the perfect paradigm for exclusion." And that is what "purified ethnocentrism" seeks: protection from Third World refugees, immigrants, Islam, and last but not least, the first full-scale war in Europe since 1945, in which everything revolves around the definition of ethnicity. According to Terkessides it is a mistake to consider culture as an issue of power, as was done in the 1970s and 1980s. He even suspects a "deal" between the establishment and its erstwhile critics: "If you'll let us govern in peace and stop bringing up the power question, then you can have culture." The result of this transformation of politics into cultural lifestyles was that "cultures" were no longer seen in their social context. Even "subversion" and "autonomy" ran aground in the early 1990s, with the option of armed struggle long forgotten (to such an extend that former terrorists could take up high profile jobs and re-appear as historical bohemian icons).

The strategy of "confusion, ambiguity and spectacle" still works, but political content is no longer discernible in it, as is the case with techno, ambient and jungle. "Independent" thought has ended in "self-satisfaction, stripped of any consequence." Postmodern strategies of difference, heterogeneity and complexity resulted in a transformation of culture, of which one no longer knows what direction it is taking. Behind slogans like "Not right, not left, just culture," Terkessides sees a very nearly fascist Weltanschauung lurking, and reconstructs its intellectual history. He considers it necessary to place contemporary media culture in a "materialistic perspective," so that struggles on the terrain of culture, in music, multimedia, computer networks, and so on, are again placed in a social, political and economic context, without relinquishing culture's autonomy.

With no persuasive or significant successors to Guattari and Foucault, and with Parisian intellectuals getting more conservative by the day, there is a retrieval of neo-Marxism and its attempts in the 1970s to foreground "ideology critique." Since the mid 1980s, we have been seeing a return to precisely the kind of leftist theorizing which the "Parisians" tried to leave behind. Foucault's "non-fascistic practice" is no longer discussed. Derrida's project to save philosophy has run aground in an interminable defense of Heidegger. Paul Virilio is seen as an anti-media, worried deacon, a Catholic who has ended up in his own "raging stillness." People find his radical critique of cyberspace and the net merely excessive. They see the net as an enrichment and can only imagine what Virilio meant by a "disturbance in the perception of what is reality." And if the Gulf War did not take place, then Jean Baudrillard no longer exists either (after Baudrillard's "No reprieve with Sarajevo," there is "No reprieve with Paris"). Terkessides identifies a "void in which people seem to consent to everything."

It is precisely this empty space which Adilkno is investigating. It is tempting to suspect an extreme-right, reactionary body of thought behind this void, in which "culture" has replaced "race." Terkessides dwells at elaborate length on the anti-parliamentarian legal philosopher Carl Schmitt and his influence on the contemporary conservative elite in Germany. Adilkno makes do for the moment without such a constructed, imaginary enemy, such as "new right" thinkers. Adilkno concerns itself with the following artifacts: almost-engagement, advanced disinterest, touching vagueness, cold passions, the fun of meaninglessness, advanced confusion, the colors of boredom, the out-of-context, electronic solitude, IKEA as cultural ideal and collective forms of disappointment. We see an ascending ideal of a society without ideas, with a "net without qualities." Here, "comfort" has become a human right and one delegates as much as possible to professionals in order to be rid of bother. There was amateurism enough in the twentieth century! The split between success and failure has arrived in the social sciences and cultural criticism, as is apparent in the following fragment from "The Society of the Debacle," Adilkno's ode to the Parisian media theorist Guy Debord (Adilkno 1998, p. 147):

> After a fascination with Evil in the 1980s, we are now in the midst of an interest in
> Failure. We no longer read about Seduction, Simulation, Perfection, Glamour and

Passion as pure self-expression. Evil had to snuff out all the Good of the 1960s, and it succeeded smashingly (cf. the breakthroughs of 1989). But then something else happened. The triumph of the dialectic, the historical synthesis of market and democracy, did not occur, and not even a new anti-thesis could be found. Good Socialism rightly gave way to the Capitalism of Failure. The system and its slaves underwent a revaluation of all values, and meanwhile nothing has changed. An indefinable situation in which nobody bothers any longer to put into words the World or the own Ego (or anything related to these). Chaos rules, and this does not lend itself to unlawful visualization. Timeless struggle takes place in the form of destructive private enterprise amid rotting cement and bankrupt government structures. The heroic radiance of the declaimed end of history is missing. The society of the spectacle has plunged us unexpectedly into the Society of the Debacle.

We can learn from Guy Debord. A heathen faith in new media, project management, surveillance, flexible scheduling, retraining, improvisation, image, and identity is the tried and true method of introducing new technologies. In the beginning there is amazement that all the strange machines and concepts function. But once they start to become widespread and really work, attention shifts to the moments at which the technologies fail, and they are written off. Once grounded in the realm of normalcy, any cyber technology loses its sparkle and has to be routinely usable. Once hardware and software begin to fail, the consumer's rage turns against the Machine and its makers. How lovely to unleash your Rage and throw all the malfunctioning machines out the window into the street en masse! Grunge and generation niX have mobilized the authenticity of elementary failure against the lycra sheen of revoked success. The breakthrough of stagnation is the surprising turn history has taken since 1989. As long as the end of progress was being announced, nothing happened. But Fukuyama the liberation philosopher couldn't foresee that bungling would get the upper hand. To be sure, self-organizing principles like chaos, artificial life, fractals, the Internet, complexity, Biosphere II, and turbulence are moving optimistically forward, but they will get stuck in their advertising hype. No consequential cancerous metastasis will be achieved — these things will remain models. Failure, on the contrary, is in principle not a model, nor a strategy. In this respect it distinguishes itself from everything that the 1980s provided in the way of ideas. Failure is not a fate: fate approaches from outside, while fiasco comes from within, impossible to program in advance. The inherent disappointment which unfolds is not a bug that can be removed from the program. In the age of over organization and a social surplus of experience, success thinking has got bogged down in flop prevention. They tried to redefine failure as an educative moment, but Philips' CD-I, nuclear power, the hasty reunification of Germany, peace in Europe . . . they were all strong concepts, lacking nothing in persuasive power, and yet went nowhere.

In order to survive one dons a mental armor. The protection against the world is no longer a sexual armor, as described by Klaus Theweleit in his monumental *Male Fantasies*, but an inconspicuous set of behaviors and precepts bent on avoiding all warm passions, a refined method and technique for dealing with "reality overload." For Europe, failure is not the opposite of success. Mild forms of crisis and stagnation are becoming the natural state of affairs. The upholding of major catastrophes such as dictatorship and world war is the actual achievement and the true aim of intergovernmental bodies such as the European Union. The Christian concept of warding off the Apocalypse, theorized by negative theologists such as Jacob Taubes, is of importance in this context, describing the forces that withhold the Apocalypse, suspending the arrival of the Final Day and the choice between heaven and hell, utopia and barbarism. In the act of warding off, both the fear and fascination for the End is being tempered. This results into a culture of relaxed stagnation, no longer obsessed with the higher, disastrous aims of enlightenment. In an Adilkno essay the dominant European mentality of limited expectations is labeled "organized innocence": a phenomenon mirroring "organized crime," and one which just as invisibly embodies modern-day Evil. Another lengthy quote from Adilkno's essay "Contemporary Nihilism—On Innocence Organized" (Adilkno 1998, p. 165):

> The middle was no longer a class which strove for an historic goal, such as revolution or fascism; it had arrived in a cold period, henceforth to be without passions. While outside it stormed and change followed change with alarming speed, one put one's

own life in "park." Without regard to history, fashion, politics, sex and the media, time could take its course. The innocent caused no problems, indeed they hated problems. "Just let things take their course." Regular folks considered themselves cogs in a larger whole, and all in all they were unashamed of it. They made sure the trains ran on time and turned homeward in the evening for a hot meal. In place of old barriers like caste, sex and religion, innocence brought in conversation-killers like tolerance, openness and harmony. Positivism became a way of life. Positive criticism served the reconstruction of politics and culture. One enjoyed oneself, was dynamically busy and had plenty of work to do. The picture of reality was simple and clear. The innocents did not embody the Good, they simply had no plan, but nor did they lack a sense of values. They never got around to crime either. And so they unintentionally became the object for strategies of Good and Evil. We speak here of a life without drama, urgency, "decision." There will never be a close race. There need never be a decision. You needn't break away just to be yourself. As the Dutch say: act normal, that's crazy enough. Innocents thrive on the rituals of everyday; these make them happy. A broken washing machine can drive a person crazy: the thing should just work. The complaint against things is that they break down, falter, fall apart, act strange, and cannot be unobtrusively replaced. The promise of undisturbed consumption is that nothing will ever happen again. In this unproblematic existence comfort is so taken for granted that it goes unnoticed. The innocent consciousness is characterized by a narrow, small-scale thinking which calls forth a universe where personal irritations erupt at the least little thing: stoplights, traffic jams, late trains, red tape, bad weather, construction noise, illness, accidents, unexpected guests and events are a repeated assault on the innocent existence. One becomes involved nonetheless in matters which one had not been expecting. This disturbance-hating mentality, which devotes itself to work and career, shuts out all risk and has elevated practicality as its sole criterion. The ideal of a wrinkle-free, spotless life presumes, touchingly, that literally everyone is pursuing it. Innocence is under continuous treatment by the doctor, the therapist, the beauty specialist, the acupuncturist, the garage manager. Innocence likes to be tinkered with. It sees it as a duty to develop itself, and retrain itself if need be. One takes a course, attends a lecture, visits the theatre, concert hall and exhibition, reads a book, follows the arrows on a walk in the woods, engages in muscle sports. Innocence is a universal human right which extends to animals, plants, buildings, landscapes and cultures. This is the condition under which the planet can finally still be saved: neither utopian nor fatalistic, but functioning normally. You can lose your innocence by committing murder, indulging in a little S/M, joining a motorcycle club, choosing art, or going undercover, but the entertainment underworld offers no solace. Only the crossing over to war and genocide is still an option that we hear much about. Yet there's no escaping the agglomeration and its dictates. Mountain bikes, cool t-shirts, clever children's clothes, computer games, graffiti, bumper stickers, sloppy sportswear, brightly colored backpacks, hair gel: these are the objets nomades of Jacques Attali's Europe, on its way to a stylized uniformity. Innocence cannot be neutralized or counterbalanced by its opposite. The only thing it cannot stand is the spoiling of the atmosphere. This rotting process within normalcy offers no alternative, commits no resistance and performs no act. And innocence finds it exhausting. One can't always be fresh and cheerful and sweep away the fog with constructive thinking. Innocence is in no danger of being wiped out by revolution or reaction. It can only decline, sink into poverty and slowly disappear from the picture. In a stagnating relationship one drags up a trash container, dumps the accumulated innocence in it, rebuilds the interior and makes a fresh, wild new start.

This is post-1989 theory, made in Europe, during the first part of the wars in former Yugoslavia (1991–1995). In Zagreb, Sarajevo, Tuzla and Belgrade people bravely try to join in, desperately believing that they are part of Europe. "Bosnians imagined that the fact they were Europeans would protect them from the horrors of war," writes David Rieff in his book *Slaughterhouse: Bosnia and the Failure of the West* (1995). For the Bosnians, Europe "was a continent on which the cosmopolitan values they stood for had become the norm." The Bosnians believed the end of communism would be succeeded by a "dull and pacifying age of consumerism." According to Rieff this led to a "cognitive dissonance," a "misunderstanding of their historical situation," a mental state which remained present in Sarajevo well into 1992, when the war broke out, and that still goes for the rest of Europe. The citizens of former Yugoslavia could not believe that the "CNN effect" would not occur in their case. They waited in vain for a live broadcast of the arrival of a rapid intervention force, come to set them free. Rieff: "People routinely speak of information and knowledge as if they were the same thing. Worse, they console themselves with the thought that once they have relevant information, they will act." Instead, "the sound bites and 'visual bites' culled bred casuistry and indifference." Rieff acknowledges that the debate is long over now. "The West chose to do anything but intervene." It chose, on the contrary, "to contain the crisis," anticipating the post destruction Cold War II paradigm that an imposed stagnation produces positive effects. The West did not want to save the Bosnian Muslims. After he has witnessed a genocide, Europe is for Rieff no longer a "civilized place. The defeat is total, the disgrace complete." The question is, why did even this message fail to get through, 50 years after Hiroshima and Auschwitz? For the first time the mental armor of the Europeans triumphed over the daily bombardment of information. According to Slavoj Zizek, the Balkans are "a new projection for Western fantasies, based on the nature of the Balkans." They are an imaginary glacis for the defense of a culture, full of communication and global dreams.

With whom could the average Westerner identify? With no broad anti-war movement, oppositional culture in former Yugoslavia is completely left to itself. The only thing that counts anymore is survival. In the long absence of political confrontations, the rage against the war machine expresses itself in a vital, ironic, high-grade cynicism. Not a nonchalant indifference; rather a form of stylized despair. The survival artists in Belgrade, Sarajevo, and Zagreb are averse to purism and every expression of political correctness comes across as foolish pettiness. It is not a protest which begs for sympathy or solidarity. The help offered by international organizations causes consolidation rather than breakthrough and offers no prospect of liberation from oppressive and dismal nationalism. In a situation in which all parties define themselves as victims it makes no sense to identify with this or that group. Once involved one automatically arrives in a gray zone. One becomes part of the black market, smokes homegrown pot, sells relief goods, is ruined by cheap heroin, or finally manages to escape to Paris, London, New York, or Amsterdam.

On the scene we become acquainted with the techno-existentialism of the few who have stayed behind. They no longer need bid farewell to modernism, as Western post-modernism has believed for decades it must do. The dominant discourse is indifferent to attempts at deconstruction and merely leaves the intellectuals to muddle on. Their supposed power is a ancient history. The minuscule opposition, which maintains itself under the yoke of repressive tolerance in the shadow of power, expresses itself in a number of "independent media." By this is meant merely that they are not property of the state or under direct influence of the governing party, which in the former Eastern Bloc is already quite a feat. Just as in Western Europe, the subculture has its own radio stations and weeklies, organizes techno parties, makes videos, posters, rock and roll and theater, and communicates via faxes and computer networks. Technologically speaking, the lag behind the West is remarkably small. New hardware and software get around with lightning speed and in this respect there is scarcely a difference any-more in Europe between a Western center and a periphery in the South and East. An example could be the Zamir computer network with almost 2000 users, providing email contact between cities like Pristina, Belgrade, Zagreb, Tuzla, and Ljubljana during the troublesome period 1992–1995. Mail was sent and received several times a day with traffic running through a server in former West Germany (Bielefeld). Hundreds of users reached nearby capitals and the rest of the world from Sarajevo by email, and anti-war groups from Zagreb and Belgrade maintained contact through the network.[8] Also worth mentioning is the well designed underground magazine *Arkzin*, published in Zagreb with a unique mix of political journalism, pop culture and con-temporary theory. There are several free radio stations in Skopje. The galaxy of inde-pendent media in Belgrade is chapter in itself. There is the weekly *Vreme* and the radio station B92.[9] Radio ZID broadcasts the sounds of the opposition in Sarajevo, criticiz-ing the Bosnian government. There is the independent Albanian weekly *Koha*, published in Pristina despite heavy Serbian repression of the Albanian majority in the province of Kosovo. Here, in "Old Serbia," President Milosevic's media campaign began in 1989 —a stroke of propaganda many see as the fatal beginning of the war. Milosevic was an expert in controlling state media and manipulating them in order to stay in power. These included several influential newspapers and the national radio and TV channels, which could be received everywhere, especially in the backward countryside, in contrast to the independent media with their inadequate distribution. In Croatia the situation was the same, and in Bosnia-Herzegovina too, with the party of Izetbegovic having authority over radio and television. Even the heroic daily paper *Oslobodenje* cannot be spoken of as completely independent. To support opposition from the West, it was first of all necessary, as Slavoj Zizek called for, to make one's own power analysis of the Balkans, one which is based on history and which views the role of the media in correct proportions.[10] It will also be necessary to make a clean sweep of the UN's quasi-neutrality and the Europeans' humanitarian aid, the slow non-intervention force. One would also have to ridicule the 19th-century diplomacy and the half-hearted support of one of the warring sides. Now that the war has acquired its own dynamic, we must not overestimate the power of the media. The "independent media" were not able to bring down the ruling tribes. At most, they were—and still are—germs of a post-political movement of the skeptical generation which has had enough of hatred, robbery and genocide. They are no longer breeding grounds for dissidents with clear-cut principles. European innocence must be conquered, the crippling identity of victimhood pushed aside, with relaxed stagnation as the best possible outcome. "Stability and cooperation" installing a long-term Brussels regime of uneasy boredom, a remote rule, so well known in the "region" from the Austro-Hungarian and Ottoman periods, which ended only less then a century ago. If, as Arthur Kroker maintains, in the new Europe, with its new, invisible, electronic warfare, everything is about "the bitter division of the world into virtual flesh and surplus flesh," then it is up to the independent media like *Zamir*, B92, and *Arkzin* to ridicule this split and, in an ironic manner, to give shape to their own local version of the universal desire towards cyberspace. B92's phrase "Don't trust anyone, not even us" could be modified: "Don't trust the Internet, and especially not our web site."[11]

## <Notes>

1. This chapter, in part, consists of lectures held at two ISEA conferences, one in Helsinki (August 1994) and one in Montreal (September 1995), both translated from Dutch by Laura Martz. "The Datadandy and Sovereign Media, An Introduction to the Media Theory of Adilkno" was published in *ISEA 94*, Proceedings, Helsinki, 1994, and in *Leonardo* 30, no. 1, 1997, pp. 57–65. "Organized Innocence and the War in the New Europe, On Electronic Solitude and Independent Media" was published in *Culture @nd Technology in the New Europe, Civil Discourse in Transformation in Post-Communist Nations*, ed. Laura Lengel (Ablex, 2000); it was published under the same title in the Proceedings of the 6th International Symposium of Electronic Art, Montreal, 1996. It appeared first in ZP Proceedings 95, Net Criticism, ed. nettime.

2. Quotes from Adilkno 1994. Online version: http://thing.desk.nl/bilwet or www.desk.org/bilwet.

3. Quotes from Bey 1992.

4. The category of the extramedial goes back to work of Adilkno member Arjen Mulder, who in 1991 published a book titled *Het Buitenmediale* in which he mainly used examples from literature. This body of thought then got used within the context of media theory in the Adilkno essay "The Extramedial, The Media Archive." More elaborations can be found in Arjen Mulder's two other studies, both in Dutch: his general media theory "Het twintigste-eeuwse lichaam" ["The Twentieth Century Body"] (1996) and a study on digital photography, "Het fotografisch genoegen" ["The Photographic Delight"] (2000).

5. The Adilkno essays after the Dutch and German editions of *The Media Archive* (1993–1997) were published (in German, under the name of Agentur Bilwet) as *Elektronische Einsamkeit* (Supposé Verlag, 1998), with an audio CD, *1000 Fehler*, published in 1999

(www.suppose.de). Most of the material is included in the English, Croatian, and Slovenian translations of *The Media Archive*.

6. The genealogy of this position can be traced back to early-1980s readings of Jean Baudrillard and Paul Virilio mixed with Antonio Negri and German magazines such as *Radikal* (1982–1984) and *Autonomie* (in particular, no. 13, 1983). Another source in this context could be Detlef Hartmann's critique of technological violence, *Die Alternative—Leben als Sabotage, Zur Krise der technologischen Gewalt* (Aktiv-Druck, 1981). What these diverse authors share is a call for disengagement with technology as such.

7. As an example of pacifist Balkan incompetence, see Slavoj Zizek referring to a debate on Austrian television between a Serb, an Albanian, and an Austrian pacifist in *Did Somebody Say Totalitarianism?* (Verso, 2001), pp. 234–236.

8. See "Zamir: Paul Stubbs, Conflict and Co-operation in the Virtual Community: Email and the Wars of the Yugoslav Succession," *Sociological Research Online* 3, no. 3 (1998) (http://www.socresonline.org.uk/socresonline/3/3/7.html).

9. For a history of the radio station B92, see Matthew Collin, *Serbia Calling, Rock 'n' Roll Radio and Belgrade's Underground Resistance* (Serpent's Tail, 2001).

10. Slavoj Zizek, interview with Geert Lovink, in InterCommunication 14 (NTT, 1995) (http://www.ntticc.or.jp/pub/ic_mag/ic014/zizek/zizek_e.html). For the first English version, see *Digital Delirium* , ed. A. and M. Kroker (St. Martin's Press, 1997). See also Slavoj Zizek, "Caught in Another's Dream in Bosnia," in *Why Bosnia?* ed. R. Ali and L. Lifschultz (Pamphleteers Press, 1993) (http://www.bard.edu/hrp/zizekessay.htm).

11. Arthur and Marilouise Kroker, "Windows on What?" (http://www.ctheory.com/event/e019.html). For an interview with Arthur Kroker, see http://www.wired.com/wired/archive/4.02/leftists.html. See also Arthur Kroker and Michael Weinstein, "The Political Economy of Virtual Reality," http://eserver.org/cyber/kroker.txt.

# Soros and the NGO Question, or The Art of Being Independent

A fear is spreading throughout Eastern Europe: the creeping, existential angst of being possessed and ruled by new, unknown forces.[1] For some, the dragon is called Brussels, NATO, the New World Order. For others it's neo-liberalism, the stock market, "Asia," globalization.

George Soros incorporates them all. He is the Hungarian-American pupil of Karl Popper, retired hedge-fund manager, billionaire turned philanthropist and founder of the Soros Foundation network.[2] The Soros network is investing heavily in education, media, culture and arts and it's hard to avoid him if you happen to work in one of these sectors. Who can afford to criticize Soros in a society with no alternative funding?

In circles of media activists and electronic artists there is acute sensitivity towards emergent institutional powers. Active groups and individuals on the edge (and the margins) of Media Related Creativity are vulnerable to new economic and political formations.[3] Temporary, freelance workers are both inside and outside of the culture industry. Within the world of foundations, everyone becomes either client or donor. There are only few permanent staff members. This makes institutional critique in Eastern Europe a rather ambivalent, dangerous activity. Everyone is in, and out, at the same time. This is causing a general feeling of uncertainty and a strong pressure to behave in an orderly politically correct matter. But who is defining what is correct and what's not, in this world of foundations and small companies were no one has been voted into office, yet have considerable power over the lives of a growing amount of project-dependent workers?

The Western critique of large size capitalist and state structures from the perspective of small groups has been well known for decades. In the past it was easy to critique Shell, MoMa, the Ministry of Culture, the Telecom and McDonald's. The lines were clear in such cases. These days the threat is more and more coming from within, without clear front lines. Power can be located anywhere. That's the popular legacy of post-structuralism. Michel Foucault for Dummies: in every friend hides a traitor; all activism is poisoned by the Will to Power and is determined, no matter how radical or honest, to betray the cause. For some power is located in the body, for others it is the media sphere, transnational capital, surveillance technology, the military entertainment complex, state subsidies, television, trade unions, religious sects, the police, or all of these at the same time. The process of simultaneous fragmentation and centralization leaves us with a blurred picture. In this stage of confusion, surrounded by a multitude of power relations, where does the old fashioned figure of Wall Street currency speculator fit in? Does critique need a clear object anyway, an artificial, imaginary focus?

Current technologies make it difficult to be fully autonomous, particularly if you are working with computers. No one has all the necessary skills combined in one person. It is next to impossible to update software, equipment and experience in all the different media. The rise of the net will only make its users only more dependent on outside forces such as bandwidth, service and software providers. With complexity and interdependency on the rise, one materialization from this landscape is the decentralized, networked, cost-effective office culture of the non-governmental organization (NGO). The first time I heard a critique of an NGO it was the case of Greenpeace. With my own eyes I had seen this organization become a megalomaniac structure of bureaucratic do-gooders. They were one of the first to "professionalize," leaving behind the more indirect and blurry tactics of the ecological movement, a charming universe of micro-initiatives which to a "communications/managerial expert" would seem lacking clear direction. As an NGO, Greenpeace was ready to deal with the governmental organizations. The professionals within Greenpeace set up a chain of branches, raised memberships, organized "campaigns" and specialized in spectacular, advertising-like media interventions while the main work was done by "volunteers." At the February 2001 World Economic Forum (WEF) in Davos, Greenpeace and other "global leaders" in the NGO sector such as Amnesty International and the World Wide Fund for Nature (WWF) were invited to discuss the direction of globalization with their business counterparts. With demonstrators outside protesting against the WEF agenda, the division between established NGOs (admired for their "web marketing expertise"—see www.ft.com) and the so-called anti-globalization activists outside, accused of violence, came to the surface.

The early NGO critiques focused on high overhead costs and salaries, internal power struggles and the misuse of funds collected by the innocent, well-meaning middle class citizenry. This process took place inside the ecological movement throughout the 1980s, and soon this managerial "corporate" approach would reach all "independent" organizations dealing with arts, culture and politics. But then the Berlin Wall fell and numerous NGOs moved into Eastern Europe, created from this "corporate-style" model. There it became really visible what the NGO was in essence all about. They are a response to downsized governments, replacing old bureaucracies while creating new ones, a process typical to the post-ideological global times. A new European saying goes like this: "We no longer work for the Party, we work for the Organization." In Western Europe NGO critique never really took off—or at least not up to this moment. The autonomous movements of the 1970s and 1980s were falling apart and their remains had turned into small NGOs themselves, even the most radical and dogmatic ones. The long march to become an Organization. These past and present political strategists tend not to focus on the organizational forms of the "struggle." What counted was, and still does, the debate around the use of violence (against buildings, police, corporations, computer networks). The same can be said of the arts and culture sectors where certain bureaucratic formulas have been spreading throughout the 1980s and 1990s without much questioning of their ideological nature.

With the Organization comes a specific kind of office management style, book keeping, social code and media strategy imported from the United States into Western Europe (and later in the East). With it comes a specific IKEA style of interior decoration and furniture: a neutral, clean, healthy, light work environment. Professional and stylish, nothing pompous. The Organization wants us to send faxes, letters, and emails and fill out applications. It wants you to have meetings with them and share in the gossip. The way of dealing with the world seems so completely self-evident, according to their rules. This "naturalization" makes it difficult to see its specific shape and program. Do you also have friends who are "playing office"? As far as I know no anthropologist has yet written about this modern set of behavior patterns. It is certainly more complicated than the mid 20th century gender drama of the boss and his secretary. Project-driven flexibility in these work places makes it hard to speak of an "office culture" in the first place. A fascinating dialectics of boredom and excitement, and of emptiness and stress is at work here.

Let's draw a line and make a difference between the two neighboring models, the "movement" and the "corporation." The NGO, of course, positions itself in between those two concepts. The movement is unpredictable, diverse, without formal leadership, a temporary social network, full of informal structures and unexpected side events. Today, movements are even more fluid than in the past. They do not seem to last longer than a couple of months. For an outsider, they look like spasmodic uprisings, while underneath there are strong currents of cultural, media driven tribes, only noticeable to the connoisseur. Movements need to gather in space as physical collections of bodies otherwise they can't exist. There are no virtual movements (yet). In times of ongoing government budget cuts in arts, culture and social services, starting your own company—so as not to rely on subsidies and grants—is constructed to appear an attractive and truly independent option. These days there is always an economic element in political work. This is even more so the case in culture. The corporate model is in essence not so much bad as it is alien to the non-profit world of the late cold war period. It seems to be an unavoidable option to turn your work into a business operation. Some work can be turned profitably, but others simply can't—and the process to find which is and which isn't is a painful one. The reality of the NGO business model is based on a steady increase of the amount of funders. Instead of having one money source, gradually organizations have to apply for five or ten grants to maintain the same budget.

Most activist NGOs are building on movements while run like businesses. Everyone takes the standard glossy corporate image for granted (the dictatorship of design). Like any corporation NGOs have their logo printed on letters and envelops. They build up their brand name with stickers and t-shirts and adds in the papers. Without a legal structure, a bank account, letterhead and an office address an NGO is truly non-existent. This even counts for virtual operations on the Internet. Turning your efforts into a business has some advantages, in terms of the possible redistribution of wealth, but it is also producing a lot of envy, anger and resentment (for those who have to do it, and for those surrounding it), mainly because there is no acceptable alternative in sight. Friends turn into clients or employees. Who's in and who's out? Why is there suddenly a board taking control? Why should this or that person turn out to be the chair(wo)man/CEO and then even starts acting as such?

There is no radical critique of NGOs as cultural organizations.[4] There is only jealousy, bad feelings and old friendships being destroyed. It is the unwritten, unreported NGO reality. The price of switching to other scales and circles, and possible "success" (and some very temporary and virtual influence) is high. In most East European countries there is little to choose, not much to contemplate about.

In Eastern Europe the subcultural undercurrents of the late 1980s did not establish themselves as money-making operations, and dissolved over the years. A small scale alternative economy, like in Northwest Europe was not a real option, mainly because there was not enough cash circulating. Initiatives were too small, too weak to immediately turn themselves into viable companies. Without being part of an oppositional or subcultural movement, the NGO style of dealing with the world appeared to be the only one left. The Soros Foundation turned out to be the most important funding body of the 1990s, particularly in the field of culture, education and media. Each of the 15 East European countries has its own offices, media programs, support structures for universities, grants for students, health initiatives, contemporary arts funding, etc. The Soros NGOs are the prime promoters of the professional non-profit institution. George Soros (in Soros et al. 1995): "The foundations had to become more professional. It is a change I have had difficulty accepting. In the beginning I wanted to have an anti-foundation foundation and for a time I succeeded." But that's long ago. Now, most Soros officials are beginning to criticize their own monopolist position and rigid NGO structure.

To break the Soros near-monopoly, alternative models could to be developed, based on financial diversity. A Soros critique could start with a critique on the NGO model itself. Through the rejection of ritual professionalism we could then turn to specific Soros policies and examine them in detail. For example: the regional Internet program.[5] Within the Soros foundations there are dozens of different models (and failures) on how to work with the net. The most common problem is the "xs4us" policy, the "closed society" (versus the hackers model of xs4all: access for all). In Eastern Europe, Internet, provided by a Soros-sponsored NGO is mainly available for officials and "organizations," not for individuals. Here we get to the essence of the NGO ideology, not just operational within the Soros Foundation network. Civil society is reduced to a limited group of NGOs, operated according to Western models, in practice facilitating a professional managerial class. A considerable part of the budget is spend on expensive connectivity, money which cannot be invested in an independent culture of Internet providers to facilitate public access and local content.

A Soros critique would first of all be a (self) critique on the inability of West European society to deal with the tremendous changes after 1989. Why is there no British, French, or German philanthropist like Soros? Why are there no flexible, local

EU funding structures? The disagreement among the Europeans is an ongoing drama, costing thousands of lives throughout former Yugoslavia and elsewhere. Another problem for a radical Soros critique is his Jewish-Hungarian background. The only well publicized critiques are coming from the nationalist, anti-Semite far right: all kinds of conspiracy theories have erupted to do with the takeover of media and the stock market through "culture" by George Soros. The repeated attacks from the nationalist right has stopped all debate. There is the serious lack of information, particular in the West, on what Soros organizations are doing. The same can be said of Mahathir, the Malaysian ruler who blames George Soros for the Asian currency crisis in 1997. Who wants to be associated with him?

The few reports in Western newspapers only deal with Soros's financial strategies. The debate about Soros's critique on capitalism in the *Atlantic Monthly* (Soros 1997) has hardly any reference to the foundations and the work they do. Even his own interview book *Soros on Soros* is poor in this respect. One gets the sense that the interviewers he wrote this book with had never been to Eastern Europe, and this might also be the case for all the finance journalists who report on Soros. While discussing the flaws of global capitalism, George Soros's analysis is of a strictly of financial, economic and global political nature. The topic of strategies and forms of organizations are carefully avoided. His own involvement and policy directives concerning the role of NGOs in the creation of "civil societies" and the special role of the media, education and the Internet remains outside of the picture. Soros critics throughout Asia probably do not even know of the existence of a Soros network and the nature of its activities. This all prolongs the imagined monopoly of the Soros Foundation in Eastern Europe and increasingly elsewhere, such as Central Asia and Southern Africa. A gradual withdrawal from Eastern Europe, already under way, and a miraculous economic prosperity, combined with EU integration could change this situation. But that all might take another decade or might never happen with the arrival of "Cold War II." Trapped in a never ending process of "transition," the Long

Stagnation regions will need Soros to be around for the time being. This makes a cultural critique of NGOs, besides the political critique of "failed accountability," all the more important.[6]

## <Notes>

1. This is an edited version of an online contribution to the nettime debate on NGOs and the role of the network of Soros Foundations Networks in Eastern Europe, nettime, May 13, 1997. For more on this debate, see "The Moderation Question" in this volume.

2. See www.soros.org. Roughly speaking, the structure of the network consists of six parts: the national foundations (mainly in Eastern Europe, Central Asia and Southern Africa), network programs (Internet, education, women, arts and culture etc.), US programs (drugs policy, crime, Death in America, youth, etc.), the Central European University in Budapest, the separate Open Society Institute (OSI) offices and other initiatives such as the Burma project, a Belarus initiative, and a Roma program. The network spent 560 million US$ over 1999, from $300 million in 1994 and $575 million in 1997 (from: *Building Open Societies*, Soros Foundations Networks Network, 1999 Report).

3. This article can only refer to a tiny part of the Soros network. It has to be read as a personal case study, build on personal experience, having worked in Eastern Europe throughout the 1990s, in close proximity to the Soros Foundations Networks. To be more precise: the network of Soros Centers for Contemporary Arts (SCCA), once a program, set up by Suzy Mészöly, and then gradually integrated in the national foundations, the Internet program, ran out of New York by Jonathan Peizer, and in some cases the media program.

4. The few existing NGO studies, mainly from political scientists, focus on the role of NGOs in decision making and criticize the NGO sector for its unaccountability. See *Neue Soziale Bewegungen, Impulse, Bilanzen und Perspektiven*, ed. A. Klein et al. (Westdeutscher Verlag, 1999); *NGOs als Legitimitätsressource, Zivilgesellschaftliche Partizipationsformen im Globalisierungsprozeß*, ed. A. Brunnengräber et al. (Leske Budrich, 2001); *Vernetzt und Verstrickt, Nicht-Regierungsorganisationen als*

*gesellschaftliche Produktivkraft*, second edition, ed. E. Altvater (Westfälisches Dampfboot, 2000); Margaret Keck and Kathryn Sikkink, *Activists Beyond Borders: Advocacy Networks in International Politics* (Cornell University Press, 1998); Peter Wahl, "NGO-Multis, McGreenpeace und die Netzwerk-Guerilla. Zu einigen Trends in der internationalen Zivilgesellschaft," *Peripherie* 18 (1998), no. 71: 55–68 (English summary: nettime, February 5, 1999).

5. See http://www.soros.org/internet/index.html. For more on the policy of the Internet program, see an email exchange between Jonathan Peizer (the head of the program) and Geert Lovink, posted on nettime January 4, 1999. A shortened version was published as "The Ins and Outs of the Soros Internet Programme in Former Eastern Europe: An E-mail Exchange with Jonathan Peizer," in *New Media Culture in Europe*, ed. F. Boyd et al. (De Balie/Virtueel Platform, 1999).

6. To raise public attention for the position of NGOs, a debate was held during the third Next Five Minute conference (Amsterdam, March 1999). Among the participants were Steve Cisler, Saskia Sassen, Kevin Dowling, Thomas Keenan, and Adriene van Heteren. From the announcement: "NGOs are regularly represented at global eco-summits, they advise different UN institutions and are used as experts in court cases. Thus, NGOs are taking over tasks that traditionally were the domain of nation states, whether democratic or not. They become part of what Saskia Sassen has referred to as a 'crisis of governance,' in which political decision making and control is shifting away from national governments towards private and public NGOs of all sorts and types." The debate tried to formulate a constructive critique, pointing out the dangers and, at the same time, analysing creative and inspiring models for building NGOs. "After all, there is a continuing need for new, critical and independent organizations that are able to challenge the debilitating and exploiting political structures that stifle large parts of the world. And why not learn from the successes and failures of Saatchi & Saatchi, Soros, the IMF, financial consulting companies and informal networks of independent radio producers?" (www.n5m.org/n5m3)

# Information Warfare: From Propaganda Critique to Culture Jamming

I recently found a book in a secondhand book shop in Amsterdam, *The Information War* by an American journalist, Dale Minor, published in 1970.[1] He defines infowar as the "seldom physical but frequently bitter conflict between reporters and government officials" who both worked in Vietnam at the time. More specifically, he views this clash between journalists and the authorities as part of a broader and more profound conflict "between the democratic imperative of full public disclosure and those forces and tendencies which act to constrict, control and manipulate the information the public gets" (Minor 1970). The "mass media"—which today play a very instrumental role in theories of information warfare—he dismisses out of hand: he argues that very little of it bears any relation to gathering and reporting news. He condemns these media not for their top-down/one-to-many model as such but rather, for their lack of critical content. For Minor, the "press" is more than a sum of its parts, it embodies an Idea: "the institution of the press is the central nervous system of democracy."

By the late 1990s, this kind of phrasing has come to sound antique, not to say empty. The "media" of which Minor was so critical have entirely pushed aside the concept of "the press" as an organizing principle of democracy, and with it all the imperatives of centrality and responsibility. Media is a business, like any other, and, like other businesses comes with a code of conduct, ethics, etc. And the censorship Minor's press faced has changed with it: censorship as such may exist under dictatorships. Yes, journalists are increasingly killed for the work they do, but generally speaking the media worldwide have turned into an innocent infotainment business. For generations grown up after Vietnam, the struggles over openness, the idea that media and democracy have an intrinsic relationship may seem odd—new, even. For the content-based work of artists, activists, and journalists this is a growing problem. The information industry needs reports (and most of all imagery), but ideas of what is salient have changed dramatically through this process of commodification and technical/editorial transformation. As technical advances have permitted "up-to-the-minute" reports, live coverage and "real-life" footage, the task and form of synthesis has shifted: synthetic, systematic analysis—which used to be the press's reason for being—is now the problem of the "information-overloaded" viewer, and ethics, once a driving force, has become a matter of regulatory compliance. More news, more indifference. Information became our neo-natural environment. Data clouds race across the sky: sometimes they're threatening, for a minute, otherwise they are just info noise. Entertainment, as time goes by.

This is the unbearable lightness of the exploding media universe: more channels, less content, less impact. The Big Digital Bang is threatening to crush (or "liberate") all meaning, to keep every cry against injustice out of the broadcasting range. That's at least the fear of a group—perhaps a diminishing group—for whom "media" means more than just a job processing other people's data. But through this data smog and processing fog, the lessons of the Cold War were learned and universalized: through this haze of the "media" we see the vague outlines and traces of invisible psychological warfare, without clear fronts and with a low-intensity paranoid conflicts on the margins. Infowar precludes the friend-enemy distinction, which, according to Carl Schmitt, forms the basis of politics. How long will this go on, we should ask? When will the protective shields of Jean Baudrillard's "silent majority" deteriorate and turn in a surprising dialectical turn stand up against Organized Trash? Today's popular indifference can be interpreted as the outcome of specific historical conjunctions (consumerism, democratization). It is not a "natural state" of the masses. The "rage against the machine" will ultimately crush the powers behind disinformation. No question. Do we simply wait and gamble on the accumulating alienation that will ultimately turn into a peaceful implosion of the media, crushed under the weight of its accumulated infotainment? Do we wait for the Western version of the 1989 implosion of the Soviet empire to recur, with global capitalism collapsing under its own omnipresence and disasters, staging another world war, or falling apart due to its decadence, following the Roman empire scenario ("Reread Gibbon"). But we are not yet there.

Since the publication of Dale Minor's *Information War* the definition of information warfare has shifted, from the press manipulating public opinion towards the specific technologies used by the military to attack the enemy. Misleading the population is only one tool in a range of "weapons" which can be used by all sides. One of the current paradigms on "war" is the solubility of the front lines and territory in general. Since the Second World War we have been living in the state of "total war" or "pure war," as Paul Virilio has called it. Theorists and historians have pointed to the intrinsic relationship between the invention of the atomic bomb, the computer and the rise of mass media (and television in particular). This historical configuration of technologies has dominated the entire postwar/Cold War era. Guerrilla movements, terrorism and civil upheavals have not been able to change the basic parameters of warfare defined by the world powers. The disintegration of the Soviet Union and the fall of the Berlin Wall has changed the political maps of entire continents, but has not brought a similar downfall of the technological paradigm of the "pure war." Quite the opposite. "1989" has only intensified the invisible and "remote" aspects of warfare. This makes Paul Virilio all the more interesting. He is one of the few thinkers that did not have to reboot his conceptual operating system. His work has only gained importance over the decades and no attempts were made so far to historicize Virilio. Rather, his "truth" revealed during the Gulf War (1991), when all of Virilio's predictions about simulated war in real time had become a reality, still echoes way into the 21st century.

This is the background to the current talk about "infowar." We witness the rise of a "military electronic complex" (miniature tactical weapons) combined with sophisticated forms of "viral" propaganda and manipulative attacks, from all sides, inside the global media and communication systems. There is no "outside" from where the attacks are being planned. Like guerrillas in the countryside, part of the peasantry, or in metropolitan areas, as anonymous city inhabitants, hackers (and their counterparts), are constantly on the move. Unlike "traditional" peace movements and antimilitarist groups, hackers have a genuine, positive attitude towards the machines. It is like a hidden, chained libido that has to be liberated by taking it away from the authorities. Keywords for this are free software, shareware, public access, and decentralized, open systems. In part, the Internet has become successful due to this hackers' ideology. But this historical configuration, written down in software and operating systems has now come to an end, or is at least in a crisis. The prime values of the early Internet, with its Usenet, virtual communities and focus on the fight against censorship are under threat. The consensus myth of an egalitarian, chaotic system, ruled by self-governing users with the help of artificial life and friendly bots, is now crushed by the take-over of telecom giants, venture capital and banks and the sharp rise in regulatory efforts by governments.

The net is becoming a paranoid sphere. It is therefore time to declare the infowar. The fight for public bandwidth, against rating systems and (self) censorship, for access for all and access to all information are not defensive strategies. There is still room for new, open standards and software. The operating system Linux can be seen as an example of a positive infowar strategy against Microsoft. There are non-commercial browsers, the "frames of our minds." This is also "info war," related to the "war on standards" (like in the case of electricity at the beginning of this century).

Another aspect of infowar could be the construction of "info weapons." Here we do not only have to think about the software used in Denial of Service (DoS) attacks. Designing info weapons could vary from traditional forms of counter propaganda, anti-spam filters, "push back" media, spamming media organizations, government departments, or corporations, to more friendly forms of infowar like public awareness campaigns, fighting censorship, spreading free software and alternative interfaces, instructing search engines, meta-tagging important content, promoting active linking and building up communities around lists and sites. The what-to-do list of net activists is long—and easily gets more sophisticated.

As Heim (1998) points out: "The Luddite falls out of sync with the powerful human energies promoting rationality for three centuries and now blossoming into the next century. The Idealist falls for the progress of tools without content, of productivity without corporeal discipline." The signposts Heim puts up to guide us in overcoming the backlash against cyberspace can be useful in this context (even if, strictly speaking, his subject is offline virtual realities). For instance, he distinguishes between virtuality in the strong and loose, popular sense, and warns that "sloppy semantics leads to false panic and confusion." Rigorous or methodical criticism, on the other hand, can help to tear away at the destructive mythologies that both sides push. The other advice he offers is also helpful. We should avoid glib exaggerations such as "now we're cyborgs" or "everything's virtual reality," reject any monolithic fear an all-persuasive technology monster, not pretend to re-present the primary world, observe closely those points where VR touches earth-centered applications. "Denouncing artificial worlds as distractions is just as off balance as wanting to dissolve the primary world into cyberspace." According to Heim, realism in VR will come from pragmatic habitation, livability, and dwelling. "Social transition to cyberspace is as important as the engineering research." Dwelling in cyberspace is certainly a challenge the established leftist baby boomers have not yet taken up.

Since the mid 1980s it has fallen out of fashion in the West to speak of "propaganda" and "media manipulation." The "manufacture of consent" (a phrase Noam Chomsky takes from Walter Lippmann) has become an abstract, invisible process, without apparent agents, despite the efforts of the Chomsky group.[2] There is no "truth" behind propaganda, just other stories, different versions. What is left is a suspicious reading of mainstream media[3] and a rise in the disbelief of the integrity of reports. Fewer and fewer social movements and organizations are capable of "beating the press." This postmodern Truth is uncontested, even among radicals. The symbiotic ties between investigative journalists, alternative press and organic intellectuals within the state or political parties become looser with every day that passes, to the point of dissolution. Grassroots initiatives have fragmented into islands of NGOs while, at same time, becoming increasingly professional in orientation and visible in the media. Counter information that could challenge corporate and governmental policies hasn't disappeared, but are quickly losing vehicles and messengers. Investigative journalists have to organize themselves in order to be heard. Their findings alone are not sufficient. We can clearly see this in the diminishing size of the alternative networks of book shops, distribution firms, publishing houses, and presses. Newer media—video, local radio, public access TV, and the Internet—haven't been able to compensate this crisis in alternative Öffentlichkeit (public sphere), in part because activists haven't been able to grasp these technologies as "media" in ways their accustomed to.

On the other hand though, activists have begun to recognize the viral qualities of information. For instance, one can, over time, undermine the images of multinationals by circulating do-it-yourself investigations in small doses; huge demonstrations, boycotts, blockades (organizational nightmares) aren't necessary. There's a historical logic to this shift from mass and class phenomena to smaller-scale efforts: proper, justified, clear arguments of the kind familiar from nineteenth-century reformist movements. It never hurts to have the long march strategies at one's disposal, but they're not sufficient. Nor does one need massive "anti" advertisement campaigns: a tiny negative info virus, targeted against the brand, can have considerable effects as companies depend more and more on public relations.[4]

This strategic move from the streets to subtler, less obvious spaces, among them cyberspace, has been discussed by the Critical Art Ensemble (1996): "Resistance like power must withdraw from the street. Cyberspace as a location and apparatus for resistance has yet to be realized. Now it is time to bring a new model of resistant practice into action." The political collective identity Luther Blissett is one such form of cultural sabotage and "semiotic terrorism." The German autonomous a.f.r.i.k.a. group has gathered these strategies together in a handbook for communication guerrilla (Autonome a.f.r.i.k.a.-gruppe et al. 1998). These strategies vary from classics like fake letters and pie throwing to ironic demonstrations of support and "image destruction campaigns." Politicized computer hackers turn up in these stories every so often, but they are still an elusive breed whose potential remains for the most part in the realm of speculation and science fiction.

The counter-strategy of guerrilla warfare has been on the rise in the last decades. Some tried to squeeze it into Deleuzean discourse.[5] Others position infowar from below in the realm of culture jamming, tactical media, net.art, visual arts practices, or performance art. In part these are creative, but nonetheless artificial constructs to compensate for the absence of lively social movements. Hit-and-run actions need a mass base to operate from; out of context, though, these semiotic sabotages are merely survival tactics with which small groups bridge long periods of boredom and lack of direction. Until events all of the sudden appear: a rave party, a sudden revolt of the unemployed, a protest against rising fascism, road constructions, nuclear transports, a local LETS group setting up a barter system, a protest against EU policies, the building of a road, the expansion of an airport, social exclusion, immigration laws, or the eviction of a squat. Things start happening. For the majority, though, these forms of resistance are all but invisible and, therefore, nonexistent. At most, we see an image of some youngsters, vaguely defined through their dress code (collapsed categories such as punk, hippies, ferals and ravers), post-lifestyle rebels rampaging against the already weakened infrastructure; and we usually see these images in a context that supports demands for more "control."

This is the trap of identity politics. Some threads of protest led into the corridors and offices of invisible NGO-network offices, other threads unravel onto the urban streets where various "factions" dressed up and merged with the fashion landscape. Neither type is the kind of "meme" that multiplies in any clear way. The diversification of oppositional politics hasn't led to a "rainbow coalition." On the contrary, it fueled and was fueled by mutual suspicion: Who has been bought up, what has been appropriated, by whom? Who's on our side and who isn't? Who's in our circle and who is not? Why do theatre if you can do Internet? Within this PC system, it has become almost impossible to work on the fly or in temporary coalitions with journalists and other media professionals. They've turned out to be on "the other side," not the mediators they once were. This shift is described in *Cracking the Movement* (Adilkno 1994), which deals with the rise and fall of the Amsterdam squatters' movement in the 1980s and its changing media tactics. But the "anti-media" attitudes that came of it, which were given explosive power by the lies of the Gulf War, haven't brought about any deeper understanding of "data deprivation" (Herbert Schiller). Nor have more recent alternatives, for example, attempts to formulate a radical "net criticism" of the nettime mailing list been able to correct this situation. Rising above this diversification are those voices booming with fairy tales and diagrams: scientific specialists, artists, and "visionaries," predicting the downfall of "top-down television" (as George Gilder did in *Life after Television*).

What is badly needed are autonomous research collectives that critically examine the social, economic, and even ecological aspects of the information technology business (so praise Adbusters!). The military-industrial complex, the nuclear and chemical multinationals, and more recently the garment industry—each is faced with a sophisticated opposition, people waging "information war" who have backgrounds as activists. But not the IT business. To build these networks, these collectives, these efforts, we need to go back to classic authors such as Noam Chomsky, Herbert Schiller, or Edward Herman—crucial thinkers on the manipulative aspect of the global media. For these authors, "infowar" isn't tied to the latest military strategies, it's the ability of the ruling class to ideologically dominate and manipulate media channels in order to dominate the world markets. Their link with the Pentagon isn't technical in nature.

This is not to suggest that the analysis we need will be simple, or that these basic questions don't or won't apply. Take the work of German media theorist Friedrich Kittler and his school. They emphasize a "military determinism" in their history of media, and focus on the primacy of US foreign policy over the global media. In this view, technological developments fit into a strategy of a US-dominated Western imperialism. It is worth noting that while both the Chomsky and Kittler schools focus on US affairs before, during, and immediately after the Second World War, the outcomes of their analyses are remarkably different. But let's not be overly concerned with old debates. It s quite clear that the media, and especially their technological branches, are still deeply rooted in the Cold War. And so are their baby boom critics. "1989" hasn't had much influence on the discourse of this generation of thinkers. Perhaps the only impact of the Berlin Wall's fall on models of infowar mass-manipulation practices was to open up new fields of operation and new "audiences."

Another example of Chomskian critique of popular journalism comes from the Australian-British correspondent John Pilger (1998). Pilger describes Tony Blair's "betrayal" of the Labor government and its ongoing assault on the underclass, the recent backlash against aboriginals in Australia, huge arms deals with Indonesia, Burma, and Iraq (also under Blair), the hidden brutal repression in East Timor and the "invisible" bombings during the Gulf War. Pilger's style is accessible, moralistic but not nagging. Far from being academic or even "subversive," he is attacking the news industry from within, from where he originates and still works, producing documentary films for mainstream (state) television. For Pilger, "manipulation" is not an abstract word: he visits the victims of the English boulevard press, like the striking dockers in Liverpool, and so on. He uses the phrase "cultural Chernobyl" to describe the disinformation that's being spread—"newszak" (like muzak), as Bob Franklin calls it. Pilger quotes George Orwell, who described how censorship in free societies is infinitely more sophisticated and thorough because "unpopular ideas can be silenced, and inconvenient facts kept dark, without any need for an official ban."

For Pilger there is only one strategy: speak out. He doesn't mention alternative models for dissident media activism. The Internet is not a serious option for investigative reporters and critics of the Chomsky class who are used to access to the old style media for the millions (despite their radical critique). Pilger writes: "Technology and the illusion of an 'information society' means more media owned by fewer and fewer conglomerates. . . . The Internet, for all its variety and potential, is essentially an elite operation as most people in the world do not own a telephone, let alone a computer." A cliché, used by many of his generation, who cannot (or do not) want to see the battle over the terms under which future generations will communicate. Which will be a fight for equal bandwidth, public access, and content, not controlled by corporations or governments. Pilger and many like him should take care of the "successor generation," a term used by "atlanticists" to bridge the old UK-US elite and the Third Way Clinton-Blair mold. Instead, Pilger (1998) quotes Edward Said: "The threat to independence in the late twentieth century from the new electronics could be greater than was colonialism. The new media have the power to penetrate more deeply into a 'receiving' culture than any previous manifestation of Western technology." The refusal to even mention the possibility of subversive back channels is striking. What is this ignorance of the "last public intellectuals" who see themselves as the moral few, speaking from established places inside the media landscape? Or do they perhaps speak out of wisdom, having gone through numerous cycles of appropriation?

For an infowar from below to be successful a radical pragmatic coalition of intellectual and artistic forces is required—forces that, so far, have been working in different directions. It is necessary to open a dialogue and confrontation between media activists, electronic artists, cultural studies scholars, designers and programmers, media theorists, journalists, those who work in fashion, pop culture, visual arts, theatre, and architecture. All these branches, discourses, and traditions, subjected to the same process of digitization times globalization. The benefits and problems of computer networking differ across these fields, but the "synergy" is visible everywhere. So far convergence has only been a techno-economic term. It is now time to think about social convergence. Even yesterday's skeptics are getting on line, just when the "early adopters" are about to drop out, bored by the predictable arguments of users, stuck in corporatized communication spaces.

In order to launch an inclusive infowar the ongoing "culture war" between disciplines, platforms, and generations has to be overcome. This doesn't mean establishing a political party or a unifying ideology. We can settle for something more practical. Mutual understanding and coordination between different forms of expression would be a huge step in itself, or many, many small steps. For the purposes of Infowar, this means new groupings and new exchanges: between artists and engineers on one side, working on an effort to formulate principles for interactive design and the old school critics of mass media content on the other side. Rtmark, Luther Blissett, Adbusters, the Electronic Disturbance Theatre, and the Critical Art Ensemble are just a few examples of groups offering—and practicing—infowar strategies.

## < N o t e s >

1.  The original version of this essay was written for the 1998 Infowar Ars Electronica Festival catalogue. More related material can be found in the online discussion, which took place in the months leading up to the conference/festival in Linz, Austria (http://www.aec.at/infowar/NETSYMPOSIUM/).

2.  A recent publication in this genre is *You Are Being Lied To*, ed. R. Kick (Disinformation Company, 2001). See also www.disinfo.com.

3.  "In the case of reading the *New York Times* most of the people I know still read it with what Paul DeMan once called a 'rhetoric of suspicion.' That is, you read it because its stories provide some standard for knowing the zeitgeist of media culture. You read it because they have a better standard of reporting bit and fragments of otherwise unrecognized information from around the world—but you and everyone else knows that 'something is being left out.' I am inter-

ested in the dynamics by which people ask what is left out." (Willard Uncapher, private correspondence, July 8, 2001)

4. The reading list of this topic is vast. Here I will mention only Klein 2000 and the work of the investigative journalist Eveline Lubbers, who is studying the responses of corporations on both street and online resistance in order to save or restore their brand value. Corporate counter-campaigns in the form of media messages, appropriation of resistance and the launch of pseudo-NGOs ("astro turf") are all on the rise. For more on Lubbers's research on corporate responses and the reference guide for activist campaigners she edited, go to www.xs4all.nl/~evel.

5. Stefan Wray, http://www.nyu.edu/projects/wray/RhizNom.html.

# Kosovo: War in the Age of Internet

What is activism? Wearing a Dazed and Confused t-shirt? You know, the lifestyle magazine. . . . Or, for that matter, one saying Help B92, the support campaign for the banned Belgrade independent conglomerate.[1] It is not the "why" but "how" which fascinates. Click here, order the damned t-shirt NOW. Engagement is a non issue for the Low Identity People, the High Intensity Crowds, the surfers without qualities. Why wonder? Enjoy, get outraged. Make War, Love Later. There are always some lost moments, not yet colonized by the "economy of attention." One enters a vague terrain of free slots of good will, yet to be filled. Once we have left behind boring political principles a universe of activism unfolds before our eyes. Cool data do not stick onto smooth surfaces. Unclassified resistance. Tell me, was it two steps forward, one step back? Or one step forward two steps back? Such a splendid feeling to end this century of European wars with. Little time for reflection, even less to concentrate and browse for new ideas. Let us move on. Welcome to angry-divided Europe in the Kosovo spring of 1999.

Clever news analysis is by far the maximum we can expect these days from the *pensee d'aujourd'hui*. The few public intellectuals left, those who did not turn into TV personalities, have little on offer at the brink of the millennium. This is the post-media era with a technological imperative going way beyond broadcasting. News is just another option within a range of menus the networked economy has imposed on its clients/users. Sooner than expected, we have slipped into the Reality of the Virtual. No *one* Baudrillard anymore to upset liberals and alike. Simulation rules; so does Reality TV. The heroic-Hegelian battle between the Real and its Virtual is over. No endgame. Both the real and the virtual are contained, subjected to the same cyber-synergetic forces. *Kosovo n'existe pas*. Not anymore.

The dirty reality and its counterpart, the clean, surgical image are intertwined into one never ending stream of infotainment. Also the newly proclaimed infowar of hackers and secret services do not prevent any Kosovo villagers from being expelled. It just opens the next, still insignificant, battleground. The yet unseen pictures from inside Kosovo will merely intensify the war. Even without shocking imagery we are faced with an evidence overload. There is no truth in the unseen. We are reaching here the point of equation: media = war. The Internet is not just an extension of the battlefield (as theories of "total war" suggest). Computer networks, including the broadcast media, are becoming the center point of military operations. Beyond the point of being mere logistics, the communication and command infrastructure is starting to direct itself. At least, that's what infowar theories predict.

During the Kosovo "conflict," the collective intelligence on the net wasn't quite ready for a full scale cyberwar. Nor were the reporters and intellectuals, such as Michael Ignatieff. In his book *Virtual Wars, Kosovo and Beyond*, Ignatieff shows a certain sensibility for the technological imperative. He tells the story of the group Télécoms Sans Frontieres which set up shop in tent in one of the camps for Kosovo-Albanian refugees in Macedonia. "They seemed the only aid workers to grasp that the Albanians did not conform to the clichés of destitution lodged in our minds by Ethiopia or the Sudan. These people were modern Europeans, with relatives and friends in every city on the content and they needed phones to activate these networks abroad. Soon the line for the phones was as long as the line for water (Ignatieff 2000). With Clausewitz, Ignatieff called Kosovo a "cabinet war." The conflict did not mobilize hundreds of thousands of soldiers. "It mobilized opinion around the world, but it was fought by no more than 1,500 NATO airmen, and the elite specialists of Serbian air defense, probably numbering no more than a thousand. Cabinet wars are fought and won by technicians. Cabinet wars do not end with parades, garlands, civic receptions, or sorrowful ceremonies at graveyards."

Will future virtual wars all be cabinet wars? Most likely not, and this is where is Ignatieff's pop use of the term "virtual" becomes problematic. He predicts that "virtual wars will not be less violent and destructive than those fought before the age of the television camera." However, "future wars may escape the scrutiny of journalists and observers altogether. If the target is the enemy's computer or banking infrastructure and the only weapons are computer viruses, no one will know the war is being fought until it is over." Unless you are a hacker, of course, or work for an ISP, a security firm, or the FBI, or, even better, if you are journalist with net skills. The Internet is not a secret—but it still is for most critical intellectuals. Ignatieff: "Virtual war is won by being spun. In these circumstances, a good citizen is a highly suspicious one." I would say: a highly technical one.

In Ignatieff's view, the citizen is still a passive consumer of images who should be taught that "media create the illusion that what we are seeing is true." Such disdain of the media user is really out of date. Ignatieff's virtual war is in fact nothing more than an updated version of the old school one-to-many television spectacle. "War becomes virtual, not simply because it appears to take place on a screen, but because it enlists societies only in virtual ways." War has been turned into "something like a spectator sport. As with sports, nothing ultimate is at stake: neither national survival, nor the faith of the economy. War affords the pleasures of a spectacle, with the added thrill that it is real for someone, but not, happily, for the spectator." A view which explain why the Internet aspect of the Kosovo is all but absent in Ignatieff's book. The same can be said of Noam Chomsky's *The New Military Humanism, Lessons from Kosovo* (1999), according to which wars are still decided on the foreign affairs pages of the *New York Times*, reducing the wide range of issues to the pro and contra of "humanitarian" interventions and other Western inconsistencies.[2]

Media never simply represent or report. Its technological nature drowns out each signal. As spin-offs from the war machine, manipulation is just another technical feature: cut & paste, import-export, delete and insert. Media as an "extension" of war, the mother of all media. It is a daily practice of media professionals, worldwide, getting lost in an uneasy propaganda theater. War as the continuation of politics with the same means: computers. The then authentic outcry in the aftermath of the Romanian television revolution can now be reinterpreted as a violent initiation into the technicality of today's live image production. The staged realities of 1999 have a similar docudrama touch, having to watch history at the speed of light, sending out very basic human impulses straight through the postmodern surfaces.

Ten years after the Romanian television revolution ("the media is with us"), the Internet is with us. Not quite. In the case of the Kosovo war, this new medium has proved particularly vulnerable. Not yet war proof. Not much "routing around the damage" as the official Internet ideology had stated. This might be due to the lack of satellite telephones, crypto software, laptops and digicams on the side of the Kosovo civilians. With the armed uprising of the KLA a few years under way in early 1999, starting in late 1996, there were few or no signs of a clandestine online press. There had not been heroic attacks from Serbian opposition on government servers. Hackers, operating on behalf of the Slav brotherhood, anti-NATO movements, or the Albanian cause, in most cases were located elsewhere (Russia, the United States, Switzerland). With Serbian "dissident" media being shut down, journalists being killed and intimidated, and Kosovo being destroyed and emptied of people, who was there to do "authentic" Internet reporting from Kosovo? It is therefore not correct to say that the Gulf War belonged to CNN, with Kosovo "the first Internet war." The screens Paul Virilio refers to in *Strategies of Deception* (2001) are remote terminals with the Balkans as the virtual theatre of operation. In a possible first "real" Internet war all sides of the conflicts, both military and civilians, inside or outside the region, will be hooked onto the net. A proliferation of access which has not yet taken place. But we're almost there. Kosovo gives us a glimpse of what is about to happen.

After Belgrade's 1996 "Internet Revolution," with B92's own Internet provider www.opennet.org continuing the banned radio signal of B92, using RealAudio,[3] journalists proclaimed an "Internet War." Chinese hackers retaliating for the NATO attack on the Chinese Embassy in Belgrade, bringing down the web sites of the US Ministry of Energy and Internal Affairs. In mid May even the rumor spread that the Yugoslav Internet as such would be shut down, which was later denied by American government officials. Internet was supposed to be good for the Yugoslav people. Slobodan Markovic, a young computer programmer, reporting almost daily to the syndicate and nettime mailing lists from Belgrade, puts the effort to shut down the Yu-Net in a broader perspective: "This attempt of shutting down Internet satellite feeds to Yugoslavia is a good reminder that Cyberspace is not situated in some kind of a vacuum and that our REAL governments CAN and WILL do anything that suits their interests. Just like corporate invertebrates, they will do all of that regardless of our communication customs and ethics we developed over years on the net."

Slobodan Markovic sums up the following incidents:

Together with Radio B92, their Internet division (opennet.org) also went down. All of Opennet's classrooms and new media labs (like the new media arts organization cybeRex) are closed. All of their Internet projects (aimed to education about Internet issues and development of Yugoslav cyberspace) are put on hold or completely canceled.—When NATO destroyed the second bridge in Novi Sad one fiber-optic cable carrying Internet traffic was broken.—When NATO hit one building in Belgrade downtown a great deal of computer equipment, belonging to BITS ISP, was totally destroyed.—NATO is targeting Post Offices in many large cities. Three days ago more than 18,000 people lost their phone connections in the city of Uzice (similar thing happened in the city of Prishtina).—NATO is using graphite bombs to COMPLETELY disable major Serbian power plants. During five days, more than half of population in Serbia (approx. 5 million of people) did not have electric power.[4]

It was hard to grasp that an entire region inside (Southeast) Europe is being turned into an information black hole. Journalists should just do their job and go there, war or no war, some said. That may be the case for CNN or BBC, with all their resources, but especially these Western news organizations are particularly vulnerable for sophisticated forms of propaganda and manipulation, especially with images. Small media may be "tactical," but they are also easy to shut down. One of the first things B92 stopped doing after being taken off the air was independent reporting. There was simply no way for them to visit "the other side." One needs a lot of courage when fellow journalists get killed on the street because of their critique of the regime. Would you have it? Would you stay, not being able to do the work properly, or go into exile, not being in touch anymore with friends, family, events. Probably old dilemmas. Most Kosovo Albanians did not even had a choice. Serbian independent media had been silenced, shut up, expressing anger over the NATO bombing in their own way, in an attempt not to stay out of tune with the Milosevic regime.

What the Internet was left with were Serbian witnesses, diaries and personal accounts, mainly from educated urban citizens.[5] Immediately, while the first bomb load was dropped, the Internet diaries started to pop up. Their psycho-geography is limited, by nature, by the very definition of the genre. They did not produce theory or a critical analysis of politics and the war situation. Add to this situation the semi-personal touch of email, and presto, you get an odd, once in a lifetime mixture of paranoia, reflection, pathetic pity, waves of despair, worrisome productions of subjectivity, with here and there valuable pictures of the everyday life under extraordinary circumstances. Here are some fragments, posted to various mailing lists.

Slobodan Markovic: YES—I AM angry and personally endangered. . . and not just physically. . . . I have dedicated all my life to computer sciences. Without that what is left for me to do? And yesterday some idiot decided to bomb all the main electric plants in Serbia. When I woke up early this morning (around 4 am) I could only sit silent in the darkness of my room, the darkness of my city, watching darkness on my computer screen! What the hell—the army is using electric power, so let's cut it out COMPLETELY, right?![6]

Marija Marjanovic: Do you still believe that they are fighting for human rights? We are in terrible position. If they are fighting only against our government why are they attacking civilians? Do we really need this aggression? Don't they have any other way to persuade our president to negotiate? Do we, civilians, have to suffer because of wrong government on one side and aggressive ways of USA to realize their strategic and economic goals on the other? We only want to live our lives normally. To work, have fun, have families, have healthy children. We are normal people that is very tired of everything that is going on here in the last ten years. Please, help us, by spreading our side of the story all over the world. Tell this to your friends. Anything that you do can be helpful. Help us only by thinking. Remember, this can happen to any poor nation. The world should not be a jungle.[7]

Baza: "good fucking morning to you too. fucking fucking fucking! early morning, 4.50, all fucking windows were shaking fucking strong, fucking close if anything happen to my son, i will fucking do something nasty, really nasty i am fucking scared, i am fucking angry, i must be fucking dangerous and do not anyone EVER dare to fucking brainwash me about fucking military targets NEVER FUCKING AGAIN i am dangerously fucking scared and ANGRY! who of you have visited novi sad and who fucking can remember the old bridge, near the fucking oldest bridge which is in danube, as remembrance of fucking WWII and thousands of jews, serbs and others fucking thrown alive in january cold water under the fucking ICE by fucking nazi destroyers? . . . We are still not stinking but shall!!! we shall be fucking stinky, and all fucking picture about fucking stinky serbs will fit finally! but it will fucking not destroy my fucking memory about the bridge and fucking fear of my little son, NEVER! there are fucking demonstrations everywhere, find a first square and START opposing madness and destroying, fucking NOWNOWNOW NOW

NOWNOWNOWNOWNOWNOWNOWNOW NOW NOWNOWNOWNOWNOWNOWNOWNOW lots of love and all the best (just to the friends) and the rest of you - happy fucking 1st of april fucking world joke fucking day."[8]

insomnia: "nato prevents humanitarian catastrophe in kosovo by creating a more grave humanitarian condition in serbia and montenegro. now it is our babies that are short of milk, now the whole population of serbia suffers from food and petrol shortages. this is no way to spread democracy. if it is, democracy is a virus that kills! i am the assistant professor of american and english literature at the university of novi sad. i have visited states and seen myself that it really is a land of opportunities. i am not one of those people who mocks american dream. still, now that i am so tense after spending two days in a damp shelter with a swollen tooth (not being able to visit my doctor in all this mess), now that i am quite tense and near the end of my tether, i do not want to be harsh, or to use harsh words on anybody. just, please, do not turn american dreams into yugoslav nightmare!"[9]

The diaries were a response to the severe censorship of the Milosevic regime. There had been a fierce (mainly financial) repression of (independent) media before March 24, 1999, the day NATO bombing started.[10] Yet, the belief in civic structures remained amazingly strong. That's what all the diary accounts have in common: a strong anger, disbelief, being completely unprepared for such a brutal act of "clean bombing." Throughout April 1999, the then banned radio station B92 worked on a lawsuit against the Serbian authorities to get back their radio station, building and equipment, which had been confiscated by a leftist patriotic student organization, Milosovic puppets.[11] This proves the strong belief in legal structure, despite all the corruption. Perhaps it was a naive, optimistic view, believing in the final victory of Law? The problem we are facing is the no longer existing distinction between war and peace. It seems hard to acknowledge for the advocates of independent media and free cyberspace that in times of war there is little or no role to play for "civil society." Besides buildings, roads, bridges, and of course lives of people, the military logic is also destroying civil structures, media first and foremost. Still, there were rather high expectations from the side of Western activists and NGOs, for example from B92 or even from Kosovars, hiding in Pristina, or somewhere in the mountains, to carry on their mission to inform the world.

With the vanishing of the very real distinction between civil and military (rule) it is especially the smaller broad/netcasters, local radio and television stations, magazines, newspapers, rooted in the local and national social structures (including its building and technological structure) which became easy targets. Not so much the established global news corporations, despite media workers increasingly becoming deadly targets. Stuck in the middle of "transitions," longing for "normalization," it seems inappropriate to demand for a militarization towards clandestine "underground" media. In wartime, all media will ultimately surrender to the military logic and will cease to exist, especially the civic, open and experimental parts of the Internet. There is no independence under (virtual) war circumstances. There is no space of "neutral" users making innocent observations. Information be instrumentalized by either party. Virtual wars do not take place in the public arena. They are not about "public opinion" but happen inside password protected servers, using encrypted communication. It is an Internet filled with secrecy and distrust, dominated by info weapons such as mailbots, Trojan horses, worms and viruses. That's a different track, beyond the by now dated, 1989 paradigm of "independent" media and light years away from the idea of Internet as public domain.

< Notes >

1. A first version of this text was written at the end of May 1999, with the NATO bombardments on former Yugoslavia two months under way, at

the height of despair, with solidarity campaigns such as HelpB92
(www.helpb92.net) in which I was involved, collapsing and general communication on all sides at an all time low. With news media reporting the
arrival of the Internet War, insiders at the civil communication front
were experiencing the exact opposite: breakdown and exhaustion. The
essay appeared first in the free newspaper *Bastard*, produced out of
Zagreb by the *Arkzin* crew (June 1999). Also published as "War in the
Age of Internet, Some Thoughts and Reports, Spring 1999," in *Ost-West
Internet—Media Revolution*, ed. S. Kovats (Campus, 1999). For more
information on the context of the essay, see the conference, exhibition,
film series and web site Carnival in the Eye of the Storm—War/Art/New
Technologies: KOSOV, April 2000, Portland, curated by Trebor Scholz
(http://projects.pnca.edu/kosovo/). For more on the role of Internet,
see Himanen 2001. In the chapter "Freedom of Speech: The Case of Kosovo"
Himanen discusses the role of B92 and the supporting role of the Dutch
Internet provider xs4all. Himanen does not problematize the silence from
within Kosovo. He does admit that "the net had only minor influence on
the general views of the war, and even less on its conduct" (p. 96).

2. For more specific media analyses in accordance with Chomsky, see
*Degraded Capacity, The Media and the Kosovo Crisis*, ed. P. Hammond
and E. Herman (Pluto, 2000).

3. David Bennahum, in *Wired* 5.04, reporting on the role of the net in
the long period of protest by the Serbian opposition around December
1996, in particular www.opennet.org, B92's Internet department.

4. Slobodan Markovic, "Tmhwk censorship!" (nettime, May 13, 1999).
Many of the diaries and discussions took place on the Syndicate mailinglist (www.v2.nl/syndicate). Because of security and privacy concerns, the Syndicate web archive for March—June 1999 has been blocked
up to this date and could therefore not be used as reference.

5. Most of the diaries were email letters; some of them had their own
web sites. A selection:
Jasmina Tesonovic, http://helpb92.xs4all.nl/diaries/jasmina/jasmina.htm;
Ivanka Besevic: www.keepfaith.com;
Vojislav Stojkovic, http://members.tripod.com/CodeMage/top.htm#diary;
Marija Marjanovic, http://www.peacefleece.com/serbia.htm;
Vladislava Gordic (insomnia), http://helpb92.xs4all.nl/diaries/diarie2.htm;
Slobodan Markovic, http://kunstradio.at/WAR/DIARY/markovic.html;
A.G.: http://www.webcinema.org/war_diaries/

6.  Slobodan Markovic, "A Just War," nettime, May 3, 1999.

7.  Marija Marjanovic, "My Side of the Story," nettime, May 4, 1999.

8.  Baza, "Fucking 1st of April Day of Fucking Joke," *Syndicate*, April 1, 1999.

9.  Insomnia, "Serbian Diary, 26 March," nettime, March 31, 1999.

10.  One of the organizations involved in the support of independent media in the former Yugoslavia has been Press Now, based in Amsterdam, founded in 1993 (www.pressnow.nl).

11.  For the full story on the occupants of B92 (April 1999—October 2000), see http://jurist.law.pitt.edu/b92files.htm.

# Towards a Political Economy

# Cyberculture in the Dotcom Age

Join the spirit of digital competition![1] The electronic gold rush is well on the way. It's now or never. Make your personal fortune today. Don't worry that Internet stocks have lost 40 percent of their value. The promised Long Boom (Dow Jones Index at 50,000) will bring prosperity to all as long as we keep the faith in the New Economy gurus. Ignore all crashes. Just hype yourself through the jungle of buzzwords, line up with the start-ups, or become one yourself . Gamble on the market of empty portal sites, useless domain name services, tiny Java applications, satellite WebTV demos, cute games for mobile phones and sell before sunset. Join the lottery of mega-mergers of the titanic telcos. Quit your job. Become a day trader. Use all your guerrilla tactics at the forefront of the micro second decision makers. Burn all the cash of your dotcom till it's time to jump off the bandwagon. Welcome to the Internet.

The early, mythological phase of digital culture is rapidly running out of its utopian energies. The Internet as a global economic model has replaced the libertarian-hippie model of a network architecture and culture that was so prominent in the early to mid 1990s. But this merely replaces one essentialist view with another. There are hardly any signs left of cyberspace as an autonomous, supranational, transgender sphere. According to the British science fiction writer Gwyneth Jones (1998), there are no indications of a rise of the cyborg, with its apparent ability to overcome patri-archal structures. The Internet has proved incapable of creating its own conscious-ness. Instead, law and order are taking command over the last pockets of digital wilderness. Logging onto the net will soon be as fascinating and meaningful as picking up the phone.

The taming of cyberculture by "clicks and mortar" businesses and their willing government executors took only a few years. The net has been a successful financial speculation market for some and left behind a scattered scene of small enterprises, stagnating networks and dead links for most of the early participants. The time of institutionalization, mega-mergers and security paranoia has arrived. These new conditions, driven by the net economy's hyper growth, bumping from boom to crash and back, will have an as yet invisible effect on the cultural new media sector (arts, design, education) which had perceived itself for so long as "ahead of the wave."

While the start-up youngsters sped towards their IPO (Initial Public Offering) epiphany and eventual sell out, the cultural sector of the new media was in panic. The accumulated cultural capital now has to be safeguarded. Where to go with all these experimental interfaces, artistic interactive installations, 3D worlds, techno samples, rich alternative content, packed in databases, stored on CD-ROMs and web sites, not designed for the market in the first place? The time to cash in came and went for everyone else, but the promised high value of "cultural content" did not.

Most money is still made with software, infrastructure and access, not with content. The interest of venture capitalists in cultural content is next to zero, with little or no cash returns or profit in sight. How to cash in when there is little or no interest in avant-garde quality concepts, with mainstream non-design and instant content proved so popular and financially successful? Back to charity? The danger of marginalization is immediate. A way back into state funded projects, museums, galleries and academia seems to be only left option for the once so mighty cultural arm of the virtual class.

The Internet has become synonymous with the New Economy. Being merely a set of standards for so-called computer-mediated communication, the handful of programmers and media lab administrators in charge of these data protocols have been easily pushed aside by corporate interests and crushed by rivalries between IT giants. The quasi-neutrality of the geek/engineer only made matters worse, in a situation of high growth where all participants faced great difficulties in keeping up. Despite previous promises the net proved incapable of armoring itself against ideology, and will from now on be associated with a very specific (American) economic agenda.

The new economy is a mix of neo-liberal state policies and entrepreneurial myths, supported (and to a certain extend corrected) by Third Way policies as defined by Tony Blair and his adviser Anthony Giddens.[2] *Business Week* came up with a what-to-do list to get a high-productivity, low-inflation economy:

- Restructure corporations to cut costs, improve flexibility and make better use of technology.

- Open financial markets to direct capital to the best uses.

- Develop venture capital and IPO markets to aid innovative companies.

- Encourage an entrepreneurial culture and make it easier to start new businesses.

- Increase the pace of deregulation, especially in telecom and labor markets.

- Adjust monetary policies and wait for inflation to appear before raising interest rates.[3]

Since the late 1990s this has become the economic program, and it is closely associated with the Internet. This can be illustrated by numerous cases in which business gurus and their financial journalists mix up these three terms: "Internet Economy," "Networked Economy," and "New Economy." The critique of this neo-liberal agenda is being reduced to the emotional intelligence level of groups that feel threatened by free trade. No word here of the neglect of social policies, problems in public education, and the decline of the "the public sphere," a crucial term if we want to understand the origin and essence of the Internet.

The notion of "the public" is all but absent in the rhetoric of the New Economy. The shadow side of the never-ending budget cuts, downsizing and restructuring are becoming apparent in the lack of skilled IT workers, worldwide. The short-term thinking of *Business Week* leads to a strange conclusion. The magazine posed the question of what could stop the New Economy from becoming a truly global phenomenon. "The main problem will be finding enough highly skilled and computer-literate workers to staff rapidly growing information industries." The believe in the growth dogma is amazing. No answer given as to who is responsible for the education mess, or how both students and teachers will reach a sophisticated level where information can be transformed into (critical) knowledge. Needless to say that the overvaluation of tech stocks is not mentioned.

Sloganomics: Those who do not know media history have the freedom to bypass it; Millennial disease: Complexity Syndrome; The Online Shopping Warrior as Kulturideal; "Digital rarity becomes indispensable"; www.j'accuse.com; "Theory is just something we don't understand, so we don't invest in it." (after Warren Buffett); The World's First Open Source Religion™; Digital Visions: The Creative Destruction of Post-Modernism (book title); "Where to click if you want to fit in" (from a site); Meet the Uncanny Prosumers; Dotcom logic: bubble or burst; Complexity as Excuse: The Showdown of Millennial Intellectuals (article); Scalable Ideas; The Poverty of e-Commerce. License or Die.

The paradoxical position of the Internet, facing both hyper-growth and conceptual stagnation, can be illustrated by the case of web design. "Just as designers have the technology to create interactive web pages packed with sound and movement such as flash/shockwave, the future seems somewhat monochrome," as Fiona Buffini says.[4] The small screens of mobile phones force design to again dramatically reduce expectations concerning color, fonts and download speed. Similar limitations are the case for interactive television. Two steps forward, one step back? Or is it one step forward, two steps back?

Web design no longer has the pioneer role in convincing a culturally savvy audience about the high performance "interactive" capabilities of the web. Sexy buttons and surprising multi-layered content, linked in ways that make surfing an exciting journey through as yet unexplored hyperspaces, have been brutally cut short, succumbing to lucid functionality. "Coolness as the single criterion for a web site's success has been dumped in favor of "the higher plane of simplicity" as main portals strive to increase speed," says Buffini.

Sites such as Yahoo!, Excite, and Amazon, search engines such as Google, and virtually all news organizations represent the new breed in screen design. With no graphic art or technical experiments, all space is used to maximize the amount of text-based information on the front page. Buffini: "Usability, it seems, has become the major task of web designers with big commercial clients." With millions of clicks a day, high ratings on the stock exchange and high, risky venture capital investment, the leading web companies cannot afford to let their customers crash on some quirky plug-in. Buffini quotes media analyst Ian Webster: "Yahoo! and Amazon deliver because they're designed to the last pixel. You can be a design snob, but these sites are among the most sophisticated. With Internet population growing, you have to design something that will work for 50 million people." In order to get this level, designers have to become neutral providers of "mass customization" for "users."

Interaction design seems to have lost its battle against interface stupidity. The office metaphor of the previous decade has been exchanged for an adaptation of the newspaper front page outlook as the dominant information architecture. In this regressive move, back to the old mass media of print, references to space or naviga-tion are no longer needed. What is presented here as a step forward, from the adult-like "grooviness" to "usability" is light years away from the Bauhaus imperatives in which sophisticated design was not seen as in conflict with mass production.

Telephone books, dictionaries and paper money all have decent typography and graphic design, so why not the world's most visited web sites? Is it perhaps the unholy alliance between geekness and money, which pushes the HTML designers of the first hour off their throne? The profession of interaction design has to adjust itself to the new circumstance, leaving behind only a niche of still interesting sites. Will the design branch rebel against this setback and push forward with a new visual language of aesthetic functionality, embedded in a broader set of social, cultural and political a priori? Or will it adjust and accept the growing division between high and low culture within cyberspace?

The so-called open and democratic character of the Internet is not a God-given fact. Throughout the 1980s and 1990s efforts were made by engineers and programmers to open up academic computer networks. Their concern not only related to access via a modem or terminals. The main battle was fought on the level of software and network architecture. After a short period during the mid 1990s, with its utopian promises, rising commercialism and radical cybercultures, a massification of the net set in. The period of dotcom mania is one of hyper growth with users turned into click rates generating "eyeballs." Open, decentralized "citizen" networks are of no use anymore in this environment. Potential customers are only interesting because of their market profile. Within the surveilled safe intranets of corporations with their entertainment and info businesses, (dissident) opinions are filtered out or at best treated as spin-off effects of virtual environments whose goal it is to generate cash flow. Communication has become unnecessary, boring and of private concern. Open communication networks based on open-source software, are increasingly becoming a threat to corporations and governments. In fact, openness has become synonymous to child pornography and computer hackers. The naive phase of "facilitation" is over and all parties are gearing up for infowar.

The response to massification and regulation is the creation of an invisible cyber elite. Already for years it has become next to impossible to discuss topics on public newsgroups. Noise levels on Usenet have risen to unbearable levels due to clumsy, arrogant, or ill-informed individuals or companies sending spam messages and advertisements to public forums. In fast growing networks people tend not to get to know each other anymore so flame wars over nothing are unleashed, in most cases without any outcome. The effect of this is a loss of confidence in the public sphere of cyberspace, with its relatively open forums and communities. As a response, business and developer groups as well as activists and researchers have started mailing lists and discussion forums within password protected sites. Who wants to discuss sophisticated concepts with all the booboos and weirdoes surfing over the web, looking for places to make trouble? Are you able to keep up with hundreds of email messages one gets in into the In box every day? What counts is exclusive, high quality information. Filter out the nonsense, whatever that may be. I do not like you and your silly opinions, so why waste precious time on opinions and attitudes one detests? The argument of an ever rising "complexity" is used as an excuse to no longer shape the network society and leave this task to large corporation and a few governments. Conspiratorial "micro politics" are proposed as an escape route to hide from the expected invasion of the online masses. At the same time the (new media) arts are looking for a comfortable refuge in old institutions such as museums and galleries. The early adopters and cyber warriors, the partisans who fought at the electronic frontiers in the roaring 1990s, are withdrawing into private realities, paralyzed by the economies of scale.

What is "cultural intelligence" in the digital age? This is a question the Vienna-based group Public Netbase has raised in their exhibition and research project www.world-information.org. Culture is an asset. Whether old or new, high or low, culture is a commodity, one of the fastest growing resources the world is currently exploiting. Arts and culture, though marginal in market capitalization, is turning now into a mysterious factor which can make and break local economies. Highly skilled workers can be based everywhere, and will indeed move on if a place turns boring or too spoiled by money (the rich only consume culture). So which concepts and ideas are "in"? What is cool and what is out? Welcome to the world of the paranoiac cultural producers. A catchy concept can be turned into an Internet start-up or exclusive contract with some media organization. Have you already been accused of cultural spying? Intellectual Property fights are all over the place. In the New Economy IT sector there is a lot of spying and intelligence work going on. To some extent this is plain robbery. Taking ideas in order to claim, patent and copyright them so that you will be the one who will make money with them in the end. So one should better beware and keep brilliant ideas for one's self. Copyright and patent them straight away, send them to your lawyer before you even tell them to your best friends. The alternative is to give them away for free in the naive hope that someone will be so generous to give you some charity pocket money in the end. You choose. That's the tragic yet realistic State of the Millennial Internet.

So far we are only dealing with the traditional definition of "culture" at the level of Samuel Huntington's *Clash of Civilizations* which is going on at the level of world religions and anthropology. In the ruling conservative definition, culture is defined by its age and ability to be endlessly recycled and marketed as "cultural heritage." But the actual "culture business" looks rather different. It is common knowledge that (pop) culture is a global market, a sophisticated machinery of rumors, memes, signs and images, driven by the never-ending desire to redefine the New in order to commodity "lifestyles." It is here that the CultureSpy™ figure appears, presenting him/herself as a curator, photographer, journalist, or project developer. The cultural spies have to be situated at the forefront of the conceptual boundaries where the 20–30 years old are pushing the limits in order to reach world fame (these days measured in click rates). The Western elites are perhaps too interwoven to unleash a real culture war on the net between, let's say, the USA and Europe. It is much easier to imagine this phenomena occurring on a strict transnational economic level. That makes the concept of "cultural intelligence" all the more interesting. Corporate spying is a booming business and so is spying among allies (Israel against the US, the US against Europe, etc.). Training a secret staff of national culture spies could already taking place. This could be an ideal project for a public-private partnership. Japanese corporations have specialized themselves in culture spying over the last decades. The West has now arrived in the age of imitating Japanese styles and strategies. Concept spying is certain one of them. Take the metaphor and run.

This is the age of implementation, not innovation. With governments withdrawing from the cultural sector and the IT sector, and a fast growing Internet business solely interested in mainstream content, the cyber avant-garde is threatened with being left alone and empty handed. All that is left for the cyber avant-garde are attempts to write and claim a history, filled with fading images and nostalgic stories. The rest are busy making money. Digital artisans, working at the conceptual sweatshops all have to compete against each other. At least, that's what the neo-liberal market ideology would like us to believe.

We are not speaking about the usual tragic cycles of appropriation here. Unlike pop cultures such as rock, punk, or rap, cyberculture—born in the late 1980s—has refrained from any gesture of resistance towards the establishment. This makes its rise and fall different—less predictable, and to a certain extent softer, though perhaps even more spectacular. The ruling market ideology generates the sweet illusion that there is enough space under the sun for all the players. Cyberculture at the dawn of the 21st century can no longer position itself in a utopian void of seamless possibilities. Collective dreams of out-of-body experiences, digital forms of consciousness and virtual gender bending have been rapidly overturned by mainstream market forces and government efforts to regulate the new media industry. No more crossing of borders with drugs, technology and fooling around with identities. Playtime for the early colonizers is over.

Now it is the turn of the civilization teams and marketeers to mark territories and set rules for just behavior so that the painful struggle for profit will not be undermined by some weirdoes who pretend that their Internet is an extension the Wild West. The economy has invaded the net, and the net itself has turned into an economy. At least that's the idea, the big picture we are confronted with in the numerous dotcom advertisements and the accompanying reportage in the old media. In order to get there, key promises such as free communication and anonymity have to be relinquished. The wild and free floating user has to be turned in a civilized, liable and accountable cyber citizen who, like any other citizen will shop, vote and pay taxes and shut his or her mouth. Internet is many. Ideally it is a network of networks. A network without qualities. In theory it could fit all wishes and desires of the world. Beware of all the worried politicians and critics, overly enthusiastic business men and whoever else is trying to reduce its functionality in the name of security or the well-being of humankind.

The Internet has a history now, going back to the early 1960s. Its pre-history in computing reaches back into the 1930s and 1940s. Its genealogy as technical media can be traced back even further, centuries ago, via Leibniz back to Raymond Lullus. The history of the "roaring 1990s" is now being written up by both business journalists and art historians. But how about the immediate future? Which strategies are available now for its further development? Fundamental research and the development of new programming languages and protocols seem to have come to a halt. A crisis in informatics as an educational program is becoming visible as both professors and their students understudy for well paid positions in the IT sector. Why do research if the overall situation will change overnight?

Only large corporations have funds and a long-term view; they will embark for a yet unknown destination and they are courageous enough to sink billions of dollars in the sand if the application turns out to be a failure and is not accepted by industry or consumers. "The Internet craze has been accompanied by far too much short-term thinking. It's time to get back to thinking in ten-year increments," says Phil Agre.[5] Time for the open source community to reveal its first Five Year Plan? Is the graphic interface killer app version of Linux already on the radar screens, or is that too ambitious?

In the official version of the Internet success story, small companies have been portrayed as the motors behind the development of the medium. But this may turn out to be a myth, despite Yahoo! and Netscape. At the end of the story, the new economy can be characterized as a process of transforming and adapting the old economy to information technology (and the Internet TCP/IP standard in particular) in all layers of capitalist production, distribution and services, including the communication patterns on the user-turned-consumer side.

The chances of David rocking Goliath are diminishing. The idea that the information age would stand for principles such as networking, customization, niche production and high-risk innovation already sounds like outdated vaporware. Instead, we witness short innovation cycles building upon even shorter cycles of creativity, set in small labs (or cultural scenes). Then comes the hunt for seed capital, possibly ending in takeovers by big players such as media giants of the print, television and film industry, telcos, cable companies, or old software firms from the 1980s.

The result for Internet standards is, relatively speaking, regression, not progress. Micro-improvements on applications are, for good or bad reasons, classified as billion dollar ideas. Because of the immense financial implications of a possible research outcome, media lab culture in many places has turned into a closed, competitive, even paranoid environment. Fights over patents and intellectual property have all but destroyed the innovative culture of the early 1990s, so naively documented in Tim Berners-Lee's book *Weaving the Web* (2000).

His call for "intercreativity" comes too late. His World Wide Web Consortium (www.w3.org) is just a tiny goodwill organization, trying to maintain its image as a neutral ground for negotiating standards. Those who will be strong enough to define the standards for datacasting and e-commerce will eventually own the net. Step by step we are approaching the final battle of the "War on Standards." With the age of web pioneers and visionaries declared history, and the net going through its phase of massification and speculation, we are approaching the next stage—codification—with a few corporations and governments left as the final players. The flip side of this development being the unleashing of "info wars," hackers turning against their former playground—a platform they once considered their own.

Tim Berners-Lee, at a technical level, took us back to the romantic period of the early 1990s; so does Margaret Wertheim (*The Pearly Gates of Cyberspace*, 1999) when it comes to the spiritual dimension. This Australian science writer, now living in Los Angeles, though not a visionary herself, can be viewed as a post mortem apologist for the "Californian Ideology," as described in the classic 1995 essay of Richard Barbrook and Andy Cameron.[6] "The Internet may seem an unlikely gateway for the soul," as the book cover states—and so it turned out to be, I would say. A tiny faction of mainly American trans-human science fiction enthusiasts are suddenly leveled onto the mainstream and portrayed as the chief architects of the Internet.

Instead of positioning the spiritual take on cyberspace as one among many metaphors, existing in parallel with others and fighting over the hegemony of this new medium, Wertheim sees an "immense spiritual yearning among many people" as the motor behind immaterialization. In the spiritualized version of the cyberspace story, VRML guru Marc Pesce and the futurist science sect the Extropians take the places of the corporates—let's say, Nicholas Negroponte or Esther Dyson.[7] What should be described in terms of experimental subcultures, dealing with the exploration of consciousness, positioned at the crossroads of religion, drugs and technology, en passant paving the way for business to take over the Internet, is mistakenly seen as the essence of the whole undertaking.

This leads Wertheim to ask: "What is it about our time and our society that is reflected in the "heavenly" appeal of cyberspace? In short, what does all this cyber-religious dreaming tell us about the state of America today?" My answer would be that it still is a deeply religious 18th century world, full of secret societies, rival schools and tribes, with little or no public intellectuals and debates. In short, there is no public space equipped to analyze superstition à la Moravec (1988) and Minsky (1986) and distinguish it from the no-nonsense business agenda of the new economy generation.

The dotcom gold diggers may perhaps not openly criticize the cyber-spiritualists for their mumbo jumbo, but they certainly would not risk including such talk in their business plans. The formulas of the earlier generation of Internet visionaries quickly expired in favor of the IPO dotcom vocabulary. Libertarians with their harsh New Age survival-of-the-fittest agendas all but disappeared into invisible think tanks, company boards and closed discussion forums. The role of these happy amateurs was taken over by strategic management consultants and other market-friendly jargon-coining professionals.

What does make Wertheim's book interesting is her historical genealogy of space, the leading metaphor of the Internet's transitional stage from myth to accessible medium in the early to mid 1990s. Having presupposed the dominant position of the School of Consciousness (if I may call these cyber-believers that), Wertheim states that "this new digital domain is an attempt to realize a technological substitute for the Christian space of Heaven." Like the early Christians, to whom Heaven was a realm in which their souls "would be freed from the frailties and failings of the flesh, so today's champions of cyberspace hail their realm as a place where we will be freed from the limitations and embarrassments of physical embodiment."

Like Heaven, "cyberspace too is potentially open to everyone": this is a crucial political statement of the libertarian factions against states that intend to use social policy to bridge the "digital divide." The market, not the state, will achieve this all on its own, the libertarians say. The main drive behind the spiritual desire associated with digitized space "is coming from people not content with a strictly materialist view." This discontent, according to Wertheim, derives from the Western scientific world picture, which is entirely monistic, "admitting the reality of the physical world alone and rebelling against the 'pointless physical void.'"

Using David Noble's *The Religion of Technology*, Wertheim states that cyber-utopianism is making a full circle, coming back to late medieval utopias of a man-made New Jerusalem—a fictional city in which technology is playing a vital role, as Noble (1999) proves. What it would mean if the Internet would drop us back into the 12th century and its totalitarian utopias is a possibility not discussed.

Wertheim clearly has more fun analyzing Dante's *Divine Comedy* as a soul space, Giotto's Arena Chapel in Padova, Einstein's relativistic space and the multidimensional spaces of contemporary physics, than she has understanding new media. It is indeed tempting to draw parallels between the 1990s cyber-gnosis school and Hermeticism or the Pythagoreans, who were interested in the numerical forms that inhered in the material world.

But Wertheim's reading of the cyberculture canon does not go beyond the obligatory classics, such as William Gibson's *Neuromancer* (1984) and Michael Bendedikt's anthology *Cyberspace: The First Steps* (1991). Some of the most obvious reference texts are quoted (Sherry Turkle, Erik Davis, Howard Rheingold). But she does not really dive into the issues, perhaps because actual cyberspace is so surprisingly secular and down to earth in its aims. Her main message is a Gnostic one: the Internet is there to leave the dirty world of physics behind.

The one techno-feature Wertheim does get excited about is 3D role-playing games such as ActiveWorlds, where she finds evidence that indeed "cyberspace is another space," referring to its non-physical nature. But the Internet is actually moving away from William Gibson's cyberspace vision, back into the hands of the media industry and their newspaper and shopping mall models. There is no money to be made with these 3D immersive environments unless they can be incorporated into PlayStation-type computer games. The now common parallel between cyberspace and the urban space hardly gets mentioned.[8] Clearly the urban parallel does not fit into Wertheim's spiritual, anti-monistic agenda, because it would only lead into social, political and economic issues of infrastructure, globalization and other earthly matters.

For those allergic to American corporatism, my sketch of the Internet as a money machine might be depressing. Time to withdraw and resign? Ignore the overall image and continue to work on what needs to be done? Sit on top of the hill, watching the state-monopoly capitalist destruction of the net passing by? Is any utopian vision of an equal (re)distribution of knowledge, resources and power not in immediate danger nevertheless to being incorporated by the same forces, this time with a Third Way label on it? We may not wish to fall back into anti-American Luddite positions, nor sell cheap, outworn solutions which may or may not have appealed to the early adopters, the so-called post-1989 Generation X.

According to Hannah Arendt (1968), this conflict, the one between utopia and negativism, cannot and should not be solved. To paraphrase Arendt's reading of Plato's *Republic*, we could say that we should not seek the immediate beauty of new media concepts. The Internet must be chaste and moderate if one is to profit from it. If we follow the analogy further, cyberspace should supplement its knowledge of ideas with knowledge of the shadow of the realm of the digital. If the Internet is to illuminate the darkness, not add to it, it must begin by taming its own utopian promises. The (self) containment of cyberspace should be rooted as a call for responsibility, not in a passive delegation of power to the state or the market.

In German, this strategy, the "civic hedging" of cyberspace, demanding a break in the release of yet another version, could be called *das Aufhalten des Netzes*. In times of hyper growth, such a proposal to hold up the development of a technology may sound conservative, but its aim is to protect that technology from being reduced to one single quality, to one single idea—shopping mall and money machine, total work and total entertainment environment. This first of all means arresting the childish dream, with its seamless possibilities of space after space, full of thrilling experiences and fortunes to be made. The aim here is to prevent the Internet turning into a nightmare (from which it then has to awake). The next version is not always going to be a better one as many of those who constantly have to download software in order to keep up may know.

In order to achieve this, the utopian vision does not have to be totally eliminated, nor do we need to withdraw into the apocalyptic pole, which states that the world and its network will collapse anyhow—with or without our interference. The conflict between utopia and negativism Hannah Arendt describes needs to be played out. The deeper we are drawn into the Virtual, the more there is a need to stage its inherent paradoxes and contradictions. To willingly suspend belief.

According to the pragmatist's view, principles are "abbreviations of past practices" (Rorty 1999, p. 23). The same can be said of the Internet dictums of open-architecture, decentralized structure, copyleft, and so on. These features, formulated under the spell of post-1968, Vietnam and the Cold War, need to be historically framed in order not to be turned into a crusty, moral belief system. It would be naive to hope for a computer network "which cannot be used by the political right, one which will lend itself only to good causes."

I am following here what Richard Rorty wrote in *Philosophy and Social Hope*. Pragmatists, according to Rorty, do not believe there is an essential essence, a "way things really are," beyond all appearances. This goes double for the "essence" of the Internet, which in pragmatic terms is neither good (liberated by the free market), nor evil (dominated by monopoly corporations). Rather, Rorty suggests we try to distinguish between descriptions (of the Internet, for example) "which are less useful and those which are more useful" To Rorty, concepts describe things, rather than reveal their essence.

We can think about this in relation to the question of the metaphors applied to the Internet. Some of them are useful and productive for a while, whereas in other contexts they may become meaningless and boring. We can think of the city metaphor, references to the (virtual) body or the Internet as a safe haven for the Self and other spiritual motifs. The future, according to Rorty, should not conform to a plan. Rorty's hero, John Dewey, posits "growth" as the only moral end. Pragmatists reject any teleology and hope that the future (of the Internet, for example) "will astonish and exhilarate. The vista not the endpoint matters." (Rorty 1999, p. 28) If we do not impose absolute values upon the directions new media might take, more realms of possibilities might reveal themselves. It is the role of theory to draw these images, not to impose them on reality.

# <Notes>

1.  This was written in the first half of 2000. A shorter, earlier version was published as "New Media Culture in the Age of the New Economy" in media_city seoul 2000 (catalogue, Seoul: media_city, 2000).

2.  See Giddens 2000.

3.  Reprinted in *Australian Financial Review*, January 22–23, 2000.

4.  *Australian Financial Review*, April 8, 2000.

5.  In a posting to *Red Rock Eater News Service*, April 8, 2000.

6.  Richard Barbrook and Andy Cameron, The California Ideology, http://media.wmin.ac.uk/HRC/ci/calif5.html.

7.  See Negroponte 1995; Dyson 1997; Pesce 2000.

8.  See e.g. William J. Mitchell, *City of Bits* (MIT Press, 1995).

# The Rise and Fall of Dotcom Mania

**I have** no opinion—and just continue shopping.
　　—Genc Greva

Disclaimer: From the perspective of critical cyberculture, there is little reason to take malicious pleasure in the massive downfall of Internet startups, however silly their business plans may have been.[1] Although populist anti-speculative sentiments and moral anti-capitalist stands are on the rise, history is not on the side of those who predicted the failure of the New Economy and, for whatever reason, stayed out of business. Let's leave the bashing of failed millionaires to IBM: "Enthusiasm is great, experience is better," it says on one of its billboards in early 2001. Another one reads: "Bad ideas don't get better online." The dotcom backlash turns into an authoritarian call for "fundamentals," as in the following *New York Times* quote: "We've just gone through this huge dot-com-Internet-globalization bubble—during which a lot of smart people got carried and forgot the fundamentals. . . . It turns out that the real secret of success in the information age is what it always was: fundamentals—reading, writing and arithmetic, church, synagogue and mosque, the rule of law and good governance."[2] It is time "e-business gets back to business" (IBM ad).[3]

No matter how crazy and fraudulent the "dotbomb" schemes were, what will replace them is certainly not going to be any better. AOL/TimeWarner and Microsoft are poised to come out of the tech crash as the big winners. The dialogue between activist techno-anarchists and libertarian entrepreneurs is a fierce one, while the one between corporate media and IT moguls is nonexistent. Those who care about civil liberty, open standards and social change, the creation of an innovative, technological culture through software development, capital investment and cultural activity should prepare for a phase of flat nihilism, dominated by just a handful of players. "Dotcom is the weakest link, goodbye." The potlatch chapter of the Internet story is over. Have a fair laugh over the build-to-flip schemes of those who lost fortunes and move on. An age of brutal normalization has set in, seen as necessary to make up for the losses and failed investments. But first, let's look back at the speculative phase of the Internet economy, also known as tulipomania dotcom.

The magic year 2000 turned out to be a turning point. The internal contradiction between the fascinating lure of the "free" and the pressure on Internet companies to come up with real revenues, finally hit the surface. Many startups found themselves in a downward spiral after the first quarter, with tax payments due, high marketing costs (billboards, TV commercials, ads in other old media), and first rounds of venture capital drying up quickly. Costs grew exponentially: "It takes $10 to create a technology, it costs $100 to create a product and $1000 to take it to market with distributor channels and marketeering materials." (Cisco CEO John Chambers) The burn rate of concepts, friendships, health, and communities was a high one. With stock options "deep out of the money" the fun was over soon. It was time to think conservatively again and put the fairy tales of risk-taking heroes aside for a while.

By mid 2000 the e-commerce hype had died, meaning that its modest growth had proved unable to reach the predicted revenues the overall Internet economy needed to go to the next round of hyper growth (and VC funding). The dependency of the IPOed companies on their overvalued stocks was the main reason why the downward spiral set in so rapidly. The speed religion of the New Economy ("Not the big will eat the small but the fast will eat the slow") turned against itself: the higher you fly the deeper you fall, with the unfortunate, some would say inevitable result that the mammoth chewed the hasty.

Forget the "business porn" (Paulina Borsook) of Red Herring, Fast Company, and Business 2.0. Perhaps with the exception of *The Industry Standard*, the Watchtowers of the New Economy have willingly been blind after what happened in the aftermath of the April 2000 NASDAQ downfall. The resemblance to Communist party news media in the former Eastern Bloc is remarkable: organized optimism, neglect of basic figures mixed with portraits of its heroes while celebrating their miraculous breakthroughs at the forefront of financial schemes. The dotcom propagandists kept on repeating their mantra of bankruptcy as a spiritually cleansing experience, hoping that the storm won't be that bad after all. The blindness of the e-commerce Pravdas is bewitching, even one year after the crash. The showcased denial of reality is worth a thorough anthropological study, assisted by clinical psychologists. Morgan Stanley analyst Mary Meeker about Priceline: "It wasn't troubled until it was troubled. It was fine on Wednesday, bad on Thursday."[4]

"We are bullish on everything positive." What was striking about New Economy believers was not the paranoia, the greed and gold-rush hallucinations but the blatant lack of self-reflection. There was a collective refusal to analyze the broader economic and political context of information technology, taking basic economic laws into account. The general news media were actively propagating the speculative bubble. As Robert J. Schiller puts it in *Irrational Exuberance* (2000, p. 95): "The role of the news media in the stock market is not, as commonly believed, simply as a convenient tool for investors who are reacting directly to the economically significant news itself. The media actively shape public attention and categories of thought, and they create the environment within which the stock market events are played out."

The presumption of the dotcom era has been that the individual entrepreneur, together with his company will succeed no matter what, as long as the Will remained unspoiled and focused. Success would come from the unlimited growth of users and their ever growing hunger for online services. As with other religions, reflexivity can be dangerous and bring the whole enterprise into trouble. Says Robert Schiller about the upward bias of stock analysts (2000, p. 31): "It is the vague, undifferentiated future, far beyond one-year forecasts, that lie behind the high market valuations. Analysts have few worries about being uniformly optimistic regarding the distant future; they have concluded that such generalized optimism is simply good for business." According to data from Zacks Investment Research only 1.0 percent of recommendations were "sells" in late 1999 (Schiller 2000, p. 30).

Doubts were not allowed. Setbacks simply happened. The dotcom attitude remained one of disbelief over the size of the tech wreck, summarized in the response on the VC site www.tornado.com, dated May 19, 2000, after boo.com's spectacular downfall: "Learn, evolve and prosper." If they did there were others to blame (mainly the "old media" press). Internal criticism was nonexistent because it could potentially undermine a company's strategy to gain value (measured in click rates) as soon as possible. Through the distribution of stock options, dotcom workers were made complicit to this "post-democratic" business model. The atmosphere was one of organized optimism, a self imposed dictatorship of the positive, comparable to a religious sect. Internal discipline was handled in ways known only in former communist parties: dissidents simply did not exist. Everybody is happy, can't you see? Shut up and party. Think of your stock options, the football table and free breakfast buffets. Don't worry, be happy. Unleash those positive energies within!

Dotcom management went like this: Be playful and don't think about anything other than accomplishing your task. Do your ping pong and write the damned code. "Negative elements" had to be marginalized and were labeled as simplistic, one-dimensional, outmoded ideologues.[5] Critique was essentially viewed as a dinosaur phenomenon, coming from those who could not keep up with the pace. Feedback, a fundamental mechanism of cybernetics, was banned because it could endanger a precarious market position. The rigid "new era" ideology of permanent success was the main reason why the dotcom crash was not anticipated by most insiders of the network revolution. It simply could not happen. Hadn't we got rid of dialectics a long time ago? Differentiation and rhizomatic growth had replaced the linear thesis-antithesis-synthesis model. In the existing age of viral guerrilla marketing there is no place for ordinary ups and downs. Long and short waves, crisis and recession, irrational exuberance, all constructs of evil minds, attempting to play down and deny the seemingly endless growth potential of the Internet economy and the global market in general. Those pointing at possible signs of a downturn are secret agents of negativism. Their constant talk of "overvalued stocks" eventually brought down the stocks.

Blame it on the Other. Sabeer Bhatia, founder of Hotmail who sold out to Microsoft, saw his second enterprise, arzoo.com, go down the drain. In April 2001 it closed operations. Bhatia: "This was necessitated by a severe downturn in the US economy which has resulted in a slowdown in corporate spending especially for any new product and services. This is not the right time to introduce such a service to our corporate partners—all of whom are engaged in what some call a 'ruthless cost-cutting' exercise." Arzoo a victim of a "ruthless exercise"? Not that its business plan was flawed. The world was simply not ready for Arzoo. Bhatia aimed at creating a virtual pool of talent that would help solve the problems of those who might encounter any IT-related troubles. "Arzoo will be used across the world by corporations to seek instant answers to their pressing technical problems. It will provide online problem-solving assistance for engineering and information technology applications to corporates," Bhatia told the Times of India on September 8, 2000. Fucked Company, a message board where rumors about down spiraling IT firms are exchanged: "Never used em, but, according to their press releases, they provided 'live, real-time interaction with experts' hmm. sounds like Usenet and EVERY FUCKING OTHER MESSAGE BOARD ON EARTH." Second Sux, responding on Fucked Company: "Anyway, I'm glad this 'genius' founder of hotmail got slapped in the ass. I mean, it was amazing enough MS gave him millions for a web-based email service that are as commonplace as dirt right now. From the interviews I saw, this mothafucka thought he was the damn Messiah after scoring that load of $$$, and the IT media whores treated him as such. Well, 2 years later, what do you fuckin know? Netbust.com! BTW, this didn't have shit to do with the economic downturn, it had more to do with something more universal—reality."

In the meantime venture capital moved on from the unsafe, open and free web to the next big thing, the proprietary wireless systems where at least a payment system already was in place. However, the VC world remained as rigorous as ever, blaming "over publicized dotcom failures and an unfriendly stock market" (www.tornado-insider.com) for the overall malaise. Lacking critical assessment it proved hard to redirect struggling companies, stubbornly sticking to the Darwinist survival-of-the-fittest world view of winners, losers and leaders. There was no time left for an evolutionary end game. For most players the curtain fell too early. NASDAQ's radical move down left behind a scattered field with no winners to identify. There was a lack of serious competitors after all. Only mature markets know serious competition, so they say. "It's the customer, stupid," is another popular post-dotcom wisdom. The users either did not come at all to a site, or, if they did, "just looked, window-shopped, compared prices, took advantage of the free stuff on offer and moved on. In dotcom speak, they failed to 'monitorize eyeballs.'"[6]

Who dares to portray Netscape as a "winner"? Michael Lewis's Silicon Valley Story "The New New Thing" wisely stops at the moment Jim Clark is becoming an after-tax billionaire after cowardly selling off Netscape to AOL. Mid 1999 Clark declared: "I've gone over the to dark side," after having purchased shares of Netscape former arch rival Microsoft. Founder Marc Andreessen doesn't mention his former darling Netscape anymore, whose IPO in 1995 kicked off the dotcom Wall Street rally. He is too busy keeping his venture new LoudCloud alive. "The jig is up," he told the *Washington Post* (December 28, 2000). "We are now in a time of great seriousness." LoudCloud reported a net loss of $60.3 million in the first quarter of 2001 and in May 2001 laid off 122 employees, 19 percent of its workforce. A LoudCloud press release: "We are beginning to recognize the leverage in our business model, which is designed to replace human capital with technological automation." By then its stock prize had dropped from $6 to $1.70. *Industry Standard*: "The results were disappointing for a company that boasts the Internet equivalent of a blue-blood pedigree. Andreessen, one of the web's first celebrities, assembled a high-powered team of former AOL and Netscape heavyweights, including AOL exec Ben Horowitz. LoudCloud sailed through early venture rounds last summer, amassing a valuation of more than $1 billion. As the Internet bubble burst, however, rain clouds formed over the company. When it went public on March 9, the company was valued at $450 million. The company is now worth $249 million and holds $205 million in cash."[7]

Jim Clark's new new thing after Netscape, the health industry portal Healtheon, merged with WebMD and fell from $105 in 1999, where Michael Lewis's account ends, to a mere $6 in mid 2001. In 2000 Clark stepped down from the board. No more talk of Healtheon/WebMD taking over IBM or Microsoft, as Michael Lewis had been speculating about at length. "Serial entrepreneur" Clark dropped from the billionaires list, ranking 334 on the Forbes 2000 Rich 400 list, from 132 in 1999. According to Forbes, Clark's wealth had shrunken from 1800 to 875 million in one year. The whole clue of Lewis's ecstatic story, Clark becoming an after tax billionaire, has fallen into pieces. Clark's latest new thing, an online service for the rich, www.mycfo.com, is not listed on the NASDAQ. The sector was cured of compulsive IPOism, as was the "anarchist outsider" Clark. Since mid 2000 no public statements of Clark could be found on the net. Michael Lewis also wisely shuts up. He is just the piano player, isn't he?

Cynicism has set in. Under the title "Pinnacles and Pitfalls of the Internet" Joseph Nocera and Tim Carvell sum up "50 sharp lessons."[8] Many of them do not go any further than stating the obvious: "A web site is not the same as a business," "Banner ads don't work," "Nobody wants to buy shampoo over the Internet," "Physical stores are wonderful things" and "We should have listened to Warren Buffett after all." The one-liners are not quite ironic nor show any vision for how to deal with the current setbacks. Rather, the business paparazzi is armoring itself for a backlash campaign against the entrepreneurial big mouths. "Youth is not the same thing as intelligence," "'Cool' is not the same as 'profitable,'" "Day trading is a sucker's game," and "The Internet has been a gift to charlatans, hypemeisters, and merchants of vapors." The mood is getting resentful: "If you have to ask "What's the business model?" there shouldn't be any stock" and "People who left good jobs for speculative options got what they wanted." In the same way as all these virtues were praised one year ago they are being denounced here. No sign of anti-cyclical intelligence. One "lesson" disturbed the traditional business community most: "Giving stuff away is an easy way to make friends and a lousy way to make money." Related is the secret wish of many CEOs that "some day email will not be free," resulting in the statement "the person to figure out e-cash will be a billionaire," thereby showing that this duo hasn't learned a thing from dotcom mania.

Dotgone entrepreneurs lacked patience to work on sustainable models. It was presumed that Moore's law would automatically apply to the Internet economy: a doubling of customers—and revenue—every 18 months. More likely every week. The rule was: become a first mover, spend a lot of money, build traffic, get a customer base, and then figure out how to make money. No time to lose till the IPO-merger-sell out. Get out as quick as you can and leave others with the mess you created. Presuming there are others. Value accumulation was believed to grow at the speed of light: "The people and companies of the new economy—from Bill Gates to Bangalore programmers—are today's global revolutionary vanguard. And the change they are spreading moves at literally the speed of light."[9] The dotcom answer to all your doubts: "you ain't seen nothing yet."

Spring 2000, with the NASDAQ losing half its value, tech stock owners must have wished Baudrillard's saying "The Year 2000 did not happen" had come true. If there is no Short Profit you can always point at the solid long-term trends, as the authors of The Long Boom did. The IPO fund metamarkets.com (connected to Long Boom): "Pessimistic pundits call the New Economy a 'fad,' and today's great bull market a 'speculative bubble.' They ignore the great trends that define the New Economy." Let history be the judge. The meta marketers have to admit that there are ups and downs in the markets. In accordance with their libertarian ideology they blame the recession on government policy. "It's always possible for something to go terribly wrong. Intense regional conflicts have the potential to reduce the value of the post-Cold War peace dividend. And while the dominant role of governments has diminished around the world, there remains the ever-present possibility of serious blunders in fiscal or monetary policy—especially in the area of taxation of new communications technologies and of international trade. But there is virtually no risk that the potential for innovation, production and wealth creation by the five billion citizens of the New Economy is anywhere near exhausted."[10] Not that anyone had suggested the end of the Internet. The libertarian presumptions of the Long Boom didn't quite work. It was the dotcom model that failed, not the Internet.

Most likely to survive are small e-commerce companies not on the dotcom radar, with modest growth expectations and real revenues, or even profits, not listed on the stock market. "Cash will be king" as Shannon Henry stated in his 2001 outlook in the *Washington Post* (December 28, 2000): "The gleeful, easy, everyone-is-getting-funded attitude has been replaced by skepticism, gloom and massive reversal of fortune. The shakeout will continue until many companies' pockets are completely emptied." There won't be many bubble ventures any time soon. What actually happened after April 2000 is the integration of the dotcom work force and expertise within the existing corporate structures. Some call it a necessary restructuring of the sector. I would rather call it a process of silent (dis)integration, disrupted and exhilarated by bankruptcies and scandals. A commentary in *The Economist* describes how the New Economy increasingly act like the old. "Yahoo! looks more like a media company every day, especially now that AOL/TimeWarner has defined the genre. At its root eBay is just a marketplace, and they are rarely valued in the bricks-and-mortal world. Eventually the two worlds begin to blur. The dotcom leaders may well be among the great companies of the future, but increasingly they will not be thought of as a class unto themselves. Nor, one suspects, will their shares."[11]

It will take a while to unravel the dark side of the electronic gold rush. Dirty deals are being uncovered made by lawyers, stockbrokers and accountants who all had multiple roles in IPO deals with firms acting as auditors, advisers, and independent experts at the same time.[12] Internet business consultants, at the center of these allegations, are always right. In rosy times they will predict infinite growth of stock values because of predicted hyper growth. In times of recession they will blame the very same market they trusted a few months earlier. Is there anyone to blame here, one wonders? Arthur Andersen, Accenture, Deloitte & Touche, etc. seem to get away with everything. There is no accountability whatsoever. It is like suing the weatherman for a bad prediction.

Take Nicolas Tingley of Morgan Stanley. In the midst of the NASDAQ crisis the *Australian Financial Review* of December 1, 2000 portrays this investment banker as an "interested bystander at the downturn of the technology sector." I am sure he would not have presented himself as such a year or so ago. Tingley is portrayed as a high-tech skeptic. He is commenting in the "Six Myths of Technology Stocks," an article in the *Wall Street Journal* (October 17, 2000), written by E. S. Browning and Greg Ip. "People desperately wanted it to be true, wanted it to be a new era. And it always is different—until it turns out it isn't." Tingley is trying to talk himself out of the episode of the short boom of 1999, blaming the overvaluation of tech stocks on "psychology." However, the agents of "psychology" remain anonymous. Morgan Stanley is certainly not one of them. No. They are, as Tingley explains, only interested in "fundamentals," focusing on "opportunities that it can understand and adequately forecast." Who then, if no US investment banks such as Morgan Stanley were the driving force behind the speculative dotcom mania? The current business rhetoric cannot answer this question, not even *Wall Street Journal*'s six myths. I will quote them here, leaving out the explanations:

> Myth No. 1: Tech companies can generate breathtaking gains in earnings, sales and productivity for years to come. . . .

Myth No. 2: Tech companies aren't subject to ordinary economic forces, such as a slower economy or rising interest rates. . . .

Myth No. 3: Monopolies create unbeatable advantages. . . .

Myth No. 4: Exponential Internet growth has just begun and, if anything, will accelerate. . . .

Myth No. 5: Prospects are more important than immediate earnings. . . .

Myth No. 6: This time, things are different. . . .

It is funny to see how the global financial discourse brokers of the *Wall Street Journal* debunk their own belief system. An unconscious collective call for punishment for those who made, and are losing millions of dollars these days, might be too simplistic. The question is rather who talked up these stocks in the first place. Most likely the same journalists, column writers, analysts and consultants, now predicting further losses. How can experts get away with such a lack of memory? Peace, love and understanding for the poor messengers and running dogs. As Carl Gunderian wrote in a private response to my call for accountability on the nettime mailing list: "Before we start marching these paid dot.flacks to the scaffold, we should remember that they merely fed the investors' capacity for greed and self-delusion. Or, as W. C. Fields once put it, you can't cheat an honest man! On the other hand, self-delusion can survive even this downturn." Dave Mandl responded on nettime: "During the New Economy mania, almost NOBODY involved in the biz (money people, dot-com entrepreneurs, financial journalists) was a naysayer. Virtually ALL of them made fun of stuffy old guys who wore ties to work and people who owned stocks in old-economy companies. There's no doubt in my mind that when the dust settles, it'll turn out that "no one" was responsible, no one really believed that Amazon was worth $600 a share, everyone thought allowing dogs into the office was silly, etc. Most of all, Wall St. will deny that they had anything to do with it. Dot-com mania 'just happened' somehow."[13]

I would therefore propose to add one myth to the Browning/Ip list:

Myth No. 7: Financial analysts, consultants and business reporters are merely bystanders.

In the Internet economy, technological change is a complex, dynamic, integrated system. Its direction is increasingly dictated by financial markets, which are no longer just "feeding" the IT industry with capital from the outside. Investment decisions of venture capitalists direct the way in which technology is being developed, thereby affecting the course of technology. A cloudy, dense information structure is intrinsically intertwined with its object (Internet technology, wireless applications, telecoms, hardware etc.). This hypersensitive environment is also open to a variety of factors such as currency exchange rates, interest rates, and even, to some extent domestic and foreign policy. And let's not forget the price of crude oil. Factors which have to be closely monitored. The media—television, print magazines, the Internet—are in constant feedback with both the financial markets and the technological sector; one big PR marketing machine. Competition does not lead to a diversification of opinions and formats. Within this turbulent climate of "digital convergence" there is little interest in independent reporting and critical research in new media and IT development.

Analysts are being called to account for a massive conflict of interest, Pamela Williams reports from New York in June 2001. "Analysts are now on trial for advising investors to buy when they themselves were selling; for propping up the prices of worthless companies; for issuing booster reports to create share price spikes while their own investment banks dumped stock; for acting as rain makers and issuing bullish reports to help win business for their investment divisions; for poor disclosure standards on personal share holdings; for regurgitating corporate press releases as independent research, and for sharing in the vast bonus pools born of the investment side of the business."[14] Analysts kept rating "a strong buy," ignoring the stormy market weather. Williams, referring to a speech of the Securities and Exchange

Commission chief Laura Unger, argues that in 2000, with the NASDAQ index dropping 60 percent, "less than 1 percent of analyst recommendations were "sell" or "strong sell." Analysts pushed the "buy" recommendations to look after their company's clients while protecting themselves by issuing occasional warnings to investors about the tech sector as a whole.

Thomas Frank, a Chicago social critic, has written a critique of the 1990s New Economy craze, *One Market Under God, Extreme Capitalism, Market Populism and the End of Economic Democracy.* He must have been finishing his manuscript in early 2000 when the NASDAQ was about to head south. Frank's analysis is merciless and systematic. He is clearly not into net activism, nor is he involved in any of the debates over Internet standards or digital rights issues. It's Frank vs. the Titanic forces of right-wing politics. A heroic tale of the Critic against the Wall St. Dragon—with insightful outcomes. Frank (2000, p. xv) points out that market populism is riven by contradictions: "It is the centerpiece of the new American consensus, but that consensus describes itself in terms of conflict, insurrection, even class war. It decries 'elitism' while transforming CEOs as a class into one of the wealthiest elites of all time. It deplores hierarchy while making the corporation the most powerful institution on earth. It hails the empowerment of the individual and yet regards those who use that power to challenge markets as robotic stooges. It salutes choice and yet tells us the triumph of markets is inevitable." Contradictions which worked at some stage—and then lost their magic.

For Thomas Frank the New Economy is a fraud. "We did not vote for Bill Gates; we didn't all sit down one day and agree that we should use his operating system. The logic of business is coercion, monopoly, and the destruction of the weak, not 'choice' or 'service' or universal affluence." The trick then becomes entrancing the public and making them believe in the benefits of a manic bull market, through "relentless incantation," a veritable army of pundits and PR men to engage in a "process of reassurance," as Frank writes (2000, p. xv), quoting Galbraith's *The Great Crash*. Remember

1998 and 1999, when nothing was capable of stopping the People's Market? Frank (ibid., p. 158) writes: "Winging above it all were the leaping, soaring Internet shares. Scattered notes of caution were far overpowered by a decade of promotional hype, of talk about the magic of communication 'mind to mind,' the technology that 'changed everything,' the place where the 'old rules' no longer applied, where the inevitabilities of Moore's Law, of Metcalfe's Law, of Gilder's Law ensured that hundred-bagger appreciations would continue to fall from the heavens."

The overall picture points at some real contradictions within digital capitalism, without a synthesis or compromise in sight. There is no Third Way solution for Digital Discontent. On the electronic frontier there is a real (conceptual) battle going on, with little or no room for the (originally Dutch) Polder model of consensus. Whereas more and more data are floating over the networks, there is a similar hyper growth of data stored away behind password protected IP walls. The pressure on the New Economy to finally come up with a real cash flow bumps into the marketing tactics of the very same breed of people who put out free content, attracting new audiences in order to build up a customer base. Two contradictory strategies, coined by Arthur Kroker as the "facilitating" and "harvesting" aspect of new technologies are colliding in a spectacular fashion. What remains from the dotcom era of wonderful nonsense is the pressing question of how information on the Internet is going to be paid for. The billions of venture capital dollars, thrown on startups didn't bring the solution of a secure payment system for content and services one step closer. It only further consolidated the ideology that everything has to be free.

Sloganism: "All hope, design could bring salvation should be eliminated" (Genc Greva). Don't stop thinking about the Internet. You are only human once. Open Monopolies for an Open Society. After the Culture Crash (book title). The Global Province: Rhetoric after Heidegger (Why do we remain in the Internet?). Virtual Failures (conference title). Empire Internet: Its Golden Dawn, Conceptual Renaissance, Nihilistic Moment. Rack Space Squatters, Unite. "I have written six theories on cybercities. They can't all be true." (Johan Sjerpstra) "We will be where the consumers are" (Chinese saying). The Will to Design: Overcoming Entertainment (T shirt). Resistance Is Fertile. Fighting Download Syndrome. Decide or Consume. Toolkit: Build your own Internet Observatory. "Extend your cozy feeling" (Baleno). Have you heard about Minorspace? Revolution 'R' Us. "No reconciliation with artificial nature" (graffiti). Lead me to the wrong side of virtuality (song). Download Your Personal Downturn Now! "Each age has its own fight against capitalism." Back to Golconda. "Accenture board of directors sentenced to death for millennial dotcom fraud."

"Napster This!" The decentralized Napster exchange of MP3 music files has put the recording industry upside down. With the *Metallica vs. Napster* court case still on, Bertelsmann and a few other record labels announced deals with Napster. By stepping up their "Zuckerbrot und Peitsche" (punish and reward) strategy, the media giants managed to even more increase their pressure on Napster to take out copyrighted material and alter its model of free content exchange into a subscription based, money making operation. Whereas post-Napster initiatives such as Gnutella and Freenet are gradually establishing themselves as true "peer-to-peer" models without any central server, MP3.com announced it would pay back the recording industry hundreds of millions of dollars for loss of copyright.

In 2000 e-commerce was scheduled to break through. A certain percentage of the created client base was supposed to reach the trust level of buying goods and services online. As an avant-garde of the free grazing herd, the early adapters would create a true Internet economy, based on real dollars, extracted from the old money economy, inserted in the net via the credit card system. Presuming that the early–mid 1990s growth would repeat itself, thousands of business were hastily founded, first in the United States, soon followed by like-minded entrepreneurs in Europe and Asia, ready to receive the first electronic consumers. Some indeed showed up. The "prosumers" purchased a bit here and there, mainly software, books, and flight tickets; not enough to match the wildly optimistic predictions. In a next round of acceleration, the B2B (business-to-business) model was introduced as a form of hype to compensate for the not fast enough growing business-to-consumer B2C revenue stream. The hugely expensive development costs for B2B were projected to be profitable only in the long run and only postponed the upcoming lag in demand of IT products and services. Hardware and infrastructure giants such as Dell and Cisco got into an overproduction mode, resulting in net losses, tumbling stocks, and massive layoffs.

The Napster madness of mid 2000 did not help to establish the badly needed stream of real dollars. According to the prophets of "free" services such as Napster would crumble the old, in this case the recording industry, and install a new economy with new rules and new players. The first may have happened to some extent but the latter certainly is a long way away. E-commerce offspring from Napster, Gnutella, Freenet and other peer-to-peer networks have been disappointingly few. Even though sales may have been substantial in individual cases for independent artists offering work for free on the web, the overall economic situation of "content providers" remains bleak. With no e-cash/micro payment system in place users will only pay for essential information. Attempts to sell .pdf documents online (such as Motley Fool's www.soapbox.com tried for a while) remained promising but did not make it outside of the banking and finance sector and closed down in the wake of the dotcom shake-out. At the end of the tech wreck phase, "free" was still the only model around.

First, in the 1980s, it was software code, and then the written word (essays, articles) which got "napsterized." With the increased capacity of chips and pipes, technology then enabled us to turn music into files of a reasonable size. The MP3 files Napster users download seem really tiny by today's standard. It will only take a few years until the free exchange of compressed feature MP4 films with a fabulous screen quality will be a fact. Watermarks against copying could split the consumer base in two—with the ones who don't care about copyright on the one hand and those who are not that techno savvy on the other hand. This is a similar split known in the case of software. Those who are somewhat clever and think they can get away with pirated software will do so, even state in public that they do not want to further financially support the Microsofts. The innocent majority will by and large agree with this but won't know what to do, until an (offshore?) Napster kind of service enters the stage. It will offer free video porn, software, exclusive financial information, anything people now pay a lot of money for.

Artists who have withdrawn (or stayed) into the world of the material objects seem to be the only ones not being affected by the inevitable napsterization of all "content." All the rest will be drawn in endless fights between the freedom of distribution and intellectual property. The answer of the libertarian gurus is a simple one: give it all away and make your living with dish washing. You may get invited to participate in some conference, exhibition, or performance, if you're lucky. The alternative is to create a micro-payment system outside of the credit-card-based old economy. That seems to be the only truly utopian option if we want to get beyond the Napster deadlock. The gift economy communities are ideal candidates to develop an open source, global platform for e-cash, a creative value clearing house, thereby making the gesture of giving away code and content a truly altruistic act, not the single remaining option.

The cultural arm of the Internet (media, the arts, academia) did not closely monitor the rise and fall of dotcom mania. "Nothing is spectacular if you aren't part of it." The Western media intelligentsia had not jumped up full of joy over the idea of stock-breeding masses. Numbed by Third Way post-Thatcherism there was no alternative developed against the tidal wave of market populism. The slaughter by greedy commerce of everything public on the net seemed inevitable. The Napster debate was the only issue where the cultural industry, faced with diminishing expectations, plagued by budget cuts and stagnating income, met the dotcom bubble. Content producers seemed divided and confused over the exploding MP3 exchange among millions of Internet users. Debates on nettime, for instance, did not show any direction or conclusion over the Napster issue. [15] Independent Internet culture, fighting over definitions what net.art might or might not be, had virtually no connections to the dotcom world.

"Information wants to be free" is coined to be the single dominant ethic in the hackers community. In his etymology of the aphorism, Roger Clarke goes back as far as John 8:32, "You shall know the truth and the truth shall make you free." In 1984, at the first hackers conference, Stewart Brand formulated the mantra in its present form. Brand: "Information wants to be free (because of the new ease of copying and reshaping and casual distribution), AND information wants to be expensive (it's the prime economic event in an information age) . . . and technology is constantly making the tension worse. If you cling blindly to the expensive part of the paradox, you miss all the action going on in the free part. The pressure of the paradox forces information to explore incessantly. Smart marketers and inventors quietly follow—and I might add, so do smart computer security people."[16] Eventually, the free part of paradox triumphed, leaving freelance content workers in despair how to earn living AND publish on the net where giving away had become the only available option.

Critique of the "free" is always in danger of being associated with media industry interests and their obsession with intellectual property. Has anyone heard the phrase "art wants to be free"? Or theory? Apart from specific censorship cases, no. Culture wants to be paid. It has to constantly fight for its existence. The free software advocates have taken the avant-garde position and see themselves on the opposite side of artists and other "content" producers such as bands, journalists and film makers. The last group is, sadly, only discussing the consequences of technologies, not shaping them, trying to keep, at best, early adapters.

"This is not an economy." (Johan Sjerpstra) The ruling "free" paradigm is a spill-over from the free software movement, whose spokesperson, Richard Stallman, once said: "When information is generally useful, redistributing it makes humanity wealthier no matter who is distributing and no matter who is receiving."[17] Against this cyber-libertarian ideology, embedded into prime code and core network architecture, there is only a weak call for content workers rights to get properly paid. Stallman's distinction between "free as in free beer" and "free as in free speech" is irrelevant for their situation. The free software movement works on the presumption that its members have a regular income. Software engineers are not short on jobs and do the voluntary free software work in their own time. In some cases they even let their bosses pay for free software development.

The few content web sites which paid its content providers closed in the dotgone aftermath. There is a "tragedy of content" in an era where the "triumph of technology" levels out and "change" has become an everyday phenomena. The Medium is still the Message, despite all marketing gurus predicting that one day, Content will be King. Despite the phenomenal growth of web pages and users, 429 million by mid 2001, the web is hardly producing unique content. Most of the web content is microwaved leftovers of old media, related to television and print media. Take the hugely popular web site of the "reality TV" series *Big Brother*. Despite its success it is not "the television program to the web site." A report on the malaise in the streaming media sector from February 2001 states: "The problem with the story of streaming media is that it started on the wrong end of the spectrum. Success will come first and foremost in enterprise and advertising. Streaming will then eventually branch out to more entertainment consumer content. Advancing content towards the general public was a mistake and the early founders have paid for it."[18]

In October 1999, at the height of the dotcom fad, the Free4What web site was launched to discuss the business model behind "free" services. The rage reached astonishing levels. Not only did free Internet providers such as FreeServe reach stock value levels of billions of dollars, users could even be paid to surf, on computers they had gotten for free. Free4What was developed during the Temp Media Lab project in Kiasma, Helsinki.[19] The starting point was a discussion the wider impact on art and culture of the free operating system Linux and open source/copyleft. There had been a steady rise of free services on the Internet, starting from email (Hotmail), web space

(Geocities) until free access services. Free4What raised issues such as privacy concerns of those using free services. If you can get paid to surf, you can as be seen as an employee, which, in theory, should have workers rights. Can users of free services complain, like consumers, about the quality which is offered to them? And the ultimate dotcom4all question: "If there can be free Internet services, why can't there be free food, free cars, free money, free houses, free electricity?" If anything remains from the period of dotcom mania, it is the question of "free" and how a sustainable Internet economy can be developed.

**< N o t e s >**

1. This was written in late 2000—mid 2001. Parts were published as "The Rise and Fall of Dotcom.mania" in *Sarai Reader 01: The Public Domain* (Sarai, 2001). The critique of the New Economy presented here got its shape in late 1999 while preparing the Tulipomania conference which I organized together with Eric Kluitenberg in De Balie, Amsterdam and Frankfurt (organized by Andreas Kallfelz) (www.balie.nl/tulipomania). Ted Byfield, Felix Stalder and David Hudson were instrumental in gaining a critical understanding of this quickly changing, fluid economic environment most cultural theorists, sadly, have little knowledge of.

2. http://www.nytimes.com/2001/01/09/opinion/09FRIE.html

3. The cynical logic of such contemporary backlash rhetoric is well documented by Robert Greene and Joost Elffers in *The 48 Laws of Power* (Profile Books, 1999). Some examples: Law 31: Control the options, get others to play with the cards you deal; Law 45: Preach the need for change, but never reform too much at once." Whereas the dotcom religion has been idealistic, utopian and arguably revolutionary in nature, the culture of cynical power, on display in the 48 Laws, has to positioned at the opposite of the spectrum. Dotcom business culture actually missed an accurate power analysis.

4. *Fortune* magazine, quoted in Pamela Williams, "Can You Trust Brokers?" *Australian Financial Review*, June 16—17, 2001. On August 3, 2001, *The Industry Standard*'s Media Grok reported about two lawsuits

against Mary Meeker: "Some investors say Meeker 'offered biased research and slanted investment advice about eBay and Seattle-based Amazon as a way to secure lucrative banking business for Morgan Stanley,' according to Bloomberg. Analysts are under the microscope right now, and Merrill Lynch recently settled arbitration against famous bull Henry Blodget. Unlike the Blodget arbitration, the cases against Meeker and Morgan Stanley are 'designed to go to court,' said the *New York Daily News*. It may not be a coincidence that these suits were filed the day after a congressional hearing that gave analysts the what-for. The SEC revealed that that 30 percent of analysts owned pre-IPO shares of companies they covered. Testimony from TheStreet.com's Adam Lashinsky suggested that financial journalists like himself aided and abetted analysts' wrongdoing. CNBC always plugged stocks 'because rising stocks meant greater viewership,' he said. TheStreet.com pointed out analyst conflicts, Lashinsky said, but 'at the same time we did our share to hype the momentum stocks of the era.'"

5.  For more on the working conditions in the dotcom sector, see Andrew Ross, "Mental Labor in the New Economy, "posted on nettime June 12, 2000 and published in *Tulipomania DotCom Reader: A Critique of the New Economy*, ed. G. Lovink and E.Kluitenberg (De Balie, 2000). See also Bill Lessard and Steve Baldwin, *NetSlaves: True Tales of Working on the Web* (McGraw-Hill, 2000); www.disobey.com/netslaves; Dana Hawkins, "Lawsuits and Workplace Monitoring," posted on nettime August 10, 2001.

6.  "Reports of the dotcom industry's death may have been exaggerated," writes John Huxley ("Down But Not Out," *Sydney Morning Herald*, March 7, 2001) in an article full of truisms such as "the dotcom disaster will look like an aberration, a mere blip, in the rise and rise of the Internet."

7.  http://www.thestandard.com/companies/dossier/0,1922,286292,00.html; http://www.thestandard.com/article/0,1902,27107,00.html.

8.  *Fortune*, reprinted in *Australian Financial Review*, December 29, 2000.

9.  Quoted from *Wired*'s *Encyclopedia of the New Economy* (http://hotwired.lycos.com/special/ene/). For a general approach on Internet time describing the hurry sickness from the user's point of view, see Gleick 1999, pp. 83–93.

10. Web site of metamarkets.com, January 2001.

11. "Is there life in e-commerce?" *Economist*, February 3, 2001, p. 18.

12. "Survey of 106 floats over 2 years," *Australian Financial Review*, December 28 and 29, 2000.

13. Geert Lovink, "The Seventh Myth," nettime, December 2, 2000; David Mandl, "re: The Seventh Myth," nettime, December 5, 2000.

14. Pamela Williams, "Can You Trust Brokers?" *Australian Financial Review*, June 16–17, 2001.

15. The Napster thread in the nettime archive started on July 23, 2000 with a posting called "Terror in Tune Town." For a summary of the debate see *net.congestion reader*, ed. G. Lovink (De Balie, 2000).

16. http://www.anu.edu.au/people/Roger.Clarke/II/IWtbF.html. The Stewart Brand quote is from an email to TBFT.com.

17. Quoted on Roger Clarke's web page (see above).

18. Paul Kushner, *streamingmedia.com newsletter*, February 26, 2001.

19. Free4What was part of the third "Nokia Country/Linux Land" week of the temp media lab project (http://temp.kiasma.fi) and was produced by a team of The Society for Old and Media including Mieke Gerritzen, Jan van den Berg, and Geert Lovink (www.waag.org/free). Richard Barbrook, Kevin Kelly, DeeDee Halleck, Patrice Riemens, Drazen Pantic, Joost Flint, Howard Rheingold, and Rishab Aiyer Ghosh joined in the debate, which was also posted to nettime (October 29, 1999).

# Hi-Low: The Bandwidth Dilemma, or Internet Stagnation after Dotcom Mania

Never enough Internet capacity can be provided to the velocity-hungry online masses.[1] The World Wide Wait community demands its natural right to surf at the promised speed of light, racing through 3D worlds, on the run to meet the perfect virtual Other. Internet traffic is booming, but where is the promised capacity?[2] But who are the agents to address the bandwidth issue? Local access providers, international telecoms, state politicians? Access policy is everything but transparent. A popular legend says: Internet capacity is gradually underused. Then why do users not get access to the vacant part of the fibber spectrum?

There exists an ambivalent attitude towards computer capacity. Five year old machines look ancient. However back then, and not that long ago, they seemed fine, state of the art. Huge sums were paid for a 486 or a Power PC. We love our old-timer hardware, the 2400-baud modem, the carefully maintained 100-Mb hard disk, packed with precious software and personal filing systems. In retrospect, yesterday's limitations are celebrated as the source of true art. So what do we want? Stumbling baroque halls of virtual reality or the genial stroke of the ascii artist? This question becomes all the more interesting in the wake of the dotcom crash. The rollout of broadband is stagnating, as is the Internet economy. On the one hand, every citizen should get the best performance network for an affordable price. On the other, why would users get a T3 line at home that service providers paid ten of thousands of dollars for a fortnight ago, comparable with the Internet access of an entire African nation?

Digirati is not a uniquely American phenomena. England has got its own breed of visionaries and Charles Leadbeater is one of them. He is promoter of "the ignorance economy,"[3] author of Living on Thin Air: The New Economy,[4] advising the Blair government in e-commerce matters and a consultant at the technology venture fund Atlas Venture. In the New Statesman of January 15, 2001, heralding the "second coming" of the Internet,[5] he states that "the Internet is not finished. We are merely seeing the end of the growth of the first Internet." What a relief amidst all the NASDAQ doom and gloom. It's that kind of salvation one can expect from a practicing priest of organized optimism. However, such escapes into bright futurism are the easy way out. The dilemma between the functionality of "low bandwidth for all" text-based systems versus high bandwidth streaming media for the few is a real one. An uneasy choice which telcos and the IT industry may struggle with for a while, with huge implications for content providers.

Against historical commonsense Leadbeater, a former Financial Times journalist, dates the "first Internet" from 1996 to 2000. Forget the 25 years or so before the World Wide Web took off. Leadbeater is well aware of this deception. He deliberately rewrites history, provoking the ascii/Linux believers by saying that the Internet was born out of the dotcom spirit of e-commerce. What Leadbeater is pushing is what we may call New Voluntarism. Forget the hackers' story of Internet rooted in military/academic informatics. Internet was born out of the Will to eBusiness. Shopping and entertainment are the true nature of humankind. They are the one and only source, engine and destiny of the net.

Unlike most New Economy prophets, Leadbeater lacks sympathy for the geniality of technology and its code magicians. What he is saying, and what many of the failed dotcom entrepreneurs would think in secret, is that Internet should shake of the yoke of technology. Applications and protocols which once pulled off this incredible global computer network were now stagnating its further development. How this liberation could be achieved is another matter.

According to Leadbeater the "first Internet" failed because the technologists and geeks, in the end, triumphed over the CEOs and their managers and usability html slaves. Early online business pioneers were of good will, ready to serve their first customers. But the general audience got scared off by geekish hocus-pocus.

Consumers, terrified by the complexity and clumsiness of this hyped-up yet incredibly self-referential environment simply left, way too early, never to come back again. No Super Bowl-style "offline" advertisement could seduce people to type in the domain names, no matter the genius of its name. The initially overpriced stock values of Internet startups, based on presupposed continuous turnover growth lost its potential customer base. By early 2000 the IT gold rush, faced with market saturation, flipped into a downward spiral. The absent clicking and sticking cyber masses triggered off the first Internet recession.

This is what the conspiracy theory of the New Economists says: blame it on the geeks. In Leadbeater's words: "The page-based Internet is boring. People want a genuinely interactive experience, with drama, excitement, games and jokes. The first Internet spent little on content and charged nothing for it. The result: hosts of bored consumers using a medium designed for geeks and nerds."

What Leadbeater is trying to sell is dreamware, this time not developed by Californian anarcho-capitalists but big media business, AOL-TimeWarner style. "The net will prosper when it is no longer the preserve of geeks, and when the speed of connections and size of bandwidth are secondary to the quality of the experience it delivers." How the news and game entertainment industry will reach supremacy while simultaneously pushing the borders of technological know-how remains unclear. In any case, the taming of geekdom is on the agenda of the virtual class—no longer just the Microsoft court case. The paranoia for monopolies has shifted to a diffuse fear for over-development in technological directions without markets.

The playful collaboration of technologists and venture capitalists has come to an end. Online creativity has shifted to other levels to express itself and moved, for example, to peer-to-peer networks and free software development. These decentralized gift economies[6] are much harder to economize compared to the heyday of "cool" web design and the ensuing portalization of online content and services. Looking down on the primitive, prehistoric past before e-commerce, the first Internet was "accessed through cumbersome personal computers and narrowband telephone lines that allowed you to download limited amounts of information," Leadbeater writes. "Its basic currency is information, mainly in text form, and searching for it is frustratingly slow and chaotic."

As an online Übermensch, just returned from the future, so kind to share a few of his thoughts with us earthlings, Leadbeater has no mercy with the "clunky" functionality of pre-millennial technology which still surrounds us. "The web pages on which the text is displayed are dense and dull; they deliver none of the excitement of a good television advertisement. They rarely make you laugh, intentionally." Someone must have fooled Leadbeater with a whole raft of false expectations. Those clever Americans perhaps? Anyway. He is really disappointed. "The Internet was supposed to be immediate, personalized, interactive and rich in content. It turned out to be slow, dense, clunky and boring."

A brief look into the political economy of bandwidth could help. The question of Internet speed is and will always be determined by economics and (cyber)geography, as the maps show,[7] not per se by the technology used at the consumer's end. Speed on the Internet is moody and in constant flux, not only depending on one's investment in hardware, locality, or available connectivity. Speed is a subjective and cultural experience. A whole range of unknown factors can bring the undisturbed surfing to a sudden halt. A broken deep-sea cable, a crucial land cable destroyed by a tractor, the US East Coast suddenly switching on their terminals or one of the main switches of MCI, AT&T, NTT, or BT gone down for a few seconds. Over the years, bandwidth has grown, however, this progress has been too slow for users to notice. The arrivals of tens of millions of newbies has eaten up the new capacity. There are recent signs of a drop in bandwidth capacity due to overpricing or a "lack of demand" as the business press calls it.[8]

Instead of analyzing the present, Leadbeater rushes back to the future: "the next Internet will be accessed everywhere, anytime, not just through hefty computers."

Leadbeater's future is going to be a Valhalla of access: "Telecommunication links will be wireless as well as well as land lines, and they will be broadband." He is promising nothing less than paradise on earth. "The second Internet will be more interactive; games and animation will become commonplace." In short: "The second Internet— wireless, ubiquitous, fast, rich in quality entertainment, drama and quality—will transform how we live, vote, shop, save, communicate and learn."

Apparently Leadbeater has not read the "13 things to know about broadband."[9] But he is well aware that he cannot deliver his technotopia overnight. "The components of the next Internet will not come together for another three years." Now, that's interesting. Three years is almost a lifetime measured in Internet time, especially if we remember the acceleration of the technological boom during the roaring 1990s. The three years in which the web established itself (1994–1997) and the even less then three years boom to bust period of dotcom mania (1998–2000). But let's suppose Leadbeater is right here. It may indeed take many years until broadband and cable modem will have penetrated Western households deep enough to create a critical user mass. Crucial time the Internet business community and most users don't have. There have been alarming editorials on the portal pages of www.streamingmedia.com about the impact the bandwidth stagnation is having on drying up net.radio and video businesses. Only those with long term strategies will survive.

A similar situation exists with the rapidly emerging peer-to-peer networks. Napster has been built up by university students using campus hard-disk space and connectivity. A vast majority of the 64 million Napster users have standard 56K modem access, are mostly interested in downloading, not exchanging files, mainly due to technical constrains. They are simply not online all the time. True peer-to-peer networks will only take off when a critical mass of its users will have a permanent, open connection to the net.[10] Until then the uploading-downloading ratio will remain unbalanced. Clerics of professional positivism will point at the ever bright future, showing bright growth figures which prove a diminishing bandwidth divide. An ever-growing amount of users may or may not yet have plenty of bandwidth at their fingertips. The question is when? Streaming media producers and users demand broadband NOW. Not next year or in a decade. The stagnating hardware industry sees broadband as a way out of the recession, speculating on the user's appetite for faster machines once they got their home DSL connection. IBM, Motorola, Intel and others even went as far to demand involvement of the US Federal Government to boost fiber digging. Broadband for everyone, from dotcom to New Deal?[11] Telcos however are reluctant to roll out broadband, deliberately delaying the upgrade of their networks to DSL levels.[12] Investments in high performance flat-rate access is not generating that much more cash, compared to the present infrastructure and revenue streams. It is anyway better to have a few well paying customers from the business sector than millions of nagging consumers paying only a few pennies for their all too comfortable stay in bandwidth paradise.

The future is taking revenge on those who have, either mentally or virtually, already arrived there. It is disappointedly empty and lonely out there: promising but without customers. Those who do not want to turn into bandwidth optimists have the option to go a few steps back and return to the productive atmosphere of low-tech tinkering. The choice between the conceptual cave of 3D streaming images and a retrograde ascii-code fundamentalism is becoming more and more attractive—and uncomfortable. Where should art projects and community networks go? Stay within the gray 56K world wide wait mainstream? Go avant-garde, requiring DSL, ending up in the sovereign atmospheres of the happy few? Jump back in history and muck around on the Unix prompt? Join the WAP debacle? Bet on an i-mode invasion from Japan? You choose. Of course we want everything, but that's a too easy an excuse. Ideally, content should be provided for all platforms. By the look of it many users are simply sticking to their PCs and wireless devices, unwilling to upgrade to newer levels which simply do not deliver the promised expectations.

The streaming media industry already seems to have made up its mind: it is withdrawing from the content-for-consumer market towards a smaller but more lucrative niche market, offering streaming media services to businesses.[13] What we see here is a return of a similar dilemma back in the early 1990s between offline multimedia 3D-interactive television/virtual reality and the real existing cyberspace, Internet, about to make its significant yet aesthetically disappointing quantum jump from a Unix kernel to the hypertext transfer protocol (HTML).

Collaborative filtering sites such as www.slashdot.org and www.plastic.com are facing the same dilemma. Apart from problematic editorial policies and the unresolved question of ownership over collaborative text databases there is the issue of those living outside of access oases not being able to contribute to important debates which are increasingly being held exclusively on online web forums. The exchange of opinions on the Internet is gradually migrating away from the email-based mailing lists and newsgroups towards web sites which require online presence, thereby indirectly undermining the (presumably) democratic and equalizing character of email as not everyone can be on the web all the time due to economical and time reasons. See the dilemm herea: stay at the level of email or jump to the online level of the web forum? It is a false but nonetheless real choice which is on the table. The net is developing in possibly conflicting directions. The image of a harmonious convergence of WebTV, PCs, and hand-held devices is not in sight. Instead of a synergy, all signs point to digital divergence, with tough choices to be made over standards and the utilization of existing, unused bandwidth. The potential of "dark fiber" is yet to be realized.[14]

## <Notes>

1. A version of this essay was "slashdotted" on February 8, 2001, resulting in a thread on the odd relationship between geek culture and the dotcom world (www.slashdot.org). Telepolis published the essay on the web in German. The English version can be found at http://www.heise.de/tp/english/inhalt/on/7121/1.html. The essay was posted on nettime March 26, 2001.

2. Source: The Net News, July 31, 2001: Net Traffic Booms. US Internet traffic is growing by an annual factor of four, according to Lawrence Roberts, respected boss of switch manufacturer Caspian Networks. It's the first accurate data-based assessment of Internet volume since 1996, when the US government controlled the network. Internet traffic expanded by a factor of 2.7 until January 2000, when it jumped to 3.6. So far this year expansion has been a factor of 4, which Roberts expects will remain steady through 2008. Roberts is an Internet guru who was in charge of developing Arpanet, precursor to the net in 1964. (Alan Farrelly).

3. "Capitalize on the Economy! We've had knowledge management. Now it's time for ignorance management," http://www.mgeneral.com/3-now/00-now/100003cl.htm.

4. Review of *Living on Thin Air*: http://www.spikemagazine.com/0100livingonthinair.htm.

5. Reprinted in *Australian Financial Review*, January 19, 2001, p. 3. Original available at www.newstatesman.co.uk.

6. For more about the role of the gift economy concept and the "cooking-pot markets" in the context of the Internet economy, see Rishab Aiyer Ghosh, "Cooking-Pot Market," in Nettime 1999 (http://www.firstmonday.dk/issues/issue3_3/ghosh/).

7. http://www.telegeography.com/Publications/tg01.html. From the Telegeography 2001 report: "International Internet bandwidth is growing faster than international Internet traffic, however. In the past few years, tremendous physical infrastructure began to come on line. Because raw bandwidth does not translate immediately into Internet capacity, however—it must first be lit, sold, deployed, and integrated into data network operations—the numbers showed what, to casual observers, appeared to be a mismatch between physical capacity and Internet capacity." See also www.cybergeography.org, www.mappingcyberspace.com, and www.architecturez.com/ae/.

8. "Bandwidth Narrows: Pan-European telecom carriers are having to curb their ambitions in a year that analysts predict will be the start of the communications shakeout. Last week, FirstMark, Viatel and GTS (Global TeleSystems) all announced they would cut their European operations. A glut of bandwidth, a lack of demand and the bottleneck of the

'local loop' to homes and offices, meant a reversal of fortunes last year. And to add to their woes, share prices were badly hit in the tech slump and extra financing became hard to come by." (http://tm0.com/sbct.cgi?s=87827715&i=295870&d=932825)

9. "13 Things to Know About Broadband" by Gerry McGovern, first published in his "New Thinking" electronic newsletter, then published in Steven Carlson's NowEurope newsletter, which was forwarded on May 13, 2000 to the nettime mailinglist (www.nettime.org). On January 13, 2001, David Garcia forwarded "13 reactions" of John Patterson to nettime in response to McGovern.

10. Statistics on the use of 56K, broadband, cable modem etc. can be found at http://cyberatlas.Internet.com/markets/broadband and at http://www.nua.ie/surveys/index.cgi.

11. Scott Thurm and Glenn R. Simpson, "Tech Industry Seeks Its Salvation," *Wall Street Journal*, June 25, 2001: "High-tech executives think they've found a cure for the industry's deepest slump in a decade: High-speed Internet access for everyone. For years, telephone and cable-TV companies have been promising to build high-speed 'broadband' networks, which let consumers and small businesses tap the Internet 20 or 30 times faster than conventional phone lines, yet the rollout has been slow. There's little agreement, even within the tech world, on the ground rules for building such networks, which would cost tens of billions of dollars. But suddenly the topic has rocketed to the top of the technology industry's agenda in Washington, where traditionally distant tech executives are asking for help." (http://interactive.wsj.com/articles/SB993418457489449631.htm) See also nettime, June 27–28, 2001.

12. "Although many providers of broadband Internet access have increased their marketing budgets to entice customers into upgrading their connections, analysts say few of the providers have been able to meet the demand that they have created. Stories abound of broadband customers waiting weeks or months to have DSL or cable-modem access installed, and Jupiter Research analyst Joseph Laszlo says the coming years will see the broadband market remain 'more supply-constrained than demand-constrained.' Analysts say the most likely reasons for providers' inability to meet demand are a lack of infrastructure and a shortage of installers and service personnel." (*Wall Street Journal*, February 12, 2001)

13.   "Perhaps the most compelling reason why streaming media will have greater success, sooner, within corporations than in front of the general public, is bandwidth. Most observers agree that, for reasons of quality, streaming video is really a broadband game, yet well over 90 percent of home Internet users in the United States are limited to dial-up access. But corporate intranets are typically built on a high-speed backbone." (Max Bloom, "Opportunities in the Enterprise," in Streamingmedia.com Europe Newsletter, February 26, 2001) In the same issue Paul Kushner writes: "The problem with the story of streaming media is that it started on the wrong end of the spectrum. Success will come first and foremost in enterprise and advertising. Streaming will then eventually branch out to more entertainment consumer content. Advancing content towards the general public was a mistake and the early founders have paid for it."

14.   "Dark fiber is optical fiber infrastructure (cabling and repeaters) that is currently in place but is not being used. Optical fiber conveys information in the form of light pulses so the 'dark' means no light pulses are being sent. For example, some electric utilities have installed optical fiber cable where they already have power lines installed in the expectation that they can lease the infrastructure to telephone or cable TV companies or use it to interconnect their own offices." (www.whatis.com)

# Bibliography

Adilkno. 1994. *Cracking the Movement*. Autonomedia

Adilkno. 1998. *The Media Archive*. Autonomedia.

Arendt, Hannah. 1968. *Between Past and Future*. Viking.

Arendt, Hannah, and Mary McCarthy. 1995. *Between Friends: The Correspondance of Hannah Arendt and Mary McCarthy*, 1949-1975. Harcourt Brace.

Autonome a.f.r.i.k.a.-gruppe/Luther Blissett/Sonja Brünzels. 1998. *Handbuch der Kommunikationsguerilla*. Verlag Libertäre Assoziation, Hamburg.

Barber, Benjamin. 1995. *Jihad vs. McWorld*. Times Books.

Benedikt, Michael, ed. 1991. *Cyberspace: The First Steps*. MIT Press.

Berlin, Isaiah. 1994. Russian *Thinkers*. Penguin.

Berlin, Isaiah. 1998. *The Proper Study of Mankind, An Anthology of Essays*. Farrar, Straus and Giroux.

Berners-Lee, Tim, with Mark Fishetti. 2000. *Weaving the Web*. Harper Business.

Bey, Hakim. 1992. *Temporary Autonomous Zones*. Autonomedia.

Bey, Hakim. 1994. *Immediatism*. AK Press.

Blaise, Clark. 2000. *Time Lords, Sir Stanford Fleming and the Creation of Standard Time*. Pantheon.

Bude, Heinz. 2001. *Generation Berlin*. Berlin: Merve.

Carey, John. 1992. *The Intellectuals and the Masses*. Faber.

Castells, Manuel. 1996. *The Information Age: Economy, Society and Culture*, volume 1: *The Rise of the Network Society*. Blackwell.

Chomsky, Noam. 1999. *The New Military Humanism, Lessons from Kosovo*. Pluto.

Critical Art Ensemble. 1996. *Electronic Civil Disobedience and Other Unpopular Ideas*. Autonomedia.

Critical Art Ensemble. 2001. *Digital Resistance*. Autonomedia.

Davis, Mark. 1997. *Gangland*. Allen & Unwin.

Dyson, Esther. 1997. *Release 2.0*. Broadway Books.

Frank, Thomas. 2000. *One Market under God, Extreme Capitalism, Market Populism and the End of Economic Democracy*. Doubleday.

Gibson, William. 1984. *Neuromancer*. Ace.

Giddens, Anthony. 2000. *The Third Way and Its Critics*. Polity.

Gilder, George. 1992. *Life after Television*. Norton.

Gleick, James. 1999. *Faster: The Acceleration of Just About Everything*. Random House.

Green, E., and A. Adam, eds. 2001. *Virtual Gender, Technology, Consumption and Identity*. Routledge,.

Hardt, Michael, and Antoni Negri. 2000. *Empire*. Harvard University Press.

Hartmann, Frank. 2000. *Medienphilosophie*. WUV.

Heim, Michael. 1998. *Virtual Realism*. Oxford University Press.

Himanen, Pekka. 2001. *The Hacker Ethic and the Spirit of the Information Age*. Random House.

Ignatieff, Michael. 2000. *Virtual War, Kosovo and Beyond*. Vintage.

Jacoby, Russell. 1987. *The Last Intellectual*. Basic Books.

Jones, Gwyneth. 1998. *Deconstructing the Starships*. University of Liverpool Press.

Kadare, Ismail. 1991. *Printemps Albanais*. Fayard.

Kaplan, Robert D. 1994. *Balkan Ghosts*. Vintage.

Kaplan, Robert D. 1996. *The End of the Earth*. Random House.

Kelly, Kevin. 1998. *New Rules for the New Economy*. Fourth Estate Limited.

Klein, Naomi. 2000. *No Logo, No Space, No Choice, No Jobs*. Flamingo.

Kroker, Arthur, and Michael Weinstein. 1994. *Data Trash: The Theory of the Virtual Class*. St. Martin's Press.

Lunenfeld, Peter. 2000. *Snap to Grid, A User's Guide to Digital Arts, Media and Cultures*. MIT Press.

Manovich, Lev. 2001. *The Language of New Media*. MIT Press.

Minor, Dale. 1970. *The Information War*. Hawthorn Books.

Minsky, Marvin. 1986. *The Society of Mind*. Simon & Schuster.

Moravec, Hans. 1988. *Mind Children*. Harvard University Press.

Negroponte, Nicholas. 1995. *Being Digital*. Knopf.

Nettime (filtered by). 1999. *Readme!, ASCII Culture and the Revenge of Knowledge*. Autonomedia.

NL-Design, ed. 2000. *Everyone Is a Designer!, Manifest for the Design Economy*. BIS Publishers. Reprinted as *Emigre* number 58, spring 2001.

NL-Design, ed. 2001. *Catalogue of Strategies*. BIS.

Noble, David. 1999. *The Religion of Technology*. Penguin.

Pesce, Marc. 2000. *The Playful World*. Ballantine.

Pilger, John. 1998. *Hidden Agendas*. Vintage.

Rheingold, Howard. 2000. *Virtual Communities*, second edition. MIT Press.

Rieff, David. 1995. Slaughterhouse: Bosnia and the Failure of the West. Simon & Schuster.

Rifkin, Jeremy. 1987. *Time Wars: The Primary Conflict in Human History*. Holt.

Rogers, Richard, ed. 2000. *Preferred Placement, Knowledge Politics on the Web*. Jan van Eyck Akademie Editions/Uitgeverij De Balie.

Rorty, Richard. 1999. *Philosophy and Social Hope*. Penguin.

Said, Edward. 1994. *Representations of the Intellectual*. Vintage.

Schiller, Robert J. 2000. *Irrational Exuberance*. Scribe Publications.

Schuler, Doug. 1996. *New Community Networks: Wired for Change*. Addison-Wesley.

Sloterdijk, Peter. 1989. *Eurotaoismus, Zur Kritik der politischen Kinetik*. Suhrkamp.

Soros, George. 1997. "The Capitalist Threat." *Atlantic Monthly*, February (http://www.theatlantic.com/issues/97feb/capital/capital.htm).

Soros, George, Byron Wien, and Krisztina Koenen. 1995. Soros on Soros: Staying Ahead of the Curve. Wiley.

Terkessidis, Mark. 1995. *Kulturkampf*. Kiepenheuer & Witsch.

Vickers, Miranda, and James Pettifer. 1997. *Albania: From Anarchy to Balkan Identity*. New York University Press.

Virilio, Paul. 2001. *Strategies of Deception*. Verso.

Waag Society for Old and New Media, ed. 2001., *Metatag, 26 Hits on Technology and Culture*. Amsterdam: The Waag.

Wertheim, Margaret. 1999. *The Pearly Gates of Cyberspace*. Doubleday.

Young, James. 1993. *The Texture of Memory, Holocaust Memorials and Meaning*. Yale University Press.